Pd 8-28-85

**Index to America:
Life and Customs —
Seventeenth Century**

FWF Useful Reference Series No. 107

Index to America: Life and Customs — Seventeeth Century

Compiled by

Norma Olin Ireland
B.A., B.S. in L.S.

F. W. FAXON COMPANY, INC./WESTWOOD, MASSACHUSETTS

MANUFACTURED IN THE UNITED STATES OF AMERICA

DEDICATION

To the memory of my father and mother, *Carl Leroy Olin* and *Jessie Latimer Olin,* who:

(1) instilled in me, at an early age, a "love of country" and an awareness of the value of history in making judgments in modern life;

(2) as direct descendants of two Pilgrims (James Chilton and Thomas Rogers) and a famous Puritan (Deacon Samuel Chapin, immortalized in the statue *The Puritan* by Augustus Saint-Gaudens), gave me a sense of pride in the heritage of 17th-century America;

(3) gave me great-grandparents who were pioneers of early Medina County, Ohio (part of that great Western Reserve migration), thus passing on a "pioneer spirit" and a love of new adventures and new places;

(4) as a farmer and a musician, gave me a "heritage of the soil," with an enduring love of nature and animals, and an "interest in the arts";

(5) gave me an appreciation of education and its corresponding values — all of which I realize had its beginning in the 17th century.

N.O.I.

PREFACE

This book, the initial volume in the four-volume series *Index to America: Life and Customs,* covers the 17th century. It is not the first volume in this series to be published; *Index to America: Life and Customs — 18th Century* was issued in 1976 because of its timeliness for our Bicentennial year. The remaining volumes to appear will be:

Vol. III — 19th century, and
Vol. IV — 20th century, 1900–1980.

Purpose and Scope

The purpose of this *Index,* and of all the other volumes in the series, is to coordinate into one work references to many of the chief publications about a particular century, concentrating on popular, recent books, but also including some older, readable volumes of historical value.

This work is designed to be used in both public and school libraries, as well as in college and university libraries. Since it is intended as a popular, rather than scholarly, compilation, we have not indexed many fine historical series and biographies or classical scholarly volumes to be found primarily in academic libraries.

Readers must remember that primarily this is an index to the life and customs of the times and not an index to historical events. Some material on specific historical events and on government, politics, and wars is, of course, included in this *Index* because such forces always influence the quality of life. Few biographies were indexed, and those which were chosen (e.g., Pocahontas, John Eliot's life with the Indians, etc.) provide information which was difficult to find in more general sources.

Foreign titles have not been indexed as, of course, this *Index* is intended mainly for use in American libraries. There is inclusion,

however, of some foreign names and organizations which were connected with the early life of the colonies.

Without conscious intent, we have indexed almost the exact number of books for this volume as we did for the one on the 18th century: 115 books, as compared to 116 for the earlier one. This *Index* is a much larger book, however, and one reason is the large number of individuals included in the present volume. In the 17th century, individuals "stood out" in the origin and development of so many aspects of life and customs.

Since Volumes I and II both contain material on life in the colonial period, there is an unavoidable degree of overlapping between some of the entries in these two volumes. References from books which cover "colonial life and times" (e.g., the Earle books) sometimes have had to be included in both volumes because specific dates were not always given to help us decide whether a certain reference would be listed more appropriately under the 17th or 18th century.

During the compilation of this book we discovered that fewer books on American life in the 17th century have been reprinted of late than on the 18th century. Perhaps this difference reflects the impetus that the approaching Bicentennial celebration gave to the publication of books on the 18th century topics in the last few years. On the other hand, there have been many *new* titles about the *Mayflower* and the 1620 landing of the Pilgrims, following the Pilgrim Anniversary in 1970.

Since we designed this *Index* to be used in American public, school, and college libraries, we selected the works to be indexed from the collections of a group of representative libraries located in California. The following libraries are listed in order of the number of volumes used: San Diego County Library (including the Fallbrook branch), San Diego Public Library, Oceanside Public Library, San Diego State College Library, California State Library, State Normal School Library, and the public libraries of Chula Vista, Coronado, National City, and Santa Ana.

In selecting books for inclusion in this *Index,* we did not use the recent age of books as a criterion, but rather books still available in libraries.

The percentage of books indexed, according to the date of publication, is as follows:

1970's — 29%,
1960's — 31%,
1950's — 18%,
1940's — 11%,
1930's — 11%.

Please note that in our "List of Collections" we have *not* indicated "out-of-print" books because many older books are still available in the libraries where this *Index* will be used. Books suitable for young people are indicated as such.

Arrangement and Subject Headings

This subject index is arranged alphabetically, word by word, in one alphabet, as have been all of our previous works. It contains over 2,500 different subject headings, not including subheadings or cross-references.

In our indexing we have followed a combination of methods: first, checking main subjects in chapters, page by page, then scanning the book's index for the inclusion of special subjects and for headings used which would be suitable for the general period or subject matter covered. However, we never depend solely on a book's index, as those of many books are full of mistakes. In those instances when we judge a particular book's index to be dependable, and when the book's index lists a great number of references on a certain subject, we sometimes use the notation *"See index"* after the book's title symbol.

Our subject headings are mostly specific, for convenient use, but some general subjects are also included, with numerous subheadings. The reader should remember that subject headings used are similar to those found in book-indexing rather than that in card catalogs. We have used the same subject headings as we used in *Index to America: Life and Customs — 18th Century* when appropriate, although there have been a few variations and adaptations to fit references to the 17th century. We have intentionally included some archaic terms of the period, with explanations in parentheses or with cross-references

because we felt that these terms reflected the spirit and atmosphere of the period. The names of a few individuals are listed in both Volumes I and II because their lives spanned part of both the 17th and 18th centuries.

We have made copious cross-references under the headings **INDIANS, JAMESTOWN, PILGRIMS, PLYMOUTH, PURITANS,** and **WOMEN,** as we felt that students might be interested in searching out all information related to these subjects. These cross-references may be found directly after each appropriate subject heading. In deciding on the choice of a main entry, the book indexed was the determining factor (i.e., how the subjects were treated therein), as well as the importance of these special topics. There is, for this reason, some overlapping under the headings **PILGRIMS** and **PLYMOUTH** because we relied on the treatment of these subjects in the books indexed.

Dates of historical events are given only when they are relevant to the subject and help clarify its meaning. Biographical data for individuals listed, including identifications and dates of lives, have not been provided because this *Index* is not a biographical dictionary.

We have made a special effort to include references to women and Indians because of the ever-increasing interest in the roles these groups played in America's history. We have compiled an appendix, "Women of the 17th Century, a Selection, " which lists the names of important women cited in the body of the *Index,* as we did a similar appendix in Volume II for Women of the 18th century. We have omitted from this appendix the names of minor female figures such as accused witches and midwives who do not figure prominently, but whose names are included in the body of the *Index.* As for the "first inhabitants" of our country, who played such a large part in our early history, a representative selection of Indians is included, as well as the names of the tribes prominent in the 17th century. Most of the books on Indians which we examined covered later periods and will be analyzed in the appropriate later volumes of this series.

Acknowledgments and Personal Note

Again we thank the staff members of the Fallbrook branch of the San Diego County Library for their fine cooperation, and this time

especially Mrs. Leona Ault, assistant, and, as always, Mrs. Dorothy Norton, Librarian, and Mrs. Betty Simmons, assistant in charge of interlibrary loans. We acknowledge, also, the use of the books from the libraries named earlier in the Preface.

The 17th century has always been our "favorite century," excepting the present, of course. Over 200 of our first immigrant ancestors have been traced back to the 1600's in our genealogical research, so perhaps we have reason for a special interest in this century. As in our previous volume, the *Index to America* is a "thank you" to this great land of ours and to the early men and women whose great courage and sacrifice made its greatness possible. We only hope their dreams and work will *not* be lost in the 20th century.

LIST OF COLLECTIONS ANALYZED

IN THIS WORK

AND

KEY TO SYMBOLS USED

ABBOT — COLONIAL
  Abbot, W. W. *The colonial origins of the United States, 1607–1763.* American Republic Series. New York, John Wiley & Sons, Inc., 1975. 134p.

*ACHESON — AMERICA'S
  Acheson, Patricia C. *America's colonial heritage.* New York, Dodd, Mead & Co., 1957. 201p.

*ADAMS — ALBUM
  Adams, James Truslow, ed. *Album of American history.* Chicago, Consolidated Book Publishers, 1944. 411p.

*ADAMS — PROVINCIAL
  Adams, James Truslow. *Provincial society, 1690–1763.* New York, Macmillan Publishing Co., ca.1927. 374p.

*ALDERMAN — STORY
  Alderman, Clifford Lindsey. *The story of the thirteen colonies.* Illustrated by Leonard Everett Fisher. New York, Random House, 1966. 188p.

*AMER. HER. — PILGRIMS
  American Heritage, ed. *The Pilgrims and Plymouth colony.* New York, American Heritage Publishing Co., Inc., 1961. 153p.

*AMER. HER. — PIONEER
  American Heritage, ed. *The* American Heritage *book of the pioneer spirit.* New York, American Heritage Publishing Co., Inc., 1959. 394p.

*AMER. HER. — THIRTEEN
  American Heritage, ed. *The* American Heritage *history of the thirteen colonies.* New York, American Heritage Publishing Co., Inc., 1967. 384p.

*AMER. HER. — TREASURY
  A Treasury of American Heritage. *A selection from the first five years of the Magazine of History.* New York, Simon & Schuster, 1960. 398p.

* *suitable for young people*

1

ANGLE — BY
  Angle, Paul M. *By these words. Great documents of American liberty, selected and placed in their contemporary settings.* New York, Rand McNally & Co., 1954. 427p.

ANNALS OF AMERICA (1)
  The Annals of America, vol. 1, 1493–1754. Discovery of a new world. Chicago, Encyclopaedia Britannica, Inc., 1968. 529p.

*ARCHER — MAYFLOWER
  Archer, Gleason L. *Mayflower heroes.* New York, The Century Co., 1931. 346p.

ARTS — AMERICA
  The arts in America. The colonial period. Louis B. Wright, et al, eds. New York, Charles Scribner's Sons, 1966. 368p.

AXTELL — AMERICA
  Axtell, James L., ed. *America perceived: a view from abroad in the 17th century.* West Haven, Conn., Pendulum Press, 1974. 236p.

BAILEY — AMERICAN (1)
  Bailey, Thomas A. *The American spirit. United States history as seen by contempories.* Vol. 1. Boston, D. C. Heath & Co., 1963. 502p.

BAILYN — NEW ENGLAND
  Bailyn, Bernard. *The New England merchants in the seventeenth century.* New York, Harper & Row, 1955. 249p.

*BEALS — JOHN ELIOT
  Beals, Carleton. *John Eliot. The man who loved the Indians (July 31, 1604–May 20, 1690).* New York, Julian Messner, Inc., 1957. 192p.

*BECK — PILGRIMS
  Beck, Barbara L. *The Pilgrims of Plymouth.* New York, Franklin Watts, Inc., 1972. 89p.

BRIDENBAUGH — CITIES
  Bridenbaugh, Carl. *Cities in the wilderness. The first century of urban life in America, 1625–1742.* 2d ed. New York, Alfred A. Knopf, 1955. 500p.

*BROOKS — DAMES
  Brooks, Geraldine. *Dames and daughters of colonial days.* 1900. Reprint. New York, Arno Press, 1974. 284p.

CAFFREY — MAYFLOWER
  Caffrey, Kate. *The Mayflower.* New York, Stein and Day, Publishers, 1974. 392p.

* *suitable for young people*

CALVERTON — AWAKE.
Calverton, V. F.   *The awakening of America.*   New York, John Day
Co., 1939.   474p.

CARMAN — HISTORY (1)
Carman, Harry J., et al.   *A history of the American people.*   Vol.
1: to 1877. 2d ed., rev.   New York, Alfred A. Knopf,
1961.   860p.

CHITWOOD — HISTORY
Chitwood, Oliver Perry.   *A history of colonial America.*   3d ed.
New York, Harper & Row, 1961.   745p.

*CHRISTENSEN — DELAWARE
Christensen, Gardell Dano, and Eugena Burney.   *Colonial
Delaware.*   New York, Thomas Nelson, Inc., 1975.   160p.

*CLARK — OLD
Clark, Imogen.   *Old days and old ways.*   New York, Thomas Y.
Crowell Co., 1928.   296p.

*COLLINS — STORY
Collins, Alan C.   *The story of America in pictures.*   New rev. ed.
Garden City, N.Y., Doubleday & Co., Inc., 1953.   480p.

CRAVEN — COLONIES
Craven, Wesley Frank.   *The colonies in transition, 1660–1713.*
New York, Harper & Row, Publishers, 1968.   363p.

CRAVEN — SOUTHERN
Craven, Wesley Frank.   *The Southern colonies in the seventeenth
century, 1607–1689.*   Baton Rouge, La., Louisiana State University Press, 1949.   451p.

DEMOS — LITTLE
Demos, John.   *A little commonwealth. Family life in Plymouth
Colony.*   New York, Oxford University Press, 1970.   201p.

DEMOS — REMARKABLE
Demos, John, ed.   *Remarkable providences: 1600–1760.*   New
York, George Braziller, Inc., 1972.   382p.

*DEXTER — COLONIAL
Dexter, Elizabeth Anthony.   *Colonial women of affairs. A study of
women in business and the professions in America before
1776.*   Boston, Houghton Mifflin Co., 1924.   204p.

DILLON — PILGRIMS
Dillon, Francis.   *The Pilgrims.* Rev. ed. of English title *A place of
habitation.*   New York, Doubleday & Co., Inc., 1975.   250p.

*DOW — DOMESTIC
Dow, George Francis.   *Domestic life in New England in the seventeenth century.*   New York, Benjamin Blom, Inc., 1972.   48p.

* *suitable for young people*

*DOW — EVERY
>Dow, George Francis. *Every day life in the Massachusetts Bay Colony.* 1935. Reprint. New York, Benjamin Blom, 1967. 290p.

*DREPPERD — PIONEER
>Drepperd, Carl W. *Pioneer America. Its first three centuries.* New York, Doubleday & Co., Inc., 1949. 311p.

*DULLES — AMERICA
>Dulles, Foster Rhea. *America learns to play: a history of popular recreation 1607–1940.* New York, Appleton-Century Co., 1940. 441p.

*EARLE — COLONIAL
>Earle, Alice Morse. *Colonial dames and good wives.* 1895. Reprint. New York, Frederick Ungar Publishing Co., 1962. 315p.

*EARLE — CUSTOMS
>Earle, Alice Morse. *Customs and fashions in old New England.* 1893. Reprint. Rutland, Vt., Charles E. Tuttle Co., 1973. 387p.

*EARLE — HOME
>Earle, Alice Morse. *Home life in colonial days.* 1898. Reprint. Stockbridge, Mass., Berkshire Traveller Press, 1974. 470p.

*EARLE — TWO CENT. (1) (2)
>Earle, Alice Morse. *Two centuries of costume in America 1620–1820.* 1903. Reprint. Rutland, Vt., Charles E. Tuttle Co., 1971. Vol. 1, 1–388p; Vol. 2, 391–824p.

FISHER — MEN (1) (2)
>Fisher, Sydney George. *Men, women and manners in colonial times* 2 vols. 1897. Reprint. Detroit, Gale Research Co., 1969. Vol. 1, 390p; Vol. 2, 392p.

FOLSOM — GIVE
>Folsom, Franklin. *Give me liberty; America's colonial heritage.* Chicago, Rand McNally & Co., 1974. 230p.

FURNAS — AMERICANS
>Furnas, J. C. *The Americans; A social history of the United States, 1587–1914.* New York, G. P. Putnam's Sons, 1969. 1015p.

GILDRIE — SALEM
>Gildrie, Richard P. *Salem, Massachusetts, 1626–1683; a covenant community.* Charlottesville, Va., University Press of Virginia, 1975. 187p.

*GILL — MAYFLOWER
>Gill, Crispin. *Mayflower remembered. A history of the Plymouth pilgrims.* New York, Taplinger Publishing Co., 1970. 206p.

* *suitable for young people*

*GLUBOK — HOME
   Glubok, Shirley, ed.   *Home and child life in colonial days.*   Abridged
      from Earle's *Home life in colonial days* and *Child life in colonial
      days.*   New York, Macmillan Publishing Co., 1969.   357p.

GOETZMANN — COLONIAL
   Goetzmann, William H., ed.   *The colonial horizon: America in the
      16th and 17th centuries. Interpretive arts and documentary
      sources.*   Reading, Mass., Addison-Wesley Publishing Co.,
      1969.   213p.

GOODWIN — COLONIAL
   Goodwin, Maud Wilder.   *The colonial cavalier, or Southern life before
      the Revolution.*   1894.   Reprint.   New York, Arno Press,
      1975.   299p.

GOULD — EARLY
   Gould, Mary Earle.   *The early American house.*   New York, Medill
      McBride Co., ca.1949, 1965.   152p.

GREENE — PROVINCIAL
   Greene, Evarts Boutell.   *Provincial America, 1690–1740.*   New
      York, Frederick Ungar Publishing Co., 1964.   356p.

*HALE — THROUGH
   Hale, Jeanne, editor-in-chief.   *Through golden windows. Stories of
      early America.*   Eau Claire, Wisc., E. M. Hale & Company,
      1958.   329p.

HALL — RELIGIOUS
   Hall, Thomas Cuming.   *The religious background of American
      culture.*   1930.   Reprint.   New York, Frederick Ungar Pub-
      lishing Co., 1959.   348p.

HAWKE — COLONIAL
   Hawke, David.   *The colonial experience.*   Indianapolis, Bobbs-
      Merrill Co., Inc., 1966.   774p.

HAWKE — U.S.
   Hawke, David, ed.   *U.S. colonial history. Readings and documents.*
      Indianapolis, Bobbs-Merrill Co., Inc., 1966.   550p.

*HILLS — HISTORY (1) (2)
   Hills, Leon Clark.   *History and genealogy of the Mayflower planters
      and firstcomers to ye olde colonie.*   2 vols. 1941.   Reprint.
      (2 vols. in 1).   Baltimore, Genealogical Publishing Co.,
      1975.   284p.

*HOLLIDAY — WOMAN'S
   Holliday, Carl.   *Woman's life in colonial days.*   1922.   Reprint.
      New York, Frederick Ungar Publishing Co., 1975.   319p.

* *suitable for young people*

6

*HOPE — NATION
  Hope of the nation. Dedicated to the restoration and expansion of
    our American heritage. Gastonia, N.C., Good Will, Inc.,
    1952. 401p.

*HOWARD — OUR
  Howard, John Tasker. Our American music. Three hundred years
    of it. 3d ed., rev. and reset. New York, Thomas Y. Crowell
    Co., 1946. 841p.

JERNEGAN — AMERICAN
  Jernegan, Marcus Wilson. The American colonies, 1492–
    1750. 1929. Reprint. New York, Frederick Ungar Publish-
    ing Co., 1959. 457p.

JOHNSTON — CONN.
  Johnston, Johanna. The Connecticut Colony . New York, Cro-
    well-Collier Press (Macmillan Publishing Co., Inc.), 1969. 136p.

KRAUS — U.S. (1)
  Kraus, Michael. The United States to 1865. Vol. 1. Ann Arbor,
    Mich., The University of Michigan Press, 1959. 529p.

*LANGDON — EVERYDAY
  Langdon, William Chauncy. Everyday things in American life, 1607–
    1776. New York, Charles Scribner's Sons, 1937. 353p.

*LAWRENCE — NEW
  Lawrence, Robert Means. New England colonial life. Cambridge,
    Mass., The Cosmos Press, 1927. 276p.

LAWRENCE — NOT
  Lawrence, Henry W. The not-quite Puritans. Some genial follies
    and peculiar frailties of our revered New England ancestors.
    1928. Reprint. Detroit, Gale Research, 1975. 228p.

*LEONARD — DEAR
  Leonard, Eugenie Andrus. The dear-bought heritage. Phil-
    adelphia, University of Pennsylvania Press, 1965. 658p.

LEYNSE — PRECED.
  Leynse, James P. Preceding the Mayflower. The Pilgrims in England
    and in the Netherlands. New York, Fountainhead Publishers,
    Inc., 1972. 286p.

*LIFE — NEW
  The Life History of the United States. The new world. Vol. 1:
    before 1775. New York, Time-Life Books, 1963. Rev.
    1974. 176p.

LOCKRIDGE — NEW
  Lockridge, Kenneth A. A New England town; the first hundred years.
    Dedham, Mass., 1636–1736. New York, W. W. Norton & Co.,
    Inc., 1970. 199p.

* suitable for young people

*McCLINTON — ANTIQUES
   McClinton, Katharine Morrison. *Antiques of American childhood.*
   New York, Clarkson N. Potter, Inc., 1970. 351p.

*MARBLE — WOMEN
   Marble, Annie Russell. *The women who came in the Mayflower.*
   Boston, The Pilgrim Press, 1920. 110p.

*MARSHALL — MAYFLOWER
   Marshall, Cyril Leek. *The Mayflower destiny: a modern curator's
   look at how the Pilgrims lived and worked in America.*
   Harrisburg, Pa., Stackpole Books, 1975. 191p.

MILLER — COLONIAL
   Miller, John C., ed. *The colonial image. Origins of American
   culture.* New York, George Braziller, Inc., 1962. 500p.

MILLER — FIRST
   Miller, John C. *The first frontier: life in colonial America.* New
   York, Delacorte Press, 1966. 288p.

MITCHELL — IT'S
   Mitchell, Edwin Valentine. *It's an old New England custom.* New
   York, Vanguard Press, 1946. 277p.

MONROE — FOUNDING (1)
   Monroe, Paul. *Founding of the American public school system. A
   history of education in the United States. From the early settlements to the close of the Civil War period.* Vol. 1. New York,
   Macmillan Publishing Co., 1940. 520p.

MORGAN — PURITAN
   Morgan, Edmund S. *The Puritan family. Essays on religious and
   domestic relations in seventeenth century New England.* New
   York, Harper & Row, 1944. 196p.

MORISON — INTELLECT.
   Morison, Samuel Eliot. *The intellectual life of colonial New
   England.* New York, New York University Press, 1956.
   Reprint. Cornell University Press, 1965. 288p.

MORISON — OXFORD
   Morison, Samuel Eliot. *The Oxford history of the American people.*
   New York, Oxford University Press, 1965. 1150p.

*MORISON — STORY
   Morison, Samuel Eliot. *The story of the "Old Colony" of the New
   Plymouth (1620–1692).* New York, Alfred A. Knopf, 1956.
   296p.

MORRIS — ENCY.
   Morris, Richard B., ed. *Encyclopedia of American history.* New
   York, Harper & Brothers Publishers, 1953. 776p.

* *suitable for young people*

MORRISON — EARLY
  Morrison, Hugh. *Early American architecture from the first colonial settlements to the national period.* New York, Oxford University Press, 1944. 619p.

MURDOCK — LITERATURE
  Murdock, Kenneth B. *Literature and theology in colonial New England.* Cambridge, Mass., Harvard University Press, 1949. 235p.

*NATIONAL — HISTORY.
  National Geographic Society. *America's historylands.* Washington, D.C., National Geographic Society, 1967. 576p.

NETTELS — ROOTS
  Nettels, Curtis P. *The roots of American civilization. A history of American colonial life.* New York, Appleton-Century-Crofts, Inc., 1938. 748p.

*NORTHEY — AMERICAN
  Northey, Sue. *American Indian.* San Antonio, Texas, The Naylor Co., 1954. 216p.

PHILLIPS — FIRST
  Phillips, Leon. *First lady of America; a romanticized biography of Pocahontas.* Richmond, Va., Westover Publishing Co., 1973. 203p.

POMFRET — FOUNDING
  Pomfret, John Edwin, with Floyd M. Shumway. *Founding the American colonies, 1583–1660.* New York, Harper & Row Publishers, 1970. 380p.

RAWSON — WHEN
  Rawson, Marion Nicholl. *When antiques were young; a story of early American social customs.* New York, Hutton, 1931. 271p.

ROTHBARD — CONCEIVED (1)
  Rothbard, Murray N. *Conceived in liberty. A new land, a new people; the American colonies in the seventeenth century.* New Rochelle, N.Y., Arlington House Publishers, 1975. Vol. 1. 531p.

ROZWENC — MAKING (1)
  Rozwenc, Edwin C. *The making of American society. An institutional and intellectual history of the United States.* Vol. 1: to 1877. Boston, Allyn & Bacon, 1972. 655p.

RUTMAN — WINTHROP'S
  Rutman, Darrett B. *Winthrop's Boston.* 1965. Reprint. New York, W. W. Norton & Co., Inc., 1972. 324p.

* *suitable for young people*

*SCOTT — SETTLERS
Scott, John Anthony.   *Settlers on the Eastern Shore, 1607–1750.*
New York, Alfred A. Knopf, 1967.   227p.

*SMITH — COLONIAL
Smith, Helen Evertson.   *Colonial days and ways, as gathered from
family papers.*   1900.   Reprint.   New York, Frederick Ungar
Publishing Co., 1966.   376p.

SMITH — 17TH
Smith, James M.   *Seventeenth-century America: Essays in colonial
history.*   Chapel Hill, N.C., University of North Carolina Press,
1959.   238p.

*SNELL — WILD
Snell, T. Loftin.   *The wild shores. America's beginnings.*   Wash-
ington, D.C., Special Publications Division, National Geographic
Society, 1974.   203p.

*SPEARE — LIFE
Speare, Elizabeth George.   *Life in colonial America.*   New York,
Random House, 1963.   172p.

SPRUILL — WOMEN'S
Spruill, Julia Cherry.   *Women's life and work in the Southern
colonies.*   New York, W. W. Norton & Co., Inc., 1972.   426p.

STARKEY — LAND
Starkey, Marion Lena.   *Land where our fathers died. The settling
of the Eastern Shore: 1607–1735.*   Garden City, N.Y., Doubleday & Co., Inc., 1962.   275p.

SWEET — RELIGION
Sweet, William Warren.   *Religion in colonial America.*   New York,
Cooper Square Publishers, Inc., 1965.   367p.

*TUNIS — COLONIAL
Tunis, Edwin.   *Colonial living.*   Cleveland, The World Publishing
Co., 1957.   155p.

*TUNIS — CRAFTSMEN
Tunis, Edwin.   *Colonial craftsmen and the beginnings of American
industry.*   Cleveland, The World Publishing Co., 1965.   155p.

TYLER — HISTORY
Tyler, Moses Coit.   *A history of American literature, 1607–1765.*
Ithaca, N.Y., Cornell University Press, 1949.   551p.

VAUGHAN — NEW
Vaughan, Alden T.   *The New England frontier: Puritans and Indians,
1620–1675.*   Boston, Little, Brown and Co., 1965.   430p.

VAUGHAN — PURITAN
Vaughan, Alden T., ed.   *The Puritan tradition in America, 1620–
1730.*   New York, Harper & Row, 1972.   348p.

* *suitable for young people*

VER STEEG — FORMATIVE
    Ver Steeg, Clarence L. *The formative years, 1607–1763.* New York, Hill & Wang, Inc., 1964. 342p.

WERTENBAKER — FIRST
    Wertenbaker, Thomas J. *The first Americans, 1607–1690.* New York, Macmillan Publishing Co., 1927. 358p.

WERTENBAKER — OLD
    Wertenbaker, Thomas J. *The old South. The founding of American civilization.* New York, Cooper Square Publishers, Inc., 1963. 364p.

WERTENBAKER — PURITAN
    Wertenbaker, Thomas J. *The Puritan oligarchy. The founding of American civilization.* New York, Charles Scribner's Sons, 1947. 359p.

*WILLIAMS — DEMETER'S
    Williams, Selma R. *Demeter's daughters. The women who founded America 1587–1787.* New York, Atheneum Publishers, 1976. 359p.

*WILLISON — PILGRIM
    Willison, George F. *Pilgrim reader: the story of the Pilgrim fathers. The story of the Pilgrims as told by themselves and their contemporaries friendly and unfriendly.* New York, Doubleday & Co., Inc., 1953. 585p.

*WILLISON — SAINTS
    Willison, George F. *Saints and strangers.* New York, Reynal & Hitchcock, 1945. 513p.

WISH — SOCIETY (1)
    Wish, Harvey. *Society and thought in early America.* Vol. 1. New York, Longmans, Green & Co., Inc., 1950. 612p.

*WOODWARD — WAY
    Woodward, William E. *The way our people lived. An intimate American history.* New York, E. P. Dutton & Co., Inc., 1944. 402p.

WRIGHT — CULTURAL
    Wright, Louis B. *The cultural life of the American colonies, 1607–1763.* New York, Harper & Row Publishers, 1957. 292p.

*WRIGHT — EVERYDAY
    Wright, Louis B. *Everyday life in colonial America.* New York, G. P. Putnam's Sons, 1965. 255p.

WRIGHT — LITERARY
    Wright, Thomas Goddard. *Literary culture in early New England, 1620–1730.* 1920. Reprint. New York, Russell & Russell, 1966. 322p.

* *suitable for young people*

A

ABIGAIL (ship)
Smith — *Colonial* p.61, 63-65

**ABNAKI (ABENAKI, WABENAKI)
INDIANS**
Caffrey — *Mayflower* p.151
Greene — *Provincial* p.110, 119, 126-127, 134
Morison — *Story* p.81, 112, 126, 134, 166, 262-263, 279, 288-289
Snell — *Wild* p.77
Vaughan — *New* p.17, 51-52, 54, 94, 98, 106, 314
Willison — *Saints* p.171, 263-264

ACADEMIES
Chitwood — *History* p.463-464

ACCESSORIES (fashion)
See also **Clothing and dress;** names of accessories
- *Women*
   Spruill — *Women's* p.124-125

ACRELIUS, ISRAEL
, *On New Sweden*
Axtell — *America* p.173-177

"ACT CONCERNING RELIGION" (1649)
Wright — *Cultural* p.76-77

"ACT OF FRAUDS" (1662)
Morris — *Ency.* p.484

"ACT OF OBLIVION AND INDEMNITY"
Vaughan — *New* p.274

**"ACTS AND ORDERS OF 1647." *See*
Rhode Island — Fundamental orders (1647)**

ADAM THOROUGHGOOD HOUSE
Morrison — *Early* p.143-147

**ADAMS, ELLEN NEWTON. *See*
Winslow, Ellen Newton Adams**

ADAMS, HENRY
- *Death, by Indians*
   Lawrence — *New* p.43

ADAMS, JOHN (colonist)
Willison — *Saints* p.315, 445, 449, 451

ADMIRALITY BOARD (Great Britain)
Jernegan — *American* p.253

ADOLESCENCE. *See* **Youth**

ADULTERY
See also **Plymouth — Adultery;
Punishment; Sin and sinners**
Holliday — *Woman's* p.278-286

"ADVENTURERS"
See also **Plymouth Company; Virginia Company of London; Weston, Thomas**
Annals of America (1) p.78-80
Beck — *Pilgrims* p.9, 11-12, 44, 51-53, 61
Caffrey — *Mayflower* p.55-58, 61-62, 82-83, 214-215
Gill — *Mayflower* p.115-120
Hawke — *Colonial* p.107-110
Hills — *History (1)* p.31-32
Marshall — *Mayflower* p.30-31
Nettels — *Roots* p.135
Pomfret — *Founding* p.147-148
Willison — *Pilgrim* p.547-548; *See also* index p.571

ADZES
Marshall — *Mayflower* p.71, 78

AESOP'S FABLES
Morison — *Intellect.* p.105-106, 108

**AGAWAM (IPSWICH),
MASSACHUSETTS**
Dow — *Domestic* p.8-9

"AGE OF FAITH"
Ver Steeg — *Formative* p.74-105
Wright — *Everyday* p.155-156

AGING. *See* **Longevity**

AGLETS (tags or ties)
Earle — *Two cent, (1)* p.174-175

AGRICULTURAL MACHINERY. *See*
Farm implements

AGRICULTURE
See also **Farmers and farming;**
Livestock; names of crops and
grains, etc.
Adams — *Provincial* p.25-51
Carman — *History (1)* p.61-69
Craven — *Southern. See* index p.435
Langdon — *Everyday* p.273-293
Nettels — *Roots* p.229-237
Wertenbaker — *First. See* index p.339
- *Boston (1630–1649)*
   Rutman — *Winthrop's. See* index
   p.297
, *Colonial*
   Wish — *Society (1)* p.49-50, 63-
   68
- *Dedham, Mass.*
   Lockridge — *New* p.10, 59, 69-
   70, 82, 89n
- *Economics*
   Rozwenc — *Making (1)* p.38-39
- *Germans*
   Miller — *First* p.165-167
- *Indians. See* **Indians — Agriculture**
- *Maryland*
   Pomfret — *Founding* p.85-86
   Wertenbaker — *First* p.37-39
- *New England*
   Jernegan — *American* p.171
   Wertenbaker — *First* p.11
- *Outlets*
   Adams — *Provincial* p.28-29
- *Plymouth. See* **Plymouth —**
   Agriculture
- *Produce*
   Bailyn — *New England* p.24, 26,
   29, 47, 59, 83, 93, 95-96, 101,
   127, 129, 149
- *South*
   Carman — *History (1)* p.64-68
   Craven — *Southern. See* index
   p.435
   Wertenbaker — *First* p.12-13

- *Virginia (1688)*
   Demos — *Remarkable* p.318-325

AINSWORTH, HENRY
Leynse — *Preced.* p.148, 157-158,
162, 185, 204, 206-208
Willison — *Pilgrim* p.32-33, 44, 185n
Willison — *Saints. See* index p.495
- *Book of Psalms*
   Howard — *Our* p.4-5

ALABAMA
- *Trade wars*
   Snell — *Wild* p.156, 160-161

ALBANY, NEW YORK
Amer. Her. — *Thirteen* p.124-126,
194-197
Craven — *Colonies* p.72-73, 79, 201,
205-207, 225, 227-229, 243-244
- *Defense*
   Craven — *Colonies* p.237, 240-
   241
- *Dutch*
   Speare — *Life* p.60-61

ALBEMARLE SOUND SETTLEMENT
See also **North Carolina**
Craven — *Colonies* p.16-17, 43, 96-
97
Folsom — *Give* p.75-77
Morris — *Ency.* p.52
Nettels — *Roots* p.159
Snell — *Wild* p.24, 151, 154

ALCOCK, SARAH
Leonard — *Dear* p.219, 248, 471, 486

ALCOHOLISM
Bridenbaugh — *Cities* p.77-78
Dow — *Domestic* p.27-29
Dow — *Every* p.107-108
Dulles — *America* p.16-17
Earle — *Customs* p.165-167
Earle — *Home* p.93-94, 161, 163-164
Lawrence — *Not* p.142-146
Miller — *First* p.185-187
Rutman — *Winthrop's* p.155, 190,
225, 239, 242, 272
Wertenbaker — Puritan p.165, 173-
174, 178
- *Law*
   Vaughan — *New* p.197

- *New England*
  Tunis — *Colonial* p.38-41
  Wertenbaker — *First* p.196-197
, *on court days*
  Wertenbaker — *First* p.202-203
- *South*
  Wertenbaker — *First* p.200-203
- *Virginia clergy*
  Wertenbaker — *First* p.128-129, 137

ALDEN, JOHN
  Caffrey — *Mayflower* p.86, 220, 249-250, 306, 312
  Collins — *Story* p.45
  Dillon — *Pilgrims* p.125, 197, 213, 217, 219
  Gill — *Mayflower* p.43, 70, 119, 130, 134, 145
  Hills — *History* (2) p.203-204
  Marble — *Women* p.28, 35, 47, 74-80
  Marshall — *Mayflower* p.28, 40, 120, 171, 175, 181, 184
  Morison — *Story* p.20-22, 128, 139, 142, 149, 160, 164, 171-172, 220, 284
  Willison — *Pilgrim. See* index p.571
  Willison — *Saints. See* index p.495

ALDEN, ELIZABETH. *See* **Pabodie, Elizabeth Alden**

ALDEN, PRISCILLA MULLINS
  Caffrey — *Mayflower* p.129, 141, 306
  Collins — *Story* p.45
  Hills — *History (1)* p.18, 20, 37, 39, 41, 47, 51-53, 57-59, 61
  Hills — *History (2)* p.203, 213-215
  Marble — *Women* p.9, 11, 31, 46, 71-77
  Marshall — *Mayflower* p.28, 120
  Morison — *Story* p.20-22, 220, 284
  Willison — *Pilgrim* p.90, 126, 149, 530, 536
  Willison — *Saints* p.130-131, 314, 407, 442, 469

ALDEN, TIMOTHY
  Willison — *Saints* p.476-477

ALDEN FAMILY
  Hills — *History* (1) *See* index p.161
  Hills — *History* (2) p.206, 208, 212; *See also* index p.243
  Marble — *Women* p.74-75, 77-79

ALDERMAN (Indian)
  Willison — *Saints* p.399-400

ALDERMAN, CLIFFORD LINDSEY
  Alderman — *Story* p.188

ALEWIVES
  Glubok — *Home* p.66-67
  Morison — *Story* p.72, 77, 168-169

ALEXANDER (Indian)
  Willison — *Saints* p.390

ALEXANDER, WILLIAM, EARL OF
  Pomfret — *Founding* p.136-139, 167, 169, 265

ALGONQUIN (ALGONKIAN) INDIANS
  See also **Abnaki Indians; Bible, Algonquin; Eliot, John; Indians — Library;** names of tribes
  Amer. Heritage — *Thirteen* p.119-120, 124, 133, 166, 194, 200
  Folsom — *Give* p.32, 34-35, 40-41
  Hawke — *Colonial* p.79, 251, 320
  Lawrence — *New* p.35, 37
  Nettels — *Roots* p.152, 202
  Smith — *17th* p.40, 42-43, 54-55
  Snell — *Wild* p.66, 70-71, 95, 98, 114
  Vaughan — *New* p.27-62, 212
- *Language*
  Folsom — *Give* p.14, 18, 33
  Vaughan — *New* p.29-30, 56, 62, 281
- *War of liberation*
  Folsom — *Give* p.35-41

ALLEN, SAMUEL
  Rothbard — *Conceived (1)* p.428-429, 464, 466-467, 473

ALLERTON, FEAR BREWSTER
  Caffrey — *Mayflower* p.28, 185, 213, 232, 239
  Dillon — *Pilgrims* p.183, 205
  Gill — *Mayflower* p.104, 122
  Marble — *Women* p.11, 37, 62
  Morison — *Story* p.129
  Willison — *Pilgrim* p.20, 79, 234, 293n, 382, 387n
  Willison — *Saints. See* index p.495

ALLERTON, ISAAC
  Caffrey — *Mayflower. See* index p.385
  Dillon — *Pilgrims* p.118, 159, 165, 196-197, 199-200, 204-205

ALLERTON, ISAAC (*continued*)
Gill — *Mayflower* p.38, 47, 70, 79, 88, 94, 111, 114-115, 119-122, 131-132, 142
Hills — *History (1).* See index p.161
Hills — *History (2)* p.173-178; *See also* index p. 245
Leynse — *Preced.* p.135-137, 206, 218, 232, 237, 253, 261, 265
Marble — *Women* p.12, 14, 37
Marshall — *Mayflower* p.27-28, 120, 167, 169-170, 183
Morison — *Story* p.11, 18, 76, 86, 117, 127-130, 134-135, 154-155
Snell — *Wild* p.108, 111
Willison — *Pilgrim.* See index p.571
Willison — *Saints.* See index p.495

ALLERTON, MARY MORRIS. *See* **Cushman, Mary Morris Allerton**

ALLERTON, REMEMBER. *See* **Maverick, Remember Allerton**

ALLERTON, SARAH. *See* **Cuthbertson, Sarah Allerton Vincent**

ALLERTON FAMILY
Caffrey — *Mayflower.* See index p.385
Hills — *History (1).* See index p.161
Hills — *History (2)* p.183-184; *See also* index p.245
Marble — *Women* p.17, 23-24, 34, 56

ALLIANCES
See also **Treaties**
, *Intercolonial*
Vaughan — *New* p.160-161
, *Interracial*
Vaughan — *New* p.17, 70-73, 125-126, 132, 150, 314
, *Intertribal*
Vaughan — *New* p.55, 130-132, 313-314

ALLIN, JOHN, REV.
Lockridge — *New* p.20n, 23, 25-26, 29-30, 32n, 34n, 35, 70, 85

ALMANACS
Earle — *Customs* p.273-275
Hawke — *Colonial* p.298
Morison — *Intellect.* p.64, 116-117
Tyler — *History* p.363-365

Wright — *Literary* p.90-91, 105, 105n, 108
- *Essays and poetry*
Morison — *Intellect.* p.124, 146-148, 230-235

ALSOP, GEORGE
Tyler — *History* p.3, 57-61
Wertenbaker — *First* p.28, 169-170, 176, 206-207, 214, 223, 229, 259, 266
- *A Charter of the province of Maryland, 1666*
Amer. Her. — *Thirteen* p.149

ALTHAM, EMMANUEL
, *on Plymouth wedding feast (1621)*
Gill — *Mayflower* p.104-105

AMADAS, PHILIP
Amer. Her. — *Thirteen* p.40-41, 46, 57-58

AMERICA
See also **Chronology**
- *17th century, end of*
Hawke — *U.S.* p.220-281

AMES, WILLIAM, REV.
Morison — *Intellect.* p.10-11, 20-21, 42, 160
Rutman — *Winthrop's* p.47, 51, 101, 283-285
Wertenbaker — *Puritan.* See index p.347

AMISH
Calverton — *Awake.* p.189

AMSTERDAM, HOLLAND
Dillon — *Pilgrims* p.71, 75, 83, 86-95, 112
Leynse — *Preced.* See index p.279
- *Congregation*
Willison — *Saints.* See index p.495

AMUSEMENTS
See also **Indians — Amusements; Puritans — Amusements; Sports and games;** names of amusements
Acheson — *America's* p.119
Bridenbaugh — *Cities* p.116-121
Chitwood — *History* p.489-491
Drepperd — *Pioneer* p.97-98

Nettels — *Roots* p.455-456
Wertenbaker — *First. See* index p.339
Wright — *Everyday* p.212-213
- *New Amsterdam*
    Bridenbaugh — *Cities* p.119
- *New England, attitude of*
    Dulles — *America* p.4-6, 12-13,
    16-17
- *New York*
    Wish — *Society (1)* p.99-100
, *Pioneer*
    Lawrence — *Society* p.12-13
- *Virginia*
    Dulles — *America* p.5, 8
    Wish — *Society (1)* p.80-81

ANABAPTISTS
Calverton — *Awake.* p.20, 162-163,
169, 181-182
Gildrie — *Salem* p.78-79, 83
Hawke — *Colonial* p.46-49, 178, 220,
302
Willison — *Saints* p.23, 32, 53, 334,
351, 380
- *Boston*
    Bridenbaugh — *Cities* p.102-103
, *German*
    Sweet — *Religion* p.15

ANATOMY
Wertenbaker — *First* p.165

ANAWON (Indian)
Morison — *Story* p.278-279
Willison — *Saints* p.400

**ANCIENT AND HONORABLE ARTIL-
LERY CO. (Boston)**
- *Founding (1638)*
    Adams — *Album* p.110

"ANCIENT BRETHREN"
Willison — *Pilgrim* p.7-10, 14-16, 32-
35, 185n
Willison — *Saints. See* index p.495

ANDERSON, RICHARD
Willison — *Pilgrim* p.309-310, 313,
366, 440-442, 448-453

ANDIRONS
Earle — *Colonial* p.285
Earle — *Home* p.62
Glubok — *Home* p.32

Gould — *Early* p.63-65
- *Cob irons*
    Earle — *Home* p.62

ANDREWES, LAUNCELOT, BISHOP
Morison — *Intellect.* p.21, 155, 157-
159

ANDREWS, RICHARD
Willison — *Saints,* p.266, 307-308,
310

ANDROS, EDMUND, SIR
Acheson — *America's* p.115-117,
130-131
Alderman — *Story* p.31-32, 62-63, 77-
78, 80, 99
Amer. Her. — *Thirteen* p.158, 164,
166, 196
Bailyn — *New England* p.169-170,
172-173, 175-176, 179-181, 187,
191, 193-134, 197
Chitwood — *History* p.175
Craven — *Colonies* p.78-79, 106, 188,
201-204, 207-208, 215-222, 225,
236
Folsom — *Give* p.64-66
Hawke — *Colonial* p.261-265; *See
also* index p.701
Jernegan — *American* p.159
Johnston — *Conn.* p.90-91, 94-98
Morison — *Intellect.* p.41, 198-199,
201-207
Morison — *Oxford* p.118-120
Morison — *Story* p.157, 263, 266-267,
282
Morris — *Ency.* p.40
Nettels — *Roots* p.235-236, 298-301,
345, 347, 352
Rothbard — *Conceived (1)* p.338-349;
See also index p.519
Rozwenc — *Making (1)* p.82-83, 93
Wertenbaker — *First* p.107, 134-136,
277
Wertenbaker — *Puritan. See* index
p.347
Willison — *Pilgrim* p.527-529
Willison — *Saints* p.403-405, 455-456
, *as prisoner*
    Collins — *Story* p.88
, *"On the rebellion against Governor
Andros" (1689)*
    Annals of America (1) p.277-282
- *Self-defense*
    Hawke — *U.S.* p.203-204

ANGLICANS
See also **Episcopalians; Puritans, as Anglicans**
Amer. Her. — *Thirteen* p.38, 154, 158, 176
Bailyn — *New England. See* index p.243 (under Anglicanism)
Beck — *Pilgrims* p.4-5, 7-8, 81
Bridenbaugh — *Cities* p.103
Carman — *History (1)* p.34-40, 86, 92-93, 97
Chitwood — *History* p.426-427
Craven — *Southern* p.130, 178-180, 228-230, 291
Folsom — *Give* p.8, 11-15, 19, 49, 65, 72-73
Greene — *Provincial* p.92-94
Leynse — *Preced. See* index p.279
Morris — *Ency.* p.547
Murdock — *Literature* p.5-6, 8, 19-28, 36-39, 44-45, 64
Nettels — *Roots* p.470, 478-479
Pomfret — *Founding. See* index p.374 (under Church of England)
Rutman — *Winthrop's. See* index p.302 (under Church of England)
Smith — *17th. See* index p.227
Ver Steeg — *Formative* p.206-207
Wertenbaker — *First. See* index p.339
Willison — *Pilgrim. See* index p.571
Willison — *Saints. See* index p.495
Wish — *Society (1)* p.4-5, 76-79, 94
Wright — *Cultural* p.83, 87
Wright — *Everyday* p.160
- *Carolinas*
  See also **Anglicans — North Carolina; Anglicans — South Carolina**
  Sweet — *Religion* p.39-40
  Wright — *Cultural* p.87-88
- *Colonial policy*
  Smith — *17th* p.166-191
- *Commissaries*
  Sweet — *Religion* p.55-56
- *England*
  Hawke — *Colonial* p.51-53
- *Liturgy, neglect of*
  Wertenbaker — *First* p.124-126
- *Maryland*
  Jernegan — *American* p.104
- *New England*
  Sweet — *Religion* p.46-48
- *New York*
  Sweet — *Religion* p.35-39
- *North Carolina*
  Sweet — *Religion* p.40

- *Pennsylvania*
  Chitwood — *History (1)* p.210
  Sweet — *Religion* p.52
- *South*
  Craven — *Southern* p.130, 178-180, 228-330
- *South Carolina*
  Sweet — *Religion* p.41
- *Virginia*
  Craven — *Colonies* p.9, 14, 32, 41-42
  Morison — *Oxford* p.91
  Nettels — *Roots* p.106-107
  Smith — *17th* p.119-142
  Sweet — *Virginia* p.29-33
  Ver Steeg — *Formative* p.88-91

ANGLO-. *See* **England and English**

ANIMALS
See also **Livestock;** names of animals
Rawson — *When p.49-53*
- *Boston (1630–1649)*
  Rutman — *Winthrop's* p.69, 88, 99, 185, 187-188, 205-207, 221, 225
, *Domestic*
  Beck — *Pilgrims* p.58, 61-62, 74
  Furnas — *Americans* p.169-171
  Gould — *Early* p.100
  Hope — *Nation* p.84-85
  Leonard — *Dear* p.129
- *New Netherland*
  Axtell — *America* p.37-41, 138-139
, *Sea — New England*
  Axtell — *America* p.31-33
, *Wild*
  Hope — *Nation* p.86
  Lawrence — *New* p.55-58
  Scott — *Settlers* p.7-9
, *Wild — New England*
  Axtell — *America* p.26-31

ANNALISTS
Morris — *Ency.* p.558-560

ANNAWON (Indian). *See* **Anawon (Indian)**

ANNE, QUEEN
Phillips — *First* p.163-171, 194

ANNE **(ship)**
Annals of America (1), p.73
Caffrey — *Mayflower,* p.184-185, 198

Morison — *Story* p.97-99
Willison — *Pilgrim* p.234, 540-545
Willison — *Saints. See* index p.495
- *Passengers*
    Caffrey — *Mayflower* p.357
    Hills — *History (1)* p.84-86
- *"Saints"*
    Willison — *Pilgrim* p.540-542
    Willison — *Saints* p.446-448
- *"Strangers"*
    Willison — *Pilgrim* p.542-545
    Willison — *Saints* p.448-450

"ANNIVERSARY DAY"
Earle — *Customs* p.231

"ANTIMONIANS"
See also **Hutchinson, Anne Marbury**
Amer. Her. — *Thirteen* p.106
Fisher — *Men (1)* p.153-159, 161
Gildrie — *Salem* p.115-116, 121-122,
    156-158, 162
Goetzmann — *Colonial* p.181-184
Morison — *Intellect.* p.29
Nettels — *Roots* p.178-180
Pomfret — *Founding* p.193, 225, 237,
    259
Rozwenc — *Making (1)* p.71
Ver Steeg — *Formative* p.49-51
Wright — *Cultural* p.82

APPALACHIAN MOUNTAINS
Hawke — *Colonial* p.77
- *Views of John Lederer*
    Axtell — *America* p.233-236

APPAREL. *See* **Clothing and dress;**
names of apparel

"APPLE BEES"
Gould — *Early* p.137
Rawson — *When* p.77

APPLES
Adams — *Provincial* p.27
Earle — *Home* p.145-147
Glubok — *Home* p.80-82
- *Applesauce and apple butter*
    Gould — *Early* p.136-137
- *Drying*
    Gould — *Early* p.137-138
- *Orchards*
    Gould — *Early* p.135

APPRENTICES
Monroe — *Founding (1)* p.40-41
Tunis — *Craftsmen* p.14-15
Wright — *Everyday* p.102-120, 133,
    137
- *Boston*
    Rutman — *Winthrop's* p.139,
    207, 220-221, 221n, 232, 242
    Woodward — *Way* p.19-20
- *Character of system*
    Monroe — *Founding (1)* p.34-35
- *Decline of system*
    Monroe — *Founding (1)* p.50-52
- *Education*
    Monroe — *Founding (1)* p.34-52
  - *New England*
      Monroe — *Founding (1)*
      p.46, 50, 105-107
      Wertenbaker — *First* p.63-64
  - *New York*
      Monroe — *Founding (1)*
      p.45-48
  - *Pennsylvania*
      Monroe — *Founding (1)*
      p.43-45
  - *Virginia*
      Monroe — *Founding (1)* p.42
- *New England. See* **Appprentices —**
Education — New England;
Plymouth — Apprenticeship
- *Villages*
    Bridenbaugh — *Cities* p.46-48

APSLEY, LUCY. *See* **Hutchinson, Lucy**
Apsley

APTUXCET (BOURNE),
    MASSACHUSETTS
Dillon — *Pilgrims* p.197-198, 219
Morrison — *Early* p.90-91
Willison — *Saints* p.264-265, 301, 338

"AQUA—VITAE" (liquor)
Earle — *Customs* p.174

ARBELLA (ARABELLA), LADY. *See*
Johnson, Arabella, Lady

***ARBELLA (ARABELLA)* (ship)**
Caffrey — *Mayflower* p.228-229
Morison — *Story* p.120
Starkey — *Land* p.1-11

ARBITRATION
- *Boston*
    Rutman — *Winthrop's* p.155,
    233-235, 257

ARCHITECTURE
See also **Builders and building;
Churches; Houses; Mansions;**
details of architecture
Carman — History (1) p.114
Furnas — Americans p.154-159
Miller — First p.174-175
Morris — Ency. p.597
Morrison — Early p.2-175, esp. p.95-
96
Wish — Society (1) p.47-48, 82, 93

- Carolinas
Morrison — Early p.165-172
, Commercial and industrial (New
England)
Morrison — Early p.89-94
, Dutch and Flemish
Arts — America p.56
Morrison — Early p.99-123

- Materials and construction
Morrison — Early p.101-104
- "Dutch colonial"
Morrison — Early p.104-118
- Albany, N.Y.
Morrison — Early p.108-114
- Long Island, N.Y.
Morrison — Early p.120-123
- English background
Morrison — Early p.15-17
- "Flemish colonial"
See also **Architecture — Dutch
and Flemish**
Morrison — Early p. 119-123
, French
Arts — America p.52
, Georgian
Wertenbaker — Puritan p.124-
127
, Gothic
Morrison — Early p.96
- Medieval tradition
Arts — America p.62-66
Morrison — Early p.5-7
- New Amsterdam
Morrison — Early p.105-107
- New England
Morrison — Early p.49-98
Wertenbaker — First p.85, 285-
288, 317-318
- New Jersey
Wertenbaker — First p.291-292
- Philadelphia
Wertenbaker — First p.290-291
, Private
Wertenbaker — First p.283-292

, Public
See also **Architecture, Com-
mercial and industrial**
Wertenbaker — First p. 292-294
- Massachusetts
Wertenbaker — First p.292-
293
- Virginia
Wertenbaker — First p.89-90
- South
Wertenbaker — First p.286-287,
317
Wertenbaker — Old p.71-82
- "Southern colonial"
Morrison — Early p.134-174
, Swedish and German
Arts — America p.60
- Virginia
Wertenbaker — Old p.75-82

ARGALL, SAMUEL, SIR
Christensen — Delaware, p.155
Craven — Southern p.85, 92, 97, 101-
102, 108, 114, 121, 369
Hawke — Colonial p.99-100, 280, 332
Phillips — First p.116-120

ARISTOCRACY
See also **Classes; Clothing and
dress — Aristocracy; Plantations
and planters; Society;** and related
subjects
Adams — Provincial p.56-65
Dillon — Pilgrims. See index p.245
Hawke — Colonial p.291-293
Nettels — Roots p.305-309
Rozwenc — Making (1) p.68
Rutman — Winthrop's. See index
p.308
Ver Steeg — Formative p.68-69

- Abbreviations and titles
Adams — Provincial p.57
, and government
Nettels — Roots p.162-163
- Boston
Bridenbaugh — Cities p.96-97
Rutman — Winthrop's. See index
p.308
- New Amsterdam
Bridenbaugh — Cities p.98-99
- New England
Wertenbaker — First p.69-71, 75,
97
- Newport, Rhode Island
Bridenbaugh — Cities p.98

- *Philadelphia*
  Bridenbaugh — *Cities* p.99-100
- *South*
  Wertenbaker — *Old* p.10, 20-22
- *Virginia*
  Calverton — *Awake.* p.212, 217-218
  Wertenbaker — *First* p.26-27, 34-36, 44-48

ARITHMETIC
See also **Mathematics**
Glubok — *Home* p.150-152

ARMAMENT
See also **Indians — Armament**
, *European*
  Vaughan — *New* p.15, 25, 52, 58, 67, 88-91, 99, 100-101, 229-231
, *Ships'*
  Marshall — *Mayflower* p.48, 56, 134

ARMINE, MARY, LADY
Earle — *Two cent. (1)* p.xv, 60

ARMINIANISM
Dillon — *Pilgrims* p.93, 99-100, 206-207
Pomfret — *Founding* p.159
Willison — *Saints* p.92-93, 356

ARMS AND ARMOR
- *Massachusetts*
  Earle — *Two cent, (2)* p.685
  Marshall — *Mayflower* p.107-108

ARMY. *See* **Militia;** names of wars; related subjects

ARNOLD, WILLIAM
Snell — *Wild* p.128-129

ART
See also **Artisans; Crafts and craftsmanship; Limners; Painters and paintings; Portraits and portrait painting; Puritans — Art; Sculpture;** related subjects and types of art
Adams — *Provincial* p.139-146
Chitwood — *History (1)* p.476
Hawke — *Colonial* p.285-288
Wright — *Cultural* p.206-207

"ARTICLES OF AGREEMENT." *See* **"Adventurers"**

ARTIFACTS
Marshall — *Mayflower* p.101

ARTILLERY. *See* **Guns**

ARTILLERY SERMONS. *See* **Sermons, "Election and artillery"**

ARTISANS
See also **Crafts and craftsmanship;** related subjects
Bridenbaugh — *Cities* p.36-38, 42-44
Earle — *Colonial* p.296-315
Folsom — *Give* p.ix, 3, 7, 9, 25, 65, 68-69, 73
- *Boston*
  Rutman — *Winthrop's* p.76, 188-190, 200, 211, 231-232, 242, 249-251
- *New England*
  Wertenbaker — *First* p.61-65, 69-70
  Wertenbaker — *Puritan* p.49-50
, *Traveling*
  Nettels — *Roots* p.249-250

ASH OVENS
Gould — *Early* p.54

ASHES
, *Use of*
  Gould — *Early* p.54

ASHLEY, EDWARD
Morison — *Story* p.135
Willison — *Pilgrim* p.359-362, 365
Willison — *Saints* p.289-291

ASPINET (Indian)
Archer — *Mayflower* p.313-315

ASPINWALL, WILLIAM
Rutman — *Winthrop's* p.54, 73-74, 79-81, 82n, 123, 167, 175-176, 226, 247

ASSEMBLIES
See also **Courts;** names of colonies
Carman — *History (1)* p.127-128
Chitwood — *History (1)* p.149
Craven — *Colonies* p.25-29, 91-92, 146, 152, 154-155, 164, 199
Folsom — *Give* p.67, 70-74, 77

ASSEMBLIES (*continued*)
- *South*
Craven — *Southern. See* index
p.435

ASSIZE COURTS
Craven — *Colonies* p.76-78

ASTROLABES
Marshall — *Mayflower* p.38

ASTROLOGY
Morison — *Intellect.* p.144, 148-149
, *in medicine*
Marshall — *Mayflower* p.122-123,
127

ASTRONOMY
Adams — *Provincial* p.123
Morison — *Intellect.* p.42, 144, 147,
244-249, 252-254
Morris — *Ency.* p.528
Wright — *Cultural* p.220-221

**ATHERTON COMPANY (Mass. and
Conn. merchants)**
Bailyn — *New England* p.117-118,
171-172
Pomfret — *Founding* p.224-225, 227
, *and Commission of 1664*
Bailyn — *New England* p.119-120

ATTICS
Adams — *Album* p.85-86
Gould — *Early* p.22
Smith — *Colonial* p.68-69

ATTWOOD, ANNE
Demos — *Little* p.37-38, 123

ATTWOOD (ATTWOOD, WOOD), JOHN
Willison — *Pilgrim* p.441, 450-453
Willison — *Saints* p.309, 329, 456

AUGSBURG, WAR OF THE LEAGUE OF.
See King William's War

AUSTIN, ANN(E)
Wertenbaker — *First* p.101-102
Wertenbaker — *Puritan* p.226-227
Williams — *Demeter's* p.124

AUTHORITY
, *Conceptions of*
Rozwenc — *Making (1)* p.63-68

- *Imperial yoke*
Rozwenc — *Making (1)* p.77-83
, *Instruments of*
Rozwenc — *Making (1)* p.53-63

AUTHORS
See also names of authors; types of
authors
- *New England women*
Earle — *Customs* p.268-269
- *"Reporters"*
Morris — *Ency.* p.558-560

AUTUMN
Gould — *Early* p.133-140

AVERY, MARY TAPPAN
Leonard — *Dear* p.176
Williams — *Demeter's* p.194

AXES
See also **Adzes**
Marshall — *Mayflower* p.71, 73
- *Helves*
Earle — *Home* p.314-315

AYRES, MRS. WILLIAM (accused witch)
Williams — *Demeter's* p.137

B

BABIES
See also **Childbearing; Children and
childhood; Christenings; Infant
mortality; Plymouth — Babies;
Puritans — Babies**
Adams — *Album* p.87
Earle — *Customs* p.1-6
Glubok — *Home* p.94-103
- *Monsters (Mass.)*
Willison — *Pilgrim* p.429-430

BACHELORS
See also **Jamestown — Bachelors;
Plymouth — Bachelors; Puritans
— Bachelors**
Earle — *Customs* p.37-38
Goodwin — *Colonial* p.54
Lawrence — *Not* p.122

BACON, ELIZABETH DUKE
Williams — *Demeter's* p.162

BACON, NATHANIEL
See also **Bacon's Rebellion**
Abbot — *Colonial* p.79-80
Acheson — *America's* p.163-165
Alderman — *Story* p.16-18
Amer. Her. — *Thirteen* p.177-179
Craven — *Colonies* p.127,130-131,
134, 139-141, 143, 145-146, 149
Craven — *Southern. See* index p.436
Fisher — *Men (1)* p.44-54
Folsom — *Give* p.44-48
Goodwin — *Colonial* p.267-269
Hope — *Nation* p.65-66
Morison — *Oxford* p.109, 111-115
Nettels — *Roots* p.334-336
Rozwenc — *Making (1)* p.76-77
Scott — *Settlers* p.98-100
Willison — *Saints* p.456
- *Death*
Tyler — *History* p.68-70
- *Epitaph*
Miller — *Colonial* p.370-371

BACON, NATHANIEL, JR.
Chitwood — *History (1)* p.75-78
Life — *New* p.56
Rothbard — *Conceived (1)* p.101-103,
105-110, 126, 144
Smith — *17th* p.103-104, 210
Starkey — *Land* p.200, 202-204
Wertenbaker — *First* p.35, 37, 200,
309

BACON'S CASTLE (Arthur Allen House)
Morrison — *Early* p.147-149
Wertenbaker — *Old* p.85

BACON'S LAWS
Jernegan — *American* p.64

BACON'S REBELLION
See also **Seneca Indians, in Bacon's
Rebellion**
Abbot — *Colonial* p.65, 79-80
Acheson — *America's* p.161-165
Amer. Her. — *Thirteen* p.177-179
Annals of America (1) p.255-261
Bailey — *American (1)* p.16-18
Calverton — *Awake.* p.226-232
Chitwood — *History (1)* p.75-78
Collins — *Story* p.39
Craven — *Colonies* p.107-108, 126-
134, 137-146, 148-153, 160, 167
Craven — *Southern* p.360-393
Fisher — *Men (1)* p.44-55
Folsom — *Give* p.32, 44-48, 72

Goetzmann — *Colonial* p.133-138
Hawke — *Colonial* p.244-250
Hawke — *U.S.* p.190-194
Hope — *Nation* p.66-68
Jernegan — *American* p.63-64
Kraus — *U.S.(1)* p.84-87
Life — *New* p.56, 64
Morison — *Oxford* p.111-115
Morris — *Ency.* p.28
National — *History.* p.61
Nettels — *Roots* p.334-336
Rothbard — *Conceived (1)* p.94, 102-
113, 126, 358, 510
Rozwenc — *Making (1)* p.75-77
Smith — *17th* p.52-55, 90, 102, 119,
140, 209, 221
Tyler — *History* p.61-70, 260, 488n,
491
Ver Steeg — *Formative* p.133-135
Wertenbaker — *First* p.4, 37, 43, 140,
304
Wish — *Society (1)* p.74-75
- *Results*
Chitwood — *History (1)* p.78
Jernegan — *American* p.64-65
Rothbard — *Conceived (1)* p.126-
130, 144-153
, *Women in*
Earle — *Colonial* p.24-25
Spruill — *Women's* p.233-236

BAKE OVENS
Gould — *Early* p.52-53

BAKER, WILLIAM A.
Gill — *Mayflower* p.65-67, 167
Marshall — *Mayflower* p.32, 48

BAKERS AND "BAKE HOUSES"
Bridenbaugh — *Cities* p.36
Earle — *Colonial* p.288-289
Earle — *Home* p.147
Tunis — *Craftsmen* p.43-44
- *Boston*
Rutman — *Winthrop's* p.189,
207, 211, 241

BALLADS
Morison — *Intellect.* p.53-54, 132
- *Ballad of 1623*
Morison — *Story* p.97-99, 115,
188
- *Writers*
Tyler — *History* p.304

BALLOTS. *See* **Suffrage**

BALLS (games)
Rawson — *When* p.81-82
, *Indian*
Northey — *American* p.20-21

BALLS AND BALLROOMS. *See* Dances
and dancing

BALTIMORE, LORDS
Sweet — *Religion. See* index p.357

**BALTIMORE, GEORGE CALVERT (1st
Lord)**
Alderman — *Story* p.81-82, 84, 89
Carman — *History (1)* p.30, 54
Chitwood — *History (1)* p.79-86
Craven — *Southern* p.175, 184, 186-
188, 190; *See also* index p.436
Fisher — *Men (2)* p.147, 149, 151-152
Hawke — *Colonial* p.108-111, 147,
208
Hawke — *U.S.* p.81-84
Hope — *Nation* p.93
Morison — *Oxford* p.79-85
Morris — *Ency.* p.28
Nettels — *Roots* p.121-123
Pomfret — *Founding* p.58, 76-80, 134-
136, 140, 148, 164, 167
Starkey — *Land* p.106-109

**BALTIMORE, CECILIUS CALVERT (2nd
Lord)**
Alderman — *Story* p.82-83, 88
Craven — *Colonies* p.9, 17, 22, 40,
43, 64, 72, 91, 160
Craven — *Southern. See* index p.436
Fisher — *Men (2)* p.154, 159-164, 169
Hawke — *Colonial* p.111-114, 181-
182, 185, 201-202, 250
Jernegan — *American* p.65-66
Morris — *Ency.* p.28-29
Pomfret — *Founding* p.58, 77, 80-83,
88-93, 96-100
Rothbard — *Conceived* (1) p.114-116,
119
Snell — *Wild* p.127-128, 131

**BALTIMORE, CHARLES CALVERT (3rd
Lord)**
Craven — *Colonies* p.27, 160-165,
190-191, 198-199, 230-231, 241
Craven — *Southern* p.193, 300-301,
410, 412, 414-415; *See also* index
p.436
Hawke — *Colonial* p.271-272, 336

BALTIMORE, MARYLAND
- *Laying out*
Collins — *Story* p.68

BANGS, EDWARD
Willison — *Saints* p.332, 448-449

BANGS, LYDIA HICKS
Willison — *Saints* p.448-449

BANISTER, JOHN
Morris — *Ency.* p.528

BANKS AND BANKING
See also related subjects
Bailyn — *New England* p.100, 183-
185, 188

BAPTISM
See also **"Half-way Covenant"**
Dexter — *Colonial* p.62-63
Willison — *Pilgrim* p.422n, 426n, 435-
436
Willison — *Saints. See* index p.496
- *Boston*
Rutman — *Winthrop's. See* index
p.298
- *Problems*
Vaughan — *Puritan* p.115-120

BAPTISTS
Chitwood — *History (1)* p.434-435
Hall — *Religious* p.101, 129-130
Morison — *Story* p.149, 163-164, 226,
232-233
Morris — *Ency.* p.548
Nettels — *Roots* p.471-472
Wertenbaker — *Puritan* p.224-245
Willison — *Saints* p.377, 382, 407,
439, 442, 445, 448, 452-453, 455,
459, 484
- *Churches. First in America*
Sweet — *Religion* p.127-131
- *Persecution*
Chitwood — *History (1)* p.120,
438-439
Sweet — *Religion* p.131-139
- *Views of John Clarke*
Vaughan — *Puritan* p.225-230
, *Welsh*
Sweet — *Religion* p.135-136

BARBADOS
See also **Puritans — Barbados**
Alderman — *Story* p.137-138, 141

Amer. Her. — *Thirteen* p.179-180, 182
Bailyn — *New England* p.68-69, 84-85, 88-89, 93, 96, 111, 133
Craven — *Colonies* p.3, 39, 55, 96, 98-99, 101, 135, 202, 233, 237
Craven — *Southern* p.137, 183, 192, 373
Morison — *Oxford* p.59-60, 100-101
Nettels — *Roots* p.124-125
Pomfret — *Founding* p.66, 99, 311-315, 317-318
Starkey — *Land* p.11, 218-219, 223-224, 229

, *and Carolina settlement*
Craven — *Southern* p.319-321, 329-333, 336, 337n, 343, 345-346, 350, 358
- *Trade*
Wertenbaker — *First* p.51, 54, 77

BARBERS AND BARBER-SURGEONS
See also **Wigs and wigmakers**
Langdon — *Everyday* p.326-327
Miller — *First* p.246
Tunis — *Craftsmen* p.41-42

BARK HOUSES.
See also **Indians — Bark houses**
Snell — *Wild* p.111

BARKER, ELIZABETH. *See* **Winslow, Elizabeth Barker**

"BARKING SPUDS" (spades)
Marshall — *Mayflower* p.77, 79

BARLOWE, ARTHUR
Amer. Her. — *Thirteen* p.40-41, 57-58

BARNS
Langdon — *Everyday* p.291

BARNSTABLE, MASSACHUSETTS
Morison — *Story* p.52, 78, 141-143, 153, 173, 219, 226-227, 233, 243, 284, 291
Willison — *Saints. See* index p.496

BARNYARDS
Rawson — *When* p.39-40

BARRELMAKING. *See* **Coopers**

BARROW(E), HENRY
Wertenbaker — *Puritan* p.20-22

Willison — *Pilgrim* p.9, 420n, 421n
Willison — *Saints* p.41-42, 61-65, 75, 89, 301, 330, 463

BARROWISM
Willison — *Saints* p.61-62, 78, 457, 459-460

BARTERING
See also **Trade and traders**
Langdon — *Everyday* p.193-194
Marshall — *Mayflower* p.170
, *with butter and cheese*
Gould — *Early* p.105

BARTLETT, MARY WARREN
Willison — *Saints* p.448, 450, 483, 486

BARTLETT, ROBERT
Hills — *History (1)* p.6, 84, 90, 94;
Hills — *History (2)* p.47, 150-151
Willison — *Saints* p.448, 450, 483, 486

BARTLETT FAMILY
Hills — *History (1) p.6, 84, 90, 94*
Hills — *History (2)* p.47, 110, 150-151, 205-206, 211-212

BASS
- *New England*
Earle — *Home* p.120-121

BASS VIOLS
, *in meetings*
Earle — *Home* p.378

BASSETT, WILLIAM
Willison — *Saints* p.191, 263, 444

BASTARDS. *See* **Illegitimacy**

BATHS AND BATHING
, *Infrequency of*
Glubok — *Home* p.103

BATTS AND BROAGS (shoes, boots)
Earle — *Two cent. (1)* p.371-388

BAULSTON, WILLIAM
Rutman — *Winthrop's* p.73, 77, 79, 81, 82n, 123, 137, 190

BAXTER, RICHARD
Morison — *Intellect.* p.22, 24, 141, 166
Murdock — *Literature* p. 37, 44-45, 47-48, 118, 133-134, 149-158, 182

"BAY HORSE." *See* **Massachusetts**

BAY PSALM BOOK
Adams — *Album* p.124
Amer. Her. — *Thirteen* p.154-155
Howard — *Our* p.5, 8-11
Morris — *Ency.* p.611
Sweet — *Religion* p.116-117
Tyler — *History* p.236-238
Wertenbaker — *Puritan* p.94-95
Willison — *Saints* p.464, 474, 481-483

BAYBERRY
Adams — *Album* p.118
Earle — *Colonial* p.303-306

BEACH, ELIZABETH
Williams — *Demeter's* p.32

BEAD BAGS
Earle — *Home* p.263

BEADLE, JOHN
Murdock — *Literature* p.101-102

BEANS
Earle — *Home* p.141, 145
Leonard — *Dear* p.132

BEARDS
Earle — *Two cent. (1)* p.349-358

BEARS
- *New Netherland*
Axtell — *America* p.37-39

"BEATING THE BOUNDS"
Glubok — *Home* p.208-210

BEAUCHAMP, JOHN
Caffrey — *Mayflower* p.220-221, 240, 259-260
Willison — *Pilgrim* p.309-310, 313, 366, 440-442, 452-454
Willison — *Saints* p. 204, 266-267, 307-308, 310, 317

BEAUTY AIDS. *See* **Cosmetics**

BEAVERS
See also **Fur trade**
Snell — *Wild* p.61, 66-67, 114
, *as currency*
Bridenbaugh — *Cities* p.52
- *New Netherland*
Axtell — *America* p.41-51

BECK, BARBARA L.
Beck — *Pilgrims* p.90

BEDDING
See also **Blankets; Coverlets**
Beck — *Pilgrims* p.56
Earle — *Customs* p.114-116
Gould — *Early* p.27-28
Leonard — *Dear* p.105-106
- *Flannel sheets*
Glubok — *Home* p.100-101

BEDS AND BEDROOMS
See also **Bedding**
Earle — *Customs* p.112-114
Earle — *Home* p.55-56
Gould — *Early* p.27-28
Langdon — *Everyday* p.34-36
Leonard — *Dear* p.105
Morrison — *Early* p.48
Spruill — *Women's* p.23-24
- *Delaware*
Christensen — *Delaware* p.33
- *Plymouth. See* **Plymouth — Beds and bedrooms**

BEER
Earle — *Customs* p.163-166
Gould — *Early* p.106
Miller — *First* p.184-185
Morison — *Story* p.20, 62, 97, 101, 115, 168, 200
- *Pilgrims. See* **Pilgrims — Beverages — Beer**

"BEES" (social functions)
See also types of bees, e.g. **Apple; Chopping; Husking; Logging; Quilting;** etc.
Holliday — *Woman's* p.118-119
Rawson — *When* p.63-78

BEISSEL, CONRAD
Calverton — *Awake.* p.199

BELCHER, ANDREW
Bailyn — *New England* p.194-197

BELLINGHAM, MRS. RICHARD
Earle — *Colonial* p.120-122

BELLINGHAM, RICHARD
Rutman — *Winthrop's* p.70, 73, 75, 77, 90n, 170, 232, 242, 247

BELLOMONT, EARL OF (Robert Coote)
Chitwood — *History (1)* p.245-246
Nettels — *Roots* p.377-378
Rothbard — *Conceived (1)* p.464-471,
473-476, 479-480

BELLOWS (belluses)
Gould — *Early* p.80

BELLS
- *Churches*
Lawrence — *New* p.186
- *Meetinghouses*
Rawson — *When* p.193-195
- *Steeples*
Speare — *Life* p.45

BENDALL, EDWARD
Rutman — *Winthrop's* p.74n, 85, 193,
222, 228, 247, 254

"BENEFITS." *See* **Remedies**

BENNETT, RICHARD
Craven — *Southern. See* index p.436

BEOTHUK INDIANS
Snell — *Wild* p.62, 66

"BERGEN HOUSE" (Brooklyn)
Morrison — *Early* p.121-122

BERKELEY, FRANCES, DAME
- *Marriages to governors*
Williams — *Demeter's* p.90

BERKELEY, JOHN, LORD
See also **"Green Spring" faction**
Calverton — *Awake.* p.212-221, 226-
227, 375
Craven — *Colonies* p.13, 54, 56, 59-
60, 64, 83-85, 106, 181
Snell — *Wild* p.141, 144, 148
, *New York grant to*
Chitwood — *History (1)* p.176-
177

BERKELEY, WILLIAM, SIR
Abbot — *Colonial p.78-80*
Acheson — *America's* p.162-164
Alderman — *Story* p.15-17, 62
Amer. Her. — *Pioneer* p.84
Chitwood — *History (1)* p.69-70, p.72-
73, 75-77, 84
Craven — *Colonies. See* index p.354
Craven — *Southern. See* index p.436

Fisher — *Men(1)* p.47-53
Life — *New* p.56, 58
Morison — *Oxford* p.92-93
Morris — *Ency.* p.27
Rothbard — *Conceived (1)* p.83-86,
90-91, 93, 98-103, 106, 108-113,
121, 128, 144, 148, 277, 510
Smith — *17th. See* index p.228
Starkey — *Land* p.121, 175, 197, 199-
205, 220
Tyler — *History* p.62-63, 67, 77-78,
491
Wertenbaker — *First. See* index p.340
Wish — *Society (1)* p.74-75, 77, 83-
84, 90
, *on Virginia (1671)*
Bailey — *American (1)* p.15-16

BERMUDA COMPANY
Pomfret — *Founding* p.304-307

BERNARD, FRANCIS
Alderman — *Story* p.163-164

BERRIES
Earle — *Home* p.145

BESOMS AND BRUSHES. *See* **Brooms**

BEST SELLERS (1640–1699)
Morris — *Ency.* p.560

BETTY LAMPS
Adams — *Album* p.81
Drepperd — *Pioneer* p.199

BEVERAGES
See also names of beverages, e.g.
Beer
Chitwood — *History (1)* p.487
Earle — *Customs* p.163-182
Earle — *Home* p.163
Furnas — *Americans* p.141-143
Gould — *Early* p.83, 105-107
Leonard — *Dear* p.148-149
Nettels — *Roots* p.238
- *Connecticut*
Johnston — *Conn.* p.51
- *Pilgrims. See* **Pilgrims —
Beverages**

"BEVERIGE" (mild drink)
Earle — *Customs* p.173

BEVERLEY, ROBERT
Smith — *17th* p.12, 109, 133, 140,
193, 219-221, 223, 225

BEVERLEY, ROBERT (*continued*)
    Tyler — *History* p.61, 75-76, 257, 491
    Wertenbaker — *First* p.31, 253-254,
        256, 269
    - *History of Virginia*
        Rozwenc — *Making (1)* p.101-
            103
    - *Indian customs and manners*
        Miller — *Colonial* p.248-256

BIBLE
    Morison — *Intellect. See* index p.277
    Murdock — *Literature. See* index
        p.229
    Willison — *Saints. See* index p.496
    , *Algonquin*
        See also **Eliot, John**
        Amer. Her. — *Pioneer* p.60-61
        Beals — *John Eliot* p.127, 137,
            151-152, 154-155, 181-182
        Vaughan — *New* p.238, 247, 274,
            276, 287, 300, 317, 320

**"BIBLE COMMONWEALTH." *See*
Massachusetts, as "Bible
Commonwealth"**

BIENVILLE, JEAN BAPTISTE, SIEUR DE
    Snell — *Wild* p.156-157

BIGOTRY. *See* Intolerance

"BILBOWES" (bilboes, footcuffs)
    Lawrence — *Not* p.134-135

BILL OF RIGHTS
    See also **"General Fundamentals"**
    , *First in America*
        Marshall — *Mayflower* p.180-181

BILLINGTON, FRANCIS
    Morison — *Story* p.64-65
    Willison — *Saints* p.133, 286, 321,
        440-441, 450

BILLINGTON, JOHN (Sr.)
    Beck — *Pilgrims* p.40-41
    Dillon — *Pilgrims* p.164, 190, 203-204
    Hills — *History (1)* p.21, 29, 37, 40,
        44, 46, 52, 54, 57, 69, 81, 89-90
    Leynse — *Preced.* p.234, 246, 261,
        263, 268
    Willison — *Pilgrim* p.125-126, 260,
        284, 355-356, 534

Willison — *Saints. See* index p.496
- *Hanging*
    Annals of America (1) p.81

**BILLINGTON, MARTHA. *See* Eaton,
Martha Billington**

BILLINGTON FAMILY
    Hills — *History (1). See* index p.162
    Leynse — *Preced.* p.234, 246-247,
        261, 263
    Marble — *Women* p.24-25, 29, 31, 69-
        70

"BILLINGTON SEA"
    Archer — *Mayflower* p.132-140

"BINDING OUT." *See* "Putting Out"

BIOGRAPHY (literature)
    Morison — *Intellect.* p.52, 121, 131,
        197
    Tyler — *History* p.374-375

BIRDS AND FOWL
    See also name of types
    Gould — *Early* p.98
    Morison — *Story* p.66-67, 77, 82, 145
    Scott — *Settlers* p.5
    - *New Netherland*
        Axtell — *America* p.41-42, 139-
            140

BIRTH RATE
    See also **Population**
    - *Dedham, Mass.*
        Lockridge — *New* p.67-68

BISHOP, BRIDGET (accused witch)
    Williams — *Demeter's* p.140

"BLACKBEARD." *See* Teach, Edward

BLACKBIRDS
    Hope — *Nation* p.86

BLACKBOARDS
    Rawsom — *When* p.146

**BLACKS. *See* Negroes; Slaves and
slavery**

BLACKSMITHS
    See also **"Farriers"**
    Marshall — *Mayflower* p.81, 172-173

Speare — *Life* p.123
Tunis — *Craftsmen* p.19-21, 58-61
- *Boston*
 Rutman — *Winthrop's* p.189-190, 211
- *New England*
 Wertenbaker — *Puritan* p.49

BLACKSTON(E), WILLIAM, REV.
Alderman — *Story* p.92-93
Beals — *John Eliot* p.70-73, 90, 96
Rutman — *Winthrop's* p.24, 28-29, 36, 39, 70, 137, 141, 213

BLACKWELL, FRANCIS
Willison — *Pilgrim* p.58n-59n
Willison — *Saints* p.109-110,136

BLACKWELL, JOHN, CAPT.
Bailyn — *New England* p.184-185, 187
Rothbard — *Conceived (1)* p.408-411, 495-496, 499, 501-502

"BLACKWELL DISASTER"
Willison — *Pilgrim* p.57-59

BLAIR, JAMES
Rozwenc — *Making (1)* p.85-86
Tyler — *History* p.488-491
Wertenbaker — *First. See* index p.340

BLANKETS
, *Children's*
 Glubok — *Home* p.100-101

BLASPHEMY. *See* **Profanity**

BLATHWAYT, WILLIAM
Bailyn — *New England* p.154, 171, 173, 177, 179, 187

BLEEDING-BASINS
Earle — *Home* p.86

BLESSING OF THE BAY **(ship)**
- *Launching, Boston (1631)*
 Nettels — *Roots* p.246

BLOCK, ADRIAN
Johnston — *Conn.* p.3-5, 15, 96
Morris — *Ency.* p.41

BLOCK ISLAND
Vaughan — *New* p.126-129, 188, 202, 221
Willison — *Saints* p.304, 449

BLOCKHOUSES
Adams — *Album* p.108-109
Morrison — *Early* p.76-79

BLOME, RICHARD
Smith — *17th* p.216-217

BLOMNAERT, SAMUEL
Christensen — *Delaware* p.25

"BLOOD ORDEAL" (for suspected murderers)
Earle — *Colonial* p.106

BLOSSOM, ANNE
Willison — *Saints* p.122, 268, 451

BLOSSOM, THOMAS
Willison — *Saints* p.122, 128, 268, 315, 451

"BLUE LAWS" (Connecticut)
Annals of America (1) p.199-203
Bailey — *American (1)* p.31-33
Lawrence — *New* p.245-246
Lawrence — *Not* p.111-115, 117-123
Sweet — *Religion* p.115-116
- *Slander*
 Lawrence — *Not* p.121-122
- *Speed (horses)*
 Lawrence — *Not* p.120

"BOARD-CLOTHS" (tablecloths)
Earle — *Customs* p.133
Earle — *Home* p.76-77
Glubok — *Home* p.40-41

BOARD OF TRADE (England)
Hawke — *Colonial. See* index p.705
Morris — *Ency.* p.57-58
- *Formation and policy (1696-99)*
 Jernegan — *American* p.253, 259-260

BOATS
See also **Ships and shipping;** types of boats
- *Laws*
 Vaughan — *New* p.196-197
- *New England*
 Langdon — *Everyday* p.213-214

BODIN, JEAN
Morison — *Intellect.* p.134-135, 148

"BOLTING ACT" (1678)
Morris — *Ency.* p.45

BOMBARDS (leather bottles)
Earle — *Colonial* p.282-283

"BOND CASTLE" (Maryland, 1649)
Morrison — *Early* p.160-162

BONDSERVANTS. See Servants, Indentured

BONGRACES (frontlets)
Earle — *Two cent. (2)* p.538-539

BONNET, STEDE, MAJOR
National — *History.* p.117

BONNETS. See Hats and hatters

BONNY, WILLIAM
Demos — *Little* p.177-178, 189

"BOOK OF GENERAL LAWES AND LIBERTYES" (1648)
Ver Steeg — *Formative* p.83-84

BOOKBINDERS
Tunis — *Craftsmen* p.98-99

BOOKS AND READING
See also **Best sellers; Censorship; Children's books and reading; Libraries; Literature; Textbooks;** related subjects
Bridenbaugh — *Cities* p.130
Earle — *Customs* p.257-263
Leonard — *Dear* p.245-246
Speare — *Life* p.167-168
Wright — *Literary* p.110-136
- *Boston, Mass.*
  Wright — *Literary* p.120-123
- *Burning, Boston*
  Earle — *Customs* p.288
- *Colleges and universities*
  Morison — *Intellect.* p.46-49
- *Etiquette*
  Earle — *Home* p.79
- *Fiction*
  Wright — *Cultural* p.143
- *First printed*
  Adams — *Album* p.124
  Earle — *Customs* p.264-265
- *History*
  Wertenbaker — *Puritan* p.87-91
  Wright — *Cultural* p.132-135
- *Indians*
  Earle — *Customs* p.265
- *Journals and diaries*
  Wright — *Cultural* p.163-164

- *Mending*
  Earle — *Customs* p.287-288
- *New England*
  Miller — *First* p.224
- *Poetry*
  See also **Poets and poetry**
  Wright — *Cultural* p.143, 171
- *Politics*
  Morison — *Intellect.* p.135, 148-149, 197-209
- *Religion.* See **Religion — Books and reading**
- *Science*
  Wright — *Cultural* p.135-136
- *"Scribbling"*
  Earle — *Customs* p.283-286
  Glubok — *Home* p.162-163
- *Sermons*
  See also **Sermons**
  Wright — *Cultural* p.139-141
- *Students' light*
  Morison — *Intellect.* p.49-56
- *Travel*
  See also **Books and reading — Journals and diaries**
  Morison — *Intellect. See* index p.287 (under Travel books)
, *Utilitarian*
  Wright — *Cultural* p.128-129
- *Virginia*
  Morison — *Oxford* p.91-92
, *Women's*
  Spruill — *Women's* p.213-216, 230

BOOKSHOPS AND BOOKSELLERS
Earle — *Customs* p.257-260
Morison — *Intellect.* p.72, 105-106n, 127-132
- *Boston*
  Bridenbaugh — *Cities* p.129-130
- *Chronology (1672-99)*
  Wright — *Literary* p.115-116

BOOTS AND SHOES. See Shoes

BORING TOOLS
Marshall — *Mayflower* p.73

BOSTON, MASSACHUSETTS (Shawmut)
Alderman — *Story* p.26-28, 30-31, 44, 76-77, 92, 115, 119
Caffrey — *Mayflower* p.152, 174, 225, 234, 271, 288-289, 304

Clark — *Old* p.25-51
Craven — *Colonies* p.18, 121, 200, 218-219, 224, 226
Earle — *Home. See* index p.454
Folsom — *Give* p.14-23, 28, 31, 37, 41, 43, 66, 76-77, 80-81, 84, 86-87, 91
Gill — *Mayflower. See* index p.201
Hawke — *Colonial. See* index p.705-706
Morison — *Story* p.81, 105, 110, 120, 139-140, 146-147, 156, 164, 201-204, 207-214, 222, 227-228, 263
Pomfret — *Founding* p.162, 202, 205-209, 212, 230, 250
Starkey — *Land* p.6, 84-86, 97, 155, 163, 182, 206-207, 213
Vaughan — *New* p.97, 101-102, 140n, 157, 159, 164, 169, 172, 207
Wertenbaker — *Puritan. See* index p.347
Willison — *Saints. See* index p.496
Woodward — *Way* p.11-37
- *Bay*
   See also **Boston . . . — Harbor**
   Willison — *Saints* p.187-188, 208, 210, 287, 382
- *Chronology (1630–49)*
   Rutman — *Winthrop's. See* index p. 298-300
- *Chronology (1663)*
   Wright — *Literary* p.79-80
- *Commerce*
   Bailyn — *New England* p.37, 40, 88-89, 95-98, 103
   Bridenbaugh — *Cities* p.30-34
- *"Common"*
   Bridenbaugh — *Cities* p.21
   Lawrence — *New* p.95-96, 106
- *Defense*
   Rutman — *Winthrop's* p.305
- *First Church*
   Bailyn — *New England* p.41-43, 141
   Rutman — *Winthrop's. See* index p.300-301
   Willison — *Saints* p.272, 355, 379, 459
- *First Town House*
   Morrison — *Early* p.88-89
   Wertenbaker — *First* p.292-293
- *Freedmen*
   Wertenbaker — *First* p.67
- *General Court*
   Beals — *John Eliot* p.81-82, 91, 93, 95, 99, 150-151

- *Harbor*
   , *Pilgrims' expedition to*
      Archer — *Mayflower* p.245-253
- *Port*
      Woodward — *Way* p.17-18
- *Life*
      Amer. Her. — *Thirteen* p.154, 158, 160
      Chitwood — *History (1)* p.479
- *Settlements*
      Marshall — *Mayflower* p.182
      Snell — *Wild* p.17, 119, 125, 127-129, 145, 148
- *Trade*
      See also **Boston . . . — Commerce**
      Amer. Her. — *Thirteen* p.100, 154-155
      Wertenbaker — *First* p.54-55

BOSTON LATIN SCHOOL
Morison — *Intellect.* p.45, 71, 76, 99, 101-112
Wright — *Everyday* p.140

BOSTON PUBLIC LIBRARY
Bridenbaugh — *Cities* p.131
Earle — *Customs* p.280

BOTTLES
- *Glass*
   Earle — *Home* p.92-93
- *Pewter*
   Earle — *Home* p.85

BOURNE, RICHARD
Morison — *Story* p.242-243
Vaughan — *New* p.288, 295, 299-300, 306

BOURNE, MASSACHUSETTS. See Aptuxet

BOWLING
- *New Amsterdam*
   Drepperd — *Pioneer* p.97

BOWLS (dishes)
Gould — *Early* p.85

"BOWLS" (game)
Jamestown (1611)
   Dulles — *America* p.3

BOWMAN, CHRISTOPHER
Willison — *Saints* p.63-64, 67, 69, 78, 110, 460

BOXES. *See* **Hemlock**

BOYLE, ROBERT
Morison — *Intellect.* p.250, 255-257, 266, 269

BOYS
- *Chores*
  Speare — *Life* p.100
- *Fights*
  Rawson — *When* p.83-84
, *in church and meetings*
  Earle — *Home* p.372-384
- *Occupations (Conn.)*
  Glubok — *Home* p.206-207

BRACELETS
Earle — *Two cent. (1)* p.57, 70-71

BRADFORD, ALICE CARPENTER SOUTHWORTH
Hills — *History (1)* p.83, 85
Hills — *History (2)* p.100, 120, 152
Marble — *Women* p.34, 36, 101-105
Willison — *Pilgrim* p.235, 510
Willison — *Saints* p.88, 236, 338, 387, 427, 447-448, 464, 474

BRADFORD, DOROTHY MAY
Dillon — *Pilgrims* p.118, 125, 147
Gill — *Mayflower* p.78
Leynse — *Preced.* p.185, 196-197, 208, 259, 266
Marble — *Women* p.7, 54
Morison — *Story* p.12, 32, 36, 47, 56
Starkey — *Land* p.48, 50-52
Willison — *Pilgrim* p.36, 78, 115, 124, 532, 555
Willison — *Saints* p.91, 122, 156-157, 438
- *Death*
  Archer — *Mayflower* p.117-118

BRADFORD, JOHN
Willison — *Saints* p.91, 122, 338, 438, 451-452

BRADFORD, WILLIAM
Amer. Her. — *Thirteen* p.90-91, 94-95, 163
Beck — *Pilgrims. See* index p.85

Caffrey — *Mayflower. See* index p.385-386
Demos — *Little* p.x, 2, 7, 10-12, 15, 27-28, 34, 61, 162, 168, 172, 174, 178, 189
Dillon — *Pilgrims. See* index p.243
Gill — *Mayflower. See* index p.201
Hall — *Religious* p.85, 90-93, 96
Leynse — *Preced.* p.265-266; *See also* index p.280
Marble — *Women* p.13, 25, 48, 53, 101-104
Marshall — *Mayflower* p.26-27, 54-55, 120, 137, 161, 166, 177, 180, 183, 185
Morison — *Intellect.* p.5, 134, 153, 155n, 177-179
Morison — *Story. See* index p.i
Murdock — *Literature* p.78-84, 91-94, 133
Pomfret — *Founding* p.101, 104-105, 118-119, 126-127, 144-145, 233
Rothbard — *Conceived (1)* p.161-162, 164, 273-274
Rozwenc — *Making (1)* p.27-29
Scott — *Settlers* p.21, 23
Smith — *17th* p.199, 201-202, 211
Snell — *Wild* p.17, 99, 101, 105-106, 108-111, 118
Starkey — *Land* p.48, 51-54, 56, 169
Vaughan — *New. See* index p.421
Wertenbaker — *First* p.192-193, 242, 276-278, 285
Wertenbaker — *Puritan* p.87-88, 169
Willison — *Pilgrim. See* index p.572
Willison — *Saints. See* index p.497
Wish — *Society (1)* p.25, 27-28, 30-33, 59
, *as governor of Plymouth*
  Archer — *Mayflower* p.207-214
- *Biography*
  Morris — *Ency.* p.637-638
- *Death*
  Willison — *Pilgrim* p.508-511
- *History*
  Gill — *Mayflower* p.157-158
, *in Austerfield (England)*
  Archer — *Mayflower* p.3-9
, *joins Separatists*
  Archer — *Mayflower* p.10-15
- *Library, personal*
  Wright — *Literary* p.27
- *"Of Plymouth Plantation" (1606–46)*
  Amer. Her. — *Thirteen* p.61-62, 146
  Annals of America (1) p.65-86

Miller — *Colonial* p.43-65
Rozwenc — *Making (1)* p.97-98
, *on morals*
Starkey — *Land* p.130-131
, *on Pilgrim exodus*
Vaughan — *Puritan* p.41-50
, *on Roger Williams*
Hawke — *U.S.* p.106
- *"The Pequot War"*
Miller — *Colonial* p.239-243
- *"Pirates in Plymouth"*
Miller — *Colonial* p.101-102
- *"Thomas Morton of Merrymount"*
Miller — *Colonial* p.103-112
Vaughan — *Puritan* p.205-207

BRADFORD, WILLIAM, JR.
Morison — *Story* p.160, 191, 218-219,
257, 264-266, 284-286, 290
Willison — *Pilgrim* p.510-511, 514,
528

BRADFORD FAMILY
Caffrey — *Mayflower. See* index p.385
Hills — *History (2)* p.103-110; *See
also* index p.248
Marble — *Women* p.54, 102

BRADSTREET, ANNE DUDLEY
Adams — *Album* p.135
Dexter — *Colonial* p.126-130
Leonard — *Dear* p.85-86, 130, 247-
248, 491-500, 536
Miller — *Colonial* p.353-356
Morison — *Intellect.* p.118-119, 211,
218-222, 224
Murdock — *Literature* p.31, 150-152
Starkey — *Land* p.5-6, 10, 86, 214
Tyler — *History. See* index p.540
Wertenbaker — *First* p.243
Wertenbaker — *Puritan* p.101-103
Williams — *Demeter's* p.29, 41-43,
94-95, 105-107, 120-121, 207
- *"To my dear and loving husband"*
Annals of America (1) p.198
- *Two poems (1650)*
Annals of America (1) p.197-198

BRADSTREET, SAMUEL
Morison — *Intellect.* p.211, 230-232

BRADSTREET, SIMON
Bailyn — *New England* p.53, 125,
138, 163, 165
Earle — *Two cent. (1)* p.xiii, 14, 140

Rothbard — *Conceived (1)* p.246,
286, 342, 368-370, 372, 376, 424,
425

BRAINTREE, MASSACHUSETTS
Rutman — *Winthrop's* p.79-84, 91-93,
95-96 and n, 200, 203, 212n, 219,
222

BRASS
Earle — *Colonial* p.283-284
Rawson — *When* p.8

BRATTLE, THOMAS
Morison — *Intellect.* p.243, 252-254,
271
Wertenbaker — *First* p.72, 113
Wright — *Literary* p.108, 108n
- *"Condemnation of witchcraft trials"*
(1692)
Annals of America (1) p.285-292

BRATTLE, WILLIAM
Wertenbaker — *Puritan* p.58-59, 152-
153, 156

BRAY, THOMAS
Sweet — *Religion* p.57-58, 57n-58n

BREADS AND BISCUITS
Earle — *Home* p.147
Gould — *Early* p.91
Lawrence — *New* p.5
Leonard — *Dear* p.143
Rutman — *Winthrop's* p.23, 174, 178,
189, 200, 207, 240
Smith — *Colonial* p.79
- *Assize law*
Bridenbaugh — *Cities* p.51
, *Dutch*
Smith — *Colonial* p.113-115
, *"Rhineinjun"*
Earle — *Colonial* p.288

BREAKFASTS
Gould — *Early* p.82

BRÉBEUF, JEAN DE
Amer. Her. — *Pioneer* p.26-27
Collins — *Story* p.78

BREEDON, THOMAS
Bailyn — *New England* p.110-111,
115-117, 120-121, 128, 138, 148

BRENT, MARGARET
Brooks — *Dames* p.59-73
Dexter — *Colonial* p.185-186
Goodwin — *Colonial* p.49-50
Holliday — *Woman's* p.299-301
Leonard — *Dear* p.66, 135, 299, 312,
321-322, 353, 415, 546
Spruill — *Women's* p.237-241
Williams — *Demeter's* p.31-32, 131-
132
, *and women's rights*
Earle — *Colonial* p.45-49

BRENT, MARY
Leonard — *Dear* p.66, 135, 299, 312,
415
Williams — *Demeter's* p.31-32

BRENTON, WILLIAM
Rutman — *Winthrop's* p.73-74, 80-82,
82n, 86, 210

BRERETON, JOHN
- *"An Account of New England"*
(1602)
Annals of America (1) p.11-14
- *"Brief and true relation of the discov-
erie of the north part of Virginia"*
(1602)
Amer. Her. — *Thirteen* p.58-59

**BREWERIES. See Distilleries and
breweries**

**BREWSTER, FEAR. See Allerton, Fear
Brewster**

BREWSTER, JOHN
Dillon — *Pilgrims* p.77-79
Gill — *Mayflower* p.23-24

BREWSTER, JONATHAN
Dillon — *Pilgrims* p.166
Gill — *Mayflower* p.93, 130, 135
Morison — *Story* p.86, 139, 216

BREWSTER, LOVE
Morison — *Story* p.183, 216

BREWSTER, MARY
Dillon — *Pilgrims* p.118, 125
Leynse — *Preced.* p.82-83, 86, 88, 95-
99, 106-107, 149, 205-207, 238-244
Marble — *Women* p.16, 60-62

Willison — *Pilgrim* p.20, 31, 79, 90,
387n, 532
Willison — *Saints. See* index p.497

**BREWSTER, PATIENCE. See Prence,
Patience Brewster**

BREWSTER, WILLIAM
Beck — *Pilgrims. See* index p.85
Caffrey — *Mayflower. See* index p.386
Dillon — *Pilgrims. See* index p.244
Folsom — *Give* p.11-13, 15
Gill — *Mayflower. See* index p.201
Hills — *History (2)* p.25-42; *See also*
index p.248
Leynse — *Preced.* p.266; *See also* in-
dex p.280
Marble — *Women* p.14-15, 31, 46, 53,
60-62
Marshall — *Mayflower* p.25-26, 31,
120, 160, 184
Morison — *Intellect.* p.114n, 133-134
Morison — *Story. See* index p.i
Snell — *Wild* p.101, 106, 108, 111
Willison — *Pilgrim. See* index p.572
Willison — *Saints. See* index p.497
- *Biography*
Willison — *Pilgrim* p.18-20
- *Death*
Amer. Her. — *Pilgrim* p.148
Willison — *Pilgrim* p.466-469
- *Library*
Earle — *Customs* p.272

BREWSTER FAMILY
Caffrey — *Mayflower. See* index p.386
Hills — *History (2)* p.25-46; *See also*
index p.248
Leynse — *Preced. See* index p.280
Marble — *Women* p.24, 47-48, 62

BRICKS
See also **Houses, Brick**
Chitwood — *History (1)* p.381
Dow — *Every* p.20
Gould — *Early* p.20, 50
Langdon — *Everyday* p.15-16
Wertenbaker — *First* p.289-292
Wright — *Cultural* p.198-199
- *Jamestown*
Adams — *Album* p.23
- *South*
Tunis — *Colonial* p.85-87

BRIDGES
Bridenbaugh — *Cities* p.20, 45
Langdon — *Everyday* p.247
Wertenbaker — *First* p.298
, *Horse*
Earle — *Home* p.331

BRIDGEWATER, MASSACHUSETTS
Willison — *Saints* p.391, 401, 410,
413, 444, 446-447

BRIGDEN, ZECHARIAH, REV.
Morison — *Intellect.* p.37, 246-247

BRISTOL, RHODE ISLAND
Demos — *Little* p.64-65, 74-79, 111,
143
Morison — *Story* p.247, 287-288, 291
- *Census (1689)*
Demos — *Little* p.194

BRITISH. *See* **England and English**

BROCK, JOHN
Morison — *Intellect.* p.139-140

BROOCHES
Earle — *Two cent. (1)* p.213

BROOMS
See also **Hemlock**
Gould — *Early* p.36, 80
Leonard — *Dear* p.101-102
- *Besoms and brushes*
Marshall — *Mayflower* p.103
, *Birch*
Earle — *Colonial* p.298-301
Gould — *Early* p.126-127
, *Indian*
Earle — *Home* p.301-304

BROWN, LYDIA HOWLAND
Marble — *Women* p.88

BROWN, PETER. *See* **Browne, Peter**

BROWN FAMILY (Providence, R.I.)
National — *History.* p.114

BROWNE, JOHN
Sweet — *Religion* p.151-152

BROWNE, MARTHA FORD
Willison — *Saints* p.191, 419, 440, 445

BROWNE, PETER
Hills — *History (1)* p.21, 29, 37, 41,
45, 69, 75, 79, 82, 90, 94
Hills — *History (2)* p.131-135
Marble — *Women* p.28, 33
Willison — *Pilgrim* p.122-123, 535,
555-556
Willison — *Saints* p.133, 162-164,
263, 315, 439-440

BROWNE, ROBERT
See also **Brownists**
Dillon — *Pilgrims* p.67-69
Willison — *Pilgrim* p.6-7
Willison — *Saints. See* index p.498

BROWNE, THOMAS, SIR
Morison — *Intellect.* p.49, 139, 154-
155

BROWNE, WILLIAM
, *and Pocahontas*
Phillips — *First* p.161

BROWNE FAMILY
See also **Brown family**
Bailyn — *New England* p.122, 125,
135, 137, 176
Hills — *History (1) See* index p.163
Hills — *History (2) See* index p.248-
249

BROWNISTS
See also **Browne, Robert; Pilgrims**
Amer. Her. — *Pioneer* p.58-59
Dillon — *Pilgrims* p.67-69, 103, 111,
119, 192-193
Willison — *Pilgrim* p.7-10, 32-34, 75
Willison — *Saints. See* index p.498

BRYDON, GEORGE M.
Smith — *17th* p.133-134

BUCCANEERS. *See* **Pirates**

"BUCKING" (thread and linen process)
Earle — *Home* p.175, 234

BUCKINGHAM, EARL OF
Phillips — *First* p.188, 193-194

BUCKNER, JOHN
Smith — *17th* p.119-120
Wertenbaker — *First* p.255-256

BUFFALOES
- *New Netherland*
  Axtell — *America* p.39

BUILDERS AND BUILDING
  See also **Architecture; Houses;**
  types of building material
  Bridenbaugh — *Cities* p.11
  Tunis — *Craftsmen* p.85-87
- *Agreements*
  Dow — *Every* p.227-228
- *Massachusetts*
  Dow — *Every* p.228-237
- *Materials, natural*
  Marshall — *Mayflower* p.86
, *Planters'*
  Wertenbaker — *Old* p.48

BULKELEY, GERSHOM
  Morison — *Intellect.* p.37, 200-208,
  250

BULKELEY, PETER
- *"A City set upon a hill" (1651)*
  Annals of America (1) p.211-212
, *on the Covenant (Mass. Bay colony)*
  Goetzmann — *Colonial* p.179-
  181

BULLIVANT, BENJAMIN
  Dow — *Every* p.176

"BUNCH-THREAD"
  Earle — *Home* p.251

BUNDLING
  Miller — *First* p.192-194
  Williams — *Demeter's* p.83
- *Connecticut*
  Fisher — *Men (1)* p.284-287
- *Massachusetts*
  Fisher — *Men (1)* p.180-181

BUNNELL, GOODWIFE
  Williams — *Demeter's* p.88

BURGHLEY, WILLIAM CECIL, BARON
  Willison — *Saints* p.23, 29, 31, 46, 62,
  64, 463

BURGOMASTERS
, *Dutch*
  Speare — *Life* p.57-59

BURIALS. *See* **Cemeteries; Death;**
  Funerals

BURLINGTON, NEW JERSEY
  Alderman — *Story* p.63-64, 67

BURRAGE, CHAMPLIN
  Willison — *Pilgrim* p.188-191

BURRAS, ANNE
  Leonard — *Dear* p.42-43
  Williams — *Demeter's* p.19

BURROUGHS, GEORGE (accused
  witch)
  Williams — *Demeter's* p.140

BUSINESS
  See also **Artisans; Commerce;**
  Crafts and craftsmanship; Guilds;
  Monopolies; Shops and shop-
  keepers; Trade and traders;
  types of business
- *Boston*
  Rutman — *Winthrop's* p.83, 193-
  194
, *Women in*
  Spruill — *Women's* p.241
  Williams — *Demeter's* p.194-195

BUSINESS DEPRESSIONS
  Rutman — *Winthrop's* p.84, 183-184,
  186, 189, 217-218, 245

BUTCHERING
  Glubok — *Home* p.85-86
  Gould — *Early* p.138-139

BUTLER, NATHANIEL, CAPTAIN
  Pomfret — *Founding* p.306-308

BUTTER
  Gould — *Early* p.104-105, 143
  Leonard — *Dear* p.145
, *Dutch*
  Smith — *Colonial* p.117-118

BUTTERMILK
, *for bleaching*
  Earle — *Home* p.175

BUTTERY (room)
  Gould — *Early* p.38

BUTTONS
Earle — *Two cent. (1)* p.192-193
, *Children's*
McClinton — *Antiques* p.64

BUZZARDS BAY, MASSACHUSETTS
Gill — *Mayflower* p.99, 118, 120, 146
Morison — *Story* p.131, 154, 224, 231-233, 243, 276, 292
Willison — *Saints* p.221-222, 264

BYLLINGE, EDWARD
Craven — *Colonies* p.106-107, 181-182, 184-185, 187, 189, 204, 244
Rothbard — *Conceived (1)* p.336-337, 397-401, 484

BYRD, VALENTINE
Folsom — *Give* p.75-76

BYRD, WILLIAM I
Craven — *Southern* p.224, 371-372, 380, 403
Morison — *Oxford* p.89-92
Wish — *Society (1)* p.92-94, 96

BYRD, WILLIAM II
Craven — *Southern* p. 252, 370-371
Wertenbaker — *First* p.27, 255, 257, 304
, *as scientist*
Wright — *Cultural* p.223

C

CABINETMAKERS
See also **Furniture**
Wertenbaker — *First* p.294

CAGES
, *as punishment*
- *Massachusetts*
Lawrence — *Not* p.132-133
, *for babies*
Earle — *Home* p.372

"CAIRNS." See "Quarns"

CALEF, ROBERT
Wertenbaker — *Puritan* p.207, 274, 285-289

CALENDARS, INDIAN. *See* **Indians — Calendars**

"CALLING" (doctrine, occupation)
See also **Perkins, William**
- *Plymouth*
Demos — *Little* p.104, 146-147
- *Three senses used*
Morgan — *Puritan* p.28-37

CALVERT, CECILIUS. *See* **Baltimore, Cecilius Calvert (2nd Lord)**

CALVERT, CHARLES. *See* **Baltimore, Charles Calvert (3rd Lord)**

CALVERT, GEORGE. *See* **Baltimore, George Calvert (1st Lord)**

CALVERT, LEONARD
Alderman — *Story* p.83, 85-86
Fisher — *Men (2)* p.163, 165, 167-169
Pomfret — *Founding* p.82, 88-90, 92-93
Starkey — *Land* p.111-112, 115-116, 123

CALVINISM
See also **Puritans**
Bailyn — *New England* p.19-23, 43
Dillon — *Pilgrims* p.79, 87-88, 93, 100-101, 126, 206, 209
Hall — *Religious* p.66, 109, 122, 124
Willison — *Saints* p.21-22, 31-32, 65, 86, 89, 92-96
Wish — *Society (1)* p.4-7, 29, 94
- *Views of Roger Williams*
Annals of America (1) p.213-216

CAMBRIDGE, MASSACHUSETTS
Rutman — *Winthrop's* p.31-32, 114, 151, 160, 165-168n
Willison — *Saints* p.312, 376, 460, 471, 473

CAMBRIDGE AGREEMENT (1629)
Chitwood — *History (1)* p.105
Morris — *Ency,* p.33
Pomfret — *Founding* p.160-161
Vaughan — *Puritan* p.58-59

CAMBRIDGE PLATFORM OF CHURCH DISCIPLINE (1648)
Annals of America (1) p.190-194
Goetzmann — *Colonial* p.184-185
Hawke — *Colonial* p.131-134, 179
Sweet — *Religion* p.103-105
Vaughan — *Puritan* p.98-115

CAMBRIDGE PRESS
Morison — *Intellect.* p.113-127
Wertenbaker — *First* p.237, 239-240
- *Books (1670)*
    Wright — *Literary* p.82-83

CAMBRIDGE UNIVERSITY
Willison — *Saints. See* index p.498

CANADA AND CANADIANS
See also **Quebec, Canada;** etc.
Abbot — *Colonial* p.115-116
- *Administration, French*
    Amer. Her. — *Thirteen* p.117,
    120-121, 164, 194
    , *and colonial wars*
        Amer. Her. — *Thirteen*
        p.124, 193, 195
- *Colonization*
    Nettels — *Roots* p.205-209
    Pomfret — *Founding* p.138-139,
    147-148
- *Exploration and first settlement*
    Amer. Her. — *Thirteen* p.24-26,
    117-124, 194
    Life — *New* p.35
- *Life*
    Amer. Her. — *Thirteen* p.117-
    119, 121, 124, 207

"CANDLE-FISH" (type of smelt)
Lawrence — *New* p.163-164

CANDLES AND CANDLEMAKING
See also **Bayberry**
Dow — *Every* p.96-97
Drepperd — *Pioneer* p.200
Earle — *Colonial* p.303, 306-308
Earle — *Home* p.34-38, 40-42
Glubok — *Home* p.18-21
Gould — *Early* p.121-124
Johnston — *Conn.* p.49
Lawrence — *New* p.162-165
Leonard — *Dear* p.98-99
Miller — *First* p.177-178
Nettels — *Roots* p.241
Speare — *Life* p.76

CANDLEWOOD
- *"Pine-knots"*
    Earle — *Home* p.32-33
    Glubok — *Home* p.16-17
    Gould — *Early* p.124
    - *Boston (1633)*
        Lawrence — *New* p.162

CANNON. *See* **Guns**

CANOES
Earle — *Home* p.325-326
Wertenbaker — *First* p.7, 309-310
, *Dugout*
    Glubok — *Home* p.331-332
    Marshall — *Mayflower* p.151,
    156-158
- *Ferries*
    Earle — *Home* p.330-331
    Glubok — *Home* p.333
, *Indian*
    Earle — *Home* p.325
    Vaughan — *New* p.49

CANONCHET (Indian)
Folsom — *Give* p.38-40
Morison — *Oxford* p.110
Morison — *Story* p.263-264, 268-269,
271-272
Rothbard — *Conceived (1)* p.347,
350-352

CANONICUS (Indian)
Morison — *Story* p.88, 91, 213
Vaughan — *New* p.55, 79-80, 118,
167, 169n, 132, 305

CAPE ANN
Gill — *Mayflower* p.52, 98, 103, 109,
111-113, 127
Willison — *Pilgrim* p.245, 254, 257-
259, 274-275
Willison — *Saints* p.152, 251-252,
257, 442, 448-449, 458, 469

CAPE COD, MASSACHUSETTS
Beck — *Pilgrims* p.15-18, 25-29, 41,
62, 64
Dillon — *Pilgrims* p.128-141, 143, 166,
174, 181, 197-198
Gill — *Mayflower* p.73-78; *See also*
index p.202
Hills — *History* (1) p.112-115
Marshall — *Mayflower* p.23, 49, 181-
182
Morison — *Story. See* index p.ii
Snell — *Wild* p.103, 105-106, 108
Willison — *Pilgrim. See* index p.573
Willison — *Saints. See* index p.498
, *Cornhill*
    Willison — *Pilgrim* p.106-108

CAPE COD INDIANS
Willison — *Saints* p.172, 187, 214,
218, 223-224, 229, 266, 388-389,
393, 396, 440, 467

CAPE FEAR COLONY
Morris — *Ency.* p.52

CAPE HENRY
- *Indian attack of English*
Smith — *17th* p.36-37, 41

CAPEN HOUSE (Topsfield, Mass.)
Dow — *Domestic.* Front, p.2, 4, 6, 8
Morrison — *Early* p.57-59

CAPITAL. *See* Finance

CAPITAL PUNISHMENT. *See* Death penalty; Hangings; Indians — Death penalty

"CAPTAIN OF THE WATCH"
- *Duties*
Earle — *Home* p.380

CAPUCHINS (garments)
Earle — *Home* p.295

CARD PLAYING
Glubok — *Home* p.189
Rawson — *When* p.92-94
Speare — *Life* p.157
Wertenbaker — *First* p.191, 269-270, 273
Willison — *Pilgrim* p.463n
Willison — *Saints* p.475
- *Boston*
Bridenbaugh — *Cities* p.116-117

CARDING (of wool)
Earle — *Home* p.194-196, 206
Gould — *Early* p.127

CAREY, SARAH. *See* Jenney, Sarah Carey

CARLETON, DUDLEY, SIR
Willison — *Pilgrim* p.39, 60-61, 187
Willison — *Saints* p.96-101

CARMEN. *See* Carters and draymen

CAROLINAS
See also **Albemarle Sound settlement (N.C.); North Carolina; South Carolina**
Annals of America (1) p.300d
Bailyn — *New England* p.147-148, 151

Carman — *History (1)* p.30-31, 55, 63, 101
Craven — *Southern* p.310-359
Fisher — *Men* p.251-253, 264-274
Hawke — *Colonial. See* index p.709
Hawke — *U.S.* p.156-163
Hope — *Nation* p.95-96
Jernegan — *American* p.72-76
Morison — *Oxford* p.94-98
Morris — *Ency.* p.51-54
Nettels — *Roots* p.124-127, 132, 137-139
Rothbard — *Conceived (1)* p.121-125
Smith — *17th* p.5, 35, 40, 42, 54, 83, 173, 178, 223
Snell — *Wild* p.24, 30-32, 141, 151-165
Starkey — *Land* p.216-235
Ver Steeg — *Formative* p.119-122
, and Maryland
Hawke — *Colonial* p.250-251
- *Barbardian "Adventurers"*
Craven — *Colonies* p.43, 55, 57-58, 88-89, 98-99
- *Charters*
Hawke — *Colonial* p.209-211
Jernegan — *American* p.73-74
Morris — *Ency. p.52*
- *"Concessions and Agreements" (1665)*
Craven — *Colonies* p.88-92
Hawke — *Colonial* p.212
Morris — *Ency.* p.52
- *Contrast between North and South*
Chitwood — *History (1)* p.193-194
- *Feudalism*
Wish — *Society (1)* p.89-92
- *First failures*
Hawke — *Colonial* p.211-212
- *Founding*
Chitwood — *History (1)* p.182-197
Kraus — *U.S. (1)* p.82-84
- *"Fundamental Constitutions" (1669)*
Chitwood — *History (1)* p.191-192
Craven — *Colonies* p.99-103, 179
Craven — *Southern* p.328, 338-342, 354, 410
Hawke — *Colonial* p.212-214
Hawke — *U.S.* p.156-159
Jernegan — *American* p.74
Morris — *Ency.* p.52

CAROLINAS (*continued*)
- *Government*
  Chitwood — *History (1)* p.191-193
  Jernegan — *American* p.74-76
- *History*
  Jernegan — *American* p.72-73
- *Indian trade and conflict*
  Morris — *Ency.* p.53
- *Opportunities and lure (1666)*
  Annals of America (1) p.240-242
  Kraus — *U.S. (1)* p.80
- *Patents, early*
  Morris — *Ency.* p.51
- *Political unrest*
  Morris — *Ency.* p.54
- *Proprietors*
  Craven — *Colonies* p.42-43, 56-57, 97-99, 135

  , *Grant to*
  Chitwood — *History (1)* p.182-183
- *Settlers*
  Collins — *Story* p.69
  Morrison — *Early* p.170
- *Success of colony*
  Hawke — *Colonial* p.214-216
- *Women*
  Leonard — *Dear* p.60-61
  Spruill — *Women's* p.11-13

CARPENTER, PRISCILLA. *See* **Wright, Priscilla Carpenter**

CARPENTER FAMILY
  Hills — *History (2)* p.121-122; *See also* index p.250
  Marble — *Women* p.101

CARPENTERS
  See also **Tools, Carpenters'**
  Rutman — *Winthrop's. See* index p.301
- *Puritans*
  Adams — *Album* p.76-77

CARR, ROBERT, SIR
  Pomfret — *Founding* p.301-303

CARRIER, MARTHA
  William — *Demeter's* p.140

CARROTS
  Earle — *Home* p.145

CARTERET, GEORGE, SIR
  Alderman — *Story* p.61-62
  Craven — *Colonies* p.54, 56, 59, 83-85, 106-107, 184, 188-189, 200, 203-204
  Craven — *Southern* p.322-323, 334, 346-347
  Pomfret — *Founding* p.301-303
  Rothbard — *Conceived (1)* p.121, 323, 325, 333, 337, 339-340, 391-392
- *Landing, New Jersey*
  Collins — *Story* p.62
, *New Jersey grant to*
  Chitwood — *History (1)* p.176-177

CARTERET, PHILIP
  Alderman — *Story* p.62-63
  Craven — *Colonies* p.84, 87-88, 93-95, 203-204
  Fisher — *Men (1)* p.379-381
  Hawke — *Colonial* p.226-227
  Hope — *Nation* p.102
  Rothbard — *Conceived (1)* p.325, 333-334, 336, 339, 390-393, 486, 489
  Snell — *Wild* p.144-145

CARTERS AND DRAYMEN
  Bridenbaugh — *Cities* p.44-45

CARVER, CATHERINE WHITE
  Leynse — *Preced.* p.83, 85, 88, 94, 99, 100-101, 150, 199, 215, 238, 266
  Marble — *Women* p.12, 57
  Willison — *Pilgrim* p.67n, 78, 147, 533
  Willison — *Saints* p.106, 122, 181, 438, 485

CARVER, JAMES
  Hills — *History (2)* p.147-149

CARVER, JOHN
  Archer — *Mayflower* p.81-82
  Beck — *Pilgrims* p.8-9, 16, 32, 37-38, 44, 67
  Caffrey — *Mayflower. See* index p.386
  Dillon — *Pilgrims* p.43-44, 109-110, 114-115, 119, 126-127, 137, 144-146, 150, 152, 155, 159
  Gill — *Mayflower* p.33-34, 38-40, 43, 47, 69-70, 75, 80, 85, 88, 142
  Hills — *History (1). See* index p.163
  Hills — *History (2). See* index p.250

Leynse — *Preced.* p.266; *See also* index p.280
Marble — *Women* p.12-13, 53, 72, 86
Marshall — *Mayflower* p.25-27, 30, 52, 120, 136, 140
Morison — *Story* p.15, 18, 35, 38, 45, 51-53, 63, 73-76, 87, 149, 171
Snell — *Wild* p.101, 106, 108
Willison — *Pilgrim. See* index p.573
Willison — *Saints. See* index p.498

CARVER FAMILY
Hills — *History (1). See* index p.163
Hills — *History (2). See* index p.250

CARVING TERMS
Earle — *Home* p.104-105

CARY, ELIZABETH
Williams — *Demeter's* p.141

"CASKET GIRLS" (clothing caskets, in La.)
Earle — *Two cent. (1)* p.99

CASSOCKS (loose coats)
Earle — *Two cent. (1)* p.175-176

CASTELL, WILLIAM
Smith — *17th* p.207-208

CASTINE, MAINE. *See* Pentagoet, Maine

"CAT WHIPPERS" (shoemakers)
Tunis — *Craftsmen* p.36-37

CATECHISMS
Morison — *Intellect.* p.79-80, 116-117
Rutman — *Winthrop's* p.149-151, 258

CATHOLICISM
See also **St. Mary's, Maryland**
Acheson — *America's* p.136-138
Chitwood — *History (1)* p.83, 86-87, 435
Folsom — *Give* p.ix, x, 5, 7-8, 11-12, 15, 19, 24, 42, 50, 64, 66, 70-74, 80, 91
Furnas — *Americans* p.60-61, 76
Hall — *Religious* p.255-256
Leynse — *Preced. See* index p.285 (under Roman Catholic church)
Morris — *Ency.* p.548
Murdock — *Literature* p.8, 10-15, 22, 24, 37-38, 40
Nettels — *Roots. See* index p.726

Pomfret — *Founding* p.61, 75-80, 87, 93-98, 231, 320
Sweet — *Religion* p.167-181
Ver Steeg — *Formative* p.6-7, 15-19, 42-44, 91-92, 141, 143-144, 216-217
Willison — *Saints* p.8, 18-29, 339, 403, 481
Wish — *Society (1)* p.77, 87-88, 98
Wright — *Cultural* p.76
- *Maryland*
  Calverton — *Awake.* p.248-249
  Morison — *Oxford* p.85
  Sweet — *Religion* p.33-34, 175-181
  Wright — *Everyday* p.160-161
- *Motive in colonization*
  Sweet — *Religion* p.10, 12
- *New York*
  Calverton — *Awake.* p.341
, *on Chesapeake*
  Fisher — *Men (2)* p.84-85, 147-229
- *Persecution*
  Alderman — *Story* p.81, 88-89, 91
  Bailey — *American (1)* p.13-14
- *Virginia, Antipathy in*
  Starkey — *Land* p.106-108, 110-111

CATS (trivets)
Gould — *Early* p.77

CATTLE
See also **Cowherds**
Beck — *Pilgrims* p.61-62
Craven — *Southern* p.19, 50, 96, 99-100, 103, 108, 191, 283, 336, 346, 357-358, 366, 376
Furnas — *Americans* p.169-171
Morison — *Story* p.31, 97-99, 112-114, 128, 138-142, 169, 175, 187-190, 197-206, 229-231, 240-241, 248
- *Boston, (1630–49)*
  Rutman — *Winthrop's. See* index p.297
- *First imported*
  Leonard — *Dear* p.129-130
- *Herding*
  Earle — *Home* p.399-301
- *New England*
  Wertenbaker — *First* p.57-58, 83
  Wertenbaker — *Puritan* p.56-57

CATTLE (continued)
- New Netherland (1650)
  Demos — Remarkable p.49-50
- Uses
  Gould — Early p.100
- Virginia
  Wertenbaker — First p.39, 41

CAUDLE (drink)
Gould — Early p.106

CAULS (headdress)
Earle — Two cent. (2) p.536

CAVALIERS
See also **Puritans, and Cavaliers**
Hawke — Colonial p.167-204
- Jamestown
  Adams — Album p.26-27
- Virginia
  Fisher — Men (1) p.64-68

CAVES
Earle — Home p.2
, of first settlers
  Dow — Every p.17-18

CELLARS
Gould — Early p.21-22
- Plymouth
  Demos — Little p.34-35

CEMETERIES
See also **Tombstones**
, Indian (Martha's Vineyard)
  Gould — Early p.104
- Jamestown
  Adams — Album p.30
- South
  Craven — Southern p.181-182,
  211-212
- Virginia
  Goodwin — Colonial p.287-288

CENSORSHIP
See also **Puritans — Censorship**
Morison — Intellect. p.122-123, 126
Wright — Literary p.167
- Massachusetts
  Wertenbaker — First p.238-240

CERAMICS. See Chinaware and porcelain; Pottery and potters

CEREAL FARMING
See also; **Corn; Rice;** etc.
Morris — Ency. p.477

CHAIR-TABLES (settles)
Langdon — Everyday p.25

CHAIRS
Earle — Customs p.109-111
Earle — Home p.310-311
Langdon — Everyday p.30-34
- Plymouth
  Adams — Album p.51
  Demos — Little p.42-43, 45
- Puritans
  Adams — Album p.84

CHAMBERS. See Rooms

CHAMPLAIN, SAMUEL DE
Amer. Her. — Pioneer p.11, 24-25
Amer. Her. — Thirteen p.24, 86, 117-121
Chitwood — History (1) p.296-300
Life — New p.34
Snell — Wild p.65-67, 72-73, 94-95, 98
- Fight for Indians
  Collins — Story p.77
- Quebec surrender
  Collins — Story p.76
- Voyages
  Morris — Ency. p.24

CHANDLER, ISABELLA CHILTON
Marble — Women p.81

CHANDLER, ROGER
Hills — History (1) p.94
Hills — History (2) p.101
Marble — Women p.81

CHANDLER FAMILY
Hills — History (1) p.94
Hills — History (2) p.101, 110, 128, 208

CHANDLERS
Tunis — Craftsmen p.37-38, 116

CHAPMEN (trunk-peddlers)
Earle — Home p.300

CHARCOAL
Gould — Early p.139-140
Marshall — Mayflower p.171

CHARGERS (platters)
Earle — *Home* p.80, 84

CHARITY **(ship)**
Morison — *Story* p.90, 99, 102-103, 111
Willison — *Pilgrim* p.199, 250, 280-282
Willison — *Saints* p.207-208, 210-211, 242, 248, 256-257, 274, 345, 446

CHARITIES
- *Views of John Winthrop*
Hawke — *U.S.* p.96-97
Vaughan — *Puritan* p.138-146

CHARITY SCHOOLS
Monroe — *Founding (1)* p.59

CHARLES I (King of England)
Alderman — *Story* p.26, 40, 74-75, 82, 86
Amer. Her. — *Thirteen* p.64-65, 87, 96, 172, 176, 180
Pomfret — *Founding. See* index p.374
Snell — *Wild* p.77, 118-119, 123, 127, 135, 151
Willison — *Pilgrim* p.301, 392, 397, 447-448, 452, 479, 487, 500
Willison — *Saints* p.42, 258, 287, 298, 300, 308, 325-326, 334, 375
- *Conflict with Parliament*
Rozwenc — *Making (1)* p.32, 54-55, 57-58, 62

CHARLES II (King of England)
Alderman — *Story* p.15, 29-31, 41, 53-54, 75-76, 99, 108, 114, 125
Amer. Her. — *Thirteen* p.136, 157-158, 169, 177, 179-180
Folsom — *Give* p.18, 26, 31, 37, 44, 48, 50, 54, 66, 75
Morison — *Oxford* p.94
Pomfret — *Founding. See* index p.374
Rothbard — *Conceived (1). See* index p.521
Rozwenc — *Making (1)* p.33-34, 77-80
Willison — *Pilgrim* p.515, 522, 526-527
Willison — *Saints* p.382-384, 401-403
- *Treatment of Virginia*
Chitwood — *History (1)* p.73-74

CHARLES RIVER
Rutman — *Winthrop's* p.24-25, 27-28, 30-31, 34-36, 194

CHARLESTON (CHARLES TOWN), SOUTH CAROLINA
Bridenbaugh — *Cities* p.8-10
Chitwood — *History (1)* p.187, 480
Hawke — *U.S.* p.160-163
Life — *New* p.59-60, 71
Morison — *Oxford* p.96
Nettels — *Roots* p.159-160
Snell — *Wild* p.24, 152-156, 160-161, 164
Starkey — *Land* p.222-223, 226, 232-233, 236, 238
- *Founding*
Morris — *Ency.* p.53
- *Houses*
Bridenbaugh — *Cities* p.10
- *Nationalities of settlers*
Morrison — *Early* p.170

CHARLESTOWN, MASSACHUSETTS
Rutman — *Winthrop's. See* index p.302
Vaughan — *New* p.96-97, 99, 104

"CHARTER OAK" (in Hartford, Conn.)
Acheson — *America's* p.116
Adams — *Album* p.131
Alderman — *Story* p.78
Hope — *Nation* p.111
Johnston — *Conn.* p.96-97

"CHARTER OF LIBERTIES" (New York, 1683)
Craven — *Colonies* p.209-210, 226
Morris — *Ency.* p.46
Sweet — *Religion* p.207

CHATHAM, MASSACHUSETTS. See Monomoy, Massachusetts

CHAUNCEY, CHARLES
Morison — *Intellect.* p.45, 74, 120, 122, 155n, 168, 172, 247
Willison — *Pilgrim* p.434-436, 461-463, 502, 562
Willison — *Saints* p.356-359, 363-364, 395, 459-460, 479
, *London's objections to*
Demos — *Remarkable* p.32-36

CHAUNCY, ELNATHAN
Morison — *Intellect.* p.49-55, 150

CHEBOBBINS (sleds)
Earle — *Home* p.415

CHEESE AND CHEESE MAKING
Earle — *Home* p.150-151, 312
Gould — *Early* p.37-38, 128-131
, *Cottage*
    Gould — *Early* p.130
, *Pineapple*
    Gould — *Early* p.131

CHEESE CLOSETS
Gould — *Early* p.130

CHEEVER, EZEKIEL
Morison — *Intellect.* p.65, 100n, 101n, 102-105, 155n, 212

CHEPIAN (Indian)
Beals — *John Eliot* p.79, 87, 126

CHEROKEE INDIANS
Smith — *17th* p.27-29, 54n

CHESAPEAKE BAY AND COLONIES
See also **Jamestown; Maryland; Virginia**
Alderman — *Story* p.7, 11, 17, 82-85
Craven — *Colonies* p.13-31, 35, 37, 39, 200
Craven — *Southern* p.53-54, 66, 73-75, 92, 108, 158, 190, 196-197, 369-370
Hawke — *Colonial* p.85-119, 179-186; *See also* index p.711
Hawke — *U.S.* p.134-148
Snell — *Wild* p.54, 79, 82-83, 99, 127-128, 132-133
- *Adjustment period*
    Hawke — *U.S.* p.134-137
- *Farms*
    Hawke — *Colonial* p.115-117
- *Government*
    Hawke — *Colonial* p.117-118, 137-148
- *Politics*
    Hawke — *Colonial* p.184-186
- *Religion*
    Hawke — *Colonial* p.118-119
- *Society*
    Hawke — *U.S.* p.84-86

CHESEBROUGH, WILLIAM
Smith — *Colonial* p.210

CHESTS
Earle — *Customs* p.116-117
Langdon — *Everyday* p.27-29

- *Plymouth*
    Demos — *Little* p.42-43, 45, 52
- *Puritans*
    Adams — *Album* p.83.

CHICABUT (Indian)
Beals — *John Eliot* p.87-88

CHICKAHOMINY CONFEDERATION INDIANS
See also **Pocahontas; Powhatan;** etc.
- *Children's clothing*
    Phillips — *First* p.7-8
- *Crime and punishment*
    Phillips — *First* p.14-15, 23-24
- *Council*
    Phillips — *First* p.13-15
- *Discipline, Family*
    Phillips — *First* p.15
- *Elders*
    Phillips — *First* p.9, 16
- *Food*
    Phillips- *First* p.25-28
- *Fruits*
    Phillips — *First* p.6, 26
- *Houses*
    Phillips — *First* p.8-9
- *Matriarchy*
    Phillips — *First* p.16-17
- *Morals*
    Phillips — *First* p.8, 15
- *Nuts*
    Phillips — *First* p.6
- *Religion*
    Phillips — *First* p.12-13, 21-23
- *Sports and games*
    Phillips — *First* p.7
- *Trade relations*
    Phillips — *First* p.140
- *Utensils*
    Phillips — *First* p.27
- *Vegetables*
    Phillips — *First* p.5-6
- *Wild fowl*
    Phillips — *First* p.6-7
- *Women*
    Phillips — *First* p.13

CHICORY
Earle — *Home* p.149

CHIESMAN, LYDIA
, *in Bacon's Rebellion*
    Williams — *Demeter's* p.162

CHILD, JOHN
Willison — *Pilgrim* p.498-499

CHILD, ROBERT
Sweet — *Religion* p.95, 102-103
Ver Steeg — *Formative* p.82-83
Wertenbaker — *Puritan* p.299-300
Willison — *Pilgrim* p.493-498
, *"On challenge to Puritan political control"*
Vaughan — *Puritan* p.219-225

CHILDBEARING
See also **Babies; Infant mortality**
Leonard — *Dear* p.209-210, 221
Spruill — *Women's* p.46-47
Wertenbaker — *First* p.183-184
- *Number of children*
Leonard — *Dear* p.79
- *Plymouth*
Demos — *Little* p.66, 131-132, 152

CHILDREN AND CHILDHOOD
See also **Babies; Boys; Childbearing; Girls; Indians; Pilgrims; Plymouth; Puritans; Youth;** special subjects, e.g. **Children's books and reading; Sports and games; Toys;** etc.
Beck — *Pilgrims* p.23, 27, 31, 51, 55, 74
Glubok — *Home* p.104-107
Speare — *Life* p.97, 113
- *Albany, N.Y.*
Speare — *Life* p.60
, *as economic necessity*
Miller — *First* p.209-210
- *Boston, Mass.*
Rutman — *Winthrop's. See* index p.302
- *Discipline*
See also **Schools — Discipline**
Glubok — *Home* p.131-135
Holliday — *Woman's* p.124-126
Leonard — *Dear* p.363-364
Miller — *First* p.211, 213-220
Morgan — *Puritan* p.57-58
Williams — *Demeter's* p.95-96
, *Dutch*
Clark — *Old* p.58-59
- *New England*
Tunis — *Colonial* p.55-56
- *Puritans*
Morgan — *Puritan* p.38

- *Education*
Beck — *Pilgrims* p.78
Glubok — *Home* p.114-120
Leonard — *Dear* p.237-238
- *Etiquette*
Glubok — *Home* p.107
, *Table*
Earle — *Home* p.101-102
Glubok — *Home* p.53-54
- *Fear, Teaching of*
Speare — *Life* p.97-100
, *Illegitimate*
- *Plymouth*
Demos — *Little* p.109, 140n, 153
- *South*
Wertenbaker — *First* p.205-206
, *Immigrant*
Leonard — *Dear* p.337-338
, *in meeting*
Earle — *Home* p.372-374
, *Indentured*
Leonard — *Dear* p.229-231
, *Kidnapping of*
Calverton — *Awake.* p.261-262
- *Laws (Mass.)*
Annals of America (1) p.200-201
- *Life*
Earle — *Customs* p.1-19
Wertenbaker — *First* p.259-261
- *Mortality*
See also **Infant mortality**
Wertenbaker — *First* p. 184-187
Williams — *Demeter's* p.93-95
- *New York*
Clark — *Old* p.69-71
- *Occupations*
Earle — *Home* p.179-180, 182, 188-189, 203-204, 261-262
- *Reverence for parents*
Morgan — *Puritan* p.59-61
- *Virginia Act for Training*
Annals of America (1) p.171

CHILDREN'S BOOKS AND READING
Earle — *Customs* p.26-27
Glubok — *Home* p.303-306

CHILDREN'S TOYS. See Toys

CHILTON, ISABELLA. See Chandler, Isabella Chilton

CHILTON, JAMES
Hills — *History (1)* p.21, 29, 37, 40, 42-44, 59, 69

CHILTON, JAMES (continued)
Hills — History (2) p.101
Leynse — Preced. p.246, 268
Willison — Pilgrim p.125, 535
Willison — Saints p.133, 141

CHILTON, MARY. See Winslow, Mary Chilton

CHILTON FAMILY
Caffrey — Mayflower p.61, 140-141
Hills — History (1) See index p.163
Hills — History (2) p.101
Leynse — Preced. p.246
Marble — Women p.81

CHIMNEYS
Bridenbaugh — Cities p.56-57
Dow — Every p.19
Earle — Colonial p.276-277
Earle — Home p.15, 52-53, 55, 68
Glubok — Home p.26-29
Gould — Early p.40, 44-55
Marshall — Mayflower p.68, 107
Morrison — Early p.39-40
Rawson — When p.3-5
Wertenbaker — First p.288-289, 291
- Base
    Gould — Early p.47-48
- Materials
    Gould — Early p.44-46
- Structure
    Gould — Early p.46
- Virginia
    Wertenbaker — Old p.78-79

CHINA
Glubok — Home p.52

CHINAWARE AND PORCELAIN
See also **Pottery and potters**
Earle — Home p.100-101
Marshall — Mayflower p.99-100

CHIP-LOGS (wood instrument)
Marshall — Mayflower p.40

CHOCOLATE (chockolett)
Earle — Customs p.182
, First (1697)
    Gould — Early p.107

CHOIR ABBEY PRESS (Pilgrim Press, Leyden)
Willison — Pilgrim p.37-40, 59-62, 551

Willison — Saints p.94-96, 99, 101-102, 330, 440, 464, 473-474

CHOPPING BEES
Earle — Home p.403-404
Glubok — Home p.318-319

CHOUART, MEDARD
Life — New p.34

CHRISTENINGS
See also **Clothing and dress — Christenings**
- Boston
    Clark — Old p.27-29

CHRISTIANITY. See Religion

CHRISTINA SETTLEMENT
Alderman — Story p.104-105, 111

CHRISTMAS
Chitwood — History (1) p.489
Lawrence — Not p.194-199
Miller — First p.84-85
Speare — Life p.159-160
Willison — Saints p.104, 160-161, 199, 377
Wish — Society (1) p.8, 31-32, 45, 99
Wright — Everyday p.211
- Boston
    Clark — Old p.38
, Dutch customs
    Leynse — Preced. p.169-174
- First (Pilgrims)
    Earle — Customs p.214-215
    Willison — Pilgrim p.118-119, 173-174
- Massachusetts
    Wertenbaker — First p.276-278
- New England
    Holliday — Woman's p.203-204
- Plymouth
    See also **Christmas — First (Pilgrims)**
    Annals of America (1) p.70
    Morison — Story p.58-59
- Puritans
    Earle — Customs p.215-216
, Objections of
    Sweet — Religion p.115
    Wertenbaker — First p.276-277
- Virginia colony
    Amer. Her. — Treasury p.36

CHRONOLOGY (dates)
- *1578–1698*
   Morris — *Ency.* p.25-62
- *1603–1699*
   Annals of America (1) p.xxvii-
   xxxix
   1675, Spirit of
   Starkey — *Land* p.197-215

CHRONOMETERS
Marshall — *Mayflower* p.38

CHUCK-FARTHING (game)
Glubok — *Home* p.186-187

CHURCH, BENJAMIN
Amer. Her. — *Pilgrims* p.141
Morison — *Intellect.* p.193-194
Morison — *Story* p.232, 274-279, 288-289
Tyler — *History* p.381-382
Willison — *Saints* p.399-400, 420-421, 450

CHURCH AND STATE
See also **Cotton, John, Rev.**
Adams — *Provincial* p.17
Goetzmann — *Colonial* p.184-186
Rutman — *Winthrop's. See* index p.302
Sweet — *Religion* p.90-91, 96-97
Wish — *Society (1)* p.24, 36-37
- *Boston*
   Rutman — *Winthrop's* p.77, 98, 141-153, 156, 257-258, 276, 278
- *Massachusetts*
   Smith — *17th* p.153-157
   Wertenbaker — *Puritan* p.70-72

CHURCH OF ENGLAND. *See* **Anglicans**

CHURCHES
See also **Excommunication; Meetinghouses; Pilgrims; Plymouth; Puritans; Religion; Women — Churches;** names of churches, denominations
Glubok — *Home* p.285-296
Nettels — *Roots* p.470-479
Rutman — *Winthrop's. See* index p.302
Wertenbaker — *Puritan. See* index p.348
- *Admission of members*
   Annals of America (1) p.191-192
   Hawke — *U.S.* p.132-133

Rutman — *Winthrop's. See* index p.302
- *Albany, N.Y.*
   Earle — *Home* p.385
- *Architecture*
   Earle — *Home* P.364-365, 385
   Wertenbaker — *First* p.293-294
- *Attendance*
   Bridenbaugh — *Cities* p.106
   Dow — *Every* p.107
- *Authority*
   See also **Church and state**
   Rozwenc — *Making (1)* p.69-72
- *Boston*
   Clark — *Old* p.30-33
, *Compulsory — Virginia*
   Rawson — *When* p.220
- *Deacons*
   Earle — *Home* p.386-387
- *Discipline*
   Rawson — *When* p.225-229
   - *New England*
      Hawke — *U.S.* p.131-134
, *Dutch*
   Earle — *Home* p.385
   Morrison — *Early* p.117
   Sweet — *Religion p.192-203*
- *Feasts*
   Willison — *Saints* p.104, 160-161, 199, 377, 462-463
, *First*
   - *English church of Separatists*
      Dillon — *Pilgrims* p.71-72, 94, 96
   - *Jamestown, first in America*
      Adams — *Album* p.25
      Godwin—*Colonial* p.195-196
- *Forts*
   Earle — *Home* p.385
, *German*
   Sweet — *Religion* p.230
. - *Indians*
   Beals — *John Eliot* p.149-152, 154
   Morison — *Story* p.243-244
- *Maryland*
   Morrison — *Early* p.164-165
- *Massachusetts*
   Annals of America (1) p.190-191
   Hawke — *Colonial* p.134-136
- *Membership, Problems of*
   See also **Churches — Admission of members; — Attendance; —Discipline**
   Vaughan — *Puritan* p.115-120

CHURCHES (*continued*)

- *New England*
  Bailyn — *New England. See*
  index p.242
  Glubok — *Home* p.285-287
  Hawke — *U.S.* p.131-132
  Smith — *17th* p.143-165
- *New York*
  Clark — *Old* p.65
  Glubok — *Home* p.295
- *North Carolina*
  Calverton — *Awake.* p.287
- *Officers*
  Rutman — *Winthrop's. See* index
  p.303
, *Opposition to*
  Calverton — *Awake.* p.164-165
- *Pews*
  Earle — *Home* p.368-369
  Rawson — *When* p.178, 189-192
- *Polity*
  Rutman — *Winthrop's. See* index
  p.303
  Vaughan — *Puritan* p.98-120
- *Seating committee*
  Glubok — *Home* p.288-289
- *Services*
  Chitwood — *History (1)* p.441-
  442
  Vaughan — *Puritan* p.78-81
- *South*
  Goodwin — *Colonial* p.189-202
- *South Carolina*
  Calverton — *Awake.* p.287-288
, *Summons to*
  Glubok — *Home* p.287-288
- *Trials*
  Smith — *17th* p.146-149
- *Virginia*
  Earle — *Home* p.381-383
  Morrison — *Early* p151-156
  Wertenbaker — *Old* p.86-89

CHURCHES OF CHRIST

- *Beginnings; views of Edward
  Johnson*
  Vaughan — *Puritan* p.74-78

CHURCHWARDENS

  Smith — *17th* p.127-128, 137

CHURNS

  Earle — *Home* p.149-150, 312
  Gould — *Early* p.104-105

CIDER AND CIDER MAKING

  Dow — *Every* p.95-96
  Earle — *Customs* p.171-172
  Glubok — *Home* p.90-91
  Gould — *Early* p.83, 135-136

CINCHONA BARK

, *as remedy*
  Wertenbaker — *First* p.179-180

CIRCUIT RIDERS

  Speare — *Life* p.148

CITIES

  See also **Towns;** names of cities
- *Government*
    Chitwood — *History (1)* p.153-
    154
- *Problems*
    Bridenbaugh — *Cities* p.55-93

"CITY OF GOD." *See* **Natick, Massachusetts**

CIVIL RIGHTS

  Craven — *Colonies* p.187-188, 195-
  196, 209
  Willison — *Pilgrim* p.492-499, 524,
  557-558

CIVILITY. *See* **Courtesy**

CLAIBORNE, WILLIAM

  Alderman — *Story* p.85-86
  Craven — *Southern. See* index p. 438
  Fisher — *Men (2)* p.167, 169-170,
  172, 174-176
  Hawke — *Colonial* p.113-114, 184-
  185
  Morris — *Ency.* p.29
  Pomfret — *Founding* p.53, 55, 58, 67-
  69, 82, 91-93, 97
  Starkey — *Land* p.111, 114-122, 124
, *and Lord Baltimore*
  Chitwood — *History (1)* p.81-83

CLAMS

- *Shells, use of*
  Earle — *Home* p.308-309

CLAPBOARD

  Marshall — *Mayflower* p.64, 68, 78
, *and wainscotting*
  Gould — *Early* p.20

CLARENDON, EDWARD HYDE, EARL OF
Craven — *Colonial* p.34, 44, 49-51, 56, 66-67, 79, 86, 97, 160, 223
Smith — *17th* p.168, 172-173, 176, 178

CLARINETS
, *in meeting*
Earle — *Home* p.378

CLARK(E), JOHN
Dow — *Every* p.176-177
Gill — *Mayflower* p.64, 75-76, 98
Pomfret — *Founding* p.218, 222-223, 225-227
Rothbard — *Conceived (1)* p.194, 196-197, 207-208, 210-212, 279-280
Sweet — *Religion* p.123, 129-130, 132-133
Willison — *Pilgrim* p.96, 104n, 110, 114
Willison — *Saints* p.119, 135, 141, 155-156, 164, 468
, *on Baptists*
Vaughan — *Puritan* p.225-230

CLARK(E), KATHERINE
Earle — *Two cent. (1)* p.xv, 57, 70-71
Earle — *Two cent. (2)* p.539

CLARKE, MARY *See* **Cushman, Mary Clarke Singleton**

CLARK(E), NATHANIEL
Morison — *Story* p.286-287
Willison — *Saints* p.404-405, 456-457

CLARK(E), RICHARD
Hills — *History (1)* p.21, 29, 38, 41, 69, 71
Hills — *History (2)* p.95

CLARK(E) FAMILY
Hills — *History (1)* p.150; *See also* index p.163-164
Hills — *History (2). See* index p.251

CLARKE'S ISLAND, MASSACHUSETTS
Gill — *Mayflower* p.76-79
Willison — *Saints* p.156-157, 159, 169, 366, 396, 405, 420, 456

CLASSES
See also **Aristocracy; Servants; Society;** etc.
Bridenbaugh — *Cities* p.96-100
Furnas — *American* p.62-64
- *Conflicts*
Rothbard — *Conceived (1)* p.261-262
- *New Jersey*
Nettels — *Roots* p.351-354
- *New York*
Nettels — *Roots* p.343-350
- *Distinctions*
Chitwood — *History (1)* p.481-482
Rozwenc — *Making (1)* p.41-51
- *Boston, Mass.*
Woodward — *Way* p.23-24
- *Swansea, Mass.*
Wertenbaker — *First* p.74-75
- *Woburn, Mass.*
Wertenbaker — *First* p.74
- *Migration*
Ver Steeg — *Formative* p.65-69
- *South*
Rozwenc — *Making (1)* p.47
Wertenbaker — *Old* p.10-11
- *Structure*
Rutman — *Winthrop's. See* index p.303
Wish — *Society (1)* p.47, 67-71
- *Massachusetts*
Pomfret — *Founding* p.202-203
- *Plymouth, Mass.*
Pomfret — *Founding* p.128-130
- *Virginia*
Monroe — *Founding (1)* p.54-55

"CLAVEL-PIECES" (mantels)
Earle — *Colonial* p.279-280
Earle — *Home* p.54

CLAYTON, JOHN
, *on agriculture, Virginia (1688)*
Demos — *Remarkable* p.318-325

CLEANING
Marshall — *Mayflower* p.100-101, 104
- *Utensils*
Marshall — *Mayflower* p.103

CLERGYMEN
See also names of clergymen
Fisher — *Men (1)* p.59-63

CLERGYMEN (*continued*)

Folsom — *Give* p.x, 8, 11-12, 14-15, 17-19, 21, 24-26, 29, 31, 33, 38-39, 41, 49, 65-66, 72-73, 78, 80-87, 92
Furnas — *Americans* p.64-68
Goodwin — *Colonial* p.197-200
Rutman — *Winthrop's. See* index p.315
Smith — *17th. See* index p.234 (under ministers)
Tyler — *History. See* index p.541
Wertenbaker — *First. See* index p.342
Wertenbaker — *Puritan. See* index p.354 (under ministers)

, *Defection in*
- *Views of John Winthrop*
Vaughan — *Puritan* p.207-211
, *Donations for*
Rawson — *When* p.209-210, 213-216
- *Harvard graduates*
Wright — *Literary* p.105
- *Maryland*
Calverton — *Awake.* p.252-253
- *Massachusetts*
Dow — *Every* p.207-209
Fisher — *Men (1)* p.134-136
Pomfret — *Founding* p.176-177
- *New England*
Jernegan — *American* p.189
- *New York*
Calverton — *Awake.* p.329-330
- *Pioneers*
Smith — *Colonial* p.34-57
- *Plymouth*
Starkey — *Land* p.93-94
Willison — *Pilgrim* p.56, 148-149, 261-273, 310-311, 319-320, 427, 436-438, 502, 516-517
, *Profession of*
Chitwood — *History (1)* p.472-473
- *"Pulpit literature"*
Morison — *Intellect.* p.156-157
- *Puritans*
Morgan — *Puritan* p.93-103
Sweet — *Religion* p.118
- *Rhetorical training*
Morison — *Intellect.* p.163-165
- *Topsfield, Mass.*
Dow — *Domestic* p.28-29
- *Virginia*
Calverton — *Awake.* p.213-214
Earle — *Home* p.384

Jernegan — *American* p.101
- *Salary (1696)*
Goodwin — *Colonial* p.214

CLERKS OF COURT
- *Maryland*
Craven — *Southern* p.507
- *Virginia*
Craven — *Southern* p.274, 280-281, 293, 383, 391n

CLIFTON. *See* **Clyfton**

CLIMATE. *See* **Weather**

CLOCK-REELS (machine, in spinning)
Earle — *Home* p.174-175, 177, 200

CLOCKS AND CLOCKMAKERS
Earle — *Customs* p.122
Earle — *Home* p.299
Furnas — *Americans* p.164

CLOGS (overshoes)
Earle — *Home* p.295
Earle — *Two cent. (1)* p.359-370

CLOSETS
See also **Cheese closets**
Smith — *Colonial* p.75

CLOTH. *See* **Fabrics**

CLOTH BARS (machine, in weaving)
Earle — *Home* p.224

CLOTHING AND DRESS
See also **Accessories; Funerals; Indians; Pilgrims; Plymouth; Puritans;** names of articles
Carman — *History (1)* p.116
Chitwood — *History (1)* p.487-488
Dow — *Every* p.60-67
Earle — *Customs* p.315-320
Furnas — *Americans* p.130-135
Glubok — *Home* p.266-278
Langdon — *Everyday* p.36-37
Lawrence — *New* p.9
Lawrence — *Not* p.3-7
Leonard — *Dear* p.157-161
Miller — *First* p.112-117
Williams — *Demeter's* p.48-49

- *Animal skins*
Earle — *Home* p.288-289
Leonard — *Dear* p.161

- *Aristocracy*
  Wertenbaker — *First* p.73-74, 279-281
- *Boston*
  Clark — *Old* p.47-48
- *Bridal*
  Earle — *Two cent. (2)* p.631-634
- *Children*
  Beck — *Pilgrims* p.73
  Earle — *Home* p.287-288
  Earle — *Two cent. (1)* p.273-275, 299-306
  Glubok — *Home* p.277-283
  McClinton — *Antiques* p.37, 39-41
  Speare — *Life* p.104-105
  Williams — *Demeter's* p.93, 96
- *Christenings*
  Earle — *Two cent. (1)* p.301-306
- *Class differences*
  Miller — *First* p.114-115
- *Coats and waistcoats*
  Earle — *Two cent. (1)* p.161-193, 255-269
- *Connecticut*
  Fisher — *Men (1)* p.270-271
  Johnston — *Conn.* p.53-54
, *Dutch*
  Speare — *Life* p.58-60
- *Frontier*
  Miller — *First* p.118-119
, *Inherited "duds"*
  Earle — *Two cent. (1)* p.10-12
- *Laws*
  Miller — *First* p.113
  - *Massachusetts, (1634)*
    Earle — *Two cent. (1)* p.61-62
  - *Massachusetts, (1650)*
    Nettels — *Roots* p.327-328
, *"Long-short"*
  Earle — *Home* p.236-237
- *Massachusetts (Inventory)*
  Earle — *Customs* p.314-315
- *Men*
  Dow — *Domestic* p.25
  Earle — *Two cent. (1)* p.28-32, 166
- *New Amsterdam*
  Clark — *Old* p.57
  Earle — *Two cent. (1)* p.100.
- *New England*
  Tunis — *Colonial* p.52-55
  Wertenbaker — *First* p.73-74, 262

- *New Netherland*
  Tunis — *Colonial* p.75-76
- *New Sweden*
  Axtell — *America* p.184-185
- *Ostentation*
  Wertenbaker — *First* p.279-281
, *Quaker*
  Earle — *Two cent. (2)* p.597-602
- *Roxbury, Mass.*
  Beals — *John Eliot* p.106
, *Shipboard*
  Marshall — *Mayflower* p.44
- *South*
  Goodwin — *Colonial* p.73-83
  Tunis — *Colonial* p.93-96
- *Virginia*
  Clark — *Old* p.8-10
  - *Prices*
    Earle — *Two cent. (1)* p.114-115
- *Women*
  Adams — *Album* p.87
  Dow — *Domestic* p.24
  Holliday — *Woman's* p.157-158
  Rutman — *Winthrop's* p.111, 259
  Spruill — *Women's* p.113-116
  - *Connecticut*
    - *Scarlet cloaks*
      Fisher — *Men (1)* p.271
  , *Dutch*
    Clark — *Old* p.58
  - *Mothers*
    - *New England*
      Earle — *Two cent. (1)* p.49-97
  - *Raillery and scolding*
    Holliday — *Woman's* p.158-159
  - *Virginia*
    Earle — *Two cent. (1)* p.97-136

CLOTHMAKING
See also **Weavers and weaving**
Beck — *Pilgrims* p.58-59, 62, 77
Chitwood — *History (1)* p.372-374
Earle — *Home* p.231-233
Jernegan — *American* p.223-224
, *Depression in*
  Smith — *17th* p.84-85

CLYFTON (CLIFTON), ANN STUFFEN
Willison — *Saints* p.59-60, 457

CLYFTON (CLIFTON), RICHARD
Beck — *Pilgrims* p.3-4

CLYFTON (CLIFTON), RICHARD (cont.)
Gill — *Mayflower* p.22, 25-26, 29-30
Leynse — *Preced.* p.17, 56-57, 61, 68-
69, 71, 77, 146, 149, 168, 182, 207-
209
Willison — *Pilgrim* p.17, 24, 26n, 30,
32, 35
Willison — *Saints. See* index p.498

CLYFTON (CLIFTON) FAMILY
Leynse — *Preced. See* index p.281

COACHES
See also **Stagecoaches and stage
lines**
Earle — *Customs* p.191-192
- *Boston*
Earle — *Home* p.331, 353-354

COASTING
Glubok — *Home* p.188-189

COATS OF ARMS
- *Founders*
- *Carolinas*
Morison — *Oxford* p.96
- *New England*
Morison — *Oxford* p.67
- *Virginia and Maryland*
Morison — *Oxford* p.80

COCHENOE (Indian)
Vaughan — *New* p.246-247

COCKFIGHTING
Glubok — *Home* p.189
Goodwin — *Colonial* p.146-148
Miller — *First* p.103

COD. See Codfish

CODDINGTON, WILLIAM
Alderman — *Story* p.97-99
Earle — *Two cent. (1)* p.xviii, 210
Hawke — *Colonial* p.147-148
Rothbard — *Conceived (1)* p.193-196,
198-199, 203, 206-208, 210, 212-
214, 241, 257-258, 349-351, 418
Rutman — *Winthrop's. See* index
p.303
Willison — *Pilgrim* p.324-325, 472-473

CODFISH
Earle — *Home* p.115-116, 120-123
Glubok — *Home* p.64, 66-67
Gould — *Early* p.99-100

National — *History.* p.81
Speare — *Life* p.116-117
Wright — *Everyday* p.82-86
- *"Cor-fish"*
Morison — *Story* p.121-124
- *New England*
- *Trade*
Jernegan — *American* p.174

COFFEE
Earle — *Customs* p.182
- *First served (1670)*
Gould — *Early* p.107

COFFEEHOUSES
Bridenbaugh — *Cities* p.109
Glubok — *Home* p.93

**COFFIN, MARY. See Starbuck, Mary
Coffin**

COFFIN, ROBERT
Willison — *Saints* p.135, 152-153, 155

COFFINS
Rawson — *When* p.243-244

COGGAN, JOHN
Rutman — *Winthrop's. See* index
p.303

COGGESHALL, JOHN
Pomfret — *Founders* p.195-196, 218-
219, 228
Rutman — *Winthrop's* p.73-74, 82n,
123, 182, 193n, 210

COIFS (headdress or cap)
Earle — *Two cent. (2)* p.537

COINS. See Currency

COKINÖE (Indian)
Beals — *John Eliot* p.113, 115, 117-
119, 121-123, 127, 134-135

COLBORNE, WILLIAM
Rutman — *Winthrop's* p.37, 54, 63,
73, 77, 79-81, 82n, 137, 210, 247

COLD HARBOR, MASSACHUSETTS
Gill — *Mayflower* p.74-75
Morison — *Story* p.48-50

COLE, JAMES
Willison — *Saints* p.321-322, 483

COLE, SAMUEL
Rutman — *Winthrop's* p.37, 73, 75, 137, 190, 213n

COLEMAN, JOHN
Christenen — *Delaware* p.56

COLIGNY, GASPER DE, ADMIRAL
Sweet — *Religion* p.25

COLLEGES AND UNIVERSITIES
See also **Books and reading; Libraries;** names of colleges and universities
Carman — *History (1)* p.101-104
Hawke — *Colonial* p.293-294
Speare — *Life* p.109-110
Vaughan — *Puritan* p.244-250
- *Academic rank*
    Morison — *Intellect.* p.34-35
- *Admission (Mass., 1672)*
    Demos — *Remarkable* p.130-135
- *Beginnings*
    Morison — *Intellect.* p.27-56
- *Curriculum*
    Chitwood — *History (1)* p.470
, *Early*
    Monroe — *Founding (1)* p.165-167
, *English*
    Morison — *Intellect.* p.18-19
, *First*
    Hope — *Nation* p.114
    - *Proposed by John Eliot*
        Annals of America (1) p.130-131
- *Life*
    Demos — *Remarkable* p.206, 208-209
    Morison — *Intellect.* p.33-34
- *Purposes*
    Morison — *Intellect.* p.31-33

COLLIER, ELIZABETH. *See* **Southworth, Elizabeth Collier**

COLLIER, MARY. *See* **Prence, Mary Collier Southworth**

COLLIER, WILLIAM
Hills — *History (1)* p.94, 120
Hills — *History (2)* p.46-48, 59, 99, 132
Willison — *Pilgrim* p.278, 379, 381, 450-451, 479, 495n
Willison — *Saints. See* index p.499

COLONIES AND COLONISTS
See also **Emigrants; Jamestown; Plymouth; Women — Colonies and colonists;** names of colonies and colonists
- *1630–1650*
    Morison — *Oxford* p.67-69
- *to 1660*
    Pomfret — *Founding* p.325-337
- *Abundance*

    - *Views of John Smith*
        Goetzmann — *Colonial* p.75
- *Administration*
    , *Imperial supervision of*
        Chitwood — *History (1)* p.406-424
        Greene — *Provincial* p.30-36, 43-44, 54-58
        Hawke — *Colonial* p.334-339
- *Assemblies. See* **Assemblies**
- *Capital procurement*
    Nettels — *Roots* p.133-140
- *Constitutional tendencies (1689)*
    Greene — *Provincial* p.63-64
- *Enemies*
    Hawke — *Colonial* p.278-281
- *Equipment requirements*
    Dow — *Every* p.4, 10-11
- *Factor and influences*
    Bridenbaugh — *Cities* p.4-6
- *First English*
    Morison — *Oxford* p.48-49
    Rozwenc — *Making (1)* p.22-29
- *Founding*
    Nettels — *Roots* p.131-161
- *Freedom of action*
    Hope — *Nation* p.119
- *Government*
    Adams — *Provincial* p.21-22
    Chitwood — *History (1)* p.146-149
, *Leaders, Plea for*
    Demos — *Remarkable* p.203-205
- *Life*
    Dow — *Every* p.225
    Gould — *Early* p.108-144
    Hawke — *Colonial* p.277-288
    Hope — *Nation* p.83-93
- *Mutual assistance*
    Vaughan — *New* p.43-44, 74-75, 84-85, 98, 103
, *Procurement of*
    Nettels — *Roots* p.140-145

COLONIES AND COLONISTS (*cont.*)
, *Proprietary*
   Carman — *History (1)* p.30-32
   Hawke — *Colonial* p.207-239
   Jernegan — *American* p.217-218
   Ver Steeg — *Formative* p.114-122
- *Conflicts*
   Nettels — *Roots* p.337-342
- *Government*
   Nettels — *Roots* p.181-190
   Rozwenc — *Making (1)* p.62-63
- *Provincial reorganization (1689–92)*
   Greene — *Provincial* p.17-29
- *Supplies*
, *Typical*
   Dow — *Every* p.239-241
- *Transition to provinces*
   Ver Steeg — *Formative* p.129-151
- *Value to England*
   Annals of America (1) p.18-20

COMAN, JOHN (accused witch)
   Wertenbaker — *First* p.148-149

COMBING (in spinning)
   Earle — *Home* p.196

COMETS
   Demos — *Remarkable* p.376-377
   Morison — *Intellect.* p.121, 248-249, 252-254
   Wertenbaker — *First* p.139-140

COMMENCEMENT DAY
- *Massachusetts*
   Wertenbaker — *First* p.278-279

COMMERCE
   See also **Exports and imports; Industry; Ships and shipping; Trade and traders;** name of localities
, *as way to wealth*
   Rozwenc — *Making (1)* p.39-41
, *Foreign*
   Chitwood — *History (1)* p.396-400
- *Regulations, enforcement of*
   Chitwood — *History (1)* p.423-424

COMMISSION FOR REGULATING PLANTATIONS
   Willison — *Pilgrim* p.392, 397n, 398-400, 447
   Willison — *Saints* p.298-300, 341, 361

COMMISSION OF 1664
   See also **Atherton Company**
   Bailyn — *New England* p.115, 119-126, 132, 153, 219
   Wertenbaker — *Puritan. See* index p.349

COMMISSIONER OF CUSTOMS
   Bailyn — *New England* p.159, 162, 165-166, 174, 177

COMMISSIONERS OF THE UNITED COLONIES
   Vaughan — *New. See* index p.422

"COMMON," THE (common field, pasture, etc.)
   See also **Boston, Mass. —** "**Common**"
   Langdon — *Everyday* p.283

COMMON LAW. *See* **Law and lawyers, Common**

"COMMON MAN" (1690)
   Adams — *Provincial* p.85-88

COMMON ROOMS. *See* **Rooms, "Common"**

"COMMONAGE" (grazing privilege)
   Rutman — *Winthrop's* p.159, 162, 197-198, 206, 223

"COMMONPLACE BOOKS"
   Demos — *Remarkable* p.350-356
   Morison — *Intellect.* p.49-55

COMMUNAL PRIVILEGES
   Earle — *Home* p.390

COMMUNICATION
   See also **Postal service; Transportation; Travel and travelers;** types of communication
   Adams — *Album* p.132

COMMUNION
   Rutman — *Winthrop's* p.16-17, 55, 107, 128, 145, 153, 251, 257, 270

COMMUNES AND COMMUNISM
   See also **Labadists; Pilgrims; Priber, Mr.**
   Calverton — *Awake. See* index p.460

- *Dedham, Mass.*
  Lockridge — *New* p.1-78
  , *Decline of*
  Lockridge — *New* p.79-90
- *Economy*
  Calverton — *Awake.* p.201-203
  , *Medieval and modern*
  Calverton — *Awake.* p.203-206
  , *Pilgrim, failure of*
  Calverton — *Awake.* p.108-109

"COMMUNITY CHEST"
, *First*
  Calverton — *Awake.* p.185

COMMUNITY LIFE. *See* name of locality, subdivision **Life of**

COMPANY FOR THE PROPAGATION OF THE GOSPEL. *See* **Society for Promoting Christian Knowledge**

"COMPANY OF ADVENTURERS." *See* **"Adventurers"**

COMPANY OF NEW FRANCE (Company of the Hundred Associates)
Amer. Her. — *Thirteen* p.120-121

COMPANY OF UNDERTAKERS FOR IRONWORKS
Bailyn — *New England* p.62-70, 119

COMPASSES
Marshall — *Mayflower* p.16, 38

COMPETITION
Wish — *Society (1)* p.1-4, 51-52, 71, 97

COMPTON, HENRY, BISHOP
Smith — *17th* p.135-136, 179, 181, 183, 187-188

CONANT, CALEB
Willison — *Saints* p.448

CONANT, ELIZABETH WESTON
Willison — *Saints* p.249, 448

CONANT, ROGER
Gildrie — *Salem* p.1-3, 5, 7-8, 24-25, 29, 34, 45-47, 60-61, 100, 104, 113, 126
Pomfret — *Founding* p.150-152
Willison — *Saints* p.249, 252, 267, 270, 272, 279, 448, 450, 458

CONCH SHELLS
, *as summons*
  Earle — *Home* p.367-368

CONCORD INDIANS
Vaughan — *New* p.250-251

CONESTOGA WAGONS
Christensen — *Delaware* p.85-86
Speare — *Life* p.140

CONFEDERATION OF NEW ENGLAND. *See* **New England Confederation**

CONFEDERATION OF NEW YORK
Nettels — *Roots* p.212-220

CONFIDENCE MEN
- *Massachusetts* (1680)
  Demos — *Remarkable* p.210-211

CONGREGATIONALISTS
See also **Cambridge Platform of Church Discipline; "Half-Way Covenant"; Puritans**
Amer. Her. — *Thirteen* p.94, 103, 155, 158
Carman — *History (1)* p.37, 86, 129
Chitwood — *History (1)* p.432
Hawke — *Colonial* p.54, 134-136, 179, 198
Life — *New* p.76, 124-125
Morison — *Intellect.* p.8, 153, 171, 274
Morris — *Ency.* p.547-548
Nettels — *Roots* p.472-474
Pomfret — *Founding. See* index p.378 (under Puritans, Puritanism)
Ver Steeg — *Formative* p.76-80
Wertenbaker — *Puritan. See* index p.349
Willison — *Saints* p.62, 104, 316, 326-327, 339, 474, 484
Wish — *Society (1)* p.6, 25, 35
Wright — *Everyday* p.164
- *Boston*
  Vaughan — *Puritan* p.329-333
- *Connecticut*
  Rozwenc — *Making (1)* p.273
- *Massachusetts*
  Chitwood — *History (1)* p.108-109
  Rozwenc — *Making (1)* p.71
- *New England*
  Sweet — *Religion* p.17-119, 271, 292

CONGREGATIONALISTS (continued)
- Origin
  Demos — Little p.3, 8-9, 17
  Hall — Religious p.16, 89, 105-108, 124
  Leynse — Preced. p.230
  Marshall — Mayflower p.60
- Polity
  Sweet — Religion p.84-85
- Puritans
  Morgan — Puritan p.79-80
, Rise of
  Sweet — Religion p.73-76
- South Carolina
  Sweet — Religion p.41

CONNECTICUT
See also **Fundamental Orders of Connecticut; Pequot War;** names of cities
Acheson — America's p.110-111
Alderman — Story p.69-71, 73-74, 76-78
Amer. Her. — Thirteen p.103, 160, 163
Annals of America (1) p.300b
Bailyn — New England. See index p.242
Calverton — Awake. p.148-159
Carman — History (1) p.29, 52, 87, 90
Chitwood — History (1) p.123-129
Craven — Colonies p.5-6, 24-25, 27-28, 44, 79, 86, 105
Folsom — Give p.17, 34, 38, 41, 65
Hawke — Colonial p.148-150; See also index p.713-714
Kraus — U.S. (1) p.64-65
Morison — Story p.146, 157, 211, 214, 223, 248-249, 264, 273, 281
Pomfret — Founding. See index p.374
Starkey — Land p.87-89, 127, 141, 169-170, 208, 213-214
Vaughan — New. See index p.422
Willison — Saints. See index p.499
, after "Glorious Revolution"
  Rothbard — Conceived (1) p.481-483
- Amusements
  Johnston — Conn. p.88
, and Dominion of New England
  Craven — Colonies p.216, 225, 234
, and Long Island
  Craven — Colonies p.46, 62, 64

, and Massachusetts
  Willison — Pilgrim p.405-409
- Annexation of New Haven
  Morris — Ency. p.37
- "Blue Laws." See **"Blue Laws" — Connecticut**
- Charter
  Chitwood — History (1) p.128-129
  Fisher — Men (1) p.253-254
  Jernegan — American p.149-150
  Johnston — Conn. p.82, 84-85, 95-96, 98-99
  Morris — Ency. p.37
  Wertenbaker — First p.106-107
- Chronology (1614-97)
  Johnston — Conn. p.129-130
- Commerce
  Wertenbaker — First p.52-55
- Democracy adopted
  Angle — By p.5-6
- Distinctions
  Johnston — Conn. p.1
- Dutch and English relations
  Collins — Story p.53
- Founding
  Fisher — Men (1) p.243
  Morris — Ency. p.34-35
  Nettels — Roots p.171-175
  Pomfret — Founding p.232-255
  Rothbard — Conceived (1) p.218-223
  Sweet — Religion p.95-96
  Wertenbaker — First p.97-98
- Historic sites
  Johnston — Conn. p.132-133
, in King Philip's War
  Craven — Colonies p.120-121
- Moral code
  Wertenbaker — First p.191
- Three river towns (Windsor, Hartford, and Wethersfield)
  Adams — Album p.98, 100
  Fisher — Men (1) p.244-248
  Johnston — Conn. p.10
- Trade establishment
  Willison — Pilgrim p.387-390

CONNECTICUT INDIANS
Vaughan — New p.116, 125, 277

CONNECTICUT RIVER AND VALLEY
Alderman — Story p.28, 41, 45, 69-72, 80
Amer. Her. — Thirteen p.103, 133, 162-163

Bailyn — *New England* p.24, 28-29, 51, 53-55
Miller — *First* p.61-64
Morison — *Story* p.134-136, 209-210, 261-262
Snell — *Wild* p.113, 129, 134-135
Vaughan — *New. See* index p.422

CONSTABLES AND SHERIFFS
Bridenbaugh — *Cities* p.63-67
Woodward — *Way* p.43-46
- *Boston*
    Rutman — *Winthrop's* p.210, 212, 212n, 213, 215, 224-228, 228n
- *Chesapeake colonies (1640–76)*
    Hawke — *Colonial* p.185-186
- *Maryland*
    Craven — *Southern* p.203, 306-307
- *Virginia*
    Craven — *Southern* p.170, 281-285, 377, 383, 391n

"CONTINENTAL SHELF"
Ver Steeg — *Formative* p.30-31

CONVICTS
- *Maryland*
    Morison — *Oxford* p.83
- *Women*
    Leonard — *Dear* p.338

COODE, JOHN
Folsom — *Give* p.72-74

COOK, ARTHUR
Rothbard — *Conceived (1)* p.409-411, 502

COOKE, DAMARIS HOPKINS
Marble — *Women* p.23, 68-69
Willison — *Saints* p.133, 441, 446

COOKE, ELIZABETH
Hills — *History (1)* p.135, 151, 153-154, 158
Hills — *History (2)* p.68, 76, 138, 140, 146, 215

COOKE, FRANCIS
Hills — *History (1)* p.156-161; *See also* index p.164
Hills — *History (2)* p.64, 69, 96, 151, 215

Leynse — *Preced.* p.205, 238, 261, 266
Marble — *Women* p.16, 89
Willison — *Pilgrim* p.129, 521, 533
Willison — *Saints. See* index p.499

COOKE, HESTER MAYHIEU
Willison — *Pilgrim* p.129, 235
Willison — *Saints* p.90, 123, 236, 446,

COOKE, JANE. *See* Mitchell, Jane Cooke

COOKE, JOHN
Willison — *Pilgrim* p.129, 521-522, 530, 533
Willison — *Saints* p.382, 407, 439, 450, 460

COOKE, SARAH WARREN
Willison — *Saints* p.439, 450

COOKE FAMILY
Hills — *History (1)* p.151-161; *See also* index p.164
Hills — *History (2)* p.215; *See also* index p.252
Marble — *Women* p.16, 24, 36, 89

COOKERY
See also **Food; Indians — Cookery; Kitchen utensils;** special subjects, colonies, etc.
Earle — *Home* p.151-152
Marshall — *Mayflower* p.94, 97
- *Books*
    Spruill — *Women's* p.209-212
, *Dutch*
    Gould — *Early* p.96
    Smith — *Colonial* p.111-112
- *Methods*
    Earle — *Colonial* p.280
    Glubok — *Home* p.83-85
- *New England*
    Tunis — *Colonial* p.37-38
- *New Netherland*
    Tunis — *Colonial* p.69-70
- *South*
    Tunis — *Colonial* p.88
- *Types*
    Langdon — *Everyday* p.20-22

COOMBS, SARAH PRIEST
Willison — *Saints* p.447

COOPER, ANTHONY ASHLEY, SIR. *See* Shaftsbury, Anthony Ashley Cooper, Earl of

COOPER, HUMILITY
Willison — *Saints* p.122, 439, 441

COOPERS
Bridenbaugh — *Cities* p.36-37
Marshall — *Mayflower* p.171, 173-177
Rutman — *Winthrop's* p.189, 199,
232, 242, 251-252
Tunis — *Craftsmen* p.22-23

COOTE, ROBERT. *See* **Bellomont,
Earl of**

COPELAND, JOHN
Wertenbaker — *Puritan* p.229-230,
232-234, 239

COPERNICAN SOCIETY
Morison — *Intellect.* p.246-247

COPPER AND COPPERSMITHS
Craven — *Southern* p.48, 53, 56, 68,
75, 84

COPPIN, ROBERT
Morison — *Story* p.32, 50-52

COQUETTES
Lawrence — *Not* p.15-18, 27-30

CORBITANT (COUNTABANT) (Indian)
Beck — *Pilgrims* p.41-42
Dillon — *Pilgrim* p.163-164, 170, 177
Marshall — *Mayflower* p.153
Morison — *Story* p.78-79
Vaughan — *New* p.75-76, 79, 324
Willison — *Pilgrim* p.208-209, 214-215
Willison — *Saints* p.186-187, 201,
213, 220-223

CORDWAINERS (shoemakers)
Tunis — *Craftsmen* p.36-37

COREY. *See* **Cory**

CORN
See also **"Samp"**
Beck — *Pilgrims* p.26, 34, 38, 59, 61
Earle — *Home* p.127-131, 133-136,
138-141
Furnas — *Americans* p.165-169
Glubok — *Home* p.70-78
Gould — *Early* p.89-90
Hope — *Nation* p.84-85
Lawrence — *New* p.6-7
Leonard — *Dear* p.139-141

Marshall — *Mayflower* p.60,143
Morison — *Story* p.47, 70-72, 78, 80,
92, 95, 111, 126, 198-200
National — *History.* p.80-81
Rutman — *Winthrop's* p.23, 63, 88,
91, 170, 180, 184-185, 188, 194,
206, 227, 271
Willison — *Pilgrim* p.146, 151, 183,
246, 259, 291-292, 305, 307
Willison — *Saints* p.149-152, 184-185,
215, 231-232, 239-240, 312-313
Woodbury — *Way* p.51
- *Caches, or caves*
Earle — *Home* p.138
- *Cobs, Uses of*
Earle — *Home* p.141
Glubok — *Home* p.77-78, 248
- *Connecticut*
Johnston—*Conn.* p.50-51
- *Dances. See* **Indians — Dances
and dancing — Corn**
- *Huskings. See* **Husking bees**
, *Indian*
Earle — *Customs* p.148-149
Earle — *Home* p.126-135
- *Kernels, Uses of*
Glubok — *Home* p.77-78
- *Plymouth*
Adams — *Album* p.46
- *Pounding*
Adams — *Album* p.57
- *Shelling*
Earle — *Home* p.140-141
Gould — *Early* p.134
- *Shucks*
Gould — *Early* p.134

CORNBURY, LORD
Rothbard — *Conceived (1)* p.474-477,
493

CORWIN, GEORGE
Gildrie — *Salem* p.61, 103-104, 106,
110-111, 113-114, 134, 138, 151,
159

CORY (COREY), GILES
Fisher — *Men (1)* p.171
Holliday — *Woman's* p.57-58
Williams — *Demeter's* p.140

CORY (COREY), MARTHA
Folsom — *Give* p.84-85

COSMETICS (beauty aids)
Earle — *Customs* p.306-308

Spruill — Women's p.127-128
Woodward — Way p.58
- Books
Spruill — Women's p.210

COSTUME. See Clothing and dress

COTILLIONS. See Dances and dancing

COTTON, ANNE
, on Bacon's Rebellion
Williams — Demeter's p.162

COTTON, JOHN, REV.
Amer. Her. — Thirteen p.90, 101, 103-104, 154
Beals — John Eliot p.48-50, 88-89, 93-95, 99, 143-144
Earle — Customs p.306-308
Earle — Two cent. (1) p.xiv, 42, 67
Earle — Two cent. (2) p.329, 417
Hawke — U.S. p.99-105, 107-111
Morison — Intellect. p.9, 11, 121, 139, 152-153, 155n, 171
Murdock — Literature p.34, 60, 120-123, 125-127, 130, 134
Pomfret — Founding p.161, 175, 181, 186-187, 193, 196, 203, 236-238, 245, 257-260, 266-267
Rozwenc — Making (1) p.37-38, 65, 71, 92, 100
Rutman — Winthrop's. See index p.304
Smith — 17th p.25, 145, 148, 151-152
Snell — Wild p.126, 129, 134
Starkey — Land p.90, 96, 98, 101-103, 136
Wertenbaker — First. See index p.342
Wertenbaker — Puritan p.21-24, 51, 63, 67, 147, 160-162, 220, 231, 239
Willison — Pilgrim p.325n-326, 395n, 418n, 424
Willison — Saints. See index p.499
Wish — Society (1) p.23, 35-38, 55, 57, 59
Wright — Everyday p.176

- Biography
Morris — Ency. p.647-648
- "Democracy as detrimental to church and state" (1636)
Annals of America (1) p.149-154
- "The divine right to occupy this land" (1630)
Annals of America (1) p.107-109

- Elegy, by John Norton
Vaughan — Puritan p.253-255
- Letter of sympathy, Plymouth (1683)
Demos — Remarkable p.165-166
- Letter to Lord Saye and Sele (1636)
Annals of America (1) p.132-133
, on Church and state
Hawke — U.S. p.102-103
Vaughan — Puritan p.147-151
, on limitation of government
Hawke — U.S. p.104-105
, on Puritan economic and social ideals
Goetzmann — Colonial p.187-190
, on Puritan theory of exclusion
Vaughan — Puritan p.201-205
, on singing psalms
Howard — Our p.10
- "Spiritual milk . . ."
Rozwenc — Making (1) p.641
- Views by John Winthrop
Hawke — U.S. p.107-111
- Views by Samuel Whiting
Hawke — U.S. p.99-102

COTTON, JOHN, JR., REV.
Willison — Pilgrim p.325, 502, 525, 529
Willison — Saints. See index p.499

COTTON
Craven — Southern p.21, 70, 119, 141, 245, 316, 336-337, 346-347, 355
Glubok — Home p.251
Leonard — Dear p.165
Speare — Life p.131-132

COUNCIL FOR NEW ENGLAND
Bailyn — New England p.5-10, 17, 50, 202-203
Chitwood — History (1) p.88-89
Gill — Mayflower p.70, 103-104, 130, 134
Jernegan — American p.121
Marshall — Mayflower p.178, 181
Nettels — Roots p.113-116
Pomfret — Founding. See index p.374
Rothbard — Conceived (1) p.375-379
Vaughan — New p.91, 117, 213, 227, 342
Willison — Pilgrim p.97-98, 158n, 229, 241, 282, 284-285, 397n

COUNCIL FOR NEW ENGLAND (*cont.*)
Willison — *Saints* p.233-234, 238, 257, 281, 286-287, 299-300, 349, 465-466, 469

COUNCIL FOR PLANTATIONS
Wertenbaker — *Puritan* p.304-307, 317-318, 320-321, 335, 337-338

COUNCIL OF MASSACHUSETTS
Bailyn — *New England* p.38-39, 103, 131, 155, 160, 169, 174-177, 180, 185-186, 188, 191, 194-195

COUNCILS FOR TRADE AND PLANTATIONS
See also **Council for Plantations**
Craven — *Colonies* p.34-35, 48, 56, 60

COUNTABANT. *See* **Corbitant (Indian)**

COUNTRY LIFE
See also **Farmers and farming**
Hawke — *Colonial* p.281-285
Wertenbaker — *First. See* index p.353 (under Rural life)

COUNTY COURTS
Craven — *Colonies* p.23-25, 74, 76, 78-79
Craven — *Southern. See* index p.439
Ver Steeg — *Formative* p.71-73

"COURT DAY"
- *South*
Wertenbaker — *First* p.202-203

COURTENAY, ARCHBISHOP
Hall — *Religious* p.18-20, 34

COURTESY
- *Laws*
Glubok — *Home* p.104-105

COURTS
See also names of colonies, names of courts, e.g. **Assemblies; Assize courts; County courts**
- *Boston*
Rutman — *Winthrop's. See* index p.305
- *Salem*
Dow — *Every* p.206-207

COURTSHIP
Chitwood — *History (1)* p.495-497
Demos — *Remarkable* p.138-149
Miller — *First* p.189
- *Boston (1663)*
Earle — *Customs* p.40-43
- *Plymouth. See* **Plymouth — Courtship**
- *Widows*
Lawrence — *Not* p.31-34, 41-48

COVENANTS
See also **"Half-way Covenant"; Bulkeley, Peter, on the Covenant**
Carman — *History (1)* p.88, 95-97
Morison — *Intellect.* p.160-161
Vaughan — *Puritan* p.76-78
Wertenbaker — *Puritan* p.19-20, 23-24, 58-59
Willison — *Saints. See* index p.499
Wright — *Cultural* p.79-81
- *Dedham, Mass.*
Lockridge — *New* p.3-16, 20n, 50-52, 80
- *Salem, Mass.*
Gildrie — *Salem. See* index p.185

COVERED WAGONS
See also **Conestoga wagons**
Wright — *Everyday* p.126

COVERLETS
- *Pennsylvania*
Earle — *Home* p.190

COWHERDS
Earle — *Home* p.399-400

COWLEY, ABRAHAM
- *Writings*
Morison — *Intellect.* p.23, 50-51

COWLS (tubs)
Earle — *Colonial* p.282

COWS. *See* **Cattle**

COYTMORE, MARTHA. *See* **Winthrop, Martha Coytmore**

CRADDOCK, MATTHEW
Bailyn — *New England* p.17-18, 27-28, 76-77
Rutman — *Winthrop's* p.45-46, 92n

"CRADDOCK HOUSE." *See* "Peter Tufts (Craddock) House"

CRADLES
Glubok — *Home* p.100-101
McClinton — *Antiques* p.137-138
, *Christening*
McClinton — *Antiques* p.33
, *Cratch*
Glubok — *Home* p.185-186

CRAFTS AND CRAFTSMANSHIP
See also **Artisans;** names of articles and types
Beck — *Pilgrims* p.62-66
Carman — *History (1)* p.75-76
Craven — *Southern* p.71, 80, 89, 104, 129-130, 242-243, 244, 272
Hawke — *Colonial* p.287
Speare — *Life* p.144-133
- *Country work*
Tunis — *Craftsmen* p.18-38
- *Home industries*
Earle — *Home* p.167, 179, 189
- *Piedmont*
Wertenbaker — *Old* p.138-140
- *Homespun, Durability of*
Earle — *Home* p.238-239
- *Honesty*
Tunis — *Craftsmen* p.16-17
- *Immigration of skilled*
Marshall — *Mayflower* p.177
- *Itinerants*
Tunis — *Craftsmen* p.36
- *Masters*
Tunis — *Craftsmen* p.15-16
- *New England*
Tunis — *Colonial* p.43-45
- *Quality*
Tunis·— *Craftsmen* p.16-17
- *South*
Craven — *Southern* p.129-130, 242-244, 272

CRANDALL, JOHN
Sweet — *Religion* p.132-133

CRANFIELD, EDWARD
Bailyn — *New England* p.168-169, 171-172, 174, 179
Rothbard — *Conceived (1)* p.362-366, 371, 374, 379, 417, 428

CRANES
Rawson — *When* p.5

CRASHAW, RICHARD
Murdock — *Literature* p.11-13, 18, 38, 45

CRAVATS (neckwear)
Earle — *Two cent. (1)* p.209-212

CREDIT AND CREDITORS
Bailyn — *New England* p.34-35, 47-48, 98, 185

CREEPERS (low andirons)
Earle — *Colonial* p.285
Earle — *Home* p.62

CRESPIN, JEAN
Morison — *Intellect.* p.46-47

CRIME AND CRIMINALS
See also **Prisons and prisoners; Punishment;** types of crime
Bridenbaugh — *Cities* p.68-78
Dow — *Domestic* p.29
Wertenbaker — *First.* See index p.342-343 (under Crime, Criminals)
Willison — *Pilgrim* p.125, 257, 306, 355-356, 442-443, 456-464, 486, 558
Wish — *Society (1)* p.30-32, 44-45, 79-80, 100
- *Essex Co., Mass.*
Lawrence — *Not* p.172-176
- *Laws*
Jernegan — *American* p.182
Nettels — *Roots* p.463-466
- *Massachusetts*
Dow — *Every* p.224-226
- *New England*
Jernegan — *American* p.183
- *Women*
Lawrence — *Not* p.162-164, 167, 170
Spruill — *Women's* p.314-323

CRISS-CROSS ROW
Glubok — *Home* p.139-140, 142

CROATAN (LUMBEE) INDIANS
Snell — *Wild* p.58
- *Raleigh's colonists*
Morison — *Oxford* p.45

CROCUS (cloth)
Glubok — *Home* p.262-263

CROMWELL, OLIVER
Rozwenc — *Making (1)* p.21, 78-80

CROPS AND GRAINS
  See also **Agriculture; Cereal farming; Farmers and farming;** names of crops and grains
  , *Control of*
    Craven — *Southern* p.238-239, 312, 398
  - *New England*
    Jernegan — *American* p.172
  - *Plymouth. See* **Plymouth — Crops and harvesting**

CROSS-CLOTHES (headdress bands)
  Earle — *Two cent. (2)* p.537-538

CROSS-STAFF (navigation instrument)
  Marshall — *Mayflower* p.381

CROUCH, NATHANIEL
  Smith — *17th* p.216-217

CRUISIE (lighting device)
  Marshall — *Mayflower* p.107

CUDWORTH, JAMES
  Morison — *Story* p.164-165, 191n, 219, 257-260, 285
  Willison — *Saints. See* index p.499

CULPEPER, JOHN
  Morris — *Ency.* p.53

CULPEPER, THOMAS, LORD
  Calverton — *Awake.* p.235-237, 295-298
  Craven — *Colonies* p.151-155, 215
  Craven — *Southern* p.376, 390-392, 395, 397-398
  Rothbard — *Conceived (1)* p.92-93, 113, 144-146, 148-150, 373-374

CULPEPER'S REBELLION (1677–1680)
  Craven — *Colonies* p.156-160, 164
  Hawke — *U.S.* p.196-198
  Morris — *Ency.* p.53

CULTURE
  See also **Art; Books and reading; Indians — Culture; Libraries; Music;** names of types
  Chitwood — *History (1)* p.233-234
  Ver Steeg — *Formative* p.93-94
  Wertenbaker — *First. See* index p.346-347
  Wright — *Literary* p.76-80
  - *Boston*
    Bridenbaugh — *Cities* p.128-131

  , *British, influence of*
    Arts — *America* p.30-31
  - *Definition*
    Morison — *Intellect.* p.3-5
  , *Dutch*
    Bridenbaugh — *Cities* p.132-133
  - *Intellectuals*
    Carman — *History (1)* p.105-106
  - *Intellect, American (1690's)*
    Adams — *Provincial* p.113-126
  - *New England*
    Jernegan — *American* p.187-191
    Wright — *Literary* p.82-109
  - *Newport, R.I.*
    Bridenbaugh — *Cities* p.132

CUMMAQUID, MASSACHUSETTS
  See also **Barnstable, Massachusetts**
  Willison — *Saints* p.212-213, 217-219, 467

CUMMAQUID INDIANS
  Willison — *Saints* p.187, 213, 218, 223, 229, 316, 424, 467

CUPBOARDS
  Earle — *Customs* p.111-112

CUPS
  , *Cocoanut*
    Earle — *Home* p.96-97

CURES. *See* **Medicine; Remedies**

CURFEW LAWS
  Bridenbaugh — *Cities* p.56

CURFEWS (fire covers)
  Gould — *Early* p.65

CURRENCY
  See also **Beavers; Money; Pine-Tree Shillings; Wampum**
  Adams — *Album* p.63, 162
  Bailyn — *New England* p.33, 48, 66, 98, 182-183
  Carman — *History (1)* p.81-83
  Langdon — *Everyday* p.195
  Nettels — *Roots* p.264-273
  Rutman — *Winthrop's* p.172n, 180, 182-184, 187, 212n, 227-228
  Massachusetts, first silver in
    Dow — *Every* p.171
  - *"N.E."*
    Dow — *Every* p.168

- *"Oak"*
    Dow — *Every* p.168

CURRIERS
Tunis — *Craftsmen* p.32-34

CURTAINS
Dow — *Domestic* p.21

CURTIS, SARAH. *See* Eliot, Sarah Curtis

CURWEN, GEORGE, CAPTAIN
Earle — *Two cent. (1)* p.xviii, 204, 207
Earle — *Two cent. (2)* p.690

CUSHENOT (trading post, on Kennebec)
Willison — *Pilgrim* p.356n, 391-392, 445

CUSHMAN, MARY CLARKE SINGLETON
Willison — *Pilgrim* p.78, 88
Willison — *Saints* p.106, 122, 444

CUSHMAN, MARY MORRIS ALLERTON (longest surviving *Mayflower* passenger)
Gill — *Mayflower* p.81
Leynse — *Preced.* p.88, 135, 237, 260, 262, 265
Marble — *Women* p.12, 56
Williams — *Demeter's* p.23
Willison — *Pilgrim* p.78, 118, 125, 383, 530, 532
Willison — *Saints* p.121-122, 125, 160, 166, 311, 314, 324-329, 407, 409, 427, 438, 444

CUSHMAN, ROBERT
Caffrey — *Mayflower. See* index p.486-387
Dillon — *Pilgrims* p.109-112, 114-115, 119-121, 161-168, 173, 185, 189, 193, 195
Gill — *Mayflower* p.32-34, 38-39, 43, 47, 61, 70, 93, 96, 114
Hills — *History (1)* p.6, 12, 15, 19, 26-30, 32-35, 58, 62-64, 79, 82-83, 116, 154
Hills — *History (2)* p.40-41, 149, 156, 173-174, 179-182, 239-240
Leynse — *Preced. See* index p.281
Marshall — *Mayflower* p.26, 30, 63, 160-161

Morison — *Story* p.15, 18, 24, 111, 166-167
Willison — *Pilgrim. See* index p.574
Willison — *Saints. See* index p.499
- *Death*
    Willison — *Pilgrim* p.289-290
- *"Reasons . . . of removing out of England, 1622"*
    Demos — *Remarkable* p.25-31

CUSHMAN, THOMAS
Gill — *Mayflower* p.93, 145
Hills — *History (1)* p.22, 47, 53, 57-58, 79, 82-83, 91, 94, 97, 153-154
Hills — *History (2)* p.106-108, 163, 167, 177-182
Willison — *Pilgrim* p.78, 88, 155, 284n, 383, 480-481, 510, 530, 538
Willison — *Saints. See* index p.499

CUSHMAN FAMILY
Caffrey — *Mayflower. See* index p.386-387
Hills — *History (1). See* index p.164-165
Hills — *History (2).* p.171, 179-182; *See also* index p.253
Marble — *Women* p.10, 16, 34

CUSTOMS (duties)
See also **Commissioner of customs; Exports and imports**
Bailyn — *New England* p.151-153, 157, 161, 164, 166, 177-178, 180
- *Collectors*
    Craven — *Colonies* p.147-148, 160, 164-165, 168, 231, 233
    Jernegan — *American* p.252

CUTHBERTSON, CUTHBERT (Godbertson, Godbert)
Willison — *Saints. See* index p.499-500

CUTHBERTSON, SARAH ALLERTON VINCENT
Willison — *Saints. See* index p.500

CUTLERS
Tunis — *Craftsmen* p.50

CUTSHAMEKIN (Indian)
Beals — *John Eliot. See* index p.188
Vaughan — *New. See* index p.423

CUT-TAILS
Earle — *Home* p.122-123

CUTTS FAMILY
Bailyn — *New England* p.82, 124-125, 131, 137, 161-162

D

"DABBADABB" (ground corn)
Scott — *Settlers* p.113

DAFFODILS
Earle — *Home* p.426-427

DAIRYING
See also **Cattle**
Furnas — *Americans* p.173

DALE, ARABELLA, LADY
Phillips — *First* p.107-110, 121-122, 126, 134, 158, 166

DALE, THOMAS, SIR
Chitwood — *History (1)* p.62-64
Craven — *Southern* p.86n, 103-105, 108-109, 116-117, 119, 121
Glubok — *Home* p.70, 293, 299
Hawke — *Colonial* p.93, 96-99, 103, 116, 127, 132
Spruill — *Women's* p.6
Wertenbaker — *First* p.210-211, 304
- *Home for Pocahontas*
Phillips — *First* p.121, 134

DALE'S LAWS (1610)
Craven — *Southern* p.96n, 105-107, 134, 178
Hawke — *Colonial* p.97, 100
Hawke — *U.S.* p.70

DAME SCHOOLS
Glubok — *Home* p.125
Monroe — *Founding (1)* p.127-134
Williams — *Demeter's* p.98-99
- *Teachers — Women*
Leonard — *Dear* p.256-257

DANCES AND DANCING
See also **Indians; Pilgrims; Puritans — Dances and dancing**
Bridenbaugh — *Cities* p.117-118
Chitwood — *History (1)* p.490-491
Glubok — *Home* p.127-128
Rawson — *When* p.95-96, 251-271

Speare — *Life* p.157-158
Wertenbaker — *Puritan* p.176-177
- *Ordination balls*
Glubok — *Home* p.128
- *Schools*
Howard — *Our* p.20-21
- *South*
Wertenbaker — *First* p.268-269
- *Views of Increase Mather*
Annals of America (1) p.272-273

DANCKAERTS, JASPER. *See* Dankers, Jasper

DANDY, ANN
Williams — *Demeter's* p.86

DANE, JOHN
- *"Declaration of . . . providences"*
Demos — *Remarkable* p.81-88

DANFORTH, SAMUEL
Morison — *Intellect.* p.121, 230-231, 248

DANFORTH, THOMAS
Beals — *John Eliot* p.166, 168, 175-180
Rothbard — *Conceived (1)* p.368-370, 372, 417, 449
Wertenbaker — *Puritan* p.282-283, 325-326

DANKERS, JASPER
Wertenbaker — *First* p.198, 249-250
- *Visit to Maryland and Virginia*
Axtell — *America* p.211-216
- *Visits to New England*
Axtell — *America* p.88-95, 107-113, 145-159

DARE, ELEANOR WHITE
Morris — *Ency.* p.25
Williams — *Demeter's* p.18-19

DARE, VIRGINIA
Amer. Her. — *Thirteen* p.42, 46
Marshall — *Mayflower* p.21
Morris — *Ency.* p.25

"DARNING"
Rawson — *When* p.111-112

DARTMOUTH (NEW BEDFORD), MASSACHUSETTS
Willison — *Saints* p.358, 382, 396, 400, 407, 439, 445-449

DATES. *See* Chronology

DAVENPORT, ELIZABETH WOOLEY
Williams — *Demeter's* p.86

DAVENPORT, JOHN, REV.
Adams — *Album* p.124
Alderman — *Story* p.73, 75-76
Bailyn — *New England* p.19, 29-30, 57, 71, 122
Hawke — *Colonial* p.138, 142, 148, 150
Johnston — *Conn.* p.37-41, 43-46, 67, 75, 84-86, 101
Morison — *Intellect.* p.121, 139, 152, 155n, 172, 247
Pomfret — *Founding* p.187, 192, 195, 237, 257, 261-262, 274, 267-270
Rothbard — *Conceived (1)* p.176, 221-222, 230, 280-282
Wertenbaker — *Puritan* p.59, 312-313

DAVENPORT, MRS. JOHN
Earle — *Colonial* p.50-55

DAVIS, JOHN
Marshall — *Mayflower* p.19, 38

DAVISON, WILLIAM, SIR
Gill — *Mayflower* p.24-25, 140
Willison — *Saints* p.35-38, 438

DAY(E), STEPHEN
Earle — *Customs* p.259
Morison — *Intellect.* p.114-116

DE LA NOYE. *See* Delano; Delanoy

DE LA WARR, LADY
Phillips — *First* p.101-102, 107-111, 158, 167
- *Jewelry, Gift to Pocahontas*
  Phillips — *First* p.110
, *on Pocahontas*
  Phillips — *First* p.108

DE LA WARR, THOMAS WEST, LORD
Craven — *Southern* p.84-85, 91, 98, 100-101, 104-105, 109, 114, 268
Hawke — *Colonial* p.93-96
Phillips — *First* p.101-102, 106-107, 111, 116-118

DE PEYSTER, LUBBETSE
Leonard — *Dear* p.440

DE VRIES, DAVID PIETERSEN, CAPTAIN
Christensen — *Delaware* p.19, 38
Fisher — *Men (2)* p.27-30, 38-49
Rothbard — *Conceived (1)* p.300-306, 310
Starkey — *Land* p.140, 144-148, 157-158
- *Delaware colony*
  Collins — *Story* p.67
, *on New Netherland*
  Axtell — *America* p.133-141
- *"Short historical notes" (1655)*
  Amer. Her. — *Thirteen* p.63

DE VRIES, MRS. RUDOLPHUS
Earle — *Colonial* p.73

DEACONS
- *Duties*
  Wertenbaker — *Puritan* p.63-64

DEANE, THOMAS
Bailyn — *New England* p.122-123, 131, 133

DEATH
See also **Cemeteries; Funerals; Infant mortality**
Demos — *Remarkable* p.165-166

DEATH PENALTY
See also **Hangings; Indians; Puritans — Death penalty**
- *Quakers*
  Wertenbaker — *Puritan* p.213-214, 234-238

DEATH RATE
See also **Plymouth**
Smith — *17th* p.8, 10, 64
Williams — *Demeter's* p.93-94, 174
Willison — *Saints* p.385-386
- *Dedham, Mass.*
  Lockridge — *New* p.67-69
- *Virginia*
  Morison — *Oxford* p.53

"DEBARKING" TREES
Marshall — *Mayflower* p.77, 79, 158

DEBT
Bailyn — *New England* p.47-49, 61, 75, 104, 185
Rutman — *Winthrop's* p.175, 182-183, 200, 218-219

DEBT (*continued*)
- *Executions. See* **Hangings**
, *Imprisonment for — New York*
Wertenbaker — *First* p.223-224

DECLARATIONS OF INDULGENCE
Craven — *Colonies* p.105-106, 221, 223

DEDHAM, MASSACHUSETTS
See also special subjects
Lockridge — *New. See* index p.201-208

DEER
Earle — *Home* p.108
Gould — *Early* p.98
, *as food*
Glubok — *Home* p.56-58
- *Fire-hunting*
Earle — *Home* p.108-109
- *New Netherland*
Axtell — *America* p.39

DEER ISLAND
Beal — *John Eliot* p.67, 74, 171-179

DEFENSE, COMMON
See also **Blockhouses; Forts**
Bridenbaugh — *Cities* p.63-68
Speare — *Life* p.83-94

DELANO (DE LA NOYE), PHILIPPE
Willison — *Pilgrim* p.155, 385n, 538-539
Willison — *Saints* p.90, 191, 314, 324, 444, 452, 486

DELANOY (DE LA NOYE), PETER
Rothbard — *Conceived (1)* p.433, 436, 446-447, 465-466, 473

DELAWARE, LORD
Acheson — *America's* p.73
Chitwood — *History (1)* p.61-62
Starkey — *Land* p.25-26, 67, 73

DELAWARE
See also **De Vries, David Pietersen, Captain**
Alderman — *Story* p.6, 103-104, 108-111, 113
Calverton — *Awake.* p.364-371
Chitwood — *History (1)* p.213-214
Christensen — *Delaware. See* index p.157-160

Jernegan — *American* p.212-213, 237-238
Monroe — *Founding (1)* p.100-101
Snell — *Wild* p.17, 113, 137-141
- *Chronology*
Christensen — *Delaware* p.151-152
- *Granted to Penn, William*
Chitwood — *History (1)* p.204-205
, *Occupation of*
Chitwood — *History (1)* p.164-165
- *Settlements*
See also **Delaware River**
Craven — *Colonies* p.60-61, 63-64

DELAWARE COMPANY
Pomfret — *Founding* p.267-268, 293-294

DELAWARE INDIANS
See also **Leni-Lenape Indians**
Alderman — *Story* p.59, 117, 123
Snell — *Wild* p.136-137, 146-147

DELAWARE RIVER
See also **New Sweden; Swedish**
Alderman — *Story* p.59-60, 63, 67, 104, 106, 108-109, 113-114, 119
Snell — *Wild* p.113, 137-138, 140-141, 148
Starkey — *Land* 141, 156, 179
- *Exploration*
Christensen — *Delaware* p.13-14
- *Settlements*
Adams — *Album* p.229
Amer. Her. — *Thirteen* p.63, 126, 128-129, 133, 135-136, 170
Christensen — *Delaware* p.18
- *"Three Lower counties"*
Christensen — *Delaware* p.70-72
Craven — *Colonies* p.197-199, 242-243
- *Trip by Capt. Thomas Yong (1634)*
Axtell — *America* p.161-172

DELLIUS, REV.
Rothbard — *Conceived (1)* p.465, 467-468, 470

DEMOCRACY
- *First documents*
Johnston — *Conn.* p.35-36

, *in colonies*
Wertenbaker — *First* p.303-304
Willison — *Saints* p.9-10, 144,
317-318, 351, 379, 404, 409,
420, 471, 480
- *Influence of frontier*
Wertenbaker — *First* p.307-308
- *Mass, clergy opposition*
Wertenbaker — *First* p.343
- *Mayflower Compact. See*
Mayflower Compact
- *Town meetings. See* **Town
Meetings**
- *Views of John Cotton*
Annals of America (1) p.149-153
- *Views of John Winthrop*
Annals of America (1) p.168-169

DEMONOLOGY. *See* **Devil; Witchcraft**

DENNISON, MARGARET
Beals — *John Eliot* p.62-64, 68, 77

DENNISON, WILLIAM
Beals — *John Eliot* p.62, 64, 68-69,
77, 101, 106

DENOMINATIONS *See* **Religion —
Denominations;** names of
denominations

DENTISTRY
Marshall — *Mayflower* p.126, 132
- *Instruments*
Marshall — *Mayflower* p.132

DENTON, DANIEL
Morison — *Intellect.* p.182-183
Tyler — *History* p.441-442

DEPRESSIONS. *See* **Business
depressions**

DERBY FAMILY
National — *History.* p.114-115

DEVIL
Folsom — *Give* p.16, 29, 78, 80-82,
98
Morison — *Intellect.* p.67-69
Wertenbaker — *First* p.164-165, 175-
176
- *Case of Elizabeth Knapp (Groton,
1672)*
Demos — *Remarkable* p.358-371

DIARIES AND DIARISTS
See also names of diarists
Wertenbaker — *Puritan* p.91-93

DICKINSON, JOHN
Alderman — *Story* p.165-166, 173

DIET. *See* **Cookery; Food;** etc.

DIGGES, EDWARD
Craven — *Southern* p.20, 252-253,
263, 267n, 296, 314

DIGGES, ELIZABETH
Leonard — *Dear* p.135, 139, 154, 246,
450
Williams — *Demeter's* p.188

DIGHTON ROCK, (Dighton, Mass.)
Morison — *Story* p.279

DILLINGHAM, JOHN
- *Home (Ipswich, Mass., 1630's),*
Dow — *Domestic* p.9-12
Dow — *Every* p.32-35, 85

DILLINGHAM, SARAH
- *Home (Ipswich, Mass., 1630's)*
Williams — *Demeter's* p.40-41

DINING BOARDS
Speare — *Life* p.73-74

DINING ROOMS
- *Virginia*
Clark — *Old* p.7

DINING TABLES
See also **Dining boards**
Glubok — *Home* p.40-41, 44
- *Plymouth*
Demos — *Little* p.41

DINNERS
Gould — *Every* p.94

DIRCKEN, LYSBERT
Williams — *Demeter's* p.31

DISCIPLINE. *See* **Children and
childhood — Discipline; Schools
— Discipline**

DISCOVERY (ship)
Hawke — *Colonial* p.89
Willison — *Pilgrim* p.183-184
Willison — *Saints* p.210-211

DISEASES
See also **Medicine; Remedies;**
names of diseases
Dow — *Domestic* p.7
Miller — *First* p.237-238
- *Virginia*
Pomfret — *Founding* p.42-43

DISHES AND UTENSILS
See also **Bowls; Jugs; Kitchen
utensils;** names of dishes, etc.
- *Plymouth*
Demos — *Little* p.42
Morison — *Story* p.176-177, 218

DISSENTERS
See also **Puritans**
Calverton — *Awake.* p.65-66
- *Origin of philosophy*
Calverton — *Awake.* p.64-65

DISTILLERIES AND BREWERIES
Bailyn — *New England* p.74, 129

DIVERSIONS. *See* **Amusements; Sports
and games,** etc.

DIVINITY. *See* **Clergymen; Religion**

DIVORCE
Miller — *First* p.205
Williams — *Demeter's* p.90-91
- *Plymouth*
Demos — *Little* p.86, 92-96, 98
- *Women's rights*
Leonard — *Dear* p.304-306

DIX, ANTHONY
Willison — *Saints* p.448-449

DOANE, JOHN
Willison — *Saints* p.311, 322, 332,
449, 456, 460

DOCHET'S ISLAND, MAINE
- *Settlement (1604–1606)*
Mitchell — *It's* p.57

DOCTORS. *See* **Physicians**

**"DOCTRINE OF SIGNATURES"
(medical plants)**
Wertenbaker — *First* p.166

DOEG INDIANS
Smith — *17th* p.42, 53-54

DOGS
Earle — *Home* p.374
Lawrence — *New* p.28-29
Morison — *Story* p.31, 46, 65, 72, 169,
198
- *"Blue laws"*
Lawrence — *Not* p. 117-119
- *Food for Indians*
Northey — *American* p.60

DOLLS
Glubok — *Home* p.192-193
Speare — *Life* p.102
, *Fashion*
McClinton — *Antiques* p.289-290
- *"Flanders babies"*
Glubok — *Home* p.192-193
- *"Letitia Penn"*
Adams — *Album* p.234
- *Pilgrims*
Adams — *Album* p.61
- *Virginia*
Clark — *Old* p.21

"DOLLY" (washing equipment)
Gould — *Early* p.114-115

DOMESTIC ECONOMY
See also **Housewives**
Dexter — *Colonial* p.55-56
- *Books*
Spruill — *Women's* p.209-212

DOMESTIC SERVICE. *See* **Servants;
Slaves and slavery**

DOMESTICITY. *See* **Families and family
life**

DOMINION OF NEW ENGLAND
See also **New England**
Amer. Her. — *Thirteen* p.196-197, 215
Bailyn — *New England* p.169-170,
172, 174-176, 192
Chitwood — *History (1)* p.220-222,
231
Craven — *Colonies* p.213-223, 225-
228, 237, 241
Hawke — *Colonial* p.229, 255-265,
273, 324, 336
Hawke — *U.S.* p.198-204
Morison — *Oxford* p.116-117

Morison — *Story* p.286-287
Nettels — *Roots* p.295-302
Rothbard — *Conceived (1)* p.376-379, 412-422
Rozwenc — *Making (1)* p.82-83
Vaughan — *Puritan* p.316-322
Ver Steeg — *Formative* p.123-125, 132, 140, 144-147
- *Overthrow*
   Rozwenc — *Making (1)* p.83

DONGAN, THOMAS
Chitwood — *History (1)* p.175-176
Craven — *Colonies* p.205-210, 216-217, 227
Hawke — *Colonial* p.225, 259, 267, 321
Nettels — *Roots* p.346-348
Rothbard — *Conceived (1)* p.384-389, 418, 420-421, 424, 439, 447
- *Instructions (1683)*
   Hawke — *U.S.* p.172-173
- *Plan for post house and riders*
   Langdon — *Everyday* p.262

DONNE, JOHN, REV.
Morison — *Intellect.* p.20, 23, 150, 155, 157, 211

DOOLING, SAMUEL
Phillips — *First* p.135-136

DOOLITTLE, WILLIAM
- *Life in Boston (1650)*
   Woodward — *Way* p.11-37

DOORS AND DOORWAYS
Glubok — *Home* p.5-6
, *Front*
   Morrison — *Early* p.40-42
- *Latches*
   Earle — *Home* p.11, 318

DORCHESTER (MATTAPAN), MASSACHUSETTS
Dillon — *Pilgrims* p.214-215
Rutman — *Winthrop's. See* index p.305
Wertenbaker — *First* p.50-51, 56-57, 71, 79-80
Willison — *Pilgrim* p.324, 405-406
Willison — *Saints* p.303, 312, 356, 445
- *Bylaws of town meeting (1645)*
   Demos — *Remarkable* p.195-199

DORCHESTER COMPANY
Bailyn — *New England* p.10, 12-14, 17-18, 76
Jernegan — *American* p.126
Morris — *Ency.* p.32
Pomfret — *Founding* p.149-151
Starkey — *Land* p.226-227, 230
Ver Steeg — *Formative* p.35

DORCHESTER INDIANS
Beals — *John Eliot* p.86-88, 104, 109, 120-121, 126, 129, 143-144

DOTEY, EDWARD
Hills — *History (1)* p.6, 20, 29, 37, 41, 49, 69-71, 88, 93, 118-119, 145, 154
Hills — *History (2)* p.94, 121, 138-143, 145, 157, 162
Willison — *Pilgrim* p.110, 382, 537, 553-554
Willison — *Saints. See* index p.500

DOTEY, FAITH
Williams — *Demeter's* p.89, 207

DOTEY (DOTY, DOTEN) FAMILY
Hills — *History (1) See* index p.165
Hills — *History (2)* p.142-143; *See also* index p.254

DOUBLETS
Earle — *Two cent. (1)* p.164-176
- *Welts (or wings)*
   Earle — *Two cent. (1)* p.167-169
, *Women's*
   Earle — *Two cent. (1)* p.90

DOVER, NEW HAMPSHIRE
Alderman — *Story* p.39-40, 42
Willison — *Saints* p.250, 279, 363, 445, 449, 458

DOWNING, LUCY WINTHROP
, *on migration*
   Williams — *Demeter's* p.30

DRAMA
See also **Puritans — Drama; Theater**
Wright — *Cultural* p.176-178
"Ye Bare and Ye Cubb"
   Morris — *Ency.* p.589

DRAYTON, MICHAEL
Tyler — *History* p.46-47
- *"Farewell Ode to Emigrants"*
   Tyler — *History* p.12-15

DRESS. *See* **Clothing and dress**

DRESS MATERIALS. *See* **Fabrics**

DRESSINGS (bands for headdress)
Earle — *Two cent. (2)* p.537-538

DRESSMAKING
Dexter — *Colonial* p.40

DRINKING VESSELS
Earle — *Home* p.85-96, 98, 321
Glubok — *Home* p.49-50
- *Jamestown*
   Adams — *Album* p.27-28
- *Types*
   Glubok — *Home* p.49-52

DRINKS AND DRINKING. *See*
Alcoholism; Beverages; names of
drinks

DRUGS
See also **Herbs; Medicine;**
Remedies
Marshall — *Mayflower* p.127-132

DRUILLETTES, GABRIEL
Morison — *Story* p.165-166

DRUMMOND, SARAH
, *in Bacon's Rebellion*
   Williams — *Demeter's* p.162-163

DRUMS
See also **Indians — Drums**
Earle — *Home* p.367-368

DUCKING STOOLS
Earle — *Colonial* p.93-95

DUDINGSTON, WILLIAM
Alderman — *Story* p.167-168

DUDLEY, DOROTHY
- *Views of Anne Bradstreet*
   Williams — *Demeter's* p.42-43

DUDLEY, JOSEPH
Bailyn — *New England* p.169-170,
   173-175, 180, 185-188, 192
Craven — *Colonies* p.172-173, 215,
   218-220, 224, 237, 240
Rothbard — *Conceived (1)* p.375-379;
   See also index p.523

Wertenbaker — *Puritan. See* index
   p.349

DUDLEY, MARY WINTHROP
Williams — *Demeter's* p.59-60, 77-80

DUDLEY, THOMAS
Bailyn — *New England* p.18-19, 26,
   160, 169
Beals — *John Eliot* p.48, 71-74, 82,
   87-88, 91-93, 95, 99-100, 104, 144
Caffrey — *Mayflower* p.53, 228-229,
   234, 239, 250
Gildrie — *Salem* p.40-41, 90-91, 98-
   99
Rutman — *Winthrop's. See* index
   p.306
Scott — *Settlers* p.28, 30, 32-34, 36
Starkey — *Land* p.4-5, 87, 99, 103,
   105
Wertenbaker — *First* p.238-239, 289
Willison — *Pilgrim* p.393-396, 475
Willison — *Saints* p.298-299, 471
- *"Hardships in Mass. Bay Colony"*
   Annals of America (1) p.118-124
, *on problems of settlement*
   Vaughan — *Puritan* p.59-63

DUELS
Wertenbaker — *First* p.267-268

DUGOUTS. *See* **Canoes, Dugout**

DUKE, ELIZABETH. *See* **Bacon, Elizabeth Duke**

DUKE'S LAWS (1665)
Chitwood — *History (1)* p.174-175
Craven — *Colonies* p.74-78, 80-82, 92
Hawke — *Colonial* p.223, 240
Hawke — *U.S.* p.168-172
Monroe — *Founding (1)*
Morris — *Ency.* p.45
Wertenbaker — *First* p.223, 239n

DUNFISH (codfish)
Earle — *Home* p.121-122

DUNKERS (DUNKARDS)
Sweet — *Religion* p.217-218

DUNSTER, HENRY
Morison — *Intellect. See* index p.280

DUNSTER-LYON PSALM BOOK
Morison — *Intellect.* p.117-118

DUNSTON, JOHN
, *on John Higginson*
Tyler — *History* p.399
, *on New England*
Axtell — *America* p.114-120
, *on William Hubbard*
Tyler — *History* p.376

DURANT, GEORGE
Craven — *Colonies* p.158-160
Folsom — *Give* p.75-77
Rothbard — *Conceived (1)* p.127-130

DUSTIN, HANNAH
Williams — *Demeter's* p.163-165

DUTCH
See also **Holland; Leyden, Holland; New Amsterdam; New Netherland;** special subjects, subdivision **Dutch**
Caffrey — *Mayflower* p.187, 217-222, 246-247, 252-253, 258
Dillon — *Pilgrims* p.87-117
Fisher — *Men (2)* p.11-13, 15, 37, 39, 48, 54-60, 119
Folsom — *Give* p.24, 44, 49, 52-53, 65, 88
Hope — *Nation* p.99-102
Nettels — *Roots* p.192-196
Smith — *Colonial* p.3-4, 11-12
Snell — *Wild* p.113-114, 129, 135, 138, 141
Vaughan — *New. See* index p.423
Williams — *Saints* p.264-266, 296-297, 299, 303, 327, 327, 335, 383, 472
Wish — *Society (1)* p.40, 92-101
Wright — *Cultural* p.46-50
, *and English*
Acheson — *America's* p.122-124
, *and New Sweden*
Rothbard — *Conceived (1)* p.311-317
, *and Quakers*
Speare — *Life* p.52-67
, *at Plymouth*
Dillon — *Pilgrim* p.198-199
Gill — *Mayflower* p.120-123
Morison — *Story* p.9-12, 130-136, 248, 263
- *Connecticut*
Johnston — *Conn. See* index p.134
- *Expansion (1640–45)*
Morris — *Ency.* p.42-43
- *Failure, reasons for*
Nettels — *Roots* p.200-205
, *in Jamestown*
Starkey — *Land* p.30-31
- *Indian relations*
Chitwood — *History (1)* p.162-163
Jernegan — *American* p.197
Vaughan — *New* p.88, 125, 142, 174-175, 229, 233, 267-268
, *Influence of*
Adams — *Provincial* p.5
- *Life*
Holliday — *Woman's* p.209-215
- *Names. See* **Names, Dutch**
- *Opposition to witch belief*
Wertenbaker — *First* p.149-150
- *Rule*
Chitwood — *History (1)* p.162
- *Settlements*
Furnas — *Americans* p.42, 73-75
Life — *New* p.81-83
New York
, *on Delaware river*
Langdon — *Everyday* p.38-47
Starkey — *Land* p.109
, *on Hudson*
Morrison — *Early* p.99-101
National — *History.* p.97-100
- *Trade*
See also **Plymouth — Dutch relations**
Dillon — *Pilgrims* p.44, 198-199, 211-212
Jernegan — *American* p.225-226
Wertenbaker — *First* p.7, 23, 42
Willison — *Pilgrim* p.300-303, 387, 389-390
- *Women*
Leonard — *Dear* p.27-28
- *Friendship with Indians*
Leonard — *Dear* p.112-113

DUTCH CROWNS (smoked meat holder)
Gould — *Early* p.80

DUTCH EAST INDIA COMPANY. *See* **East India Company**

DUTCH OVENS
Earle — *Home* p.66
Gould — *Early* p.74

DUTCH REFORMED CHURCH
See also **Reformed Dutch Church**
Folsom — *Give* p.24-26, 53, 65-66
Nettels — *Roots* p.476-477
Sweet — *Religion* p.189-190, 192-203, 206-209
Willison — *Saints* p.65, 89-90, 104

DUTCH WEST INDIA COMPANY. *See*
West India Company

DUXBURY, MASSACHUSETTS
Gill — *Mayflower* p.73, 131-132, 140, 142, 146-147, 166, 177
Morison — *Story* p.139-142, 152-153, 162, 185, 201, 204, 226, 271, 204, 226, 271, 275, 291
Willison — *Saints. See* index p.500

DYER, MARY
Earle — *Colonial* p.119-120
Fisher — *Men (1)* p.159-160
Folsom — *Give* p.22, 28-31, 40, 49
Leonard — *Dear* p.349, 372, 376-377
Rothbard — *Conceived (1)* p.193, 196, 241, 243-244, 340, 455
Starkey — *Land* p.98, 104, 179, 212
Sweet — *Religion* p.144, 147
Wertenbaker — *Puritan* p.229, 234-237
Williams — *Demeter's* p.125-129, 147-148
Willison — *Pilgrim* p.429-430, 519
Willison — *Saints* p.379, 472

DYER, WILLIAM
Willison — *Pilgrim* p.430

DYES
Glubok — *Home* p.245-246
Gould — *Early* p.127-128
Rawson — *When* p.122-125
- *South*
Craven — *Southern* p.30, 35, 45, 56, 81, 141

E

EARTHQUAKES (1638)
Willison — *Pilgrim* p.443

EAST INDIA COMPANY
Acheson — *America's* p.125
Leonard — *Dear* p.28

Leynse — *Preced.* p.64, 91, 133-134, 146, 166, 172
Pomfret — *Founding* p.278-280
Rozwenc — *Making (1)* p.14-15, 20

EAST INDIA SCHOOL
Craven — *Southern* p.143-144
Monroe — *Founding (1)* p.64-65

EAST JERSEY. *See* **New Jersey — East Jersey**

EASTHAM (NAUSET), MASSACHUSETTS
Morison — *Story* p.51, 140, 145, 158, 203, 220, 224-226, 234, 243
Willison — *Saints* p.154, 332, 340, 357, 363, 389, 391, 439, 441-442, 445, 448-450, 453
- *History*
Hills — *History (1)* p.108-111

EASTLANDERS (Indians). *See* **Wampanoag Indians**

EASTON, NICHOLAS
Rothbard — *Conceived (1)* p.194, 210, 212-213, 348, 418

EATING. *See* **Food;** names of meals

EATON, FRANCIS
Hills — *History (1)* p.21, 37, 41, 44, 54, 69-70, 90-91, 93, 99
Marble — *Women* p.12, 48, 58
Marshall — *Mayflower* p.29, 63
Willison — *Saints* p.148, 263, 315, 384, 441, 450

EATON, MARTHA BILLINGTON
Willison — *Saints* p.441

EATON, NATHANIEL
Earle — *Colonial* p.123-129

EATON, SARAH
Marble — *Women* p.12, 16

EATON, THEOPHILUS
Johnston — *Conn.* p.37-38, 41-42, 44-45
Miller — *Colonial* p.115-117
Pomfret — *Founding* p.258-259, 261-262, 268, 270, 293

Rothbard — *Conceived (1)* p.221-222,
230, 232, 241, 312
- *Biography, by Cotton Mather*
Vaughan — *Puritan* p.255-261
- *Books, Bequest of*
Morison — *Intellect.* p.145-146

EATON FAMILY
Hills — *History (1). See* index p.165-
166

EATON FREE SCHOOL
Monroe — *Founding (1)* p.65

"EBULUM" (drink)
Earle — *Customs* p.173

ECONOMY (economics)
See also names of localities, e.g.
Plymouth; Puritans
Adams — *Provincial* p.25-47
Vaughan — *Puritan* p.172-179
Wertenbaker — *First. See* index p.344
- *Diverse patterns*
Rozwenc — *Making (1)* p.37-41
- *Effect of geography on*
Wertenbaker — *First* p.2-21
- *Foundations*
Nettels — *Roots* p.222-230
- *Impetus for colonization*
Wertenbaker — *First* p.2-21
- *Restriction by England*
Carman — *History (1)* p.131-134

EDUCATION
See also **Academies; Children and
childhood; Colleges and universi-
ties; Indians; Plymouth; Puritans;
Scholars and scholarship;
Schools;** names of colleges and
universities; special subjects
Dillon — *Pilgrims. See* index p.245
Drepperd — *Pioneer* p.216-217
Hawke — *Colonial* p.293-298
National — *History.* p.117
Rozwenc — *Making (1)* p.85-103
Speare — *Life* p.105-109
Williams — *Demeter's. See* index
p.350
Wish — *Society (1)* p.32-33, 53-57,
83-84, 95, 107-108
Wright — *Literary* p.99-109
- *Act of 1642*
Hawke — *Colonial* p.295-296
Leonard — *Dear* p.258

, *and Church*
- *Virginia*
Monroe — *Founding (1)* p.57
- *Apprentices. See* **Apprentices —
Education**
, *as social control*
Rozwenc — *Making (1)* p.88-90
- *Boston, Mass.*
Bridenbaugh — *Cities* p.121-122
Starkey — *Land* p.85
, *by barter*
Morison — *Intellect.* p.36-37
- *Carolinas*
Starkey — *Land* p.236
- *Charlestown*
Bridenbaugh — *Cities* p.126
Chesapeake colonies
Ver Steeg — *Formative* p.102-103
- *Class character*
Monroe — *Founding (1)* p.55-56
Rozwenc — *Making (1)* p.87-88
- *Curriculum, Liberal*
Morison — *Intellect.* p.41-43
, *Dutch*
See also **Education — New
Netherland**
Jernegan — *American* p.235-
237
- *Foundations (1647)*
Bailey — *American (1)* p.69
- *Girls*
Willison — *Saints* p.387, 478
- *Laws*
See also **Education — Act of
1642**
Leonard — *Dear* p.258-260
Morison — *Intellect.* p.65-79
- *Connecticut*
Monroe — *Founding (1)*
p.123-124
- *New Jersey*
Jernegan — *American* p.237
- *Maryland*
Jernegan — *American* p.108
Wright — *Cultural* p.109-110
- *Massachusetts*
Morison — *Intellect.* p.58, 63, 66-
69, 76
Wertenbaker — *Puritan* p.135-
158
Wright — *Cultural* p.101-103
Wright — *Literary* p.16-24
- *Middle Colonies*
Chitwood — *History (1)* p.458-
460
Monroe — *Founding (1)* p.101

EDUCATION (continued)
- *New Amsterdam*
    Bridenbaugh — *Cities* p.124-126
    Leonard — *Dear* p.268-269
- *New England*
    Caffrey — *Mayflower* p.289-299, 301
    Chitwood — *History (1)* p.455-457
    Hawke — *U.S.* p.230-235
    Jernegan — *American* p.189-190
    Morison — *Intellect.* p.57-58
    Rozwenc — *Making (1)* p.86-87
    Tunis — *Colonial* p.63-64
    Ver Steeg — *Formative* p.101-102
    Willison — *Saints* p.384-385, 387-388, 478
    Wright — *Cultural* p.103-104
- *New Hampshire*
    Monroe — *Founding (1)* p.124
- *New Haven*
    Monroe — *Founding (1)* p.123-124
- *New Netherland*
    Williams — *Demeter's* p.100-101
    Wright — *Cultural* p.105-106
- *New Sweden*
    Jernegan — *American* p.237
- *New York*
    Clark — *Old* p.62-63
- *Newport, R.I.*
    Bridenbaugh — *Cities* p.123
- *Pennsylvania*
    Clark — *Old* p.76-82
    Starkey — *Land* p.190, 192
    Wright — *Cultural* p.107-108
- *Philadelphia*
    Bridenbaugh — *Cities* p.123-124
, *Popular support of*
    Morison — *Intellect.* p.37-41
- *Quakers*
    Jernegan — *American* p.238
    Rozwenc — *Making (1)* p.90-91
, *Religious. See* **Religion — Books and reading; Religion — Education**
- *Rhode Island*
    Bridenbaugh — *Cities* p.127
    Morison — *Intellect.* p.69-70, 77, 107
- *"Saints"*
    Morgan — *Puritan* p.45-61
, *Secondary*
    Monroe — *Founding (1)* p.136-154
- *South*
    Chitwood — *History (1)* p.461-462
    Goodwin — *Colonial* p.221-230
    Jernegan — *American* p.105-109
    Miller — *First* p.232-233
    Tunis — *Colonial* p.96
- *English scheme*
    Monroe — *Founding (1)* p.53-68
- *Virginia*
    Clark — *Old* p.18-20
    Hawke — *U.S.* p.235-237
    Jernegan — *American* p.106
    Miller — *First* p.233-236
    Rozwenc — *Making (1)* p.85-86, 90
    Wright — *Cultural* p.99-100
- *English scheme*
    Monroe — *Founding (1)* p.54-55
- *Views of Berkeley, (1671)*
    Monroe — *Founding (1)* p.53-54
- *Women*
    Leonard — *Dear* p.239-244
    Williams — *Demeter's* p.98-99, 104-105
- *Virginia*
    Clark — *Old* p.19

EELS
    Earle — *Home* p.117
- *Traps*
    Marshall — *Mayflower* p.89

EFFINGHAM, HOWARD, LORD
    Craven — *Colonies* p.155-156, 213, 234, 236

ELEAZER ARNOLD HOUSE (Lincoln, R. I., 1687)
    Morrison — *Early* p.66-67

ELECTIONS
See also **Politics**
- *Boston*
    Rutman — *Winthrop's. See* index p.306

ELEGIES
    Morison — *Intellect.* p.224-226

ELIOT, ANN(E) (HANNAH) MONTFORT
    Beals — *John Eliot. See* index p.189

Leonard — *Dear* p.219, 471, 486
Williams — *Demeter's* p.173

ELIOT, JOHN, REV.
Amer. Her. — *Pioneer* p.60-61, 63-65
Beals — *John Eliot. See* index p.189-
190
Morison — *Intellect.* p.81n, 119-120,
123, 125, 136
Morison — *Story* p.242-244, 249
Morris — *Ency.* p.36-37
Pomfret — *Founding* p.196, 199, 217-
218
Rutman — *Winthrop's* p.73, 103,
104n, 114, 124-125
Vaughan — *New. See* index p.423
Willison — *Saints* p.367n, 371, 388-
389, 392, 396, 398, 401, 476
- *"A College proposed for Massachu-
setts Bay"*
Annals of America (1) p.130-131
- *Death*
Beals — *John Eliot* p.185
- *"Puritan Missions to the Indians"*
(1646)
Annals of America (1) p.180-183
- *"Records of the First Church of Rox-
bury, Mass." (1643–46)*
Demos — *Remarkable* p.373-376
- *Sermons*
Beals — *John Eliot* p.79-81, 92,
99, 102, 106, 121, 123-126,
130, 134, 154
- *Indian language*
Beals — *John Eliot* p.122-
126
- *Work with Indians*
Amer. Her. — *Treasury* p.66-73
Beals — *John Eliot. See* index
p.189-190
Starkey — *Land* p.209-210
Vaughan — *Puritan* p.261-267

ELIOT, SARAH CURTIS
Beals — *John Eliot* p.11, 31, 37-38,
45-46, 83, 156

ELIOT FAMILY
Beals — *John Eliot* p.189-190

***ELIZABETH DE LO* (ship)**
- *Passengers (1635)*
Demos — *Remarkable* p.38-39

ELLWOOD, THOMAS
Wertenbaker — *First* p.209-210

EMIGRANTS
See also **Colonies and colonists; Mi-
gration; etc.**
Hawke — *Colonial* p.68-81
National — *History.* p.113-120
- *"How and where they went"*
Hawke — *Colonial* p.72-77
- *"What they found"*
Hawke — *Colonial* p.77-81
- *"Who and why"*
Hawke — *Colonial* p.68-72

ENCYCLOPEDIAS
Wright — *Cultural* p.129

ENDICOTT (ENDECOTT) JOHN
Amer. Her. — *Pilgrims* p.121-123
Caffrey — *Mayflower* p.224, 226, 229,
234, 247, 261-262
Collins — *Story* p.49
Earle — *Two cent. (1)* p.xiii, 5
Earle — *Two cent. (2)* p.300, 355
Gildrie — *Salem. See* index p.185
Morison — *Story* p.119, 156, 210-211
Morris — *Ency.* p.32-33
Pomfret — *Founding* p.151-152, 154,
156-158, 162, 165, 167-168
Rothbard — *Conceived (1)* p.168,
174, 180, 202, 207, 228, 234, 239,
242-243, 245, 248, 342
Snell — *Wild* p.118, 124-125
Starkey — *Land* p.9, 94, 101, 212
Wertenbaker — *First* p.102, 104, 278,
297-298
Wertenbaker — *Puritan* p.30, 163,
203, 227, 230, 232-233, 239
Willison — *Pilgrim* p.315-317, 327,
410-411, 446-448, 472, 473n, 518
Willison — *Saints* p.253, 267, 270-
273, 283-284, 299, 304, 346, 348,
377, 379, 449, 471

ENFIELD, CONNECTICUT
Wertenbaker — *Puritan. See* index
p.350

ENGLAND AND ENGLISH
Folsom — *Give* p.ix, 6, 9, 18, 28, 32,
34, 38, 44, 53, 65, 80
Hawke — *Colonial. See* index p.720-
721
Hawke — *U.S.* p.250-256
Pomfret — *Founding. See* index p.375
Wertenbaker — *First. See* index p.344
- *Civil war (1641)*
Gill — *Mayflower* p.139-145

ENGLAND AND ENGLISH (*continued*)
- *Classes, average village*
  Hills — *History (2)* p.195
- *Colonial administration*
  See also **Plymouth — English relations**
  Carman — *History (1)* p.16-58
  Craven — *Colonies.* See index p.356
  Greene — *Provincial* p.3-16
  Jernegan — *American* p.144-250
  Netells — *Roots* p.289-295
  Rozwenc — *Making (1)* p.81-82
- *Commercial policy (1606–90)*
  Jernegan — *American* p.257-261
  Rozwenc — *Making (1)* p.79-81
- *Commissioners, visit to New England*
  Willison — *Saints* p.383-384, 475-478
- *Dutch relations*
  Morris — *Ency.* p.44
  Nettels — *Roots* p.277-284, 358-365
- *Expansion policy*
  Rozwenc — *Making (1)* p.15-22
  Ver Steeg — *Formative* p.29-52
- *French relations*
  Morris — *Ency.* p.59-62
  Nettels — *Roots* p.358-365
- *Kings, and prerogative*
  Jernegan — *American* p.250-251
  Rozwenc — *Making (1)* p.53-54
, *of "Forefathers"*
  Hills — *History (2)* p.190-202
- *Literary men, and colonists*
  Wright — *Literary* p.62-75
- *Parliament*
  Rozwenc — *Making (1)* p.54-55
- *Political institutions (1600)*
  Chitwood — *History (1)* p.143-146
- *Political theories*
  Rozwenc — *Making (1)* p.64
- *Privy Council*
  Jernegan — *American* p.251-252
- *Revolution of 1688*
  Chitwood — *History (1)* p.216-217
- *Social discontent*
  Rozwenc — *Making (1)* p.31-32
- *West country, immigrants from*
  Smith — *17th* p.79-80,84,86,88
- *Women*
  Leonard — *Dear* p.24-26, 42
  Spruill — *Women's* p.340

ENGLISH, PHILIP
  Langdon — *Everyday* p.220

ENLIGHTENMENT (movement)
  Ver Steeg — *Formative* p.217-221, 228-229

EPENOW (Indian)
  Marshall — *Mayflower* p.134

EPIDEMICS
  See also **Smallpox;** etc.
  Bridenbaugh — *Cities* p.87-88
  Clark — *Old* p.75-76
  Langdon — *Everyday* p.328
  Wertenbaker — *First* p.180-181
- *Virginia*
  Wertenbaker — *First* p.178-180

EPISCOPALIANS
  See also **Anglicans**
  Alderman — *Story* p.88-89

EPITAPHS
  Earle — *Customs* p.383-386
  Wertenbaker — *First* p.244

ERASERS
  Rawson — *When* p.160

ESSEX, ROBERT DEVEREUX, EARL OF
  Willison — *Saints* p.34-35, 37, 39, 465

ESTABLISHED CHURCH. *See* **Anglicans; Episcopalians**

ESTY, MARY
  Williams — *Demeter's* p.140

ETHICS
, *In curriculum*
  Morison — *Intellect.* p.41-42

ETIQUETTE
  See also **Books and reading — Etiquette; Children and childhood — Etiquette; Courtesy**
  Leonard — *Dear* p.228-229
- *Girls*
  Willison — *Saints* p.371-372
- *Massachusetts (1686)*
  Fisher — *Men (1)* p.181-182
, *Table*
  Marshall — *Mayflower* p.99
- *Women, Books on*
  Spruill — *Women's* p. 213-216

EUPRAXIA (EUPHRASIA) (plant)
Morison — *Intellect.* p.43-44

EUROPE. *See* names of countries, nationalities

EVANGELISM. *See* **Circuit riders: Clergymen**

EVELYN, JOHN
Morison — *Intellect.* p.144-145

EXCOMMUNICATION (church)
Annals of America (1) p.192-193
Smith — *17th* p.146, 150-151, 155-156
- *Proceedings*
Demos — *Remarkable* p.221-239

EXECUTIONS. *See* **Death penalty; Hangings**

EXETER COMPACT (New Hampshire, 1639)
Demos — *Remarkable* p.192-193
Morris — *Ency.* p.36

"EXPEDITION OF 1623"
- *Building of forts*
Jernegan — *American* p.196-197

EXPLORATION
See also **Pilgrims — Exploration and discoveries;** names of explorers
Life — *New* p.29-47

EXPORTS AND IMPORTS
Dow — *Every* p.246-250, 255-257
Nettels — *Roots* p.251-252
- *"Enumerated goods" (forbidden)*
Bailyn — *New England* p.127, 148-150, 164-165, 178
- *South*
Jernegan — *American* p.94

EYEGLASSES
- *Sellers*
Tunis — *Craftsmen* p.48-50

F

FABRICS
See also types of fabrics, e.g. **Cotton; Wool; Clothmaking**

Dow — *Domestic* p.24
Leonard — *Dear* p.169-170
Spruill — *Women's* p.114
- *Names*
Dow — *Every* p.70-83
- *New England*
Tunis — *Colonial* p.45-46
- *Plymouth*
Demos — *Little* p.54
- *Slashing*
Earle — *Two cent. (1)* p.172-173

FAIR DAY. *See* **Fairs**

FAIRBANKS HOUSE
Earle — *Home* p.22-23
Morrison — *Early* p.52-54

FAIRS
Beck — *Pilgrims* p.64-66
Bridenbaugh — *Cities* p.28-29
Rawson — *When* p.100-109

"FALL LINE" (settlement 100 miles inland line)
Ver Steeg — *Formative* p.30

FALSEHOOD
See also **Perjury**
- *New England, laws against*
Jernegan — *American* p.183-184

FAMILIES AND FAMILY LIFE
See also **Plymouth; Puritans**
Beck — *Pilgrims* p.55-56, 74, 77-79
Marshall — *Mayflower* p.60-62
Miller — *First* p.60-61
Nettels — *Roots* p.441-449
Rutman — *Winthrop's* p.96-97, 139, 147-149, 221, 256-257, 277
Wish — *Society (1)* p.49-50, 93-94
- *Boston*
Rutman — *Winthrop's* p.58, 76, 79, 82, 138, 140, 144, 146-147, 210, 212
- *Domesticity*
Adams — *Provincial* p.10-12
- *New England*
Wertenbaker — *First* p.83-85
- *Size*
Earle — *Customs* p.23-24
Wertenbaker — *First* p.182-184
Williams — *Demeter's* p.94-95

"FAMILISTS"
Calverton — *Awake.* p.189-191

FAMINE. *See* **Jamestown; Plymouth**

FANCYWORK. *See* **Needlework**

FANS
Earle — *Two cent. (1)* p.124-125
Spruill — *Women's* p.124

FARM IMPLEMENTS
Chitwood — *History (1)* p.358-359
Drepperd — *Pioneer* p.51, 56
Langdon — *Everyday* p.296-298
Marshall — *Mayflower* p.144-145
- *Plymouth. See* **Plymouth — Farm implements**

FARMER, MARY
Williams — *Demeter's* p.195

FARMERS AND FARMING
Amer. Her. — *Thirteen* p.44, 104, 106-107, 132-133, 141-142, 154, 163, 165-166, 171-176, 183
Carman — *History (1)* p.61-67
Chitwood — *History (1)* p.357-358
Dow — *Every* p.91-100
Folsom — *Give* p.3, 14, 16-18, 32-33, 36, 44, 46-48, 52, 54, 71-73, 75-77
Hope — *Nation* p.84-86
Nettels — *Roots* p.313-319; *See also* index p.730
Rutman — *Winthrop's. See* index p.307
Smith — *17th* p.68, 70-72, 75, 82
- *Chesapeake colonies*
Hawke — *U.S.* p.85-86
- *Debts*
Nettels — *Roots* p.330
- *Growth*
Wertenbaker — *Puritan* p.184-190
- *Middle Colonies, tenant farming*
Jernegan — *American* p.218-219
- *New England*
Nettels — *Roots* p.235
- *New Netherland, supplies for (1650)*
Demos — *Remarkable* p.50-51
- *New York*
Carman — *History* p.63-64
- *Pennsylvania Germans*
Langdon — *Everyday* p.63-67
- *Plymouth. See* **Plymouth — Farmers and farming**
- *Salem, Mass.*
Gildrie — *Salem* p.116-122, 124-125, 129-130, 134, 141, 157, 166
- *South, back country*
Wertenbaker — *Old* p.14-15
- *South Hadley, Mass.*
Wertenbaker — *Puritan* p.186-187
- *Versatility*
Chitwood — *History (1)* p.370
- *Virginia*
Carman — *History (1)* p.64-65, 67

FARRIERS (horseshoers)
Tunis — *Craftsmen* p.21

FASHION
See also **Accessories; Clothing and dress;** articles of fashion
- *Laws*
Dow — *Domestic* p.23
- *London*
Goodwin — *Colonial* p.80-83
- *Puritans*
Speare — *Life* p.35-36

FAUNCE, JOHN
Willison — *Saints* p.235, 447, 449, 460

FAUNCE, PATIENCE MORTON
Willison — *Saints* p.235, 447, 449, 460

FAUNCE, THOMAS
Willison — *Saints* p.411, 431, 447, 449, 460

FAYERWEATHER, THOMAS
Earle — *Two cent. (1)* p.xviii, 211

"FEE SIMPLE" (of land grants)
Carman — *History (1)* p.52-53
- *New England*
Jernegan — *American* p.169

"FEMME COVERT" (married women's legal protection)
Williams — *Demeter's* p.301

"FEMME SOLE." *See* **Spinsters; Widows**

FENCES
Dow — *Every* p.100
Earle — *Home* p.25, 401-402
Furnas — *Americans* p.152-153
Gould — *Early* p.110-112
Rutman — *Winthrop's* p.39, 44, 63, 75, 96, 204, 214, 225
- *Boston*
Rutman — *Winthrop's* p.35, 203-204, 225, 228

- *Laws*
　Craven — *Southern* p.212-213, 370n
- *New England*
　Glubok — *Home* p.13-14, 317-318
- *Plymouth*
　Morison — *Story* p.200-201, 228, 241
- *South — Laws*
　Craven — *Southern* p.212-213, 370n
- *Viewers*
　Glubok — *Home* p.317-318

FENDALL, JOSIAS
　Craven — *Southern,* p.297-299, 441-442
　Nettels — *Roots* p.338-339
　Pomfret — *Founding* p.99-100, 300

FENWICK, GEORGE
　Johnston — *Conn.* p.59-60, 62-63, 67
　Pomfret — *Founding* p.234, 251, 259, 261, 264

FERRIES
　See also **Canoes — Ferries**
　Speare — *Life* p.134
- *Massachusetts*
　Wertenbaker — *First* p.297-298

FERTILITY. *See* **Childbearing**

FESTIVALS. *See* **Fairs; Holidays and festivals; Indians — Festivals**

FICTION
- *Romances*
　Morison — *Intellect.* p.129-132, 138, 148

FIELDS
- *New England, town*
　Wertenbaker — *Puritan* p.50-54

FINANCE
　Bailyn — *New England* p.3-8, 10-11, 17-18, 23-24, 31, 34, 51, 78-79, 81-82, 87-88
　Chitwood — *History (1)* p.402-403
　Nettels — *Roots* p.264-273
- *"Joint-stock" method — South*
　Craven — *Southern* p.54-55, 59, 82-90, 102-103, 111-113, 118-119, 122-123, 145, 185

- *Plymouth. See* **Plymouth — Finance**

FINE ARTS. *See* **Art; Drama; Music;** etc.

FINES
　Rutman — *Winthrop's. See* index p.307
- *Boston*
　Rutman — *Winthrop's. See* index p.307

FINNISH
　See also **Women — Swedish and Finnish**
　Alderman — *Story* p.61, 65, 103, 105, 111
　Christensen — *Delaware* p.25, 31
- *Delaware*
　Starkey — *Land,* p.154-156
- *New Sweden*
　Snell — *Wild* p.24, 137-139

FIRE BUCKETS
　Earle — *Home* p.16-19
　Glubok — *Home* p.8-9

FIRE DOGS
　Earle — *Home* p.62
　Marshall — *Mayflower* p.98-99

FIRE FRAMES
　Rawson — *When* p.7

FIRE IRONS
　Drepperd — *Pioneer* p.25-33

FIRE PLATES
　Earle — *Home* p.54-55

FIREARMS. *See* **Guns**

FIREPLACES
　See also **Chimneys;** names of accessories
　Dow — *Domestic* p.15-17
　Dow — *Every* p.40-41, 91-93
　Earle — *Colonial* p.276-280
　Furnas — *Americans* p.135-139
　Gould — *Early* p.44-55
　Miller — *First* p.175-176
　Morrison — *Early* p.44-45
- *Equipment*
　Earle — *Home* p.53
　Gould — *Early* p.65, 67-81
　Marshall — *Mayflower* p.96-99

FIREPLACES (continued)
- *Hearths*
 Gould — *Early* p.60-61
 Marshall — *Mayflower* p.68, 94-99
 Rawson — *When* p.5-6
- *Kitchens*
 Glubok — *Home* p.26-33
 Langdon — *Everyday* p.19-23
- *Lintels*
 Gould — *Early* p.61-62
- *Plymouth*
 Demos — *Little* p.30, 33, 39-40, 46
- *Virginia*
 Clark — *Old* p.6

FIRES AND FIREFIGHTING
 Bridenbaugh — *Cities* p.55-61
 Glubok — *Home* p.24-25
 Langdon — *Everyday* p.13-14
 Speare — *Life* p.93-94
- *Boston*
 Bridenbaugh — *Cities* p.59-61
 Lawrence — *New* p.195-197
 - *Codes, First*
  Bridenbaugh — *Cities* p.58
 - *Engines, First*
  Earle — *Home* p.19
, *for cooking*
 Holliday — *Woman's* p.118
- *New England*
 Earle — *Home* p.15-16
- *Pilgrims*
 Marshall — *Mayflower* p.96
- *Plymouth*
 Caffrey — *Mayflower* p.193
 Willison — *Pilgrim* p.123-124, 242, 243
 Willison — *Saints* p.164-165, 200

FIRESIDE INDUSTRIES. *See* **Artisans; Crafts and craftsmanship; Needlework; Spinning; Weaving;** etc.

FISH (as food)
 Earle — *Customs* p.146-148
, *Smoking*
 Marshall — *Mayflower* p.91

FISHER, LEONARD EVERETT
 Alderman — *Story* p.188

FISHER, MARY
 Spruill — *Women's* p.249-250
 Wertenbaker — *First* p.101-102
 Williams — *Demeter's* p.124

FISHERIES
 Bailyn — *New England. See* index p.243
 Gill — *Mayflower. See* index p.202
- *Massachusetts*
 Nettels — *Roots* p.242-244
- *New England*
 Jernegan — *American* p.172-173
, *Northern*
 Pomfret — *Founding* p.13, 109, 112, 118, 131-136, 140-142
, *Rise of*
 Rothbard — *Conceived (1)* p.267-270

FISHING AND FISHERMEN
 See also **Fish (as food); Ice fishing;** names of fish
 Adams — *Album* p.31-33, 92
 Bailyn — *New England* p.78, 82, 99, 124, 130
 Caffrey — *Mayflower* p.284-285
 Carman — *History (1)* p.28, 72-75
 Chitwood — *History (1)* p.384-385
 Earle — *Home* p.116-117, 119-123
 Furnas — *Americans* p.26-27
 Glubok — *Home* p.64-69
 Gould — *Early* p.98-100
 Rutman — *Winthrop's* p.177, 183, 187-188, 191, 207, 251
 Scott — *Settlers* p.6
 Wish — *Society (1)* p.112-114
 Wright — *Everyday* p.27-28, 44-46, 80-91, 190, 197-200
- *Connecticut*
 Wertenbaker — *First* p.50-51
- *Indians. See* **Indians — Fishing**
- *Maine*
 Snell — *Wild* p.76-77, 121
- *New England*
 Amer. Her. — *Thirteen* p.66-67, 87, 96, 106, 154
 Caffrey — *Mayflower* p.284-285
 Earle — *Home* p.115-125, 130
 Leonard — *Dear* p.128
 Wertenbaker — *First* p.50-51
- *New Netherland*
 Axtell — *America* p.140-141
- *Pilgrims*
 Beck — *Pilgrims* p.17, 25, 34, 61, 74, 77
 Furnas — *Americans* p.26
 Marshall — *Mayflower* p.145, 148, 166
- *Plymouth*
 Miller — *First* p.32.

Morison — *Story* p.15-20, 62-63, 77, 96, 114, 121-127, 141, 167-169, 188, 201-202, 224-226, 291
Willison — *Pilgrim* p.103-104, 120, 146, 166n, 169, 188-190, 233, 250, 257-258, 274-275, 280-281, 358-359, 362-363
Willison — *Saints* p.206, 232, 242, 251-252, 289-290, 325
- *Virginia*
  Clark — *Old* p.23-24

FITZHUGH, WILLIAM
Goetzmann — *Colonial* p.127-128
Wertenbaker — *First* p.27, 46-48, 205, 257-258, 287
Wish — *Society (1)* p.63-86, 88-89
- *Letters*
  Goetzmann — *Colonial* p.128-132
- *Letters on Virginia (1686)*
  Demos — *Remarkable* p.124-126
- *Orchard and plantation*
  Adams — *Provincial* p.27, 30

FIVE NATIONS. *See* **Iroquois Indians**

FLAILERS
Earle — *Home* p.312-314

FLASKETS (flower baskets)
Earle — *Colonial* p.293

FLAT-CAPS
Earle — *Two cent. (1)* p.218-219

FLAX
See also **Linen industry**
Adams — *Album* p.116
Craven — *Southern* p.35, 45, 56, 108, 140, 163, 253, 312, 316, 346-347
Earle — *Colonial* p.309-315
Earle — *Home* p.166-181
Glubok — *Home* p.229-233
Gould — *Early* p.131-133
Langdon — *Everyday* p.292-293
Leonard — *Dear* p.162-164
- *Beetling*
  Earle — *Home* p.172
- *Bobs*
  Earle — *Home* p.168
- *Brake*
  Earle — *Home* p.169-170
- *Breaking (separation of fabric)*
  Gould — *Early* p.132

- *Bun*
  Earle — *Home* p.169
- *Massachusetts*
  Earle — *Home* p.179-180
- *New England*
  Tunis — *Colonial* p.48-49
- *Seed*
  Earl — *Home* p.167-168, 176
- *South*
  Craven — *Southern* p.35, 45, 56, 108, 140, 163, 253, 312, 316, 346-347
- *Swingling*
  Earle — *Home* p.171-172
- *Thread*
  Earle — *Home* p.174-175
- *Wheel*
  Earle — *Home* p.167, 174, 177

FLETCHER, BENJAMIN
Chitwood — *History (1)* p.245
Craven — *Colonies* p.243, 253, 256, 268, 280-282
Rothbard — *Conceived (1)* p.447, 460, 464-470, 474-477, 481, 485, 498-501, 506

FLINTLOCK RIFLES. *See* **Guns**

FLIP (drink)
Earle — *Colonial* p.289-290
Earle — *Customs* p.178-179
Gould — *Early* p.106

FLIP DOGS (loggerheads)
Earle — *Colonial* p.289
Gould — *Early* p.80

FLIRTING. *See* **Coquettes**

FLOOR COVERINGS
Smith — *Colonial* p.78

FLOORS
Dow — *Domestic* p.20
Dow — *Every* p.44
Gould — *Early* p.21
- *Plymouth*
  Demos — *Little* p.32, 46

FLORIDA
Collins — *Story* p.71-72

FLOUR AND FLOUR MILLS
Nettels — *Roots* p.248-249

FLOWERDIEU, TEMPERANCE
Leonard — *Dear* p.44

FLOWERS
See also **Gardens**
- *"Bouncing Bet"*
Earle — *Home* p.447
- *Folk names*
Earle — *Home* p.441-442
, *Old time*
Earle — *Home* p.421-430, 441
- *Plymouth*
Morison — *Story* p.67, 76-77, 80
- *Seeds, sold by women*
Earle — *Home* p.440-441

FLYNT, MARGERY HOAR
Williams — *Demeter's* p.176

FOLGER, PETER
Morison — *Intellect.* p.227-228
Tyler — *History* p.272-274

FOOD
See also **Indians; Pilgrims; Plym-
outh;** names of food
Beck — *Pilgrims* p.43, 46-47, 74, 77-
78
Chitwood — *History (1)* p.487
Dow — *Domestic* p.16
Glubok — *Home* p.56-87
Gould — *Early* p.82, 97-105
Lawrence — *New* p.5-8
Marshall — *Mayflower* p.88-89, 91, 94
Miller — *First* p.182-188
Rutman — *Winthrop's* p.63, 75, 172-
174, 178, 190
Williams — *Demeter's* p.43-46
, *and child mortality*
Wertenbaker — *First* p.186-187
, *from forests*
Earle — *Home* p.108-114
, *from sea and river*
Earle — *Home* p.124-125
- *Habits*
Wish — *Society (1)* p.48-49
- *Maryland*
Wertenbaker — *First* p.39-40
- *Massachusetts*
Dow — *Every* p.42
- *Inventories*
Dow — *Domestic* p.17
, *Native*
Nettels — *Roots* p.147

- *New England*
Tunis — *Colonial* p.35-41
Wertenbaker — *First* p.84-85
- *Year's supply*
Dow — *Domestic* p.6
- *New Netherland*
Tunis — *Colonial* p.69-70
- *Pocahontas' influence*
Phillips — *First* p.125-126
- *Preservation*
Leonard — *Dear* p.145-147
, *Shipboard*
Dow — *Every* p.6, 9-10
- *South*
Tunis — *Colonial* p.88-89
Wertenbaker — *First* p.39-40
- *Supply requirements*
Dow — *Every* p.3, 11
Earle — *Customs* p.146-158
, *Swedish*
Christensen — *Delaware* p.34
- *Women*
Leonard — *Dear* p.118-154

FOOT STOVES
Earle — *Home* p.375, 386
Glubok — *Home* p.290, 295–296

FOOTBALL
Earle — *Customs* p.239
, *First*
Drepperd — *Pioneer* p.97
- *Indians*
Glubok — *Home* p.190-191

FOOTCUFFS. See "Bilbowes"

FOOTPATHS. See Trails — Footpaths

FOOTWEAR. See Shoes

FORBES, ALEXANDER
Wertenbaker — *First* p.118-119

**FORD, MARTHA. See Browne, Martha
Ford**

**"FOREFATHER'S DAY (Pilgrims'
landing)**
Earle — *Customs* p.231
Morison — *Story* p.54
Willison — *Pilgrim* p.115n,566
Willison — *Saints* p.2, 156n, 411-416,
421-423, 425-426, 464-465, 484-
485

"FOREFATHER'S SONG"
Annals of America (1) p.116-117

FOREROOMS. *See* **Parlors**

FOREST
Furnas — *Americans* p.17-19, 23-36
Hawke — *Colonial* p.77
, *and colonization*
Wertenbaker — *First* p.15-18
- *"Forest primeval"*
Gould — *Early* p.104
Nettels — *Roots* p.146-147
- *Industries*
Chitwood — *History (1)* p.375-377
, *Influence of*
Wertenbaker — *First* p.307-311
- *New England*
Amer. Her. — *Treasury* p.56-65
Wertenbaker — *First* p.11
- *Products*
Jernegan — *American* p.173-175

FORKS
Earle — *Customs,* p.136-137
Earle — *Home* p.77-78
, *First*
Earle — *Home* p.77
- *Plymouth*
Demos — *Little* p.42

FORREST, ANNE
Leonard — *Dear* p.42-44, 126, 129, 157, 304
Williams — *Demeter's* p.19

FORTS
See also **Blockhouses; Plymouth**
Glubok — *Home* p.12-14
Morison — *Early* p.75-79
- *Caroline*
Folsom — *Give* p.4-7
- *Casimir*
Christensen — *Delaware* p.41-42
- *Christina*
Acheson — *America's* p.127
Christensen — *Delaware* p.27-29
- *Crailo House*
Morison — *Early* p.110
- *Good Hope*
Willison — *Pilgrim* p.389-390
- *Halifax*
Morison — *Early* p.76
- *Orange*
Axtell — *America* p.72-88
- *St. George. See* **Sagadahoc, Maine**

- *Saybrook. See* **Saybrook, Connecticut**
- *Trinity*
Christensen — *Delaware* p.44-46

FORTUNE (ship)
Annals of America (1) p.69-70
Archer — *Mayflower* p.258-271
Beck — *Pilgrims* p.44-45
Caffrey — *Mayflower* p.153-155, 157-158, 167
Dillon — *Pilgrims* p.166-168, 185
Gill — *Mayflower* p.92-93, 101, 130
Morison — *Story* p.85-90, 117, 171
Willison — *Pilgrim* p.154-171
Willison — *Saints. See* index p.501
- *Colonial papers*
Willison — *Pilgrim* p.171
- *Passengers (1621)*
See also **Fortune — "Saints";**
Fortune — "Strangers"
Caffrey — *Mayflower* p.355-356
Hills — *History (1)* p.79-83
- *Pirates' seizure*
Willison — *Pilgrim* p.170-171
- *"Saints"*
Willison — *Pilgrim* p.538-539
Willison — *Saints* p.444-445
- *"Strangers"*
Willison — *Pilgrim* p.539-540
Willison — *Saints* p.445-446

FOSTER, JOHN
Hawke — *Colonial* p.287
Morison — *Intellect.* p.124-126

FOSTER'S CASTLE (New Kent Co., 1685–1690)
Morison — *Early* p.149-150

"FOUNDING FATHERS." *See* Pilgrims; Plymouth

FOWL. *See* **Birds and fowl;** names of various types

FOX, GEORGE
Craven — *Colonies* p.183-185
Hawke — *Colonial* p.227, 230, 232
Snell — *Wild* p.145, 151, 154
Sweet — *Religion* p.22, 153-154

FOX, JABEX, and JOHN
Morison — *Intellect.* p.94-95

FRANCE
  See also **Company of New France;**
  French
  Bailyn — *New England* p.90, 93, 116,
    130, 144-148, 150, 155, 164
  Life — *New* p.34-35

FRANCHISE. *See* **Suffrage**

FRANCISCANS
  See also **Schools — Franciscans**
  Willison — *Saints* p.75, 78-79, 109-
    110, 117, 136, 344, 457-458, 460

FRANKLIN, BENJAMIN
  , *in Philadelphia*
    Collins — *Story* p.65
  , *on his apprenticeship*
    Monroe — *Founding (1)* p.50

FRAUDS. *See* **"ACT OF FRAUDS" (1662)**

"FREE SCHOOLS"
  - *Virginia*
    Monroe — *Founding (1)* p.63-67

FREE SOCIETY OF TRADERS
  (Pennsylvania)
  Craven — *Colonial* p.198-199

FREEDMEN
  , *Future of*
    Wertenbaker — *First* p.28-29, 32-
      33
  - *Maryland*
    Wertenbaker — *First* p.28-29

FREEDOM OF CONSCIENCE
  Folsom — *Give* p.18

FREEDOM OF RELIGION. *See* **Religious**
  freedom

FREEDOM OF THE PRESS
  Folsom — *Give* p.44
  Wish — *Society (1)* p.17-18

FREEDOM TO WORSHIP. *See* **Religious**
  freedom

FREEHOLDING
  Goetzmann — *Colonial* p.104-106
  Rozwenc — *Making (1)* p.34-36

FREEMAN, EDWARD
  Willison — *Saints* p.309, 317, 362,
    456-457

FREEMAN FAMILY
  Hills — *History (1). See* index p.166
  Hills — *History (2)* p.48-50; *See also*
    index p.257

FREEMEN
  Beck — *Pilgrims* p.67-68
  Demos — *Little* p.7, 82, 148
  Rutman — *Winthrop's. See* index
    p.307
  Ver Steeg — *Formative* p.41-42
  - *Boston*
    Rutman — *Winthrop's. See* index
      p.308
  - *Connecticut*
    Johnston — *Conn.* p.54-56
  - *Massachusetts*
    Fisher — *Men (1)* p.132
    Nettels — *Roots* p.169-171
    Woodward — *Way* p.24
    Wright — *Everyday* p.164-165
  - *New England*
    Jernegan — *American* p.167
  - *Oath (Mass., 1634)*
    Annals of America (1) p.148
  - *Plymouth. See* **Plymouth —**
    Freemen

FRENCH
  See also **Canada; France; Hugue-**
  nots; Indians — French relations;
  Nova Scotia; Plymouth — French
  relations; Walloons
  Acheson — *America's* p.170-172
  Caffrey — *Mayflower* p.167, 241-243,
    253-255
  Carman — *History (1)* p.15-16
  Wright — *Cultural* p. 51-57
  - *Artisans and laborers*
    Furnas — *Americans* p.29
  , *as war menace*
    Hawke — *Colonial* p.316-321
  - *Attempts at colonization*
    Marshall — *Mayflower* p.23
  - *English relations*
    Greene — *Provincial* p.106-118
  - *Exploration and colonies*
    Collins — *Story* p.74-85
    Furnas — *Americans* p.25, 41-42
  - *Migration to America*
    Nettels — *Roots* p.385-386
  , *in North America*
    Beck — *Pilgrims p.17-18, 82*
  - *Settlements, St. Lawrence Basin*
    Chitwood — *History (1)* p.297-
      300

- *Traders*
  Furnas — *Americans* p.25, 37, 41-42
- *Women*
  Leonard — *Dear* p.26
  Williams — *Demeter's* p.34

FRENCH AND INDIAN WAR (Seven Years' War)
Alderman — *Story* p.58, 65, 90, 101, 111, 122-123, 134
Collins — *Story* p.86-89

FRETHORNE, RICHARD
- *Letter from Virginia (1623)*
  Demos — *Remarkable* p.68-72

FRIENDS, SOCIETY OF. *See* Quakers

FRIENDSHIP (fishing vessel)
Caffrey — *Mayflower* p.235-236, 240, 242, 259
Willison — *Pilgrim* p.362-365, 368-369, 377, 453

FRONTENAC, LOUIS DE BAUDE, COUNT
Amer. Her. — *Thirteen* p.195-196, 200
Chitwood — *History (1)* p.301-302
- *Attack on Quebec*
  Collins — *Story* p.83

FRONTIER
See also names of localities
Carman — *History (1)* p.55-56
- *Expansion*
  Morris — *Ency.* p.409-411
, *First (Connecticut Valley)*
  Adams — *Album* p.97
, *Influences of*
  Wish — *Society (1)* p.44, 63-86
- *Life*
  Hawke — *U.S.* p.158-160
  Miller — *First* p.135-142

"FROW"
Marshall — *Mayflower* p.71, 78

FRUIT
See also **Indians — Fruit; Plymouth — Fruit;** names of fruits
Adams — *Provincial* p.27
Beck — *Pilgrims* p.59, 77
Furnas — *Americans* p.174-175
Langdon — *Everyday* p.279-280
Scott — *Settlers* p.4-5

- *New England*
  Axtell — *American* p.22
- *New Netherland*
  Axtell — *America* p.37

FUEL. *See* names of fuel

FULLER, BRIDGET LEE
Gill — *Mayflower* p.104
Marble — *Women* p.16, 37, 94-96
Marshall — *Mayflower* p.29, 127-128
Williams — *Demeter's* p.99
Willison — *Saints* p.102, 366, 384, 387, 439, 447

FULLER, EDWARD
Caffrey — *Mayflower* p.41, 54, 140
Hills — *History (I)* p.21, 29, 37, 40, 43-44, 69
Leynse — *Preced.* p.269

FULLER, SAMUEL
Caffrey — *Mayflower* p.41, 54, 56, 71-72, 111, 203, 234, 248, 279
Dow — *Every* p.174
Gill — *Mayflower* p.38, 47, 69, 91, 129
Hills — *History (1)* p.21-22, 29, 37, 39-40, 43, 45-46, 50, 52, 54, 56-57, 69, 90-91, 93, 143, 149
Hills — *History (2)* p.41, 99, 122, 173-174
Leynse — *Preced.* p.267; *See also* index p.282
Marble — *Women* p.14, 16, 53, 95-96
Marshall — *Mayflower* p.29
Morison — *Story* p.63, 79, 119, 185-186, 215, 231, 259
Rutman — *Winthrop's* p.18-19, 26-27, 49, 51, 53, 281-282
Willison — *Pilgrim. See* index p.575
Willison — *Saints. See* index p.501

FULLER, SUSANNA. *See* **Winslow, Susanna Fuller White**

FULLER FAMILY
Hills — *History (1). See* index p.166
Hills — *History (2). See* index p.257
Marble — *Women* p.12, 24, 95-96
Willison — *Saints. See* index p.501

FULLERS
Tunis — *Craftsmen* p.35

FUNDAMENTAL CONSTITUTIONS (1669). *See* Carolinas — "Fundamental Constitutions" (1669)

FUNDAMENTAL ORDERS OF CONNECTICUT (1639)
Acheson — *America's* p.110
Angle — *By* p.6-9
Annals of America (1) p.157-159
Carman — *History (1)* p.90
Johnston — *Conn.* p.34-36, 117, 125
Nettels — *Roots* p.173-174
Vaughan — *Puritan* p.156-161

FUNDAMENTAL ORDERS OF RHODE ISLAND (1647). *See* Rhode Island — "Fundamental Orders"

FUNERALS
See also **Cemeteries; Tombstones**
Earle — *Customs* p.364, 367-370
Rawson — *When* p.235-250

- *Clothing and dress*
Earle — *Two cent.(1)* p.188, 190-191
Earle — *Two cent. (2)* p.650-654
- *Cost*
Rawson — *When* p.242
- *Customs*
Rawson — *When* p.245-246
- *Elegies*
Wright — *Literary* p.85-89
- *Gloves*
Rawson — *When* p.240
- *Hatchments*
Earle — *Two cent.(2)* p.650-651
- *Jewelry*
See also **Funerals — Rings and seals**
Rawson — *When* p.240-241
- *New England*
Glubok — *Home* p.301
- *Pilgrims*
Willison — *Saints* p.402, 480-481
- *Rings and seals*
Goodwin — *Colonial* p.291
- *Sermons*
Earle — *Customs* p.367-368
- *South*
Goodwin — *Colonial* p.288-289
- *Virginia*
Spruill — *Women's*, p.87

FUR TRADE
See also **Hunting and trapping; Plymouth — Fur trade; Puritans — Fur trade**
Adams — *Album* p.66
Amer. Her. — *Thirteen* p.66-67, 87, 91, 97, 117-121, 124-125, 127, 135, 163, 182, 193-194, 208-209
Beck — *Pilgrims* p.17-18, 42, 52, 64
Caffrey — *Mayflower* p.152, 170, 181, 194-195, 209, 212-213, 218, 245, 258-259, 266
Carman — *History (1)* p.69-71
Craven — *Colonies* p.61-62, 112-116, 206
Dillon — *Pilgrims* p.162, 195-200, 221
Furnas — *Americans* p.36
Gill — *Mayflower. See* index p.203
Marshall — *Mayflower* p.155, 166-168
Morison — *Story* p.81, 96, 101, 112, 125-130, 134-137, 166, 204, 219
Smith — *17th* p.49, 52-53, 58, 60
Vaughan — *New* p.213-220, 232-234
Wertenbaker — *First* p.6, 9, 306-307, 309
Wertenbaker — *Puritan* p.196-197
Willison — *Pilgrim. See* index p.575
Willison — *Saints. See* index p.501
Wright — *Everyday* p.26-28, 97-100, 120

- *Albany, N.Y.*
Craven — *Colonies* p.205-206
- *Atlantic coast*
Snell — *Wild* p.66-67, 70-71, 77, 94, 113-114, 138-140
- *French*
See also **French — Traders**
Chitwood — *History (1)* p.302-303
- *Maine islands*
Bailyn — *New England* p.14, 58
- *Massachusetts*
Bailyn — *New England* p.14, 27, 55-57
- *Monopoly*
Bailyn — *New England* p.22-27, 30, 52-53, 55-56

- *Disintegration of*
Rothbard — *Conceived (1)* p.252-253
- *New Hampshire*
Bailyn — *New England* p.49-51
- *New Netherland*
Jernegan — *American* p.225-226

- *Rhode Island*
  Bailyn — *New England* p.14, 49,
  58-60
- *Skins and furs*
  Adams — *Album* p.118
- *Virginia*
  Calverton — *Awake.* p.226-227,
  233

FUR TRADE COMPANY OF 1645
Bailyn — *New England* p.52-53

FURNITURE
See also **Cabinetmakers;** names of
pieces of furniture
Adams — *Album* p.118
Arts — *America* p.253-265
Beck — *Pilgrims* p.55-56
Drepperd — *Pioneer* p.247-252, 255,
257
Langdon — *Everyday* p.24-36
Leonard — *Dear* p.106
Smith — *Colonial* p.11-16
Spruill — *Women's* p.24
Woodward — *Way* p.25-26
- *Anglo-Dutch style*
  Arts — *America* p.265
, *Hall*
  Morrison — *Early* p.45-47
- *Inventories*
  Earle — *Customs* p.108-109
- *New England*
  Tunis — *Colonial* p.34-35
  Wertenbaker — *First* p.294-295
- *New York*
  Clark — *Old* p.55-56
- *Pilgrims*
  Marshall — *Mayflower* p.104-105
, *Pioneer*
  Lawrence — *New* p.25
- *Plymouth*
  Adams — *Album* p.55
- *South*
  Tunis — *Colonial* p.87-88
  Wertenbaker — *First* p.295-296

G

GAINSBOROUGH, ENGLAND
Gill — *Mayflower* p.21-26, 29-30

GALLUP, JOHN
Smith — *Colonial* p.85-88

GALLUP FAMILY
Smith — *Colonial* p.208-209

GALOSHES
Earle — *Two cent.(1)* p.366-367

GAMBLING
See also **Card playing; Lotteries**
Goodwin — *Colonial* p.143-144
Wertenbaker — *Puritan* p.164, 169,
179
- *Laws — Virginia*
  Morison — *Oxford* p.90

GAME. *See* **Animals, Wild; Hunting and
trapping;** names of game

GAMES. *See* **Amusements; Sports and
games**

GAMING. *See* **Gambling**

GOALS. *See* **Prisons and prisoners**

GARDENS
See also **Vegetables — Gardens**
Beck — *Pilgrims* p.58-59, 77
Gould — *Early* p.113
Rutman — *Winthrop's* p.36, 39, 89,
91-93
- *Boston*
  Clark — *Old* p.36
- *Box-borders*
  Earle — *Home* p.430-431
, *Flower*
  Earle — *Home* p.443-445
  - *New England*
    Glubok — *Home* p.324-329
- *New York*
  Clark — *Old* p.54-55
- *Plymouth. See* **Plymouth —
  Gardens**
- *South*
  Goodwin — *Colonial* p.41-42
- *Virginia*
  Leonard — *Dear* p.214

GARDINER, LION
Johnston — *Conn.* p.17, 23, 59-60
Vaughan — *New* p.117, 128-130, 141,
310

GARDYNER, GEORGE
Smith — *17th* p.208

GARRISONS. *See* **Forts;** names of forts

GARRETS. *See* **Attics**

GATES, THOMAS, SIR
Alderman — *Story* p.9-10
Craven — *Southern* p.64, 81, 92, 97, 100, 102-105, 109, 116
Hawke — *Colonial* p.94-98
Wertenbaker — *First* p.210-211, 304

GAYHEAD INDIANS
Gould — *Early* p.104
Willison — *Saints* p.187, 223, 366-367, 388

GEESE
Earle — *Home* p.257-259
- *Plucking*
    Glubok — *Home* p.201-202
    Gould — *Early* p.125

GENEALOGY
- *Bible*
    Adams — *Album* p.85

GENERAL COURT OF NEW ENGLAND.
    See **New England — General Court**

"GENERAL FUNDAMENTALS"
Morison — *Story* p.152-153

"GENTLEMEN"
, *in colonization*
    Smith — *17th* p.66, 68, 71
- *New England*
    Hawke — *U.S.* p.223-226
, *Southern*
    Hawke — *U.S.* p.220-223
- *Virginia*
    Miller — *First* p.110

"GENTLEMEN ADVENTURERS." *See* **"Adventurers"; Plymouth Company; Virginia Company of London**

"GENTRY." *See* **Aristocracy**

GERMAN REFORMED CHURCH
Nettels — *Roots* p.476-477

GERMANS
See also **Palatinates**
Adams — *Provincial* p.6-7
Alderman — *Story* p.119, 127, 129, 145, 152
Carman — *History (1)* p.43, 57

Folsom — *Give* p.54, 65-66, 86
Wright — *Cultural* p.58-59
, *as farmers*
    Miller — *First* p.165-167
- *Emigrants*
    Nettels — *Roots* p.384-385
    Ver Steeg — *Formative* p.167
- *Pennsylvania*
    See also **Pennsylvania Dutch**
    Chitwood — *History (1)* p.210
- *Women*
    Leonard — *Dear* p.29

GERMANTOWN, PENNSYLVANIA
Starkey — *Land* p.194-195

GIBBONS, EDWARD
Bailyn — *New England* p.37, 60-61, 84, 101, 103, 110
Rutman — *Winthrop's* p.73, 82n, 85, 124, 137, 185, 199

GILBERT, HUMPHREY, SIR
Craven — *Southern* p.31-33, 36-39
Dillon — *Pilgrims* p.44-45, 47, 127, 185
Morison — *Oxford* p.43-44

GINGER
Craven — *Southern* p.20-21, 245, 336-337, 346-347

GINSENG
- *Jamestown*
    Adams — *Album* p.16

GIRLING, CAPTAIN
Willison — *Pilgrim* p.402-403
Willison — *Saints* p.301-302

GIRLS
, *in Church*
    Earle — *Home* p.372
    Glubok — *Home* p.289-290
- *Occupations*
    Glubok — *Home* p.190-206, 211-212
    Speare — *Life* p.101

GITON, JUDITH. *See* **Manigault, Judith Giton**

GLASS
Bailyn — *New England* p.74
Chitwood — *History (1)* p.380-381
Earle — *Home* p.23, 46-47, 92, 366

Glubok — *Home* p.49-50
Langdon — *Everyday* p.199-200
Speare — *Life* p.125
Wertenbaker — *First* p.18-19
- *Jamestown*
Adams — *Album* p.18
- *New Amsterdam*
Hale — *Through* p.85-91
- *Painting*
See also **Pearl painting**
Rawson — *When* p.125-126

"GLORIOUS REVOLUTION" (1688–1692)
Hawke — *Colonial* p.265-273
Hawke — *U.S.* p.204-219
Rothbard — *Conceived (1)* p.131-143
Ver Steeg — *Formative* p.124-125
- *Carolinas*
Rothbard — *Conceived (1)* p.135-143
- *England*
Craven — *Colonies* p.212-246
- *Maryland*
Rothbard — *Conceived (1)* p.131-135
- *Middle Colonies*
Hawke — *Colonial* p.266-269
- *New England*
Hawke — *Colonial* p.265-266
Morris — *Ency.* p.40
- *Northern colonies*
Rothbard — *Conceived (1)* p.423-451
- *Pennsylvania*
Morris — *Ency.* p.49
- *South*
Hawke — *Colonial* p.269-273

GLOUCESTER, MASSACHUSETTS
Langdon — *Everyday* p.228

GLOVER, ELIZABETH
Morison — *Intellect.* p.115-116

GLOVER, JOSÉ
Morison — *Intellect.* p.114-115

GLOVER, "WITCH"
Williams — *Demeter's* p.138

GLOVES, FUNERAL. *See* **Funerals —
Gloves**

GOATS. *See* **Plymouth — Goats and
sheep**

GOD
See also **Churches; Indians —
Gods; Religion;** etc.
Smith — *17th* p.19, 24, 91, 143-145,
148, 205, 218, 220

GODBERTSON, GODBERT. *See* **Cuthbertson, Cuthbert**

***GODSPEED* (ship)**
Hawke — *Colonial* p.89
Leynse — *Preced.* p.28

GOFFE, WILLIAM
Alderman — *Story* p.75-76
Johnston — *Conn.* p.75-77

GOLDENROD
, *as dye*
Earle — *Home* p.193

GOLF, "MIDGET"
- *Manhattan, N.Y. (1652)*
Bridenbaugh — *Cities* p.120

GOLOE-SHOES
See also **Galoshes**
Earle — *Two cent. (1)* p.359-370

GOOD, DORCAS
Williams — *Demeter's* p.140

**GOOD, SARAH (Goodwife, Goody
Good)**
Folsom — *Give* p.82-83, 87
Williams — *Demeter's* p.139

GOODMAN, JOHN
Willison — *Pilgrim* p.122-123, 555-556
Willison — *Saints* p.123, 163-164,
335, 439

GOODWIFE, GOODY GOOD. *See* **Good,
Sarah**

GOODWIN, JOHN A.
Marble — *Women* p.27, 60, 62, 70,
103

GOODWIN, MARTHA
, *Cured by Cotton Mather*
Williams — *Demeter's* p.138

GOOKIN, DANIEL, CAPTAIN
Beals — *John Eliot. See* index p.190

GOOKIN, DANIEL, CAPTAIN (*cont.*)
Vaughan — *New. See* index p.423
Willison — *Saints* p.396-397

GOOSE, MRS.
Williams — *Demeter's* p.194

GORGAS. *See* **Gorges**

GORGES, FERDINANDO, SIR
Bailyn — *New England* p.1, 3-10, 50, 95, 98, 119, 124
Gill — *Mayflower* p.51, 55, 57, 103, 127, 134
Hawke — *Colonial* p.88-89, 108, 141-142, 151
Pomfret — *Founding* p.19, 112, 121-122, 132, 137, 139-140, 151-152, 164, 167-171
Rothbard — *Conceived (1)* p.42-43, 45, 159, 163, 172, 175, 224-226, 356, 358
Vaughan — *New* p.4, 9-11, 13-17, 23, 88-89, 212, 228
Willison — *Pilgrim* p.97, 145, 158n, 241n, 339n, 350, 353-354, 396-397, 400-401, 471, 479
Willison — *Saints. See* index p.501

GORGES, ROBERT
Caffrey — *Mayflower* p.189, 191-193
Willison — *Pilgrim* p.241-243
Willison — *Saints* p.238-239

GORGETS (front frills)
Earle — *Two cent. (1)* p.205-209

GORTON, SAMUEL
Alderman — *Story* p.97-98
Fisher — *Men (1)* p.303-307
Pomfret — *Founding* p.213-216, 218, 221, 225, 228
Rothbard — *Conceived (1)* p.197-209, 233, 350, 418
Willison — *Pilgrim* p.431-434, 496, 498
Willison — *Saints* p.352-354, 396, 474

GOSNOLD, BARTHOLOMEW, CAPTAIN
Dillon — *Pilgrims* p.129, 133-134, 142
Marshall — *Mayflower* p.22-23, 133

GOSPEL SOCIETY
Willison — *Saints* p.334, 388-389, 478

GOSSIPS
, *Punishment for*
Miller — *First* p.258

GOTT, CHARLES
Willison — *Pilgrim* p.317-318

GOULD, THOMAS
Wertenbaker — *Puritan* p.242-243

GOURDS
Earle — *Home* p.96, 309
Glubok — *Home* p.51, 213

GOVE, EDWARD
- *Revolt against oppression*
Calverton — *Awake.* p.159

GOVERNMENT
See also names of localities
Carman — *History (1)* p.121-128
- *Autocratic theories*
Rozwenc — *Making (1)* p.66-67
, *County*
Chitwood — *History (1)* p.149-151
, *Evolution of*
- *Views of Israel Stoughton*
Vaughan — *Puritan* p.151-156
, *Limitation of*
- *Views of John Cotton*
Hawke — *U.S.* p.104-105
- *Quaker conceptions*
Rozwenc — *Making (1)* p.68

GOVERNORS
See also names of governors
Chitwood — *History (1)* p.147-148
Craven — *Colonies. See* index p.356
Hope — *Nation* p.63-64
, *Dutch*
Jernegan — *American* p.199
- *South*
Craven — *Southern. See* index p.441

GRADY, KATHERINE
Williams — *Demeter's* p.143

GRAIN
See also **Crops and grains;** names of grain
Adams — *Provincial* p.26-27
Rutman — *Winthrop's. See* index p.308
- *New England*
Wertenbaker — *Puritan* p.54-55

- *New Netherland*
  Tunis — *Colonial* p.70-71
- *Pennsylvania*
  Langdon — *Everyday* p.277
- *Plymouth. See* **Plymouth — Crops and harvesting**

"GRAINS" (prongs)
Earle — *Colonial* p.292-293

GRAMMAR SCHOOLS. *See* **Schools, Grammar**

"GRAND MODEL." *See* **Carolinas — "Fundamental Constitutions"**

GRAPHITE
Bailyn — *New England* p.74, 107

GRAVESTONES. *See* **Tombstones**

GREAT BRITAIN. *See* **England**

GREAT HOPE **(ship)**
Morison — *Story* p.136
Willison — *Saints* p.301-302

"GREAT LAKE" (of the Iroquois)
Bailyn — *New England* p.28-29, 49-53, 107

"GREAT MIGRATION." *See* **Migration**

"GREAT RIVER." *See* **Connecticut River and Valley**

"GREAT SHIPPE"
Johnston — *Conn.* p.65-66, 101

"GREAT SWAMP FIGHT" (1675)
See also **King Philip's War**
Morison — *Story* p.263-268, 284
Smith — *Colonial* p.86, 208

GREEK (in schools)
Morison — *Intellect.* p.42, 44-48, 87, 98, 106, 107n

GREEN, JOSEPH
Commonplace Book, Extracts
Demos — *Remarkable* p.350-356

GREEN, SAMUEL
Morison — *Intellect.* p.116-117, 119-121, 123, 178, 327n

GREEN GATE CHURCH (in Holland)
Willison — *Pilgrim* p.41-45, 287-290, 298, 313, 317, 319, 321-323
Willison — *Saints. See* index p.501

"GREEN SPRING" FACTION (of Gov. Berkeley)
Smith — *17th* p.100, 140

GREENWOOD, JOHN
Wertenbaker — *Puritan* p.20-22
Willison — *Saints* p.33, 41-42, 61-64, 301

GRIDDLE CAKES
Gould — *Early* p.98

GRIDIRONS
Earle — *Home* p.61
Gould — *Early* p.77-78

GRIP **(ship)**
Christensen — *Delaware* p.26-27, 29

GROSEILLIERS, SIEUR DES
Life — *New* p.34

GUERCHEVILLE, MADAME DE
Leonard — *Dear* p.61-62

GUILDS
Wish — *Society (1)* p.1-2, 51

GUILFORD, CONNECTICUT
Pomfret — *Founding* p.211, 264-266, 270

GUILT. *See* **"Ordeal of touch"**

GUNPOWDER PLOT
Wish — *Society (1)* p.5-6

GUNS
Drepperd — *Pioneer* p.37-38
Marshall — *Mayflower* p.107, 109-112, 146
- *Equipment*
  Marshall — *Mayflower* p.110
- *Flintlock and rifle*
  Speare — *Life* p.90-91
- *, Historic*
  Marshall — *Mayflower* p.109
- *Muskets*
  Adams — *Album* p.95-96
  Marshall — *Mayflower* p.111-112, 146

GUNS (*continued*)
- *Patereros (cannon)*
  Marshall — *Mayflower* p.55
- *Pilgrims*
  Adams — *Album* p.47
- *Plymouth*
  Willison — *Pilgrim* p.337-338

GUSTAVUS II (king of Sweden)
Christensen — *Delaware* p.18, 24

GUTTERS (in houses)
Earle — *Home* p.9

GUY, JOHN
Pomfret — *Founding* p.132-133, 305

GUY FAWKE'S DAY
Earle — *Customs* p.229-230
Speare — *Life* p.161
Wright — *Everyday* p.208
- *New York*
  Clark — *Old* p.68-69

H .

HACKLING. *See* **Hetchling**

HADDON, ELIZABETH
Williams — *Demeter's* p.189-190

HAIRDRESSING
- *Girls*
  Glubok — *Home* p.278
, *Long*
  See also **Hair, Men's**
  Woodward — *Way* p.43
, *Men's*
  Dow — *Domestic* p.24
  Earle — *Customs* p.289-290
  Lawrence — *Not* p.17
  Wertenbaker — *First* p.73-74, 280
- *Powder*
  Earle — *Two cent. (2)* p.512-513
- *Puritans. See* **Puritans — Hairdressing**
- *Restorers*
  Earle — *Customs* p.296-297
, *Women's*
  Earle — *Customs* p.290
  Earle — *Two cent. (2)* p.507-508
  Rutman — *Winthrop's* p.133

HAKES (hooks)
Earle — *Home* p.53

HAKLUYT, RICHARD
Craven — *Southern. See* index p.441
Rothbard — *Conceived (1)* p.38-40, 43
Smith — *17th* p.122, 197, 206
Wertenbaker — *First* p.2, 16, 19-20, 80

HALF-MOON (ship)
Christensen — *Delaware* pg.13-14

"HALF-WAY COVENANT" (baptism)
Abbot — *Colonial* p.69
Craven — *Colonies* p.2-3
Fisher — *Men (1)* p.265-266
Monroe — *Founding (1)* p.117-118
Morgan — *Puritan* p.103
Morison — *Intellect.* p.121, 172
Morris — *Ency.* p.547-548
Nettels — *Roots* p.474
Rothbard — *Conceived (1)* p.272
Rutman — *Winthrop's* p.269-270, 276-277
Sweet — *Religion* p.106-108, 271-272
Ver Steeg — *Formative* p.85-87
Wertenbaker — *First* p.110-111
Wertenbaker — *Puritan* p.312-313
Wish — *Society (1)* p.30-31, 42

HALL-SYMONDS LETTERS
Earle — *Two cent. (1)* p.140-159

HALLEY, EDMUND
, *and comet*
  Morison — *Intellect.* p.148, 153-154

HALLS
Demos — *Little* p.30, 32, 39, 46, 48
Dow — *Domestic* p.18-20
Gould — *Early* p.24
Morrison — *Early* p.42-47

HAMMOND, JOHN
Tyler — *History* p.3, 53-54, 57
Wertenbaker — *First* p.229-230, 286

, *on Virginia and Maryland ("Leah and Rachel," 1656)*
  Amer. Her. — *Thirteen* p.147-148
  Axtell — *America* p.195-211

HAMOR, RALPH
- "A true discourse of the present es-
tate of Virginia, 1615"
Amer. Her. — Thirteen p.140

**HAMPTON COURT CONFERENCE
(1604)**
Willison — Saints p.47-49, 51

**HANDICRAFTS. See Artisans; Crafts
and craftsmanship; names of
crafts**

**HANDIWORK. See Needlework; Spin-
ning; Weavers and weaving**

HANDKERCHIEFS
- Plymouth
Demos — Little p.38

HANDMAID (ship)
Willison — Pilgrim p.321-322, 546
Willison — Saints. See index p.501

HANDWRITING. See Penmanship

HANGINGS
Lawrence — Not p.139
Rutman — Winthrop's p.175
, for heresy
Wertenbaker — First p.101-105
, for witchcraft
Wertenbaker — First p.150-162
- New England
Wertenbaker — First p.215-216
- South
Wertenbaker — First p.214-215

HARBORS
See also names of cities; harbors
Bridenbaugh — Cities p.3-4
, Natural
Furnas — Americans p.21

HARD, ELIZABETH
Leonard — Dear p.68

HARDING
Rutman — Winthrop's p.73-75, 82n,
90, 253

HARLOW, EDWARD
Marshall — Mayflower p.134

HARRIS, ELIZABETH
Leonard — Dear p.393-394

HARRIS, WILLIAM
Hawke — Colonial p.147
Rothbard — Conceived (1) p.188,
197, 199-200, 215, 217, 348-350

HARRISON, JOHN
Marshall — Mayflower p.38

HARRISON, SARAH
Williams — Demeter's p.81, 84

HARTFORD, CONNECTICUT
Alderman — Story p.70-71
Amer. Her. — Thirteen p.103-104
Pomfret — Founding p.233-234, 236,
239, 245, 251
Starkey — Land p.88-89, 169, 213
Vaughan — New p.117-118, 138-139,
164-165, 340

HARVARD, JOHN
, Legacy of
Bailey — American (1) p.70

HARVARD COLLEGE
Amer. Her. — Thirteen p.99, 139-140,
153-155, 157
Bailey — American (1) p.70
Caffrey — Mayflower p.228, 269, 281-
283, 291-292, 296, 299, 304
Chitwood — History (1) p.465-466
Collins — Story p.52
Glubok — Home p.42, 44, 109, 112,
115
Hawke — U.S. p.233-235
Hope — Nation p.114
Jernegan — American p.189
Langdon — Everyday p.319-320
Monroe — Founding (1) p.166
Morison — Intellect. See index p.281
National — History. p.117-118
Rozwenc — Making (1) p.86, 90
Smith — 17th p.189-190, 215, 218,
224
Vaughan — New p.223, 253, 281-284,
287, 289, 307, 333
Ver Steeg — Formative p.103-104
Wertenbaker — First. See index p.345
Wertenbaker — Puritan. See index
p.351
Willison — Saints p.502
Wish — Society (1) p.53-54, 61, 95
Wright — Cultural p.116-118
Wright — Everyday p.141-144
Wright — Literary p.18-22, 99-105,
108

HARVARD COLLEGE (*continued*)
- *Architecture*
  Morrison — *Early* p.82, 85-87
- *Charter and founding*
  Annals of America *(1)* p.195-196
  Vaughan — *Puritan* p.245-247
- *Food and drink*
  Gould — *Early* p.88-89
- *Indian Seminary*
  Beals — *John Eliot* p.155
  Morrison — *Early* p.87-88
- *Laws, liberties, and orders*
  Vaughan — *Puritan* p.248-250
- *Library*
  Morison — *Intellect.* p.146-147
  Wright — *Literary* p.40, 43, 135
- *Life*
  Earle — *Colonial* p.125-128
, *Priority of*
  Morison — *Intellect.* p.27
- *Stoughton Hall (1698–99)*
  Morrison — *Early* p.88

HARVEST FESTIVALS. *See* **Holidays and festivals; Indians — Festivals; Plymouth; Thanksgiving Day**

HARVEY, JOHN, SIR
  Chitwood — *History (1)* p.69
  Hawke — *Colonial* p.106-107, 109, 112, 114, 243
  Pomfret — *Founding* p.203
  Smith — *17th* p.90, 95-97, 126
  Starkey — *Land* p.77, 107, 114, 116-118
  Wertenbaker — *First* p.36, 130, 176, 179

HARVEY, WILLIAM
  Hawke — *Colonial* p.298-300

HATHERLEY (HATHERLY), TIMOTHY
  Caffrey — *Mayflower* p.220, 235-240, 242
  Willison — *Pilgrim* p.313, 363-366, 377, 438, 494n, 495n, 508, 521
  Willison — *Saints. See* index p.502

HATHORNE, WILLIAM
  Gildrie — *Salem. See* index p.186

HATS AND HATTERS
  Gould — *Early* p.142-143
, *Beaver*
  Earle — *Two cent. (1)* p.224
- *Bonnets*
  Earle — *Two cent. (1)* p.242-243
- *Caps*
  Earle — *Two cent. (1)* p.215-235
, *Monmouth*
  Earle — *Two cent. (1)* p.219-221
, *Montero*
  Earle — *Two cent. (1)* p.221-223
- *Church objections*
  Earle — *Home* p.285-286
- *Hatbands*
  Earle — *Two cent. (1)* p.123-124, 150
, *Men's*
  Earle — *Two cent. (2)* p.567
- *New Netherland*
  Tunis — *Colonial* p.65-66
- *Plymouth*
  Demos — *Little* p.56-57
, *Steeple-crowned*
  Earle — *Two cent. (1)* p.234

HAY
  Rutman — *Winthrop's* p.36, 69, 84, 88, 91, 93, 159, 197, 205

HAY-WARDS
  Earle — *Home* p.402
  Glubok — *Home* p.318

HAYWARD, JOHN
, *as first letter carrier*
  Langdon — *Everyday* p.261

HEADDRESS. *See* **Cross-Clothes; Coifs; Hairdressing**

HEADRIGHTS (land acreage system)
  Craven — *Colonies* p.90-91, 97-98, 178, 185
  Craven — *Southern. See* index p.442
  Jernegan — *American* p.85-86
  Morison — *Oxford* p.81, 86
  Ver Steeg — *Formative* p.56
- *Carolinas*
  Craven — *Southern* p.325, 327-328, 331, 338, 350-352
- *Indians. See* **Indians — Headrights**
- *Maryland*
  Craven — *Southern* p.191-192, 219, 328n

- *South*
  - *Abuses of system*
    Craven — *Southern* p.210
- *Virginia*
  Carman — *History (1)* p.54-55
  - *Origins*
    Craven — *Southern* p.121,
      128, 175-177, 365

HEALE, GILES
Marshall — *Mayflower* p.48, 119-120

HEALTH. See Hygiene; Sanitation

HEARTH AND HOME INDUSTRIES. See Crafts and craftsmanship; Spinning; Weavers and weaving

HEARTHS. See Fireplaces — Hearths

"HEARTLAND"
See also **New Sweden; Pennsylvania**
- *View from abroad*
  Axtell — *America* p.161-193

HEATING
See also **Fireplaces; Foot stoves; Stoves**
Drepperd — *Pioneer* p.232
Earle — *Home* p.69-72
- *Meetinghouses*
  Rawson — *When* p.222-223
- *New England*
  Tunis — *Colonial* p.41-43

HEBDEN, KATHARINE
Williams — *Demeter's* p.173-174

HEBREW
, *in curriculum*
  Morison — *Intellect.* p.42, 44-45

HELMONT, J. B.
Morison — *Intellect.* p.52, 138-250

HEMLOCK
- *Brooms and Boxes*
  Earle — *Home* p.304-305, 310

HEMP
Adams — *Album* p.116
Craven — *Southern* p.45, 56, 70, 108,
  163, 313, 315n-316, 347

Earle — *Home* p.167, 169
Glubok — *Home* p.229-231
Leonard — *Dear* p.173-175, 183, 184
- *South*
  Craven — *Southern* p.45, 56, 70,
    108, 163, 312, 313n, 316, 347

HENCHMAN, HUMPHREY, BISHOP
Smith — *17th* p.171-172, 181

HENDRICKSEN, CORNELIUS
Christiansen — *Delaware* p.16-17

HENRICO, UNIVERSITY OF
- *Failure of 1st university, Va.*
  Wright — *Everyday* p.135

HENRY WHITEFIELD HOUSE (Guilford, Conn., 1639–40)
Morrison — *Early* p.69-71

HERBS
See also **Remedies**
Adams — *Album* p.58, 93
Beck — *Pilgrims* p.58-59, 77-78
Earle — *Customs* p.346-348
Lawrence — *New* p.2-4
Marshall — *Mayflower* p.123-124
- *Methods and tools*
  Marshall — *Mayflower* p.129
- *Pilgrims*
  Marshall — *Mayflower* p.94

HERDING
Earle — *Home* p.399-401, 403
- *Fence-herds*
  Glubok — *Home* p.317-318

HERESY
See also **Baptists; Quakers,** names
  of heretics
- *New England*
  Wertenbaker — *First* p.98-105
- *Punishment*
  Wertenbaker — *First* p.215, 220
, *Suppression of*
  Rothbard — *Conceived (1)* p.182-
    189, 237-250
- *Views of John Winthrop*
  Annals of America (1) p.154-156

HETCHELING (of flax)
Earle — *Home* p.172

"HEX" SYMBOLS
- *Pennsylvania Dutch*
  Adams — *Album* p.242

HEYLYN, PETER
  Smith — *17th* p.207-208

HEYWOOD, THOMAS
  , *and Pocahontas*
  Phillips — *First* p.161

HIBBENS (HIBBINS), ANNE
  Demos — *Remarkable* p.221-239
  Williams — *Demeter's* p.136-137

HICKS, MARGARET
  Willison — *Saints* p.449

HICKS, PHEBE. *See* **Watson, Phebe Hicks**

HICKS, ROBERT
  Hills — *History (1)* p.80, 83, 91, 93
  Hills — *History (2)* p.70-72, 132
  Marble — *Women* p.35, 96
  Willison — *Saints* p.445, 449

HICKS FAMILY
  Hills — *History (1). See* index p.167
  Hills — *History (2). See* index p.260

HIGGINSON, FRANCIS
  Gildrie — *Salem* p.8-10, 13-15, 21, 32, 146
  Willison — *Saints* p.271, 346-347, 469
  - *Catalogue of . . . things, planters, New England*
    Demos — *Remarkable* p.42-43
  , *on New England*
    Axtell — *America* p.13-21
  , *on Salem*
    Dow — *Domestic* p.5-8
  - *"On the riches of New England" (1629)*
    Annals of America (1) p.95-99

HIGGINSON, JOHN
  Bailyn — *New England* p.140-142
  Gildrie — *Salem* p.123, 136, 142-148, 150, 152, 154, 163
  Tyler — *History* p.168, 179, 399-400
  Wertenbaker — *Puritan* p.83-84, 155, 173, 211, 243

- *"The cause of God and the people in New England, 1663"*
  Amer. Her. — *Thirteen* p.151

HIGHER EDUCATION. *See* **Colleges and universities**

HIGHWAYS
  See also **Indian trails; Roads**
  Bridenbaugh — *Cities* p.13-18
  - *King's highways*
  , *Oldest (Boston)*
    Langdon — *Everyday* p.246

HILL, VALENTINE
  Bailyn — *New England* p.35, 37, 51, 80, 82, 101, 110, 124

HILTON, WILLIAM
  Willison — *Saints* p.225, 235, 246, 249-250, 279, 445, 449, 458

HINCKLEY, THOMAS
  Morison — *Story* p.173, 183n, 219, 243, 284-287, 290
  Willison — *Pilgrim* p.528-529
  Willison — *Saints* p.374, 402-407, 410, 428, 455-456

HINESTROSA, FRANCISCA
  Williams — *Demeter's* p.17

HINGES
  Earle — *Home* p.9, 318

HINGHAM, MASSACHUSETTS
  Wertenbaker — *First. See* index p.346

HISTORIANS
  See also **Women — Historians**
  Morris — *Ency.* p.558-559, 560
  , *English — of America*
    Smith — *17th* p.195-225
  - *New England*
    Tyler — *History* p.3, 100-136, 374-381
    Wright — *Cultural* p.155-162
  - *Virginia*
    Tyler — *History* p.61-68

HISTORY. *See* **Books and reading — History**

HOAR, MARGERY. *See* **Flynt, Margery Hoar**

HOBAMOCK (HOBAMOK, WAMPA-NOAG) (Indian)
Archer — *Mayflower* p.272-273
Beck — *Pilgrims* p.41, 45, 48
Caffrey — *Mayflower* p.149-150, 176, 179, 163-164
Dillon — *Pilgrims* p.162-163, 169-170, 177-178, 180
Marble — *Women* p.22, 58
Marshall — *Mayflower* p.27, 153, 159, 168
Vaughan — *New* p.75-76, 80-85
Willison — *Pilgrim* p.141-142, 174-175, 207-212, 215-216, 220-222, 385
Willison — *Saints* p.185-187, 200-203, 220-224, 226-227, 240, 314

HOCKING, CAPTAIN
- *Affair — killing on Kennebec (1634)*
  Willison — *Pilgrim* p.390-396
  Willison — *Saints* p.297-299, 443

HOG ISLAND
Rutman — *Winthrop's* p.70, 76, 84-85, 85n, 92

HOGS
Craven — *Southern* p.19, 96n, 100, 103, 212, 346, 357-358, 364
Earle — *Home* p.125, 311, 402-403
Furnas — *Americans* p.172
Gould — *Early* p.101-103
Langdon — *Everyday* p.283-284
- *"Hog reeves" (inspectors)*
  Earle — *Home* p.402-403
- *South*
  Craven — *Southern* p.19, 96n, 100, 103, 212, 346, 357-358, 364
- *Stealing*
  Craven — *Southern* p.213-214
  - *South*
    Craven — *Southern* p.213-214

HOLDEN, CHRISTOPHER
Wertenbaker — *Puritan* p.229-230, 232-234

HOLIDAYS AND FESTIVALS
See also **Indians — Festivals;** names of holidays and festivals
Earle — *Customs* p.231-233
Leonard — *Dear* p.236

Miller — *First* p.84-86
Rawson — *When* p.229-230
Speare — *Life* p.159-161
Spruill — *Women's* p.87-88
Wright — *Cultural* p.188
Wright — *Everyday* p.205-211
, *Dutch*
  Speare — *Life* p.161
- *Views of Judge Sewall*
  Holliday — *Woman's* p.203-204

HOLLAND
See also **Dutch; New Amsterdam; Pilgrims**
Craven — *Colonies* p.34, 36, 59-60, 73, 104-106, 200, 202, 227
Craven — *Southern. See* index p.442
Folsom — *Give* p.ix, 11, 44, 53, 64-67
Gill — *Mayflower. See* index p.203
Hawke — *Colonial. See* index p.731
Rutman — *Winthrop's* p.101, 133, 138, 174, 187, 199, 231
Starkey — *Land* p.139-140

HOLLIS, THOMAS
Sweet — *Religion* p.138-139

HOLMES, JONATHAN
- *Diary, extract (Middletown, N.J., 1737)*
  Demos — *Remarkable* p.147-148

HOLMES, OBEDIAH (Obadiah)
Sweet — *Religion* p.131-134
Wertenbaker — *Puritan* p.224-226

HOLMES, WILLIAM
Johnston — *Conn.* p.7-10, 14-15
Pomfret — *Founding* p.232-233
Willison — *Saints* p.296-297, 306, 320

HOLT HOUSE (in Lewes, Del.)
Christensen — *Delaware* p.153

HOLY DISCIPLINE
See also **Brownism**
Williams — *Saints. See* index p.502

"HOLY EXPERIMENT"
See also **Philadelphia; Pennsylvania**
Folsom — *Give* p.49-54
Morison — *Oxford* p.126-131
Rothbard — *Conceived (1)* p.402-411

HOME FURNISHINGS
  See also **Furniture; Houses —**
  Interiors; Plymouth — Home
  furnishings
  Chitwood — *History (1)* p.486-487
  Miller — *First* p.178-179
  - *List*
    Smith — *Colonial* p.72-73
  - *Maryland*
    Spruill — *Women's* p.27-28
  - *New England*
    Lawrence — *New* p.20-21
    Wertenbaker — *First* p.83-85,
    295
  - *Planters, Wealthy*
    Wertenbaker — *First* p.46-47,
    295-296
  - *South*
    Goodwin — *Colonial* p.26-30
  - *Virginia*
    Clark — *Old* p.5-6
  - *Yeomanry*
    Wertenbaker — *First* p.40-41

HOME INDUSTRIES. *See* **Crafts and**
  craftsmanship; Spinning; Weav-
  ers and weaving; etc.

HOME LIFE. *See* **Families and family life**

HOMES. *See* **Houses; Log cabins; Man-**
  sions; etc.

HOMINY
  Earle — *Home* p.131

HONEY
  Earle — *Home* p.110-111

HOODS
  Earle — *Two cent. (1)* p.237-253

HOOKER, SUSANNA
  Beals — *John Eliot* p.35, 38, 43-44,
  54, 56, 58-62, 76, 88, 98

HOOKER, THOMAS
  Acheson — *America's* p.110-111
  Alderman — *Story* p.69-71, 73-74
  Amer. Her. — *Thirteen* p.103-104
  Beals — *John Eliot. See* index p.190

HOOKER, THOMAS, REV.
  Calverton — *Awake.* p.148-152
  Carman — *History (1)* p.90
  Fisher — *Men (1)* p.244-247

Johnston — *Conn.* p.11-18, 20, 22,
  24, 32-34, 36, 43, 48, 67, 126
Life — *New* p.78-80, 86, 90
Morgan — *Puritan* p.98-99, 117-118
Morison — *Intellect.* p.139, 151-152,
  155n, 171
Murdock — *Literature* p.34-35, 59-60
Nettels — *Roots* p.172-173
Pomfret — *Founding* p.187, 192, 195,
  199, 203, 235-240, 242-249, 257-
  258
Rothbard — *Conceived (1)* p.172,
  185, 218-221, 231
Rozwenc — *Making (1)* p.66, 71
Rutman — *Winthrop's* p.47, 51, 103,
  112, 180, 184, 217-219, 263
Wertenbaker — *Puritan* p.34, 81-82,
  217, 259
Wish — *Society (1)* p.23, 35-36
Wright — *Everyday* p.165-166
  - *House and furnishings*
    Smith — *Colonial* p.9-10
  , *on Puritans preaching*
    Vaughan — *Puritan* p.82-92

HOOKS
  Gould — *Early* p.68-69

HOPKINS, CATHERINE WHELDON
  Willison — *Saints* p.441

HOPKINS, CONSTANCE. *See* **Snow,**
  Constantia Hopkins

HOPKINS, DAMARIS. *See* **Cooke, Da-**
  maris Hopkins

HOPKINS, EDWARD
  Bailyn — *New England* p.29-30, 36,
  38, 55, 72, 94, 206

HOPKINS, ELIZABETH
  Gill — *Mayflower* p.69
  Marble — *Women* p.9, 68-69
  Williams — *Demeter's* p.22-23

HOPKINS, GILES
  Willison — *Saints* p.133, 316-317, 441

HOPKINS, MATTHEW
  Wertenbaker — *First* p.144, 151, 154

HOPKINS, OCEANUS
  Willison — *Pilgrim* p.110n, 535-536
  Willison — *Saints* p.133, 437, 441

HOPKINS, STEPHEN
Caffrey — *Mayflower. See* index p.388
Dillon — *Pilgrims* p.136, 144-146, 152-153, 159-162
Gill — *Mayflower* p.47, 74-75, 82, 91, 131
Hills — *History (1)* p.137-141; *See also* index p.168
Hills — *History (2). See* index p.261
Leynse — *Preced.* p.233-234, 246, 252-253, 256-257, 269
Marshall — *Mayflower* p.28, 140, 184
Morison — *Story* p.36, 51, 69, 77, 140, 149, 168-170, 193
Willison — *Pilgrim* p.105, 110, 126, 129, 139-141, 248n, 378, 382, 535, 552-554
Willison — *Saints. See* index p.502

HOPKINS FAMILY
Caffrey — *Mayflower* p.388
Hills — *History (1)* p.137-146; *See also* index p.168
Hills — *History (2) See* index p.261
Leynse — *Preced. See* index p.282
Marble — *Women* p.22, 24, 30, 68-69
- *House*
Marshall — *Mayflower* p.54

HOPS
Craven — *Southern* p.45, 50, 70, 140, 253, 357
- *South*
Craven — *Southern* p.45, 50, 70, 140, 253, 357

HORN
- *Carving*
Earle — *Home* p.321-322
- *Utensils*
Earle — *Home* p.88, 96

HORNBOOKS
Adams — *Album* p.121
Glubok — *Home* p.138-141
McClinton — *Antiques* p.75
Rawson — *When* p.153
Speare — *Life* p.106

HORNSMITHS
Tunis — *Craftsmen* p.54-55

HORSE RACING
Langdon — *Everyday* p.288, 331-332
- *Henrico Co., Va.*
Wertenbaker — *First* p.264-265

- *New York*
Wertenbaker — *First* p.272-273
- *Virginia*
Wertenbaker — *First* p.263-265

HORSES
Adams — *Provincial* p.31
Bailyn — *New England* p.50, 85, 89, 100, 127
Craven — *Southern* p.19, 50, 96n, 100, 212, 283, 370, 381, 406
Earle — *Customs* p.185-187, 191
Speare — *Life* p.137-138
- *Boston*
Rutman — *Winthrop's* p.6, 91, 169, 185, 205, 247
- *Conestoga*
Langdon — *Everyday* p.290
- *First, in New England*
Langdon — *Everyday* p.288
- *Laws*
Vaughan — *New* p.196-197, 231
- *Plymouth. See* **Plymouth — Horses**
- *Riding*
Goodwin — *Colonial* p.148-150
- *South*
Craven — *Southern* p.19, 50, 96n, 100, 212, 283, 370, 381, 406
- *Transportation*
Glubok — *Home* p.333-334
- *Virginia*
Fisher — *Men (1)* p.71-72

HOSPITALITY
- *Maryland*
Earle — *Home* p.396-397
- *Planters*
Wertenbaker — *First* p.269
, *Southern*
Earle — *Home* p.397-398

HOTELS. *See* **Inns and innkeepers**

HOUGHTON, ROBERT
Bailyn — *New England* p.79-80

HOUSE OF HOPE (Dutch fort)
Johnston — *Conn.* p.7-9

HOUSE OF SEVEN GABLES (TURNER HOUSE) (Salem, Mass., 1670)
Morrison — *Early* p.64-66

HOUSE-RAISING
Glubok — *Home* p.320-321
Morrison — *Early* p.27-28
Rawson — *When* p.67-68

HOUSECLEANING
Gould — *Early* p.113

HOUSEHOLD ARTICLES
See also **Dishes and utensils;**
Kitchen utensils; name of articles
- *Aids*
Marshall — *Mayflower* p.93
- *Hints*
Rawson — *When* p.16-19
- *New England*
Dow — *Domestic* p.6
- *Requirements, 1st year*
Dow — *Every* p.3
- *South*
Craven — *Southern* p.94-95

HOUSEKEEPERS
- *Qualifications*
Earle — *Home* p.252-253

HOUSELOTS. *See* **Land — Lots**

HOUSES
- *See also* **Architecture; Bark houses;**
Log cabins; Mansions; Wigwams;
names of famous houses
Bridenbaugh — *Cities* p.10-11
Carman — *History (1)* p.113-116
Chitwood — *History (1)* p.483-486
Glubok — *Home* p.2-14
Hawke — *Colonial* p.285-286
Langdon — *Everyday* p.12-13, 15
Miller — *First* p.173-175
Morrison — *Early* p.20-22
Rutman — *Winthrop's. See* index
p.309
Scott — *Settlers* p.36-37
Williams — *Demeter's* p.38-42
Woodward — *Way* p.27-29

- *Amsterdam (old)*
Smith — *Colonial* p.91-106
- *Boston*
Adams — *Album* p.80-81
Lawrence — *New* p.29-31
Rutman — *Winthrop's. See* index
p.309
, *Brick*
Morrison — *Early* p.139-140
Wertenbaker — *First* p.290-292

, *Dutch*
Morrison — *Early* p.103-104
- *Maryland*
Morrison — *Early* p.158
- *New England*
See also names of brick
houses
Morrison — *Early* p.71-75
- *Cabins and cottages*
Morrison — *Early* p.9-12
- *"Cape Cod"*
Morrison — *Early* p.67-68
- *Carolinas*
Morrison — *Early* p.165-172
, *Common*
Marshall — *Mayflower* p.54
- *Connecticut*
Fisher — *Men (1)* p.268-269
Johnston — *Conn.* p.46-49
Smith — *Colonial* p.91-106
Wertenbaker — *First* p.317-318
- *Delaware*
Christensen — *Delaware* p.31-33
- *Dugouts*
Morrison — *Early* p.9
, *Dutch*
Hale — *Through* p.72-75
Langdon — *Everyday* p.44-45
Speare — *Life* p.53-54
- *Farmhouses*
Nettles — *Roots* p.316-319
- *Interiors*
Scott — *Settlers* p.37
, *First*
See also **Houses —**
Jamestown; Houses —
Pilgrims; Houses —
Plymouth; Houses — Puritan
Langdon — *Everyday* p.2-9
Lawrence — *New* p.19-33
Morris — *Ency.* p.597-598
Wertenbaker — *First* p.283-286
, *Frame*
Morrison — *Early* p.14-15, 22-30
- *New England*
See also names of famous
frame houses
Morrison — *Early* p.51-68
- *Virginia*
Morrison — *Early* p.138-139
, *Functional*
Wright — *Cultural* p.199
, *Historic*
See also names of historic
houses
Drepperd — *Pioneer* p.17-19, 21

- *Massachusetts*
    Adams — *Album* p.133
- *New England*
    National — *History.* p.88-89
- *Huts, Conical*
    Lawrence — *New* p.21-22
- *Interiors*
    Earle — *Customs* p.108-118
    Woodward — *Way* p.40
    Wright — *Cultural* p.199
- *New Netherland*
    Tunis — *Colonial* p.67-69
- *Maryland*
    Earle — *Home* p.11
    Morrison — *Early* p.157-165
    , *Largest in colonies (St. Mary's
        City, 1639)*
        Morrison — *Early* p.158-159
    , *Most remarkable*
        Morrison — *Early* p.160
- *Massachusetts*
    Glubok — *Home* p.9-11
    Wertenbaker — *First* p.283-288
- *New England*
    Dow — *Every* p.20-21
    Hope — *Nation* p.87-88
    Morrison — *Early* p.20-48
    Smith — *Colonial* p.66-69
    Tunis — *Colonial* p.29-33
    Wertenbaker — *First* p.287-288,
        317-318
- *New Jersey*
    Wertenbaker — *First* p.291-292
- *New Netherland*
    Hale — *Through* p.72-75
    Williams — *Demeter's* p.50
- *New Sweden*
    Axtell — *America* p.184
- *New York*
    Clark — *Old* p.53-54
    Earle — *Home* p.7-11
- *North and South contrasted*
    Williams — *Demeter's* p.49-50
- *One-room*
    Gould — *Early* p.15-39
- *Overhang*
    Morrison — *Early* p.28-30
- *Peasants*
    Marshall — *Mayflower* p.64-67
- *Pennsylvania*
    Wertenbaker — *First* p.290-291,
        318
- *Philadelphia, Pa.*
    Bridenbaugh — *Cities* p.10
- *Pioneers*
    Drepperd — *Pioneer* p.12-15

, *Plank*
    Snell — *Wild* p.62, 111
- *Rentals*
    Winthrop's. *See* index p.317
- *Rhode Island*
    Bridenbaugh — *Cities* p.9-10
, *Row*
    Snell — *Wild* p.111-112
- *South*
    Goodwin — *Colonial* p.15-42
    Wertenbaker — *First* p.286-287,
        317
    - *Cottages*
        Tunis — *Colonial* p.81-82
, *Stone*
    Wright — *Cultural* p.199
    , *Dutch*
        Morrison — *Early* p.102
    - *New England*
        See also names of stone
            houses
        Morrison — *Early* p.68-71
- *Sudbury, Mass. (1680)*
    Woodward — *Way* p.39-41
- *Thatched (wattle and daub)*
    Snell — *Wild* p.82, 92-93, 106
- *Types*
    Glubok — *Home* p.4-6, 38-39
    - *Virginia*
        Morrison — *Early* p.140-143
- *Virginia*
    Clark — *Old* p.4-5
    Morrison — *Early* p.150-151
    Spruill — *Women's* p.21-23
    Wertenbaker — *Old* p.74-82
    , *Oldest*
        Morrison — *Early* p.143-147,
            150-151

HOUSEWIVES

Leonard — *Dear* p.409-410
Spruill — *Women's* p.83-84
, *Dutch*
    Earle — *Two cent. (1)* p.104-106
    Smith — *Colonial* p.109-122
- *Landowners*
    Leonard — *Dear* p.134-137

HOUSEWRIGHTS

Tunis — *Craftsmen* p.24-25

HOWARD, FRANCIS LORD

Rothbard — *Conceived (1)* p.146-149

HOWLAND, ARTHUR, JR.

Willison — *Pilgrim* p.520-521
Willison — *Saints* p.321, 380-381

HOWLAND, ELIZABETH TILLEY
Hills — *History (1)* p.21, 34, 37-38, 40, 47, 51, 53-54, 57-61
Hills — *History (2)* p.130
Marble — *Women* p.85-88
Willison — *Pilgrim* p.520-521
Willison — *Saints* p.122, 427, 439, 443

HOWLAND, JOHN
Caffrey — *Mayflower* p.108, 117, 124, 220, 249-250, 312
Dillon — *Pilgrims* p.144-146, 197, 213
Gill — *Mayflower* p.69, 119
Hills — *History (1)* p.87
Hills — *History (2)* p.162-163
Marble — *Women* p.5, 35, 58, 85-88
Marshall — *Mayflower* p.28-29, 44, 170
Morison — *Story* p.35, 38, 45, 128, 134, 149, 171, 276
Willison — *Saints*. *See* index p.502

HOWLAND, THOMAS SOUTHWORTH
Willison — *Saints* p.412-413, 420, 483

HOWLAND FAMILY
Hills — *History (1)*. *See* index p.168
Hills — *History (2)* p.160-163; *See also* index p.261-262

HOWLAND HOUSE
Willison — *Saints* p.386, 483

HUBBARD, WILLIAM
Morison — *Intellect.* p.124-125, 180-186
Smith — *17th* p.211, 213-215, 219
Tyler — *History*. *See* index p.544
Wertenbaker — *Puritan*. *See* index p.352
- *"The happiness of a people" (1676)*
  Annals of America (1) p.248-254

HUDDLESTON, JOHN, CAPTAIN
Willison — *Pilgrim* p.180-181

HUDSON, HENRY
Acheson — *America's* p.125
Chitwood — *History (1)* p.159-160
Christensen — *Delaware* p.13-14
Jernegan — *American* p.195-196
- *Landing*
  Collins — *Story* p.57
- *Voyages*
  Marshall — *Mayflower* p.23
  Morris — *Ency.* p.24

HUDSON RIVER AND VALLEY (New York)
Alderman — *Story* p.47-49, 58-60
Amer. Her. — *Thirteen* p.63, 107, 117, 124-125, 128-129, 133, 136
Amer. Her. — *Treasury* p.172-177
Gill — *Mayflower* p.37-38, 52, 69-70, 118, 137, 145
Hope — *Nation* p.100-102
- *Dutch*
  Amer. Her. — *Treasury* p.178-179
  National — *History.* p.97-100

HUDSON'S BAY COMPANY
Collins — *Story* p.79

"HUGGERY" (mock battle with Indians)
Willison — *Pilgrim* p.154-155, 169, 183-184, 229

HUGUENOTS
Adams — *Provincial* p.7-8
Alderman — *Story* p.127, 136
American Her. — *Thirteen* p.26-27, 33, 55-57, 107, 119-121, 128, 165, 182
Bridenbaugh — *Cities* p.93, 95, 102-103, 250
Carman — *History (1)* p.14-15, 43
Craven — *Colonies* p.177-178
Craven — *Southern* p.9, 11-12, 355
Folsom — *Give* p.4-5, 8-9, 11-12, 65-66
Furnas — *Americans* p.76-77
Jernegan — *American* p.312
Leonard — *Dear* p.26, 60-61
Leynse — *Preced.* p.24-26, 28, 32, 118, 126
Nettels — *Roots* p.385-386
Smith — *Colonial* p.4-5, 7-8
Starkey — *Land* p.216-217, 226-228, 237
Sweet — *Religion* p.24-25
Wish — *Society (1)* p.91-92
Wright — *Cultural* p.52-56
Wright — *Everyday* p.123
- *Characteristics*
  Smith — *Colonial* p.7-8
- *Courtesy games*
  Smith — *Colonial* p.164-166
- *Escape of a family*
  Smith — *Colonial* p.125-138
- *Florida*
  Collins — *Story* p.71

- *Life*
    Smith — *Colonial* p.155-156
- *Migration*
    Ver Steeg — *Formative* p.168-169
- *New Rochelle, N.Y.*
    Clark — *Old* p.83-93
    Smith — *Colonial* p.141-152
- *Schools*
    Smith — *Colonial* p.161-162
- *South Carolina*
    Chitwood — *History (1)* p.188
    Fisher — *Men (2)* p.265, 273, 286-287
- *Women (South Carolina)*
    Spruill — *Women's* p.13-14

HULL, JOHN
    Bailyn — *New England* p.23, 73, 87-88, 91, 101, 108, 110, 117, 131, 134-135, 143, 151-152, 183, 186
    Dow — *Every* p.169-171
    National — *History.* p.114
    Wertenbaker — *Puritan* p.91-92, 174, 199, 203-204, 226-227, 255, 302-303
    Wright — *Cultural* p.31-34, 37
    Wright — *Everyday* p.175

HULL, MASSACHUSETTS. *See* **Nantasket, Massachusetts**

HUMANISM
- *New England*
    Morison — *Intellect.* p.16-17, 46-55, 62

HUMOR
    Hawke — *Colonial* p.307-308

HUMPHREY, JOHN
    Pomfret — *Founding* p.151, 154, 158, 160-161, 163-164, 168
    Rutman — *Winthrop's* p.100-101n, 102-103, 135, 136n, 284

"HUNDRED, THE" (Adventurers' Society)
- *Maryland*
    Craven — *Southern* p.201-202
- *Virginia*
    Craven — *Southern* p.120n, 122-123

"HUNDRED FAMILY" LAW (grammar schools)
    Morison — *Intellect.* p.88-89

HUNGER. *See* **Jamestown — Starvation; Plymouth —"Starving time"**

HUNT, ROBERT
    Chitwood — *History (1)* p.426-427

HUNT, THOMAS, CAPTAIN
    Marshall — *Mayflower* p.134, 151
- *Kidnapping of Indians*
    Willison — *Saints* p.183-184

HUNTING AND TRAPPING
    See also **Indians — Hunting and trapping; Plymouth — Hunting and trapping**
    Beck — *Pilgrims* p.43, 74
    Dulles — *America* p.24-26
    Earle — *Customs* p.236-238
    Furnas — *Americans* p.171-172
    Glubok — *Home* p.56-61, 69-70
    Speare — *Life* p.154
    Wright — *Cultural* p.189
- *Traps and snares*
    Marshall — *Mayflower* p.147
- *Virginia*
    Clark — *Old* p.22-23

HURON INDIANS
    Snell — *Wild* p.36-37, 95, 98, 114

HURRICANES. *See* **Plymouth — Hurricanes (1635)**

"HUSBANDMEN." *See* **"Familists"**

HUSBANDS. *See* **Plymouth — Husbands; Puritans — Husbands, authoritative role; Women — Husbands**

HUSKING BEES
    Dulles — *America* p.26
    Earle — *Home* p.136
    Furnas — *Americans* p.168-169
    Gould — *Early* p.135
    Rawson — *When* p.76-77
    Speare — *Life* p.154-155
- *Indians, Woodland*
    Northey — *American* p.87-88

HUTCHINSON, ANNE MARBURY
Abbot — *Colonial* p.47, 51-52, 126
Acheson — *America's* p.107-109
Amer. Her. — *Pioneer* p.63
Amer. Her. — *Thirteen* p.104, 106, 132-133
Beals — *John Eliot* p.98-101
Brooks — *Dame* p.1-29
Carman — *History (1)* p.91, 93
Chitwood — *History (1)* p.117-119
Dexter — *Colonial* p.142-146
Earle — *Colonial* p.111-119
Fisher — *Men (1)* p.152-158
Folsom — *Give* p.19-23, 28, 49, 81
Hawke — *Colonial* p.145-147, 162, 169
Hawke — *U.S.* p.112-119
Holliday — *Women's* p.39-47, 57, 291-292
Jernegan — *American* p.132-134
Leonard — *Dear* p.31, 117, 349, 369-370, 372-373, 473, 493-494, 529
Life — *New* p.78-81
Nettels — *Roots* p.178-179
Pomfret — *Founding* p.188-189, 193-197, 204, 213-215, 218, 236-237, 259-260
Rothbard — *Conceived (1). See* index p.525
Rutman — *Winthrop's* p.118-124, 130, 142, 152
Smith — *17th* p.146, 153-155, 203
Snell — *Wild* p.116, 129, 134
Sweet — *Religion* p.90, 92-94
Ver Steeg — *Formative* p.49-51
Wertenbaker — *First* p.91, 99-101
Wertenbaker — *Puritan* p.89-90, 219-223
Williams — *Demeter's* p.29-30, 115-119, 125
Willison — *Pilgrim* p.458n
Willison — *Saints* p.157, 352, 472
Wish — *Society (1)* p.38-39
Wright — *Cultural* p.82

- *Biography*
Morris — *Ency.* p.679-680
- *Flight*
Bailey — *American (1)* p.27-28
Rothbard — *Conceived (1)* p.190-196
- *Trial*
Morris — *Ency.* p.34
, *and aftermath*
Hawke — *U.S.* p.115-119

- *Views of Thomas Hutchinson*
Goetzmann — *Colonial* p.181-184

HUTCHINSON, LUCY APSLEY
Murdock — *Literature* p.133-134

HUTCHINSON, THOMAS
Earle — *Two cent. (1)* p.39-40, 43-45
Willison — *Pilgrim* p.564-565
Willison — *Saints* p.428-429

HUTCHINSON, WILLIAM
Rothbard — *Conceived (1)* p.190, 193-196
Rutman — *Winthrop's* p.73-74, 74n, 78-81, 82n, 193n
Starkey — *Land* p.96-97, 103

HUTCHINSON FAMILY
Bailyn — *New England* p.35, 37, 40, 88-90, 101, 137

HUTERIANS (Huterites)
Calverton — *Awake.* p.182-183

HYGIENE
See also **Sanitation**
- *Code of public health, Philadelphia*
Bridenbaugh — *Cities* p.92
- *Hingham, Mass.*
Wertenbaker — *First* p.181-182
, *Ideas of*
Wertenbaker — *First* p.166-167

HYLLES, THOMAS
Glubok — *Home* p.150-151

HYMNS
See also **Bay Psalm Book;** "**Old Hundred**" **(psalms)**
- *New England reformers*
Howard — *Our* p.7

I

ICE FISHING
Rawson — *When* p.86-89

IDLENESS
Woodward — *Way* p.14
, *Detestation of*
Dulles — *America* p.3-21

- *Laws*
  Wertenbaker — *Puritan* p.165-166
  Woodward — *Way* p.44-45

ILLEGITIMACY ("bastardy cases")
Spruill — *Women's* p.314-323

ILLITERACY
Wertenbaker — *First* p.254, 259

ILLNESS. *See* **Sickness**

IMMIGRANTS AND IMMIGRATION
See also **Colonies and colonists;**
names of localities; nationalities
Hawke — *U.S.* p.49-59
Kraus — *U.S. (1)* p.92-97
Smith — *17th* p.6-7, 9, 11, 63-89
- *Place of origin*
  Smith — *17th* p.78-79
- *Provision checklist (1630)*
  Demos — *Remarkable* p.42-43
, *Reasons for*
  Hawke — *U.S.* p.49-50
- *Social origins*
  Smith — *17th* p.64-89

IMMORALITY
See also **Punishment**
Holliday — *Woman's* p.278-286
- *Laws against*
  Spruill — *Women's* p.314-315
- *New England*
  Wertenbaker — *First* p.192-200
- *Reaction against code*
  Wertenbaker — *First* p.346
- *South*
  Wertenbaker — *First* p.200-207

IMPERIALISM
, *New (1650–70)*
  Hawke — *U.S.* p.148-154

IMPORTS. *See* **Exports and imports**

IMPRISONMENT. *See* **Prisons and prisoners**

INDENTURED SERVANTS. *See*
Servants, Indentured

INDEPENDENCE. *See* **Liberty**

"INDEPENDENTS" (Cromwell's religious group)
Willison — *Saints* p.10, 31, 49, 326-327, 333-334, 342, 473

"INDIAN BOWLS"
Earle — *Colonial* p.295

INDIAN TRAILS
Chitwood — *History (1)* p.387
Earle — *Customs* p.199, 205-206
Earle — *Home* p.329-330
Glubok — *Home* p.332-333
Langdon — *Everyday* p.241-242

INDIANS
See also names of tribes, individuals;
Indians subdivision, under following subjects: **Bible, Algonquin;
Books and reading; Brooms;
Byrd, William I; Canoes; Cemeteries; Churches; Corn; Eliot, John;
Football; Harvard College —
Indian Seminary; Hunt, Thomas,
Captain; Husking bees; Labadists; Maple sugar; Natick, Massachusetts; Oglethorpe, James
Edward; Pumpkins; Puritans;
Quakers: Smith, John, Captain;
Spoons; Trees —Debarking;
Trees — Felling; Weavers and
weaving; Williams, Roger**
Adams — *Album* p.6-7
Alderman — *Story. See* index p.183
Amer. Her. — *Pioneer. See* index
p.397
Amer. Her. — *Treasury* p.8-19
Bailyn — *New England* p.1, 5, 10-14
Beck — *Pilgrims. See* index p.87
Calverton — *Awake.* p.70-97
Craven — *Colonies* p.108-116
Craven — *Southern. See* index p.442
Dillon — *Pilgrims* p.43, 122, 128, 148,
150, 152-156, 159, 163-165, 168-171, 174-175, 195-196, 205, 218
Gill — *Mayflower. See* index p.203
Hawke — *Colonial* p.79-81; *See also*
index p.732-733
Hope — *Nation* p.64-65, 83-84, 123
Life — *New* p.8-27; *See also* index
p.174
Miller — *Colonial* p.248-289
Pomfret — *Founding. See* index p.376
Rutman — *Winthrop's. See* index
p.310

104

INDIANS (continued)

Scott — *Settlers* p.11-18
Smith — *17th*. *See* index p.232
Snell — *Wild* p.10, 42, 44-46, 54, 76, 90, 95, 98, 114, 118
Vaughan — *New* p.15-17, 58-65, 77-79, 97, 186; *See also* index p.424
Ver Steeg — *Formative* p.33-35
Wertenbaker — *First* p.231-232, 259, 308-311
Williams — *Demeter's*. *See* index under "Native Americans"
- *Agriculture*
  Chitwood — *History (1)* p.356-357
  Marshall — *Mayflower* p.142-143, 151-152
  Smith — *17th* p.23
- *Amusements*
  See also **Indians — Sports and games**
  Northey — *America* p.18-21
  Vaughan — *New* p.49-50
, *and Anglo-French conflict*
  See also **Indians — Dutch relations; Indians — English relations**
  Nettels — *Roots* p.359-362, 364, 368-372
, *and "civilization"*
  Axtell — *America* p.88-95
, *and Miles Standish*
  Dillon — *Pilgrim* p.176-181
- *Armament*
  Vaughan — *New* p.38-39
, *as neighbors*
  Lawrence — *New* p.34-43
- *Attempted voyage to England*
  Calverton — *Awake*. p.81-82
- *Balance of power*
  Ver Steeg — *Formative* p.154-155
- *Bark houses*
  Northey — *American* p.44-50
- *Benefactors*
  See also **Indians — Missions and missionaries**
  Marshall — *Mayflower* p.133-159
- *Betrayal*
  Calverton — *Awake*. p.79-80
- *Bush burning (New Netherland)*
  Axtell — *America* p.34-35
- *Calendars*
  Northey — *American* p.43

- *Cannibalism*
  Vaughan — *New* p.53, 58, 64, 141, 165
- *Cape Cod*
  Dillon — *Pilgrims* p.134-135, 138-141, 143-144, 146
  Vaughan — *New* p.23, 57, 65-67, 75
, *Captives of*
  Miller — *Colonial* p.257-289
  Morris — *Ency*. p.560
  - *Mary Richardson*
    Demos — *Remarkable* p.285-310
  - *Women*
    Leonard — *Dear* p.63, 110-112
- *Capture by European explorers*
  Marshall — *Mayflower* p.134
- *Carolinas*
  Starkey — *Land* p.226
- *Caves*
  Earle — *Home* p.138
- *Character*
  See also **Indians (various character traits)**
  Goodwin — *Colonial* p.132-133
  Vaughan — *New* p.25, 43-46
  - *Virginia*
    Axtell — *America* p.54-55
- *Children*
  Hawke — *U.S.* p.55-56
  Northey — *American* p.27-31
, *Christianizing of*. *See* **Indians — Missions and missionaries; Michaëlius, Jonas; Indians; "Praying"**
- *Clans*
  Nettels — *Roots* p.152
- *Clothing and dress*
  Hawke — *U.S.* p.54
  Northey — *American* p.10-17
  Vaughan — *New* p.47-48
- *Connecticut*
  See also **Connecticut Indians**
  Hope — *Nation* p.83
  Vaughan — *New* p.125, 130, 133-134, 138-143, 151-153, 156, 159, 164, 169, 172-174, 191, 196, 203-205, 207, 230-231
- *Cookery*
  See also **Indians — Food**
  Earle — *Home* p.131-136
  Hawke — *U.S.* p.56-57
  Northey — *American* p.53-55

- *Beans*
  Earle — *Home* p.145
- *Cooperation*
  Calverton — *Awake.* p.77-78
  Smith — *17th* p.15-60
- *Council*
  Nettels — *Roots* p.154
- *Crafts and craftsmanship*
  Hawke — *U.S.* p.58-59
- *Cruelty*
  Calverton — *Awake.* p.82-85
  Vaughan — *New* p.40-41, 64, 130, 133
- *Culture*
  Caffrey — *Mayflower* p.120-122
  Calverton — *Awake.* p.70-71
  Smith — *17th* p.33, 44, 56-59
- *Customs. See* **Indians — Life** (and related topics)
- *Dances and dancing*
  - *Corn*
    Earle — *Home* p.138
    - *Woodland Indians*
      Northey — *American* p.90-92
      - *Fish*
        Northey — *American* p.92
      - *Great Feather dance*
        Northey — *American* p.91-92
      - *Trotting*
        Northey — *American* p.92
      - *War*
        Northey — *American* p.92
- *Death penalty*
  Smith — *17th* p.45-46
- *Dedham, Mass.*
  Lockridge — *New* p.4, 59, 72, 83-84
- *Delaware*
  Calverton — *Awake.* p.367-368
- *Description*
  Amer. Her. — *Thirteen* p.40, 55, 58-59, 63, 67, 120, 132, 142-144, 164
  - *"Four best things"*
    Earle — *Home* p.304
- *Disputes*
  Calverton — *Awake.* p.85-89, 410-411
  Vaughan — *New* p.37-38, 40, 54-55, 109

- *Drums*
  Northey — *American* p.23-25
- *Dutch relations*
  Morris — *Ency.* p.44
  Starkey — *Land* p.141-142
- *Education*
  See also **Commissioners of the United Colonies; Indians — Schools**
  Craven — *Southern* p.132, 142-143
  Starkey — *Land* p.63
  Willison — *Saints* p.364, 388-389, 475-476
  , *Refusal of*
    Northey — *American* p.39-40
- *Endurance*
  Earle — *Home* p.137
- *English relations*
  Starkey — *Land* p.20-21
- *Families*
  See also names of families, e.g. **Algonquin; Iroquois; Muskogeans**
  Nettels — *Roots* p.152
- *Festivals*
  - *Woodland Indians*
    Northey — *American* p.83-84
    - *Corn*
      Northey — *American* p.85-92
    - *Harvest*
      Northey — *American* p.87
    - *Hunting feast for young*
      Northey — *American* p.71
    - *Planting*
      Northey — *American* p.85
    - *Tobacco*
      Northey — *American* p.89
    - *Wild strawberries*
      Northey — *American* p.88-89
- *"First Americans"*
  Folsom — *Give* p.9-10, 17, 22-23, 25, 34, 38, 41-42, 44-46, 48-49, 53, 75, 79-81, 88
  Hale — *Through* p.9-13
- *Fishing*
  Marshall — *Mayflower* p.145, 148-149

INDIANS (*continued*)
- *Virginia*
    Axtell — *America* p.57-58
- *Food*
    See also **Indians — Cookery;
    Indians — Fruit;** etc.
    Vaughan — *New* p.31-32, 327
    - *Storage*
        Northey — *American*
        p.55-62
    - *Woodland Indians*
        Northey — *American*
        p.51-71
- *Forest*
    Collins — *Story* p.15
- *Forts*
    Hawke — *U.S.* p.56
    Speare — *Life* p.84-85
- *French relations*
    Amer. Her. — *Thirteen* p.119-
    120, 124, 133, 193-195, 200-
    201
    Morris — *Ency.* p.59
- *Friendliness*
    Calverton — *Awake.* p.79-80, 85
    Northey — *American* p.8-9
- *Fruit*
    Northey — *American* p.58
- *Gentleness*
    Calverton — *Awake.* p.78-79
- *Gods*
    - *"Great Spirit" (Man in the sky;
    Man above)*
        Northey — *American* p.32
    - *"Oke" (chief god, devil)*
        Axtell — *America* p.62-66
- *Guerilla warfare*
    Hawke — *Colonial* p.279
- *Guns*
    Caffrey — *Mayflower* p.222-224,
    231-232
    Vaughan — *New* p.22, 27, 91, 95,
    197-198, 227, 330, 336
- *Headrights*
    Hawke — *Colonial* p.183
- *Hostility*
    Amer. Her. — *Thirteen* p.61-63,
    82, 128, 176, 201
    Marshall — *Mayflower* p.135-
    141, 153-155
- *Houses and moving*
    See also **Indians — Bark
    Houses; Wigwams**
    Earle — *Home* p.3-4
    Marshall — *Mayflower* p.141-142

Vaughan — *New* p.46-47
- *Virginia*
    Axtell — *America* p.55-56
- *Hunting and trapping*
    Marshall — *Mayflower* p.143,
    145, 147
    Northey — *American* p.65-71
    - *Virginia*
        Axtell — *America* p.58-59
- *Independence*
    Calverton — *Awake.* p.75-77
- *Justice, ideas of*
    Starkey — *Land* p.144
- *Labor*
    - *Division between wife and
    husband*
        Williams — *Demeter's* p.3,
        5-7
    - *Habits*
        Vaughan — *New* p.31-32,
        49-50
    - *Men's work*
        Marshall — *Mayflower* p.151
- *Lands*
    See also **Indians — Headrights**
    Amer. Her. — *Thirteen* p.104,
    106, 129, 135, 163, 166
    Dillon — *Pilgrims* p.156
    Vaughan — *New* p.33, 104-109,
    112, 116
    Willison — *Saints* p.391-392
    - *Defense of buying*
        Bailey — *American (1)* p.34-
        35
    - *Titles*
        Folsom — *Give* p.17-18, 33,
        46
- *Languages*
    Axtell — *America* p.70-71
    Beals — *John Eliot* p.119-120
    Smith — *17th* p.36, 38, 40-43, 54-
    55
    Vaughan — *New* p.59
- *Laws*
    , and authority
        Hawke — *U.S.* p.57-58
    , Ten
        Beals — *John Eliot* p.128
- *Library*
    Vaughan — *New* p.276-279
- *Life*
    See also **Indians;** related topics
    Hope — *Nation* p.16-18
    Marshall — *Mayflower* p.141-151
    Miller — *Colonial* p.248-256
    Nettels — *Roots* p.150-152

- *"Feast and famine"*
  Marshall — *Mayflower* p.149
, *of simplicity*
  Calverton — *Awake.* p.70-
  71, 74-76
- *Liquor*
  Calverton — *Awake.* p.87-88,
  354, 410
  Lawrence — *Not* p.153-155
  Starkey — *Land* p.146, 168
  Vaughan — *New* p.45, 70, 72,
  197, 219, 227, 230-232, 269,
  328
  - *Virginia*
    Axtell — *America* p.61-62
- *Maine*
  Beck — *Pilgrims* p.17, 34, 42
  Vaughan — *New* p.32, 52, 103,
  106, 202, 213-214, 303
- *Maps*
  - *Chesapeake region*
    Hawke — *Colonial* p.98
  - *Eastern U.S.*
    Nettels — *Roots* p.149
  - *Seventeenth century, early*
    Hawke — *Colonial* p.74-75
- *Marriages*
  Hawke — *U.S.* p.55-56
- *Massachusetts*
  Beck — *Pilgrims* p.42, 82
  Dillon — *Pilgrims* p.169, 178-180
  Gill — *Mayflower* p.92, 95, 99-
  100
  Morison — *Story* p.81, 93-95,
  126, 209
  Snell — *Wild* p.72-73, 99, 106,
  108, 110-111, 113-114
  Vaughan — *New. See* index
  p.425
  - *Tribe*
    Willison — *Pilgrim* p.150-
    151, 174-175, 201-207,
    215-223
    Willison — *Saints. See* index
    p.504
- *Massacres*
  Chitwood — *History (1)* p.65-66
  Craven — *Southern* p.232, 362-
  363
  - *Virginia*
    See also **Jamestown —
    Indians — Massacres
    (1622)**
    Dillon — *Pilgrims* p.172
    Pomfret — *Founding* p.41-42

- *Medicine*
  Marshall — *Mayflower* p.150-151
  Vaughan — *New* p.34-35
  Wertenbaker — *First* p.170
  - *"Medicine men." See* **Indians
    — Powwows**
- *Plants*
  Marshall — *Mayflower*
  p.150-151
- *Messages*
  Northey — *American* p.35-38
- *Migrations, seasonal*
  Vaughan — *New* p.30-31
- *Missions and missionaries*
  See also **Eliot, John; Indians,
  "Praying"; Michaëlius, Jonas**
  Amer. Her. — *Thirteen* p.121,
  128-129, 163-164
  Annals of America (1) p.92-94,
  180-183
  Calverton — *Awake.* p.94, 152
  Chitwood — *History (1)* p.451
  Craven — *Colonies* p.117-118,
  123
  Morris — *Ency.* p.36-37
  Nettels — *Roots* p.206, 209, 217-
  219
  Vaughan — *New* p.19-21, 24, 60-
  61, 232-233, 235-308
  Vaughan — *Puritan* p.261-267
  Wright — *Everyday* p.160
  - *Jesuits*
    Adams — *Album* p.35
  - *South*
    Craven — *Southern* p.77-78,
    80-82, 114n, 115, 192-
    193, 196, 231-233
- *Music*
  Calverton — *Awake.* p.92-93
  Howard — *Our* p.620-622
  Northey — *American* p.22-26
  - *Themes*
    Howard — *Our* p.236, 357-
    359, 381-383, 389, 407-
    408
  - *Virginia*
    Axtell — *America* p.61
- *Musical instruments*
  See also **Indians —** names of
  various instruments
  Northey — *American* p.23-25
- *Name, Origin of*
  Calverton — *Awake.* p.178-179
- *New England attitude*
  Calverton — *Awake.* p.51

INDIANS (*continued*)

- *New Netherland*
    Axtell — *American* p.144-145
    - *"Journal of New Netherland"*
    (1647)
        Amer. Her. — *Thirteen*
        p.142-143
- *New Sweden*
    Axtell — *America* p.181-184
- *Pennsylvania*
    Calverton — *Awake.* p.354-356
- *Physical welfare*
    Lawrence — *New* p.37, 41
- *Plague*
    Nettels — *Roots* p.157
    Starkey — *Land* p.58
- *Plains*
    Collins — *Story* p.16
- *Political organizations*
    Vaughan — *New* p.32-34, 294
- *Population*
    Craven — *Colonies* p.109-110
    Vaughan — *New* p.28-29, 52-54,
    329
    - *1620s*
        Hope — *Nation* p.18
- *Powwows (medicine men)*
    Beals — *John Eliot* p.79, 126-128
    Vaughan — *New* p.34-36, 250,
    257-258
, *"Praying"*
    Amer. Her. — *Pioneer* p.60-61,
    64
    Beals — *John Eliot. See* index
    p.191
    Folsom — *Give* p.33, 36, 40-42
    Miller — *First* p.36
    Vaughan — *Ne v* p.234-308, 346-
    347
    - *Plymouth*
        Morrison — *Story* p.243-244,
        249-250, 282-283
- *Rattles (musical instruments)*
    Northey — *American* p.24-25
- *Religion*
    See also **Indians — Gods; Mis-
    sions and missionaries;
    "Praying"**
    Axtell — *America* p.69-70
    Northey — *American* p.32-34
    Vaughan — *New* p.34-37, 61
    - *New Sweden*
        Axtell — *America* p.182-183
    - *Virginia*
        Axtell — *America* p.62-66

- *Reservations*
    Calverton — *Awake.* p.96-97
- *River tribes*
    Vaughan — *New* p.56-57, 125,
    134-135, 203-204, 216, 301-
    302
- *St. Lawrence*
    Annals of America (1) p.138b-
    138i
- *Scholarships refused*
    Northey — *American* p.39-40
- *Schools*
    Monroe — *Founding (1)* p.64
- *Segregation, Failure of*
    Hawke — *Colonial* p.183
- *Sex among*
    Calverton — *Awake.* p. 74-75
- *Slaves and slavery, Attempts for*
    Amer. Her. — *Thirteen* p.155,
    163, 182, 202
    Calverton — *Awake.* p.76, 76n-
    77, 125-126
    Craven — *Southern* p.358, 366,
    368, 385, 391n 402
    Furnas — *American* p.117, 119
    Miller — *First* p.144-147
    Vaughan — *New* p.32, 150, 189,
    199, 207, 212, 319, 332
    - *South*
        Craven — *Southern* p.358,
        366, 368, 385, 391n, 402
    - *Views of John Eliot*
        Beals — *John Eliot* p.103
- *Smoke signals*
    Northey — *American* p.35-37
- *South*
    Craven — *Southern. See* index
    p.442
- *South Carolina*
    Calverton — *Awake.* p.88
- *Spoons*
    Earle — *Home* p.88
- *Sports and games*
    See also **Balls (games), Indian**
    Northey — *American* p.18-21
    - *"Game of the bowl"*
        Northey — *American* p.19-
        21
    - *"Hoop and pole game"*
        Northey — *American* p.20
    - *"Peach-stone game"*
        Northey — *American* p.19-
        21
- *Squaws. See* **Indians — Women**
- *Taxes, opposition to*
    Beals — *John Eliot* p.142-143

- *Temperament*
  Nettels — *Roots* p.151-152
- *"Ten commandments"*
  Beck — *John Eliot* p.128
- *Towns*
  Vaughan — *New* p.38-39
  , *and buildings*
  Hawke — *U.S.* p.56
- *Trade*
  See also **Byrd, William I;**
  Plymouth — Indian trade;
  Wampum
  Amer. Her. — *Thirteen* p.34, 66,
  74, 97, 118-120, 135, 163, 193,
  201
  Craven — *Southern. See* index
  p.442
  Marshall — *Mayflower* p.161-163
  Vaughan — *New* p.6, 52, 62, 98,
  105-109, 125, 197, 211-234,
  327-329
  - *South*
    Craven — *Southern. See*
    index p.442
  - *South Carolina*
    Craven — *Colonies* p.135-
    136, 177
  - *Virginia*
    Axtell — *America* p.61
    Craven — *Colonies* p.114-
    115, 135
- *Treaties*
  Collins — *Story* p.60
  Dillon — *Pilgrims* p.155-156
  - *Plymouth*
    Gill — *Mayflower* p.82-85
  - *Virginia*
    Smith — *17th* p.52, 55, 178
- *Tribes*
  See also **Indians** — names of
  localities; names of tribes
  Christensen — *Delaware* p.10
  Nettels — *Roots* p.152-154
- *Views from abroad*
  Axtell — *America* p.53-95
- *Views of Robert Beverley*
  Miller — *Colonial* p.248-256
- *Virginia*
  Annals of America (1) p.138a-
  138g
  Goetzmann — *Colonial* p.109-
  113
  Hawke — *Colonial* p.101, 103-
  104, 182-184, 243, 245, 249
  Starkey — *Land* p.197-198
  Wish — *Society (1)* p.75-76

- *Government*
  Axtell — *America* p.66-69
- *Names*
  Axtell — *America* p.56
- *Ornamentation (adornment)*
  Axtell — *America* p.54-55
- *Priests*
  Axtell — *America* p.63-66
- *Relations*
  Pomfret — *Founding* p.53-
  54, 69-70
- *Sacrifices of children*
  Axtell — *America* p.64-65
- *Tools*
  Axtell — *America* p.57
- *Travel*
  Earle — *Home* p.325
- *Uprisings*
  Hawke — *Colonial* p.182-
  183
- *Views of John Smith*
  Axtell — *America* p.53-69
  Miller — *Colonial* p.221-230
  Starkey — *Land* p.37-38
- *Wars*
  See also names of wars
  Amer. Her. — *Pioneer* p.64-65
  Caffrey — *Mayflower* p.261-265,
  270-274
  - *Histories*
    Morison — *Intellect.* p.183-
    194
  - *Virginia*
    Axtell — *America* p.59-61
- *Women*
  See also **Chickahominy Con-**
  federation; Indians —
  Women; "Squaw Sachem"
  of Massachusetts; "Matri-
  archate." (Iroquois Indians);
  Women — Indian relations
  Calverton — *Awake.* p.71-75, 85
  Earle — *Two cent. (1)* p.127-128
  Goodwin — *Colonial* p.129-130
  Hawke — *U.S.* p.18-20, 29, 54-55
  Marshall — *Mayflower* p.151
  Smith — *17th* p.57
  Spruill — *Women* p.177-178
  Vaughan — *New* p.45, 49-50, 89
  Williams — *Demeter's. See* index
  under Native American women
  , *as workers*
  Nettels — *Roots* p.151
  , *Friendship to*
  Leonard — *Dear* p.108

INDIANS (continued)
- *Views of Edward Johnson*
  Williams — *Demeter's* p.10
- *Virginia*
  Axtell — *America* p.54-56
- *Woodland*
  See also **Indians — Dances and dancing; — Festivals; Food; Husking bees; New Year's Day**
  Northey — *American* p.41-103
- *Travel*
  Northey — *American* p.75-78

INDIGO
Craven — *Southern* p.119, 141, 316, 336-337, 347, 355-356
Earle — *Home* p.193
- *South*
  Craven — *Southern* p.119, 141, 316, 336-337, 347, 355-356

"INDIVIDUAL ENTERPRISE"
Nettels — *Roots* p.222-229
Rozwenc — *Making (1)* p.37-38

INDIVIDUALISM
Dow — *Domestic* p.25-26
Hope — *Nation* p.92
Nettels — *Roots* p.454-455
- *Restraints*
  Nettels — *Roots* p.456-457

INDUSTRY
See also **Artisans; Business; Commerce; Crafts and craftsmanship; Manufacturing;** names of individual industries, etc.
Chitwood — *History (1)* p.371-385
Collins — *Story* p.54-55
Nettels — *Roots* p.242-250
- *Middle Colonies*
  Jernegan — *American* p.239
- *New England*
  Jernegan — *American* p.171-174
- *South*
  Jernegan — *American* p.91-93

INEQUALITY. See **Classes; Intolerance**

INFANT MORTALITY
Spruill — *Women's* p.47

INFLATION
Willison — *Pilgrim* p.445-446

INGHAM, MARY
Williams — *Demeter's* p.137-138

INGLE, RICHARD
Morris — *Ency.* p.29

INGOLDESBY, RICHARD
Rothbard — *Conceived (1)* p.444-447, 474, 476

INHERITANCE
Demos — *Remarkable* p.167-173

INK
Glubok — *Home* p.159-160
Rawson — *When* p.152

"INNER LIGHT" (Penn's religion)
Jernegan — *American* p.209

INNS AND INNKEEPERS
See also **Taverns;** names of inns and innkeepers
Rutman — *Winthrop's. See* index p.310
- *Architecture*
  Morrison — *Early* p.92

INOCULATION, SMALLPOX
See also **Smallpox**
- *Views of Cotton Mather*
  Miller — *Colonial* p.118-131
- *Views of Increase Mather*
  Vaughan — *Puritan* p.285-287

INSECTS
Furnas — *Americans* p.22

INSTRUMENTS
- *Philosophical, mathematical and scientific*
  Drepperd — *Pioneer* p.91

INTELLECTUAL LIFE. See **Books and reading; Colleges and universities; Culture; Drama; Education; Libraries; Literature; Music; etc.**

INTERIOR DECORATION. See **Furniture; Houses — Interiors**

INTERMARRIAGE
Bailyn — *New England* p.135-138, 180
Vaughan — *New* p.208-209

INTOLERANCE
See also **Plymouth; Puritans**
Chitwood — History (1) p.439-440
Leonard — Dear p.117
Wertenbaker — Puritan. See index
p.355
- Maryland
Bailey — American (1) p.11-14
Jernegan — American p.104
Ver Steeg — Formative p.216
- Religious minorities
Morris — Ency. p.37
- Views of Nathaniel Ward
Miller — Colonial p.175-178
- Views of Thomas Morton
Annals of America (1) p.125-129

INVENTIONS AND INVENTORS
See also names of inventions and
inventors
Wright — Cultural p.215
- First — Women
Earle — Home p.138-139, 260

INVENTORIES
Dow — Every p.34-38, 41-43
Goodwin — Colonial p. 290-291
Marshall — Mayflower p.114, 117
Wertenbaker — First p.40-41
- Boston
Dow — Every p.258-262
- Maryland
Wertenbaker — First p.40-41
- New England
Dow — Domestic p.36-48
- Rhode Island
- Typical estate, Providence
(1682)
Demos — Remarkable
p.122-124
- Salem, Mass.
Dow — Domestic p.31
Dow — Every p.262-283

IPSWICH, MASSACHUSETTS
See also **Agawam, Massachusetts**
Dow — Every p.32-33, 35
Rutman — Winthrop's p.42, 75, 144,
174, 176, 178, 220n, 235n, 249,
250n, 264
- Petition for leader (1637)
Demos — Remarkable p.204-205

IRIS
, as dye
Earle — Home p.193-194

IRISH
See also **Scotch-Irish**
Hall — Religious p.122-126, 142
Wright — Cultural p.65-66

IRON INDUSTRY
See also **Company of Undertakers
for Ironworks; Saugus, Mass. —
Ironworks**
Bailyn — New England. See index
p.244
Chitwood — History (1) p.379-380
Craven — Southern p.48, 56, 68, 70,
85, 102, 109, 140-141, 312, 314
Furnas — Americans p.29, 32-33
Langdon — Everyday p.158-162
Nettels — Roots p.247-248
- First foundry (Lynn, Mass., 1643)
Gould — Early p.67
- Household articles See also **Irons;**
names of articles
Earle — Customs p.142
Rawson — When p.8
- Jamestown, Va.
Adams — Album p.22
- Middle Colonies
Jernegan — American p.224
- Plymouth
Morison — Story p.203, 206-208,
226
- Saugus, Mass.
National — History. p.82-85
- South
Craven — Southern p.48, 56, 68,
70, 102, 312, 314
- Virginia
Craven — Southern p.85, 109,
141
Langdon — Everyday p.158-159

IRONING ("smoothing")
Gould — Early p.117-120

IRONS
Gould — Early p.118-120
, Crimping
Gould — Early p.121

IROQUOIS INDIANS
See also **"Great Lake" (of the Iroquois);** names of tribes
Craven — Colonies p.107, 124-126,
134-135, 205-206, 230
Greene — Provincial p.111-113, 120,
129-132, 134

IROQUOIS INDIANS (*continued*)

Hawke — *Colonial* p.79-80; *See also* index p.733
Nettels — *Roots* p.152
Snell — *Wild* p.95, 98, 114
Vaughan — *New* p.29-30, 52, 55
, *and Samuel de Champlain*
   Nettels — *Roots* p.206-207
, *as "Matriarchate"*
   Williams — *Demeter's* p.354
- *Breakfasts*
   Northey — *American* p.62-63
- *Council*
   Northey — *America* p.97-100
- *Dutch relations*
   Nettels — *Roots* p.202, 207, 225
- *English relations*
   Amer. Her. — *Thirteen* p.119-120, 166, 193-195, 197, 200
   Chitwood — *History (1)* p.176
- *"Five Nations"*
   Fisher — *Men (2)* p.89-99
   Northey — *American* p.93-101
- *French relations*
   Amer. Her. — *Thirteen* p.124, 196, 200
- *Fur trade*
   Nettels — *Roots* p.225, 359-362, 369
- *"Long house"*
   Northey — *America* p.100-101
- *War*
   Morris — *Ency.* p.60, 62

"ISLE OF ERRORS" (Rhode Island)
Fisher — *Men (1)* p.303

IYANOUGH (Indian)
Caffrey — *Mayflower* p.149, 173, 180
Willison — *Saints* p.212-213, 218, 229, 316, 424, 467

J

JABEZ WILDER HOUSE (South Hingham, Mass.)
Morrison — *Early* p.67-68

JACKNIVES. *See* Knives

JACKS (jugs)
Earle — *Colonial* p.282
Earle — *Home* p.64
Gould — *Early* p.71

JACOBSEN, MARCUS ("Long Finn")
Christensen — *Delaware* p.56

JAILS. *See* Prisons and prisoners

JAMES I (King of England)
Acheson — *America's* p.82-84
Alderman — *Story* p.7, 21, 81-82
Amer. Her. — *Thirteen* p.48, 70-71n, 75, 80-82, 88, 106
Caffrey — *Mayflower* p.14, 17, 21, 24, 39, 47, 247
Dillon — *Pilgrim. See* index p.246
Leynse — *Preced. See* index p.282
Morison — *Story* p.15, 44, 72-73, 120, 157, 179
Phillips — *First* p.187-193
Rozwenc — *Making (1)* p.19, 26, 42, 53-56
Willison — *Pilgrim* p.50, 53, 57, 61, 131n-132n
Willison — *Saints. See* index p.503

JAMES II (King of England)
Alderman — *Story* p.31-32, 34, 54, 63, 77, 88, 120
Amer. Her. — *Thirteen* p.158, 162, 166, 173, 193, 196-197
Folsom — *Give* p.54, 64, 66-67, 73
Johnston — *Conn.* p.85-86, 88-89, 94-95, 98
Morison — *Story* p.285-287
Rothbard — *Conceived (1). See* index p.525
Willison — *Saints* p.403-405, 455

JAMESTOWN, VIRGINIA
See also subjects, with Jamestown (subdivision), as follows: **"Bowls" (game); Bricks; Cavaliers; Cemeteries; Drinking vessels; Dutch; Ginseng; Glass; Iron industry; Log cabins; Mulberry; Persimmons; Pocahontas; Potatoes; Powhatan; Profanity; Sassafras; Tableware; Tobacco**
Acheson — *America's* p.69-78
Adams — *Album* p.12-30
Alderman — *Story* p.7, 9-11, 16-17
Amer. Her. — *Thirteen* p.48, 59-60, 71-72, 74-75, 78-82, 85
Amer. Her. — *Treasury* p.21-40
Annals of America (1) p.232b
Bailey — *America (1)* p.7-11
Carman — *History (1)* p.27-28
Collins — *Story* p.33-34

Craven — *Southern* p.60-92; *See also* index p.443
Folsom — *Give* p.8-10, 44, 47
Furnas — *American* p.30, 49-53, 57
Gill — *Mayflower* p.32, 51-52, 65, 97-98
Hawke — *Colonial* p.89-94; *See also* index p.734
Hawke — *U.S.* p.63-65
Kraus — *U.S. (1)* p.38-46
Leonard — *Dear* p.42-46, 109, 121
Leynse — *Preced.* p.30-31, 211, 228
Life — *New* p.37, 49-50, 52-56, 62, 64, 95
Marshall — *Mayflower* p.22, 24, 177
Morison — *Oxford* p.50-54
Morris — *Ency.* p.26
National — *History.* p.47-61
Pomfret — *Founding* p.27-35, 378
Rozwenc — *Making (1)* p.23-26
Smith — *17th.* See index p.232
Snell — *Wild.* See index p.201
Speare — *Life* p.6-8
Starkey — *Land* p.12-26, 65-66, 84, 204, 206
Tunis — *Colonial* p.21-22
Willison — *Saints* p.110, 139, 465, 467
Wright — *Everyday* p.24-26, 38, 40, 43-44, 55, 70-71, 157
- *Adultery*
 Phillips — *First* p.105
- *Anglicans*
 Phillips — *First* p.103-104
- *Bachelors*
 Spruill — *Women's* p.8-10
- *Charters*
 Chitwood — *History (1)* p.50, 59-60
- *Church*
 Wertenbaker — *First* p.293
- *Crimes and criminals*
 Phillips — *First* p.104-105
- *Crops*
 Phillips — *First* p.79
- *Deaths, Causes of*
 Miller — *First* p.238-239
- *End of company control*
 Morris — *Ency.* p.26-27
- *Epidemics*
 Phillips — *First* p.78
 Wertenbaker — *First* p.178-179
- *Featherbeds*
 Phillips — *First* p.125
- *Founding*
 Chitwood — *History (1)* p.53-54

- *Government, representative*
 Chitwood — *History (1)* p.64
- *Hardships*
 Bailey — *American (1)* p.7-9
 Chitwood — *History (1)* p.54-55, 57-59
- *Houses*
 Adams — *Album* p.24-25
 Langdon — *Everyday* p.5-7, 14
 Morrison — *Early* p.135-138
 Spruill — *Women's* p.20-21
 Wertenbaker — *First* p.283-286, 290
- *Hunting and agriculture*
 Phillips — *First* p.104
- *Hygiene*
 Wertenbaker — *First* p.166-167
- *Indians*
 See also **Chickahominy Indians; Pocahontas; Powhatan**
 Phillips — *First* p.75
 Starkey — *Land* p.20
 - *Massacres*
  Adams — *Album* p.22
  Bailey — *American (1)* p.10-11
  Collins — *Story* p.37
  Craven — *Southern* p.146-147, 161-162
  Life — *New p.55, 62*
  Starkey — *Land* p.64-66, 74-75
- *Jail*
 Phillips — *First* p.105
- *Laws and decrees*
 Phillips — *First* p.105-106
- *Legislature, First colonial*
 - *Views of John Pory*
  Annals of America (1) p.40-46
- *Life*
 Hope — *Nation* p.61-63
- *Lighting*
 Phillips — *First* p.145-146
- *Manufactures*
 Wertenbaker — *First* p.18-19
, *Military*
 Chitwood — *History (1)* p.62-64
 Phillips — *First* p.104
- *Money*
 Adams — *Album* p.19
- *Private enterprise*
 Phillips — p.104
- *Religion*
 Phillips — *First* p.103-104

JAMESTOWN, VIRGINIA (*continued*)
- *Restoration*
  Adams — *Album* p.24
- *Slaves and slavery*
  Chitwood — *History (1)* p.64-65
  Adams — *Album* p.20
- *Sports and games*
  Phillips — *First* p.106
- *Starvation (1608-10)*
  Annals of America (1) p.21-31
  Bailey — *American (1)* p.9-10
  Chitwood — *History (1)* p.60-61
  Hawke — *Colonial* p.95-96
  Hawke — *U.S.* p.68-70
- *Statehouses*
  Wertenbaker — *First* p.292
- *Surrender*
  Collins — *Story* p.38
- *Taverns*
  Wertenbaker — *First* p.300-301
- *Trials of leader*
  Demos — *remarkable* p.57-67
- *Wives brought over*
  Chitwood — *History (1)* p.65
  Hope — *Nation* p.63
  Spruill — *Women's* p.8-10
  Starkey — *Land* p.70
- *Women*
  Furnas — *Americans* p.52-53
  Leonard — *Dear* p.121-122
  Phillips — *First* p.87, 102-103
  Miller — *First* p.27-29
  , *First in Virginia*
    Spruill — *Women's* p.1-2
  , *Suffering of*
    Spruill — *Women's* p.4-5

JANEWAY, JAMES
Glubok — *Home* p.304-305

JANSEN BROTHERS
Hale — *Through* p.85-91

JAQUET, JEAN PAUL
Christensen — *Delaware* p.49-51

JEFFREYS, HERBERT
Craven — *Colorado* p.146, 150-151, 153

JENNEY, JOHN
Marshall — *Mayflower* p.171
Willison — *Saints* p.90, 236, 322, 329, 447, 456

JENNEY, SARAH CAREY
Willison — *Saints* p.236, 322, 447

"JEREMIADS" (moralistic sermons)
Miller — *First* p.267-268

JERKINS (jackets)
Earle — *Two cent. (1)* p.164-175

JERSEYS. *See* **New Jersey**

JESUITS
Amer. Her. — *Pioneer* p.11, 26-27
Chitwood — *History (1)* p.302-303
- *Controversy*
  Chitwood — *History (1)* p.86-87
- *Endurance of tortures*
  See also **Jogues, Isaac, Father**
  Bailey — *American (1)* p.43-46

JEWELRY
See also names of jewelry; **Funerals — Jewelry**
Earle — *Two cent. (1)* p.72-73
Glubok — *Home* p.274-275
Spruill — *Women's* p.125-126

JEWS
See also names of individuals
Amer. Her. — *Thirteen* p.128, 165
Bridenbaugh — *Cities* p.94-95, 101-102, 104
Carman — *History (1)* p.92
Chitwood — *History (1)* p.338-339
Dillon — *Pilgrims* p.25, 88-89, 101
Folsom — *Give* p.24-27, 53, 65-66, 70, 88
Furnas — *Americans* p.95
Leonard — *Dear* p. 392
Morris — *Ency.* p.548
Ver Steeg — *Formative* p.214
Wish — *Society (1)* p.91-92, 94
- *Carolinas*
  Starkey — *Land* p.222
- *Delaware*
  Calverton — *Awake.* p.369
- *New Amsterdam*
  Starkey — *Land* p.165-166
  - *Exclusion from military service (1655)*
    Annals of America (1) p.221
- *Rhode Island*
  Alderman — *Story* p.100

JOB OF BOONDA (learned Negro)
Calverton — *Awake.* p.273

JOGUES, ISAAC, FATHER
- *Endurance of Jesuit tortures*
  Bailey — *American (1)* p.43-46
- *Views on New Netherland*
  Axtell — *America* p.141-145

JOHN WARD HOUSE (Salem, Mass., 1684)
Morrison — *Early* p.62-64

JOHNNYCAKES
See also **Bannocks**
Leonard — *Dear* p.142
Woodward — *Way* p.56

JOHNSON, ARABELLA (ARBELLA), LADY
Gill — *Mayflower* p.127-129
Starkey — *Land* p.5-6, 9-10, 78
Williams — *Demeter's* p.29

JOHNSON, EDWARD
Bailyn — *New England* p.30, 74, 105, 108-109
Rutman — *Winthrop's* p.119, 186, 188-189, 220, 245, 262n-263, 263n
Smith — *17th* p.199, 204-205, 218
Wertenbaker — *First* p.52, 66, 91, 112, 242, 248-249, 283-284
Wertenbaker — *Puritan* p.89-90, 193, 197, 201-202, 204, 208-209
, *on Anne Hutchinson*
  Williams — *Demeter's* p.119
, *on Churches of Christ*
  Vaughan — *Puritan* p.74-78
, *on Sarah Simmes*
  Williams — *Demeter's* p.75
, *on women gathering food*
  Williams — *Demeter's* p.43-45
- *"The Pequot war"*
  Miller — *Colonial* p.244-247
- *"Sions [sic] saviour in New England" (1654)*
  Annals of America (1) p.217-219
- *"Wonder working providers"*
  Goetzmann — *Colonial* p.160-169

JOHNSON, FRANCIS
Leynse — *Preced.* p.82, 96, 146-150, 161-162, 207-209, 215, 228-229
Willison — *Pilgrim* p.32-34
Willison — *Saints. See* index p.503

JOHNSON, GEORGE
Leynse — *Preced.* p.148-150, 161
Willison — *Saints* p.34, 64-67, 457, 463

JOHNSON, ISAAC
Rutman — *Winthrop's. See* index p.311
Willison — *Pilgrim* p.326-327

JOHNSON, THOMAS H.
Murdock — *Literature* p.153, 168, 170, 217, 219

JOHNSON, THOMASINE BOYES
Earle — *Two cent. (1)* p.52-59
Willison — *Saints* p.66-67, 70, 79, 457

JOINERS
Tunis — *Craftsmen* p.26-28

JOLLIET, LOUIS
Amer. Her. — *Pioneer* p.27

JONES, CHRISTOPHER, CAPTAIN
Caffrey — *Mayflower. See* index p.388
Dillon — *Pilgrims* p.124, 141, 148-149, 152-153, 158
Gill — *Mayflower* p.44, 60-61, 68-70, 72, 74, 78, 80, 82, 85-86
Hills — *History (1)* p.16, 18, 23-25, 51, 53, 64, 67, 70-71, 78
Hills — *History (2)* p.203, 213-214
Leynse — *Preced.* p.244-245, 247, 250, 255, 258-259, 261
Marble — *Women* p.5, 72
Marshall — *Mayflower* p.32, 49, 134-135
Morison — *Story* p.31-32, 36-39, 42-43, 48-49, 62-66
Willison — *Pilgrim* p.84n, 96, 119, 127, 130, 139, 184
Willison — *Saints. See* index p.503

JONES, HUGH
Wertenbaker — *First* p.45, 263-264

JONES, MARGARET
See also **Winthrop, John, on Margaret Jones**
Leonard — *Dear* p.382
Williams — *Demeter's* p.135
Willison — *Pilgrim* p.430-431

JONES, THOMAS
Willison — *Pilgrim* p.183-184, 485n
Willison — *Saints* p.211

JONES FAMILY
Hills — *History (2)*. See index p.263

JONES RIVER, MASSACHUSETTS
Willison — *Saints* p.159, 313, 338,
410, 418, 428

JORESEY, SARAH
Leonard — *Dear* p.56

JOSSELYN, JOHN
- *"An account of two voyages to New
England, 1674"*
Amer. Her. — *Thirteen* p.149-150
- *on Maine*
Axtell — *American* p.101-107

JOURNEYMEN
Tunis — *Craftsmen* p.15

JOY, GEORGE
Morison — *Intellect.* p.226-227

JUDGES
- *Laymen*
Miller — *First* p.263

JUDICIARY
- *Massachusetts*
Dow — *Every* p.200-201

JUGS
Earle — *Customs* p.137-138
- *Stoneware*
Earle — *Home* p.98

JURIES
Rutman — *Winthrop's* p.43, 64, 173-
174, 233, 235-236

JUSTICES OF THE PEACE
Craven — *Southern* p.167-170, 285-
286, 288n, 293
Ver Steeg — *Formative* p.70-71
- *Origins, Virginia*
Craven — *Southern* p.167-170
- *South*
- *Responsibilities*
Craven — *Southern* p.285-
286
, *Title of*
Craven — *Southern* p.293

K

KALM, PEHR
, *on New Sweden*
Axtell — *American* p.177-186

KALMAR NYCKEL (ship)
Christensen — *Delaware* p.26-28

KATTENANIT (Indian)
Beals — *John Eliot* p.173-175

KEAYNE, ROBERT
Bailyn — *New England* p.35-39, 41-
44, 70, 87, 97, 102, 110-111, 122,
134, 138, 209
Bridenbaugh — *Cities* p.131
Rutman — *Winthrop's*. See index
p.311
- *"Apologia" (Economics)*
Vaughan — *Puritan* p.176-179
- *Case, 1639 (Fair prices, excess
profits)*
Bridenbaugh — *Cities* p.49-50

KECOUGHTON INDIANS
Starkey — *Land* p.13, 28, 32

KEITH, GEORGE
Sweet — *Religious* p.59

KELPIUS, JOHN
Calverton — *Awake.* p.199, 200n

**KEMBLE, SARAH. See KNIGHT, SARAH
KEMBLE**

KENDALL, GEORGE, CAPTAIN
Phillips — *First* p.63, 78, 81

**KENNEBEC RIVER SETTLEMENT
(Maine)**
Bailyn — *New England* p.14, 24-25,
28, 58
Morison — *Story* p.112, 134, 137, 154,
165-166, 204, 218, 288
Snell — *Wild* p.73, 76-77
Willison — *Pilgrim* p.97, 286, 298,
310, 352, 356, 391-392, 445
Willison — *Saints*. See index p.503

KENT ISLAND
Alderman — *Story* p.85-86
Craven — *Southern* p.173, 196-198,
202-203, 250, 261, 303, 369

KEPLER, JOHANNES
Morison — *Intellect.* p.245-248, 250-251, 253-254

KETTLES
Holliday — *Woman's* p.108

KIAWAH INDIANS
Snell — *Wild* p.155

KIDD, WILLIAM, CAPTAIN
Fisher — *Men (2)* p.279-283
Langdon — *Everyday* p.221-223
Nettels — *Roots* p.377-378

KIDNAPPING
Vaughan — *New* p.9, 15-16, 59-60, 65, 133-134, 142, 200

KIEFT (KIEFFT), WILLIAM
Amer. Her. — *Thirteen* p.63, 132-133, 142
Hawke — *Colonial* p.219
Pomfret — *Founding* p.82, 287-288, 291-292
Rothbard — *Conceived (1)* p.302-315, 319
Starkey — *Land* p.137-138, 142-149, 153

KIERSTEDE, SARAH, MADAME
Leonard — *Dear* p.56, 112-113

KING GEORGE'S WAR
Collins — *Story* p.89

KING PHILIP'S WAR
See also **"Great Swamp Fight";
Philip, King (Indian); Plymouth —
King Philip's War**
Amer. Her. — *Pioneer* p.60, 63-65
Amer. Her. — *Thirteen* p.144, 162-164
Caffrey — *Mayflower* p.258, 280, 301
Chitwood — *History (1)* p.140-141
Craven — *Colonies* p.107-108, 116-124, 128, 166
Demos — *Little* p.15-16, 175
Gill — *Mayflower* p.146-147
Hawke — *Colonial* p.157, 251-256, 260, 265, 273; 302-303, 307, 331
Jernegan — *American* p.150-152
Kraus — *U.S. (1)* p.91-92
Morison — *Intellect.* p.39, 97, 183-197, 228-230
Morison — *Oxford* p.107-111

Morison — *Story* p.160, 165, 168, 227-229, 232, 238, 245, 251, 254-255, 258-279, 281-284
Morris — *Ency.* p.38-39
Rothbard — *Conceived (1)* p.344-354, 357, 373, 380, 418
Scott — *Settlers* p.42, 58
Smith — *17th* p.25, 211-212
Vaughan — *New* p.62, 194, 229-230, 232, 234, 284, 287, 292, 295, 298, 310-314, 324, 330, 335
Willison — *Pilgrim* p.414, 523-526
Willison — *Saints.* See index p.503
-*Causes and results*
Hawke — *U.S.* p.194-195
- *New England maps*
Hawke — *Colonial* p.252
- *Views of Increase Mather*
Goetzmann — *Colonial* p.200

KING WILLIAM'S WAR
Amer. Her. — *Thirteen* p.193-197, 200-201
Chitwood — *History (1)* p.307-309
Greene — *Provincial* p.119-134
Hawke — *Colonial* p.268, 321-329, 334, 337
Hawke — *U.S.* p.250-254
Morison — *Intellect.* p.88, 207-208
Morison — *Story* p.288-289
Rozwenc — *Making (1)* p.108
- *Aftermath*
Starkey — *Land* p.210

KING'S COMMISSIONERS (1664-1666)
Morris — *Ency.* p.38

KINGSBURY, MRS. JOSEPH
Williams — *Demeter's* p.120

KINSHIP
Bailyn — *New England* p.35-36, 79-80, 82, 87-91

"KITCHEN JUNKETS" (parties)
Rawson — *When* p.92-93

KITCHEN UTENSILS
See also **Pilgrims — Kitchen utensils; Plymouth — Kitchen utensils;** names of utensils, materials
Earle — *Colonial* p.280-284
Earle — *Home* p.56
Glubok — *Home* p.29-30
Gould — *Early* p.66-71, 76

KITCHEN UTENSILS (*continued*)
Langdon — *Everyday* p.21
Marshall — *Mayflower* p.99
-*Metals*
  Earle — *Customs* p.142

KITCHENS
Adams — *Album* p.88-89
Earle — *Home* p.52
Hope — *Nation* p.89-90
Morrison — *Early* p.47-48
Lawson — *When* p.10-12
- *Plymouth*
  Adams — *Album* p.52
  Demos — *Little* p.33, 47
- *Poetry*
  Earle — *Home* p.73-75
- *South*
  Goodwin — *Colonial* p.29-30
- *Virginia*
  Spruill — *Women's* p.25-26

KLEIN, HERBERT S.
, *on Virginia's institutions*
  Goetzmann — *Colonial* p.85-96

KNIGHT, EDGAR W.
Morison — *Intellect.* p.34-35, 58

KNIGHT, SARAH KEMBLE, MADAME
Brooks — *Dames* p.75-101

KNITTING
Earle — *Home* p.190, 201, 261-262
Glubok — *Home* p.225-226
Leonard — *Dear* p.169
Rawson — *When* p.119-121

KNIVES
Gould — *Early* p.88
- *Jackknives*
  Earle — *Home* p.307-308
  Glubok — *Home* p.194-105, 212-213
- *Plymouth*
  Demos — *Little* p.41

KNOCKERS
Earle — *Home* p.29

KUYTER, JOACHIM
Rothbard — *Conceived (1)* p.208-210, 313

L

LABADIE, JEAN DE
Calverton — *Awake.* p.195-196

LABADISTS
See also **Dankers, Jasper; Sluyter, Peter**
Calverton — *Awake.* p.194-198
Earle — *Home* p.118-119
- *Visit to Indians (1679–80)*
  Axtell — *America* p.88-95
- *Women*
  Calverton — *Awake.* p.197-198

LABOR
See also **Apprentices; Servants; Slaves and slavery;** types of labor
Miller — *First* p.143-145
Morris — *Ency.* p.517
Rutman — *Winthrop's. See* index p.311
Ver Steeg — *Formative* p.186-189
Wertenbaker — *First. See* index p.347
Wish — *Society (1)* p.7, 50-51, 67-69, 97
, *Family*
  Adams — *Album* p.90
, *Free*
  Chitwood — *History (1)* p.339-340
, *Gospel of*
  Wright — *Cultural* p.23-30
- *Itinerant workers*
  Gould — *Early* p.142
- *Massachusetts*
  Calverton — *Awake.* p.127-128
- *New England*
  Jernegan — *American* p.170
  Wertenbaker — *First* p.65, 68-69
- *South*
  - *Classes*
    Jernegan — *American* p.96-97
  - *Problems*
    Jernegan — *American* p.86-88
  - *Villages*
    Bridenbaugh — *Cities* p.48-49

LACE MAKING
Glubok — *Home* p.227
, *Black*
  Earle — *Two cent. (1)* p.77-78

LADDERS. *See* **Plymouth — Ladders**

LADIES. *See* **Women**

LADIES' BOOKS. *See* **Books and reading — Women**

LADIES CALLING **(authority on nature & duties of women)**
Spruill — *Women's* p.213-215

LAKE, MARGARET
Smith — *Colonial* p.61-62, 207-208
- *Clothing and dress*
Smith — *Colonial* p.76-77

LAMBERTON, GEORGE, CAPTAIN
Pomfret — *Bounding* p.260, 267-268, 270, 293-294

LAMPS
See also **Betty lamps; Phoebe lamps**
Earle — *Customs* p.125
Earle — *Home* p.43-47
Leonard — *Dear* p.98
- *Bull's-eye*
Earle — *Home* p.45
- *Pilgrims*
Marshall — *Mayflower* p.105-107

LANCASTER, MASSACHUSETTS
Vaughan — *New* p.235-236

LANCASTERIAN SYSTEM (punishment)
Glubok — *Home* p.134-135

LAND, WILLIAM
Wertenbaker — *Puritan* 27, 32-34, 296

LAND
See also **Headrights; Plymouth — Land; "Walking Purchase"**
Acheson — *America's* p.95-100
Adams — *Provincial* p.12-14
Carman — *History (1)* p.51-55, 57
Craven — *Southern. See* index p.443
Hawke — *Colonial. See* index p.737
Nettels — *Roots* p.329-330
Rutman — *Winthrop's. See* index p.311
Vaughan — *New* p.30-31, 152, 297
Ver Steeg — *Formative* p.54-58, 60-62

- *Carolinas*
Craven — *Southern* p.325-328, 330-333, 338-339, 346, 348-350
- *Dedham, Mass.*
Lockridge — *New* p.8-10, 17, 70-72, 82-83
- *Grants*
- *Map (1606, 1609, 1620)*
Hawke — *Colonial* p.90
- *Maryland*
Wertenbaker — *First* p.29-30
- *Middle Colonies*
Jernegan — *American* p.218-222
- *Pilgrims*
Beck — *Pilgrims* p.8, 16, 44
- *Lots*
- *Boston, Mass.*
Rutman — *Winthrop's. See* index p.309
, *Field, division of*
Wertenbaker — *Puritan* p.50-54
, *Home, division of*
Wertenbaker — *Puritan* p.45-47
- *Women, single; servants and slaves*
- *Carolinas*
Williams — *Demeter's* p.32-33
- *Maryland*
Williams — *Demeter's* p.31-32
- *Massachusetts*
Williams — *Demeter's* p.25
- *Maryland*
Craven — *Colonies* p.22-23
Craven — *Southern* p.191-192, 210n, 219, 328n
Pomfret — *Founding* p.83-84
- *Middle Colonies*
Jernegan — *American* p.217-222
- *New England*
Craven — *Colonies* p.19-20, 221-222
Jernegan — *American* p.169-170
Wertenbaker — *First* p.55-59
- *New York*
Craven — *Colonies* p.80, 82, 201
- *Occupancy right (1691)*
Annals of America (1) p.282-284

LAND (continued)
- *Pennsylvania*
  Craven — *Colonies* p.193-194
  Ver Steeg — *Formative* p.176
- *Pilgrims*
  Willison — *Saints* p.161-162,
  231-232, 262, 265-266, 313,
  315, 317, 319, 391-392, 401
- *Plymouth*
  Annals of America (1) p.77-78
- *Public sale*
  Craven — *Colonies* p.178-179,
  185-186, 194
- *South*
  Craven — *Southern. See* index
  p.443
  Jernegan — *American* p.83-86
  Tunis — *Colonial* p.79-80
  Wertenbaker — *First* p.26-31
- *Speculation*
  Carman — *History (1)* p.57-58
- *Tenure*
  Craven — *Colonies* p.21-22
- *Titles*
  Folsom — *Give* p.16-17, 23, 80
  , *from Indians. See* **Indians —
  Lands-Titles**
- *Virginia*
  Carman — *History (1)* p.54-55
  Craven — *Southern* p.116-117,
  121, 127-131, 174-176, 278,
  313
  - *Wives*
    Williams — *Demeter's* p.20
- *Women*
  See also **Land — Lots —
  Women**
  Earle — *Colonial* p.50-52
  Leonard — *Dear* p.134-136, 309-
  313

LANDGRAVES
- *South, Titles* of
  Craven — *Southern* p.339-341,
  350, 354

LANDHOLDING
, *Great*
  Rozwenc — *Making (1)* p.32-34
- *Middle Colonies*
  Chitwood — *History (1)* p.366-
  367
- *New England*
  Chitwood — *History (1)* p.363-
  366

- *South*
  Chitwood — *History (1)* p.367-
  370

LANGUAGES
See also **Indians — Languages;**
  names of languages
  Hawke — *Colonial* p.78, 221, 305-309
, *Learned*
  Morison — *Intellect* p.44-48

LARDERS
  Gould — *Early* p.38

**LA SALLE, RENÉ ROBERT CAVELIER,
  SIEUR DE**
  Amer. Her. — *Pioneer* p.29-31, 81
  Chitwood — *History (1)* p.303
  Morison — *Oxford* p.117-118
, *and Mississippi River*
  Collins — *Story* p.82
- *Murder*
  Collins — *Story* p.82

LATCHSTRINGS
  Gould — *Early* p.20
  Woodward — *Way* p.41

LATHAM, WILLIAM
  Hills — *History (1)* p.21, 29, 36, 38,
  49-50, 52-54, 91, 154
  Hills — *History (2)* p.162, 215-216

LATIN LANGUAGE
- *Harvard*
  Wertenbaker — *First* p.247-249
, *in schools*
  Morison — *Intellect.* p.42, 98,
  100n, 105-107, 164

LATIN GRAMMAR SCHOOLS
  Monroe — *Founding (1)* p.136-154
- *Connecticut*
  Monroe — *Founding (1)* p.151
- *Massachusetts*
  Monroe — *Founding (1)* p.146-
  149
- *Masters*
  Monroe — *Founding (1)* p.154-
  155
- *New Hampshire*
  Monroe — *Founding (1)* p.151-
  152

- *New Haven*
    Monroe — *Founding (1)* p.151
- *New Netherland*
    Monroe — *Founding (1)* p.144-145
- *Pennsylvania*
    Monroe — *Founding (1)* p.146
- *South*
    Monroe — *Founding (1)* p.140-144
- *Virginia*
    Monroe — *Founding (1)* p.140-141

LATOUR, FRANCES MARY JACQUELINE
Brooks — *Dames* p.31-58

"LATTENWARE" (type of brass)
Earle — *Colonial* p.283

LAUD, WILLIAM (Archbishop of Canterbury)
Hawke — *Colonial* p.71, 140-142, 150, 168, 335
Morison — *Intellect.* p.13, 21, 114-115
Morris — *Ency.* p.33, 57
Willison — *Pilgrim* p.326, 350, 392, 400-401, 435n, 447-449, 452, 487
Willison — *Saints* p.298, 300-301, 308, 316, 325-327, 333, 356-357, 401

LAUD COMMISSION (1634–41)
Morris — *Ency.* p.57

LAUNDRY
See also **"Dolly"**
Gould — *Early* p.114-115
Leonard — *Dear* p.106-107
Nettels — *Roots* p.241-242
Williams — *Demeter's* p.23

LAW AND LAWYERS
See also **Curfew laws; Pilgrims — Laws; Plymouth — Laws; Women — Law and lawyers;** special subjects
Adams — *Provincial* p.14-17
Chitwood — *History (1)* p.154-158
Hawke — *Colonial* p.292-293, 295
Lawrence — *Not* p.122-123
Vaughan — *New. See* index p.425
Woodward — *Way* p.54

, *Biblical*
    Bailey — *American (1)* p.31-35
    Morrison — *Intellect.* p.116-117, 130, 142, 147
, *Capital*
    - *New England (1641)*
        Hawke — *U.S.* p.127-128
    - *Codification*
        Chitwood — *History (1)* p.114
, *Common*
    Smith — *17th* p.158-159, 163
    , *and Puritans*
        Smith — *17th* p.157, 160-161
    - *Dedham, Mass.*
        Lockridge — *New* p.13, 15-16, 23, 48-49
, *English*
    Vaughan — *New* p.186-191, 195-196, 208-210, 320
, *Lack of*
    Adams — *Provincial* p.14, 16
    - *Massachusetts*
        Vaughan — *Puritan* p.161-172
    - *New England*
        , *and liberties (1648)*
            Hawke — *U.S.* p.129-130
    - *Puritans*
        Wish — *Society (1)* p.42-45
    - *South*
        Goodwin — *Colonial* p.243-259
    - *Sudbury, Mass. (1680)*
        Woodbury — *Way* p.43-45
    - *Virginia*
        Pomfret — *Founding* p.35, 39, 70-71
        Wish — *Society (1)* p.73-74
    - *Wartime restrictions*
        Vaughan — *New* p.132, 330
    - *Women*
        Leonard — *Dear* p.415-416
        , *Protection for — Massachusetts*
            Williams — *Demeter's* p.82, 84-85

***LEAH AND RACHEL* (Virginia and Maryland)**
Morison — *Oxford* p.85
- *Tract by John Hammond*
    Tyler — *History* p.54-57

LEARNING. *See* Education; Schools; etc.

LEATHER
See also **Shoemakers; Tanners and tanning**
Adams — *Album* p.117
Chitwood — *History (1)* p.374
Glubok — *Home* p.50
Marshall — *Mayflower* p.116-117
Rutman — *Winthrop's* p.92, 188, 200, 207, 244, 247-248
Wright — *Everyday* p.128

LECHFORD, THOMAS
Rutman — *Winthrop's* p.127, 161, 167, 169, 176, 196, 218, 234, 251, 256-257
, *on church services*
Vaughan — *Puritan* p.78-81

L'ECLUSE, JEAN DE, ELDER
Willison — *Saints* p.67, 78, 91

"LECTURE DAY"
Earle — *Customs* p.234-236
National — *History.* p.77
Woodward — *Way* p.59, 62-64

LECTURES
- *Restrictions*
Dulles — *America* p.7

LEDERER, JOHN
Amer. Her. — *Pioneer* p.84-85
, *on Appalachian Mountains*
Axtell — *America* p.233-236

LEDERER, WILLIAM
Craven — *Colonies* p.114-115

LEE, MARY
Williams — *Demeter's* p.143-144

LEE, SAMUEL
Morison — *Intellect.* p.143-145, 147, 236, 266-267

LEGGE, WILLIAM
Earle — *Two cent. (1)* p.xvii, 177, 181

LEISLER, JACOB
Amer. Her. — *Thirteen* p.166-167, 196-197
Calverton — *Awake.* p.324n, 327-328, 329n-330n
Craven — *Colonies* p.228-230, 237-240, 281-282

Fisher — *Men (2)* p.80-94
Folsom — *Give* p.64-67, 88
Hawke — *U.S.* p.209-212
Morison — *Oxford* p.120-122
Morris — *Ency.* p.46
Nettels — *Roots* p.348-350
Rothbard — *Conceived (1)* p.383, 429, 433-447, 461, 466, 468-469, 473-474, 476, 495, 510
, *Defense of*
Hawke — *U.S.* p.212-217

LEISLER'S REBELLION (1688–1691)
Amer. Her. — *Thirteen* p.166-167, 173
Craven — *Colonies* p.225-230
Hawke — *U.S.* p.209-317
Jernegan — *American* p.206
Morris — *Ency.* p.46
Nettels — *Roots* p.348-350
Sweet — *Religion* p.107-108
Ver Steeg — *Formative* p.112, 133, 140-141

LEISTER, EDWARD
Willison — *Saints* p.134, 142-143, 189, 443

LEMONS
Craven — *Southern* p.19, 35, 45, 141, 346

LENI-LENAPE (DELAWARE) INDIANS
Christenson — *Delaware* p.7, 9-10, 29
Folsom — *Give* p.53-54
- *"Walum Olum" (history)*
Christenson — *Delaware* p.9-10

LEONARD (LENNARDSON), SAMUEL
Williams — *Demeter's* p.164

LEONARD BROTHERS (Henry and James)
Morison — *Story* p.207

"LETITIA HOUSE" (home of William Penn)
Adams — *Album* p.233

LEVERETT, JOHN
Morison — *Intellect.* p.41, 49-52, 275
Wertenbaker — *Puritan* p.152-153, 156-158

LEVERETT, THOMAS
Rutman — *Winthrop's. See* index p.312

LEVERIDGE, WILLIAM
Vaughan — *New* p.288, 298-299

LEWES, DELAWARE
- *Historic sites*
  Christensen — *Delaware* p.153

LEYDEN, HOLLAND
See also **Pilgrims — Holland**
Adams — *Album* p.40-41
Amer. Her. — *Pilgrims* p.52-65
Dillon — *Pilgrims* p.90, 93-117
Gill — *Mayflower. See* index p.203
Leynse — *Preced. See* index p.283
Morison — *Story* p.10-14, 20, 97, 117-119, 242
Willison — *Saints. See* index p.503
- *Bell Alley*
  Willison — *Saints* p.83, 93, 181, 259, 341
- *Church congregation*
  Marshall — *Mayflower* p.25-26, 30-31
- *Life*
  Leynse — *Preced.* p.191-209

LEYDEN, UNIVERSITY OF
Willison — *Saints* p.92, 99, 341-342,458, 461

LIBERTY
, *Limits of*
  Hawke — *U.S.* p. 97-99
- *Massachusetts*
  - *Children*
    Annals of America (1) p.166
- *New England*
  Hawke — *U.S.* p.124-127
  - *Animals*
    Hawke — *U.S.* p.127
  - *Children*
    Hawke — *U.S.* p.127
  - *Churches*
    Hawke — *U.S.* p.128-129
  - *Foreigners and strangers*
    Hawke — *U.S.* p.127
  - *"The free man"*
    Hawke — *U.S.* p.126-127
  - *Judicial proceedings*
    Hawke — *U.S.* p.126
  - *Servants*
    Hawke — *U.S.* p.127

- *Women*
  Hawke — *U.S.* p.127
, *of conscience*
  See also **Toleration**
  Willison — *Pilgrim* p.2, 31, 56-57, 491-498, 522
  Willison — *Saints. See* index p.503
- *Views of Gov. Winthrop*
  Bailey — *American (1)* p.28-29
- *Views of Roger Williams*
  Bailey — *American (1)* p.35-37

LIBRARIES
See also **Puritans — Libraries**
- *Boston*
  Morison — *Intellect.* p.145
- *Harvard*
  Wertenbaker — *First* p.247
- *Massachusetts*
  Wertenbaker — *First* p.240-242
- *New England*
  Wertenbaker — *First* p.240-242
- *New Haven*
  Morison — *Intellect.* p.145-146
, *Private*
  Adams — *Provincial* p.115-116
  Earle — *Customs* p.272
  Morison — *Intellect.* p.46, 133-149
  Ver Steeg — *Formative* p.98-99, 233-234
  Wright — *Cultural* p.135-136
  Wright — *Literary* p.27-39, 52-61
- *Alcock, George*
  Morison — *Intellect.* p.49n, 108, 137-138
- *Boston*
  Bridenbaugh — *Cities* p.129
- *Bradford, William*
  Wright — *Literary* p.58-59
- *Clergymen*
  Wright — *Literary* p.48-51
- *Dudley, Thomas*
  Wright — *Literary* p.39
- *Harvard, John*
  Wright — *Literary* p.30-31
- *Home, typical*
  Woodward — *Way* p.32-33
- *Lee, Samuel*
  Morison — *Intellect.* p.143-145
  Wright — *Literary* p.127-130
- *Mather, Increase*
  Wright — *Literary* p.130-133

LIBRARIES (*continued*)
- *Mather family*
  Wright — *Literary (1)* p.126-127, 130
- *Merchant*
  Hope — *Nation* p.89
- *Winthrop, John, Jr.*
  Morison — *Intellect.* p.134-136
  Wright — *Literary* p.30, 32
, *Public*
  Adams — *Provincial* p.116-118
- *Virginia*
  Wertenbaker — *First* p.257-258
- *Women*
  Leonard — *Dear* p.245-246

LIDGET, CHARLES
Bailyn — *New England* p.135, 138, 190-193

LIGHT AND LIGHTING
See also **Candles and candlemaking; Lamps; Rushlights**
Drepperd — *Pioneer* p.199-200, 203
Furnas — *Americans* p.162
Glubok — *Home* p.16-21
Langdon — *Everyday* p.23-24
Lawrence — *New* p.162-165
- *Devices*
  Marshall — *Mayflower* p.106-107
, *Dutch*
  Smith — *Colonial* p.119-120
- *New England*
  Tunis — *Colonial* p.41-43

LIGHTNING
Wertenbaker — *First* p.140-141, 162

LILBURNE, JOHN
Earle — *Two cent.(1)* p.xvii, 173

LIMESTONE
Adams — *Provincial* p.40-41

LIMNERS (painters)
Morris — *Ency.* p.596
Tunis — *Craftsmen* p.109

LINCOLN, EARL OF
Beals — *John Eliot* p.10, 34, 43-44, 47-52, 55

LINEN INDUSTRY
Earle — *Home* p.234, 238
Glubok — *Home* p.260-262, 275-277

Leonard — *Dear* p.162-164
Spruill — *Women's* p.24-25
Wertenbaker — *First* p.76

***LION* (ship)**
Caffrey — *Mayflower* p.232, 245, 247

LIQUOR
See also **Alcoholism; Distilleries and breweries; Indians — Liquor;** names of liquor
Woodward — *Way* p.61-62
- *Plymouth*
  Willison — *Saints. See* index p.503
- *Sale, law for*
  Vaughan — *New* p.46, 189-190, 194, 197, 227, 330-336

LITERACY
Morison — *Intellect.* p.82-85
- *Men and women compared*
  Williams — *Demeter's* p.108
- *Plymouth*
  Demos — *Little* p.22, 72

LITERATURE
See also **Authors; Books and reading; Publishers and publishing; Puritans — Literature;** types of literature
Chitwood — *History (1)* p.474-475
Hawke — *Colonial* p.164, 305-308, 311
Miller — *Colonial* p.353
Murdock — *Literature* p.1-2, 202
Rozwenc — *Making (1)* p.85-103
Ver Steeg — *Formative* p.95-96
- *Colonial period (1607-76)*
  Tyler — *History* p.5-253
- *Colonial period (1676-99)*
  Tyler — *History* p.260-287
- *Early narratives*
  Rozwenc — *Making (1)* p.96-97
, *Historical*
  Morison — *Intellect.* p.121, 124, 177-197, 209
- *New England*
  Wright — *Literary* p.82-109
- *Problems*
  Murdock — *Literature* p.2, 29, 38-39
, *Promotional*
  Amer. Her. — *Thirteen* p.33-34, 38-39, 79, 147-148, 169-170, 180, 182, 200

, *Religious. See* **Religion — Books and reading**
- *Rhode Island*
    Morison — *Intellect.* p.154
- *Virginia*
    Wertenbaker — *First* p.256-257
, *Weakness of*
    Murdock — *Literature* p.202-203, 206-207

LITTLE JAMES (ship)
*See also **Anne** (ship)*
Annals of America (1) p. 73
Caffrey — *Mayflower* p.185, 188, 194-195, 209-210
Gill — *Mayflower* p.104-106, 111-113
Morison — *Story* p.97-101, 117, 123-126
Willison — *Pilgrim* p.234, 249-250, 280-281, 540-545
- *Passengers (1623)*
    Caffrey — *Mayflower* p.357-359
    Hills — *History (1)* p.86

LITTLETON, MASSACHUSETTS. *See* **Nashoba**

LIVESTOCK
See also names of animals
Adams — *Provincial* p.30-32
Chitwood — *History (1)* p.359-360
Langdon — *Everyday* p.280-284
Miller — *First* p.168-169
Morris — *Ency.* p.477
- *Branding and earmarks*
    Craven — *Southern* p.213-214, 305
    Wertenbaker — *First* p.218, 220, 230
- *Carolinas*
    Starkey — *Land* p.225
- *New Netherland*
    Starkey — *Land* p.141
- *Plymouth*
    Marshall — *Mayflower* p.91, 164-165
    Starkey — *Land* p.86
    Willison — *Pilgrim* p.245, 250, 279, 292, 296, 385, 417, 449-450
- *Transportation difficulties*
    Starkey — *Land* p.128-129
- *Virginia*
    Starkey — *Land* p.28

LIVINGSTON, ROBERT
Rothbard — *Conceived (1)* p.380, 387-388, 435-436, 441-443, 465, 468, 473-476, 480
- *Manor*
    Smith — *Colonial* p.185-196

LLOYD, THOMAS
Rothbard — *Conceived (1)* p.406, 408-411, 496-498, 500, 502

LOBSTERS
Earle — *Home* p.117-118

LOCKE, JOHN
Starkey — *Land* p.216, 220-221

LOCKSMITHS
Tunis — *Craftsmen* p.61-63

LOG CABINS
Dow — *Every* p.13-15
Furnas — *Americans* p.147-151
Snell — *Wild* p.24, 139-140
Starkey — *Land* p.154-155
, *and barns*
    Adams — *Album* p.243
- *Delaware*
    Christensen — *Delaware* p.31-33
, *First*
    Dow — *Every* p.13
- *Forms*
    Earle — *Home* p.5-7
- *Germans*
    Wertenbaker — *Old* p.72-73
, *Lack of*
    Dow — *Domestic* p.3-4
    Morrison — *Early* p.12-13
    Wright — *Cultural* p.197-198
    - *Jamestown*
        Wertenbaker — *Old* p.72-73
    - *New England*
        Wertenbaker — *Puritan* p.115
- *Maryland*
    Morrison — *Early* p.157
- *New England*
    Lawrence — *New* p.22-23
- *New Sweden*
    Wertenbaker — *Old* p.72
- *North Carolina*
    Morrison — *Early* p.166-170
, *Swedish*
    Gould — *Early* p.16
    Morrison — *Early* p.13

LOG ROLLING
Earle — *Home* p.389, 404, 406
Lawrence — *New* p.17

LOGGERHEADS (flip irons)
Earle — *Colonial* p.289

LOGGING BEES
Earle — *Home* p.416-417

LOGIC
Morison — *Intellect.* p.42-43, 166

LOGS
See also **Lumbering;** related subjects
Marshall — *Mayflower* p.40, 77-79
- *Debarking*
  Marshall — *Mayflower* p.77
- *Sawing, shaping*
  Marshall — *Mayflower* p.78
  Morrison — *Early* p.33-34
- *Squaring*
  Marshall — *Mayflower* p.79

LOLLARDS AND LOLLARDISM
Hall — *Religious* p.69, 87-89, 128n, 128-129

LONG ISLAND, NEW YORK
Adams — *Album* p.107
Alderman — *Story* p.69, 72-73, 80
Craven — *Colonies. See* index p.358
Pomfret — *Founding* p.265-267, 273, 298-299, 302-303
, *Resettlement in*
  Morris — *Ency.* p.43

LONGEVITY
See also **Pilgrims — Longevity;**
  Plymouth — Longevity
- *Articles of Agreement (Conn., 1686)*
  Demos — *Remarkable* p.155-156

"LORDS OF TRADE" (English)
Abbot — *Colonial* p.71-73
Craven — *Colonies* p.148-149, 151, 165-167, 169, 177, 191, 210, 214, 235, 243
Craven — *Southern* p.322, 391, 395-397, 412, 414
Hawke — *Colonial. See* index p.740
Morris — *Ency.* p.57
Smith — *17th* p.179-180, 182, 185, 187-188
Ver Steeg — *Formative* p.123

"LOST COLONY." *See* **Roanoke Colony**

LOTHROP, ISAAC
Willison — *Saints* p.409, 413-414, 416, 418

LOTTERIES
Goodwin — *Colonial* p.144-145

LOUIS XIV (king of France)
Chitwood — *History (1)* p.300

LOUISIANA
See also **"Casket Girls"**
- *Women (1699)*
  Leonard — *Dear* p.57

LOVE. *See* **Courtship; Marriage;**
  Puritans — Love

LOVELACE, FRANCIS
Hawke — *Colonial* p.223, 225
- *Intercolonial post plan*
  Langdon — *Everyday* p.259-261

LUDLOW, ROGER
- *Letter, on frontier*
  Adams — *Album* p.97

LUDWELL, PHILIP (SR.)
Craven — *Colonies* p.153-154, 156, 234, 243

LUDWELL, THOMAS
Wertenbaker — *First* p.42-43

LUG-POLES (in chimneys, fireplaces)
Earle — *Colonial* p.277, 279

LUMBEE INDIANS. *See* **Croatan Indians**

LUMBERING
See also **Logs; Sawmills;** related subjects
Bailyn — *New England. See* index p.248
Carman — *History (1)* p.69, 71-72
Craven — *Southern* p.35, 48, 102, 108, 141, 336, 346n
Gould — *Early* p.110
Marshall — *Mayflower* p.73-77, 82-83
Nettels — *Roots* p.244-245
Tunis — *Colonial* p.89-91
, *First export*
  Langdon — *Everyday* p.9-10

- *Maine*
  Mitchell — *It's* p.3-43
- *Middle Colonies*
  Jernegan — *American* p.223-224

LUTHER, ELEAZER
Lockridge — *New* p.29, 43n, 45-46, 62, 84

LUTHER, MARTIN
Willison — *Saints* p.8, 19, 27, 92, 371, 462

LUTHERANS
Amer. Her. — *Thirteen* p.107-109, 136, 171
Folsom — *Give* p.7, 25, 53
Morris — *Ency.* p.548
Sweet — *Religion* p.189, 200, 204–205
Willison — *Saints* p.21-22
- *New Amsterdam*
  Bridenbaugh — *Cities* p.101

LYDFORD (LYFORD), JOHN, REV.
Dillon — *Pilgrims* p.189-193
Gill — *Mayflower* p.106, 109, 111-112, 127
Marshall — *Mayflower* p.183
Morison — *Story* p.102-103, 111, 117, 124-125, 150
Pomfret — *Founding* p.115-116
Willison — *Pilgrim* p.261-273, 274n, 315, 339n
Willison — *Saints. See* index p.504

LYE MAKING
Earle — *Home* p.254
Gould — *Early* p.113-114
Marshall — *Mayflower* p.101-102

LYFORD, JOHN. See Lydford, John

LYNDE, SIMON
Bailyn — *New England* p.187-188

LYNN, MASSACHUSETTS
Bailyn — *New England* p.27, 30, 62, 65-71, 179
Rutman — *Winthrop's* p.89, 186, 208, 251, 260

LYON, RICHARD
Morison — *Intellect.* p.117-118

LYON **(ship)**
Willison — *Pilgrim* p.362, 379, 416

M

MACK, MRS.
Leonard — *Dear* p.114

MAGAZINES
Morison — *Intellect.* p.126, 146, 257

MAGISTRATES
Hawke — *Colonial* p.686-698
Rutman — *Winthrop's. See* index p.312
- *Salem, Mass.*
  Gildrie — *Salem* p.37-38, 40-41, 99

"MAGUNKAQUOG" (Hopkinton, Mass.)
Vaughan — *New* p.292

MAHICAN INDIANS. See Mohegan Indians

"MAID LOTS." See Land — Lots — Women

MAIL SERVICE. See Postal service

MAINE
See also **Fisheries; Fur trade**
Alderman — *Story* p.33-34
Amer. Her. — *Thirteen* p.24, 66-67, 85-87, 124, 158, 195, 200
Bailyn — *New England. See* index p.245
Chitwood — *History (1)* p.137-138
Craven — *Colonies* p.18, 63, 79, 86, 107, 121, 160, 166, 207, 214-216, 244
Gill — *Mayflower. See* index p.203
Morison — *Story* p.70, 90, 104, 111-112, 122-127, 134-136, 166, 279, 288-290
Morris — *Ency.* p.32, 36
Pomfret — *Founding* p.170-172
Snell — *Wild* p.54, 99, 117, 120-121
Vaughan — *New* p.8, 11, 87, 201
Willison — *Saints. See* index p.504
- *Coast*
  Adams — *Album* p.37-38
, *Duke of York's rights in*
  Craven — *Colonies* p.63, 79, 215-216
- *Explorations*
  Beck — *Pilgrims* p.17-18, 21
- *Flowers*
  Mitchell — *It's* p.146-148
- *Islands*
  Mitchell — *It's* p.44-64

MAINE (*continued*)
, *Jurisdiction of Massachusetts in*
   Craven — *Colonies* p.18, 86, 167,
   169, 214, 244
- *Northeast*
   Adams — *Album* p.65-66
- *Settlements*
   Jernegan — *American* p.116, 138
   Leonard — *Dear* p.61-62
   Snell — *Wild* p.67, 73, 76-77
- *Thanksgiving, First. See*
   **Thanksgiving Day, First —
   Monhegan Island, Me.**
- *Township order on religious liberty*
   Annals of America (1) p.91
- *Views of John Josselyn*
   Axtell — *America* p.101-107

MAIZE. *See* **Corn**

MAKEMIE, FRANCIS
   Sweet — *Religion* p.254-255

MALARIA
   See also **Cinchona bark**
   Wertenbaker — *First* p.178-180
- *Virginia*
   Wertenbaker — *First* p.178-180

MAN. *See* **"Common man"**

MANAHOAC INDIANS
   Smith — *17th* p.43, 46, 48-49

MANHATTAN ISLAND, NEW YORK
   Fisher — *Men (2)* p.13-102
   Hope — *Nation* p.100, 106
   Small — *Wild* p.101, 111-113, 138,
   141, 144
- *Purchase*
   Collins — *Story* p.59
   Dillon — *Pilgrims* p.198
   Jernegan — *American* p.197
   Leonard — *Dear* p.55-56
- *Settlements*
   Collins — *Story* p.58
- *Views of Jonas (Johannis)*
   Michaëlius
   Axtell — *America* p.69-72

MANIGAULT, JUDITH GITON
   Williams — *Demeter's* p.52-53, 178

MANN, RACHEL
   Morison — *Story* p.251-252

MANN, RICHARD. *See* **More, Richard**

MANNERS. *See* **Etiquette**

MANOMET, MASSACHUSETTS
   Willison — *Pilgrim* p.142, 205-207
   Willison — *Saints* p.213, 219-220, 225

MANOMET INDIANS
   Willison — *Saints* p.187, 223, 229,
   264

MANORS. *See* **Mansions**

MANSIONS
   Wertenbaker — *Puritan* p.2-7, 41
- *Life*
   Smith — *Colonial* p.185-196
- *Maryland*
   Craven — *Southern* p.191-192,
   195, 200-201, 219-220
   Pomfret — *Founding* p.83-84, 86-
   87
- *South*
   Tunis — *Colonial* p.84-85

MANTEO (Indian)
   Snell — *Wild* p.54-55, 58

MANUFACTURING
   See also **Industry;** names of individ-
   ual types
   Bailyn — *New England. See* index
   p.245
   Carman — *History (1)* p.75-76, 137-
   138
   Dow — *Every* p.120-121
- *Connecticut*
   Wertenbaker — *First* p.76-83
, *Household*
   Nettels — *Roots* p.237-239
- *Laws*
   Chitwood — *History (1)* p.381-
   382
- *Massachusetts*
   Wertenbaker — *First* p.76-83
- *New England*
   Jernegan — *American* p.173-174
- *South, types*
   Jernegan — *American* p.91-92

MAPLE SUGAR
   Furnas — *Americans* p.174-175
   Gould — *Early* p.108-110
- *Indians*
   Northey — *American* p.72-74

- *"Sugaring off"* gatherings
  Rawson — *When* p.96-98

MAPLE WOOD
- *Bowls*
  Earle — *Home* p.82, 318-320

MARBLEHEAD, MASSACHUSETTS
  Willison — *Pilgrim* p.382-383
  Willison — *Saints* p.311, 437-438

MARBURY, ANNE. *See* Hutchinson, Anne Marbury

MARCH, ELIZABETH. *See* Warren, Elizabeth March

***MARGARET AND JOHN* (ship)**
  Goodwin — *Colonial* p.101-102

MARIGOLDS
  Earle — *Home* p.427-428

MARKETS AND MARKETING
  Bridenbaugh — *Cities* p.27-28
  Gould — *Early* p.144
  Rutman — *Winthrop's* p.312
  - *Boston, First*
    Lawrence — *New* p.189

MARKHAM, WILLIAM
  Rothbard — *Conceived (1)* p.402, 411, 495-496, 499-503

MAR-PRELATE, MARTIN
  Willison — *Saints* p.39-41, 65, 462

MARLBOROUGH, MASSACHUSETTS
  Willison — *Saints* p.366, 398, 415, 459

MARQUETTE, JACQUES, FATHER
  Amer. Her. — *Pioneer* p.27

MARRIAGE
  See also **Pilgrims — Marriage; Plymouth — Marriage; Puritans — Marriage; Weddings; etc.**
  Chitwood — *History (1)* p.495-497
  Craven — *Southern* p.13-14, 179, 273-275, 305
  Demos — *Remarkable* p.138-149
  Lawrence — *Not* p.82-95
  Smith — *17th* p.74, 142, 165
  Williams — *Demeter's*. *See* index p.353

, *and property*
  Nettels — *Roots* p.442-443
- *Articles of agreement (Calvert Co., Md., 1669)*
  Demos — *Remarkable* p.148-149
, *as family matter*
  Spruill — *Women's* p.143-146
, *as proprietary colony*
  Life — *New* p.57-58, 61, 68
  Nettels — *Roots* p.337-339
, *by clergymen (1692)*
  Nettels — *Roots* p.442
- *Children (under-age; secret)*
  Spruill — *Women's* p.140-141
- *Contracts (prenuptial and postnuptial)*
  Williams — *Demeter's* p.88-89, 91
  - *Hartford, Conn. (1654)*
    Demos — *Remarkable* p.145-147
  - *South*
    Craven — *Southern* p.274-275
- *Dedham, Mass.*
  - *Rate*
    Lockridge — *New* p.14, 59, 66-68, 95-96
, *Forbidden (English Act)*
  Spruill — *Women's* p.141-142
- *Laws*
  Holliday — *Woman's* p.260-261
- *Maryland statute*
  Hawke — *U.S.* p.143-144, 147
- *Massachusetts*
  - *Customs, regulations*
    - *Views of John Winthrop*
      Hawke — *U.S.* p.124
  - *Laws*
    Annals of America (1) p.203
- *New England*
  Miller — *First* p. 200-201
- *Separations*
  Spruill — *Women's* p.342-344
- *Settlements*
  See also **Marriage — Contracts**
  - *Boston*
    Woodward — *Way* p.31
- *South*
  Craven — *Southern* p.179, 305
  Holliday — *Woman's* p.270-272
  - *Bans*
    Craven — *Southern* p.273, 305

MARRIAGE (*continued*)
- *Licenses*
  Craven — *Southern* p.273-274
- *Virginia*
  Hawke — *U.S.* p.76, 138
- *Women*
  Leonard — *Dear* p.78
  Nettels — *Roots* p.444-445

MARSHES
Rutman — *Winthrop's. See* index p.312-313

MARSHFIELD, MASSACHUSETTS
Morison — *Story* p.36, 139-142, 156, 173, 217, 227, 256
Willison — *Saints. See* index p.504

**MARTHA'S VINEYARD, MASSACHU-
SETTS**
Vaughan — *New* p.15-16, 36, 54, 65, 242, 259, 284, 286-287, 295, 297-298, 300, 303, 314
Willison — *Saints* p.187, 223, 366, 388, 410, 452, 459

MARTIN, CHRISTOPHER
Caffrey — *Mayflower* p.49, 51, 60, 86, 99-100, 132, 141
Dillon — *Pilgrims* p.116, 119-120, 150
Gill — *Mayflower* p.39, 43, 47, 70, 80-81
Hills — *History (1). See* index p.170
Hills — *History (2)* p.217-218; *See also* index p.265
Leynse — *Preced.* p.232, 240, 244-245, 253, 263
Willison — *Pilgrim* p.72-73, 84n, 85-86, 120-121, 126, 536
Willison — *Saints. See* index p.504

MARTIN, SUSANNA
Williams — *Demeter's* p.140

MARVELL, ANDREW
- *"Bermudas" (1655)*
  Annals of America (1) p.222

MARYLAND
See also **Baltimore, Lords (I, II, III)**; names of cities; special subjects
Acheson — *America's* p.136-138
Alderman — *Story* p.82-90, 113, 115, 170
Annals of America (1) p.235h

Calverton — *Awake.* p.238-256
Carman — *History (1)* p.54, 64-65
Chitwood — *History (1)* p.79-87
Craven — *Colonies. See* index p.358
Craven — *Southern* p.183-223; *See also* index p.444
Folsom — *Give* p.50, 67, 70-74
Hawke — *Colonial* p.742
Hawke — *U.S.* p.81-84
Jernegan — *American* p.65-72
Kraus — *U.S. (1)* p.69-71
Miller — *First* p.46-49
Morison — *Oxford* p.79-85
Morris — *Ency.* p.28-30
Nettels — *Roots* p.122-123; *See also* index p.736
Pomfret — *Founding* p.75-100; *See also* index p.377
Rothbard — *Conceived (1)* p.114-120, 126-127, 131-135
Smith — *17th* p.40, 42, 51, 53-54, 66, 83, 131
Snell — *Wild* p.17, 99, 123
Starkey — *Land* p.109, 112-116, 123-124, 187, 201
Tunis — *Colonial* p.25
Ver Steeg — *Formative* p.42-45
Wertenbaker — *First. See* index p.348
, *and Carolina*
  Hawke — *Colonial* p.250-251
- *Assembly*
  Craven — *Colonies* p.10, 26-27, 232
  Hawke — *U.S.* p.143-148
  Jernegan — *American* p.68
  Pomfret — *Founding* p.89-91
- *Boundary disputes*
  Jernegan — *American* p.69
  Snell — *Wild* p.128, 132-133
- *Charter*
  Hawke — *Colonial* p.110-111
  Jernegan — *American* p.66-67
  Pomfret — *Founding* p.78-79, 81, 300
- *Civil War (1654)*
  Chitwood — *History (1)* p.85-86
- *Economy*
  Wertenbaker — *First* p.304-306
- *Explorations*
  Jernegan — *American* p.67
- *Feudalism*
  Wish — *Society (1)* p.87-89

- *Founding*
    Jernegan — *American* p.65-66
    Snell — *Wild* p.124, 127-128
    Sweet — *Religion* p.168-171
- *Government, royal*
    Craven — *Colonies* p.241-242
- *Governor and officials*
    Jernegan — *American* p.67-68
- *"Hundreds" (parish subdivision)*
    Chitwood — *History (1)* p.154
- *Life*
    Earle — *Two cent. (1)* p.107-109
- *Plantations and planters.* See
    **Plantations and planters —
    Maryland**
- *Political difficulties*
    Craven — *Colonies* p.160-165
- *Prosperity*
    Wertenbaker — *First* p.41-42
- *"A Relation of Maryland" (1635)*
    Amer. Her. — *Thirteen* p.142
- *Revolution of 1689 (English)*
    Chitwood — *History (1)* p.227-
    229
    Craven — *Colonies* p.230-232
    Hawke — *U.S.* p.217-219
    Jernegan — *American* p.71-72
    Morris — *Ency.* p.29-30
- *Settlements*
    Amer. Her. — *Thirteen* p.142,
    169, 172-174
    Jernegan — *American* p.70-76
    Leonard — *Dear* p.64-66
    Morris — *Ency.* p.28-29
- *Women*
    Calverton — *Awake.* p.253-256
    Spruill — *Women's* p.10-11

MARYLAND TOLERATION ACT (1649)
    Acheson — *America's* p.137
    Annals of America (1) p.88-90
    Bailey — *America (1)* p.11-15
    Fisher — *Men (2)* p.169-170
    Morison — *Oxford* p.84
    Nettels — *Roots* p.186
    Pomfret — *Founding* p.93-94, 96, 98
    Sweet — *Religion* p.26-27
    Ver Steeg — *Formative* p.91-92, 216

MASKS
    Earle — *Two cent. (1)* p.156-157

MASON, JOHN, CAPTAIN
    Acheson — *America's* p.112-113
    Alderman — *Story* p.39, 72-73
    Johnston — *Conn.* p.24-29, 31

Pomfret — *Founding* p.133, 144, 153,
    164-165, 169-170, 259, 276
Vaughan — *New* p.139, 141-143, 150-
    153, 169, 207, 289, 310, 324-325

MASON, ROBERT T.
    Rothbard — *Conceived (1)* p.285,
    356, 360-362, 364-366, 368, 371,
    376, 415, 428, 449

**MASSACHUSETTS (Bay Colony;
    Commonwealth)**
    See also **Boston, Mass.; Council of
    Massachusetts; Pilgrims; Plym-
    outh; Puritans**
    Acheson — *America's* p.111-113
    Alderman — *Story. See* index p.184
    Amer. Her. — *Thirteen* p.91, 95-96,
    98, 102, 106, 132-133, 162-163
    Annals of America (1) p.232e,f
    Arts — *America* p.21-26
    Beck — *Pilgrims* p.61-62, 81-82
    Caffrey — *Mayflower* p.228, 230, 249,
    273, 295-296, 303-304
    Calverton — *Awake.* p.119-145
    Carman — *Hist. (1)* p.29-30, 96, 101
    Chitwood — *History (1)* p.109, 231-
    233
    Craven — *Colonies. See* index p.358
    Demos — *Little* p.9, 16, 18, 53, 78,
    92, 98, 146, 163, 175
    Fisher — *Men (1)* p.130
    Folsom — *Give* p.13-15, 17-19, 21-
    23, 28, 30-31, 36-38, 41, 52, 64, 80,
    84, 86, 88
    Gill — *Mayflower* p.55, 98-99, 106,
    119, 129-131, 135-136, 140-141,
    145-146
    Hawke — *Colonial* p.134-142; *See
    also* index p.742
    Kraus — *U.S. (1)* p.52-57
    Lawrence — *New* p.15
    Miller — *First* p.39-46
    Morison — *Story. See* index p.iv
    Morris — *Ency.* p.32-34, 36
    Pomfret — *Founding* p.178-209; *See
    also* index p.377
    Rozwenc — *Making (1)* p.29, 31, 40,
    58-59, 62
    Rutman — *Winthrop's. See* index
    p.312-314
    Scott — *Settlers* p.29-30
    Snell — *Wild* p.4, 17, 72-73, 117, 119,
    124, 128-129, 135
    Starkey — *Land. See* index p.271

MASSACHUSETTS (Bay Colony; Commonwealth) (*continued*)

Tunis — *Colonial* p.24-25
Vaughan — *New. See* index p.425
Ver Steeg — *Formative* p.38-39
Wertenbaker — *First. See* index p.348-349
Willison — *Pilgrim. See* index p.578
Willison — *Saints* p.407-408; *See also* index p.504

- *Act of 1647*
 Rozwenc — *Making (1)* p.86-87
- *Agents*
 Craven — *Colonies* p.45, 172, 245
- *Aims, views of John Winthrop*
 Goetzmann — *Colonial* p.169-179
, *and colonial wars*
 Amer. Her. — *Thirteen* p.164, 197, 200-201
, *and Dominion of New England*
 Craven — *Colonies* p.214-215, 219-221
, *and 1664 investigation*
 Craven — *Colonies* p.66-67
, *and the Restoration*
 Craven — *Colonies* p.6, 44-46
- *Annexation of Maine (1665–69)*
 Morris — *Ency.* p.38
, *as "Bible Commonwealth"*
 Nettels — *Roots* p.168-169
 Ver Steeg — *Formative* p.37-38
 - *View from abroad*
 Axtell — *America* p.97-126
- *Beginnings*
 See also **Massachusetts — Charters; Massachusetts — Founding; Massachusetts — Settlements**
 Abbot — *Colonial* p.35-53
 Chitwood — *History (1)* p.102-103
 Jernegan — *American* p.125-128
 Morris — *Ency.* p.33
 Nettels — *Roots* p.118-121
 Pomfret — *Founding* p.149-177
 Vaughan — *Puritan* p.54-63
- *Boundaries*
 Pomfret — *Founding* p.228-229
- *Capital laws*
 Annals of America (1) p.200
- *Charters*
 Annals of America (1) p.100-103
 Beck — *Pilgrims* p.82-83

Rutman — *Winthrop's* p.41, 46, 114, 137
Snell — *Wild* p.119, 127
, *Annulment of*
 Bailyn — *New England* p.158-159, 169, 192
 Craven — *Colonies* p.209-210, 220
 Morris — *Ency.* p.33-34, 40
, *New*
 Bailyn — *New England* p.170, 175-176
 Beck — *Pilgrims* p.82-83
 Craven — *Colonies* p.241, 244-246
 Vaughan — *Puritan* p.322-324
 Wertenbaker — *First* p.108-109
- *Commerce*
 Wertenbaker — *First* p.11
- *Commission of 1664*
 Bailyn — *New England* p.120-121
- *Conformity*
 Bailey — *American (1)* p.27-31
- *Constitutionalism (1661)*
 Annals of America (1) p.231-232
- *Contrast with Virginia*
 Calverton — *Awake.* p.215-221
- *Court of Assistants*
 Dow — *Every* p.200-202, 204-205
 Rutman — *Winthrop's. See* index p.313
- *Deputies*
 Rutman — *Winthrop's* p.81-82, 159-161, 168, 168n-169, 172-173, 223-224, 250, 250n, 261, 268
- *Dissensions and persecutions*
 Jernegan — *American* p.131-134
- *Ecclesiastical laws*
 Annals of America (1) p.201-202
 Smith — *17th* p.143-165
- *Economy*
 Demos — *Remarkable* p.250-254
 Pomfret — *Founding* p.205-209
- *Educated men*
 Wright — *Literary* p.16-18
- *English relations*
 Amer. Her. — *Thirteen* p.157-158
 Craven — *Colonies* p.165-174
- *Expansion*
 Jernegan — *American* p.148

- *Explorations*
  Amer. Her. — *Thirteen* p.66, 87-90, 99-100
  Beck — *Pilgrims* p.17-18, 21-23
  Willison — *Saints* p.200-203, 212
- *Founding*
  Morison — *Intellect.* p.7, 17
  Morison — *Oxford* p.64-67
  Rothbard — *Conceived (1)* p.165-173
- *Freehold tenure*
  Rozwenc — *Making (1)* p.34-35
- *General court*
  Bailyn — *New England* p.20, 32-33, 38-39, 48, 51, 62-63, 85-86, 92-93, 97, 103-104, 120-121, 140, 158, 176, 189
  Chitwood — *History (1)* p.109-114
  Lockridge — *New* p.15, 17, 29, 35, 38, 45-46
  Morison — *Intellect. See* index p.281
  Rozwenc — *Making (1)* p.58-61, 86
  Rutman — *Winthrop's. See* index p.313
  Starkey — *Land* p.91, 94, 98-104
- *Government*
  Abbot — *Colonial* p.52-53, 68
  Amer. Her. — *Thirteen* p.100-101, 103, 157-158, 162
  Annals of America (1) p.217-220
  Hawke — *Colonial* p.136-140
  Hope — *Nation* p.81
  Jernegan — *American* p.129-131
  Morris — *Ency.* p.33
  Pomfret — *Founding* p.174-177, 182-183, 205-206
  Snell — *Wild* p.119, 125, 127
- *Governors*
  See also names of governors
  Rutman — *Winthrop's* p.26, 41-42, 165, 165n-166, 169-171, 173, 176
- *Hardships, views of Thomas Dudley*
  Annals of America (1) p.118-124
- *History*
  Smith — *17th* p.203-206, 210-215, 217-219, 224-225
- *King Philip's war*
  Craven — *Colonies* p.120-121, 123
- *Laws*
  Morison — *Intellect.* p.66, 88

Rutman — *Winthrop's. See* index p.313-314
- *Letters (1630)*
  Demos — *Remarkable* p.73-75
- *Magistrate's role*
  Pomfret — *Founding* p.178-180, 188, 211
- *Marshall*
  Rutman — *Winthrop's* p.37, 43, 73, 166, 175, 234-235
, *Migration from*
  Wertenbaker — *First* p.97-98
- *Non-conformists*
  Snell — *Wild* p.117-118, 125-126
- *Population*
  Wertenbaker — *First* p.313
- *Royal commission*
  Jernegan — *American* p.154-155
- *Settlements*
  Acheson — *America's* p.88-89
  Gill — *Mayflower* p.145-146
  Hope — *Nation* p.80
  Vaughan — *Puritan* p.59-63
- *Suffrage*
  Chitwood — *History (1)* p.109-110
- *Theocracy*
  Rothbard — *Conceived* p.174-181, 251-259, 263-266, 341-343
  Wertenbaker — *First* p.93-98
- *Treasurer and treasury*
  Rutman — *Winthrop's* p.105, 165, 167, 171-172, 210-212, 237
- *Women*
  Holliday — *Women's* p.7-9
  Leonard — *Dear* p.61-62
  Willison — *Pilgrim* p.150-151
  - *Liberties*
    Annals of America (1) p.166

MASSACHUSETTS BAY COMPANY
See also "**Undertakers**"
Acheson — *America's* p.88
Amer. Her. — *Thirteen* p.97-98, 101
Caffrey — *Mayflower* p.214
Carman — *Hist.(1)* p.26-27, 29, 52
Chitwood — *History (1)* p.103-104
Dillon — *Pilgrims* p.204, 207-212
Dow — *Every* p.5, 20, 239
Gill — *Mayflower* p.128
Hawke — *Colonial* p.129-132
Morris — *Ency.* p.33
Nettels — *Roots* p.118-120, 135-137, 169-171

MASSACHUSETTS BAY COMPANY
(continued)
Pomfret — *Founding. See* index p.377
Rutman — *Winthrop's. See* index
    p.314
Scott — *Settlers* p.28-30
Ver Steeg — *Formative* p.35-37
Willison — *Saints* p.267, 272, 310,
    470-471
- *Charter*
    Abbot — *Colonial* p.38-39, 50-51,
        74
    Jernegan — *American* p.126-127
    Pomfret — *Founding* p.153-154,
        160-161, 164-170, 172-176,
        256
    Rozwenc — *Making (1)* p.57-58,
        78, 82, 93
    Vaughan — *Puritan* p.54-58
- *Expedition*
    Pomfret — *Founding* p.156, 161-
        162, 178, 199, 205, 210
- *Government*
    Pomfret — *Founding* p.163, 173-
        177
- *Organization*
    Pomfret — *Founding* p.154-156

MASSACHUSETTS BODY OF LIBER-
TIES (1641)
Abbot — *Colonial* p.52
Annals of America (1) p.163-167
Dow — *Every* p.200, 211
Gildrie — *Salem* p.92-93
Hawke — *Colonial* p.124-127, 138,
    177, 297
Lawrence — *Not* p.24-26, 114-115
Morris — *Ency.* p.36
Rozwenc — *Making (1)* p.71-72

MASSACRES. *See* Indians —
    Massacres; names of massacres

MASSASOIT (Indian)
Alderman — *Story* p.25, 28, 93-94
Archer — *Mayflower* p.195-206
Beck — *Pilgrims* p.21, 34, 37, 39-43,
    48, 81
Caffrey — *Mayflower. See* index p.388
Dillon — *Pilgrims* p.154-156, 161-163,
    165, 168-171, 177-178, 186, 212
Folsom — *Give* p.35-36
Gill — *Mayflower* p.82-85, 91-92, 95-
    96, 99-100
Leonard — *Dear* p.50

Marshall — *Mayflower* p.135-138,
    140-141, 149, 153, 159
Morison — *Story. See* index p.iv
Scott — *Settlers* p.41-42
Snell — *Wild* p.99, 108, 110, 117, 128
Starkey — *Land* p.60-61, 197, 206
Vaughan — *New* p.54, 70-78, 81-82,
    84-86, 96, 112-113, 118, 187, 210,
    241, 258, 298, 300, 305, 324, 456
Willison — *Pilgrim* p.134-137, 139-
    142, 152-153, 175-177, 388n, 523
Willison — *Saints. See* index p.504
, *and Pilgrims*
    Archer — *Mayflower* p.201-206,
        215-229, 290
    Marshall — *Mayflower* p.135-138
    Northey — *American* p.72-74
    Willison — *Pilgrims* p.176-177
, *Demand for Squanto's death*
    Archer — *Mayflower* p.282-289
- *Illness and death*
    Archer — *Mayflower* p.325
    Willison — *Pilgrim* p.207-214
    Willison — *Saints* p.220-222, 390
, *Winslow and Hopkins' visit to*
    Marshall — *Mayflower* p.140-141

MASTERSON, EDMUND
Hills — *History (2)* p.218

MASTERSON, RICHARD
Willison — *Saints. See* index p.504

"MASTING" (marking trees for masts)
Fisher — *Men(1)* p.326-327

MATAOKO (Indian)
Phillips — *First* p.43-47, 111
- *Opposition to Pocahontas' wedding*
    Phillips — *First* p.140-141

MATERIALISM
Rutman — *Winthrop's* p.21-22, 143,
    243, 248, 256, 260, 275, 277-278

MATHEMATICS
See also **Arithmetic**
, *in schools*
    Morison — *Intellect.* p.19, 32, 78,
        139-140, 142, 144, 147, 242-
        243, 249

MATHER, COTTON, REV.
Adams — *Album* p.113
Amer. Her. — *Thirteen* p.154-155,
    160-162, 207

Caffrey — *Mayflower* p.229, 279, 283, 290, 304
Carman — *History (1)* p.94, 96
Chitwood — *History (1)* p.234-235
Dow — *Every* p.102
Earle — *Two cent. (1)* p.xiv, 42-43
Earle — *Two cent. (2)* p.330-332, 417
Fisher — *Men (1)* p.166-169, 172
Folsom — *Give* p.64, 78, 80-82, 86, 92
Glubok — *Home* p.38, 145, 303-305
Leonard — *Dear* p.79, 218, 265, 362-363, 386
Morison — *Intellect. See* index p.283
Murdock — *Literature. See* index p.232
Rozwenc — *Making (1)* p.38, 102-103
Smith — *17th* p.145, 215, 217-218, 221, 223, 225
Tyler — *History. See* index p.545
Wertenbaker — *First. See* index p.349
Wertenbaker — *Puritan. See* index p.353
Willison — *Saints. See* index p.504
Wish — *Society (1)* p.31, 35, 40, 42, 45, 56, 58-59
Wright — *Everyday* p.1, 152, 154, 177-179
- *"An exemplary Christian"*
    Miller — *Colonial* p.115-117
, *as father*
    Williams — *Demeter's* p.95-96
, *as historian*
    Wright — *Cultural* p.161-162
- *"Inoculation for smallpox"*
    Miller — *Colonial* p.118-131
- *"Life of Theophilus Eaton"*
    Vaughan — *Puritan* p.255-261
- *"Magnalia"* . . .
    Rozwenc — *Making (1)* p.99-101
- *"Memorable providence relating to witchcraft and possession"*
    Williams — *Demeter's* p.138
, *on amusements*
    Dulles — *America* p.14, 17, 20, 25
, *on Anne Bradstreet*
    Williams — *Demeter's* p.107-108
, *on Christianizing Negroes*
    Vaughan — *Puritan* p.261-267
, *on courtship*
    Lawrence — *Not* p.54-66
, *on female education*
    Williams — *Demeter's* p.108

, *on New England's "woeful decade"*
    Williams — *Demeter's* p.149, 160-161
, *on remarkable salvations*
    Vaughan — *Puritan* p.274-276
, *on witchcraft and trials*
    Goetzmann — *Colonial* p.204-213
    Holliday — *Woman's* p.50-51, 56, 58
    Rozwenc — *Making (1)* p.95-96
- *Tract on Mercy Short*
    Williams — *Demeter's* p.150-152
- *"Witchcraft in Salem"*
    Miller — *Colonial* p.185-189
- *"Wonders of the invisible world" (1693)*
    Annals of America (1) p.297-298

MATHER, ELEAZER
    Wertenbaker — *Puritan* p.87, 169-170, 176, 203, 224

MATHER, INCREASE
    Amer. Her. — *Thirteen* p.154-155, 158, 160
    Bailyn — *New England* p.140-141
    Caffrey — *Mayflower* p.279, 294, 304
    Chitwood — *History (1)* p.223
    Craven — *Colonies* p.3, 21, 222, 236, 245-246
    Folsom — *Give* p.41, 69, 80-81, 93
    Morgan — *Puritan* p.101-102, 118
    Morison — *Intellect. See* index p.283
    Morison — *Story* p.289-290
    Murdock — *Literature* p.34, 45, 65, 95-96, 127-128, 178
    Rothbard — *Conceived* p.342, 368, 371, 413, 417, 424-425, 427-429, 446, 449, 452-455, 457, 459, 461, 472
    Rozwenc — *Making (1)* p.94-95
    Smith — *17th* p.152, 190, 211-212
    Sweet — *Religion* p.48, 109-111
    Tyler — *History. See* index p.545
    Ver Steeg — *Formative* p.146-147
    Wertenbaker — *First. See* index p.349
    Wertenbaker — *Puritan. See* index p.353
    Willison — *Pilgrim* p.414, 526, 528-529
    Willison — *Saints. See* index p.504
    Wright — *Everyday* p.177-178
, *and Harvard College*
    Wright — *Literary* p.99-100

MATHER, INCREASE (*continued*)

, *and Spanish language*
Wright — *Literary* p.106-107
- *"Arrow against profane and promis-cuous dancing"*
Annals of America (1) p.272-273
- *Defense of inoculation*
Vaughan — *Puritan* p.285-287
- *"Insufficiency of evidence against witches" (1693)*
Annals of America (1) p.293-296
, *on drinking*
Dulles — *America* p.17-18, 20
- *"Witchcraft in Salem"*
Miller — *Colonial* p.179-185

MATHER, NATHANIEL
Morison — *Intellect.* p.253, 268-269

MATHER FAMILY
Tyler — *History* p.316-337
- *Literature*
Wright — *Literary* p.160-162, 165-166
- *Quotations*
Wright — *Literary* p.140-148

MATHEWS, SAMUEL
Goetzmann — *Colonial* p.117-120
Smith — *17th* p.94-96, 98
Wertenbaker — *First* p.44-45, 47

"MATHOGLIN." *See* **"Metheglin"**

MATIANUCK (Windsor, Conn.)
Willison — *Pilgrim* p.390, 406-409

MATOAKA. *See* **Pocahontas**

"MATRIARCHATE" (of Iroquois Indians)
Williams — *Demeter's* p.354

MATS
Rawson — *When* p.114-116

MATTAPAN, MASSACHUSETTS.
See **Dorchester, Massachusetts**

MATTAPONI INDIANS
Smith — *17th* p.40, 46, 55, 58

MATTERHORN (Indian)
Starkey — *Land* p.156

MATTHEWS, MARGARET
, *Quaker wedding of*
Williams — *Demeter's* p.84

MATTRESSES
Beck — *Pilgrims* p.56
, *Developed by Pocahontas*
Phillips — *First* p.125

MAVERICK, MOSES
Willison — *Saint* p.121, 311, 438

MAVERICK, REMEMBER ALLERTON
Willison — *Saints* p.121-122, 311, 438

MAVERICK, SAMUEL
Bailyn — *New England. See* index p.246
Rutman — *Winthrop's* p.24-25, 70-71, 78, 90, 94, 142, 185, 253-254
Willison — *Saints* p.382-384, 477

MAY, CORNELIS JACOBSEN
Morris — *Ency.* p.41

MAY, DOROTHY. *See* **Bradford, Dorothy May**

MAY DAY
, *and Puritans*
Wertenbaker — *First* p.277-278

MAYFLOWER **(ship)**
See also **Pilgrims; Plymouth**
Acheson — *America's* p.85-86
Alderman — *Story* p.20-23
Amer. Her. — *Pioneer* p.58-59
Amer. Her. — *Thirteen* p.88, 90, 94, 99
Beck — *Pilgrims. See* index p.87
Caffrey — *Mayflower* p.229, 288
Carman — *Hist. (1)* p.28-29
Chitwood — *History (1)* p.93-94
Dillon — *Pilgrims* p.viii, 38, 80, 103, 117, 158-159, 164, 168, 173, 183, 185
Dow — *Every* p.7, 15, 31, 44
Furnas — *Americans* p.20, 47-48, 54, 57
Gill — *Mayflower* p.1-67
Leynse — *Preced.* p.11-12, 15-17, 207, 232, 234, 236-237, 240, 244-263
Marshall — *Mayflower* p.31-32, 42-48, 119

Morison — *Story* p.16, 19, 26-66, 76, 82, 85-87, 120, 220
Rozwenc — *Making (1)* p.27-28
Snell — *Wild* p.94, 101-106
Willison — *Pilgrim. See* index p.578
Willison — *Saints. See* index p.504
, at Southampton
   Caffrey — *Mayflower* p.80
- Bill of lading (1654)
   Caffrey — *Mayflower* p.363-364
- Charter
   Caffrey — *Mayflower* p.79
   Gill — *Mayflower* p.39
- Deaths aboard
   Dillon — *Pilgrims* p.127, 147
- Democracy
   Calverton — *Awake.* p.103-104
- Departure
   Adams — *Album* p.41
   Annals of America (1) p.67-68
   Caffrey — *Mayflower* p.87-88
   Collins — *Story* p.42
- Design and measurements
   See also **Mayflower —Tonnage and displacement**
   Caffrey — *Mayflower* p.66-69, 94-96, 109-110
   Dillon — *Pilgrims* p.123-124
- Earlier voyages
   Caffrey — *Mayflower* p.11-12, 65-67
- Explorations
   Dillon — *Pilgrims* p.129-147
   Gill — *Mayflower* p.70-85
   Jernegan — *American* p.119-120
- Food allocations
   Caffrey — *Mayflower* p.109
- Landing
   Hills — *History (1)* p.66-71
   Willison — *Saints* p.137-138, 437, 465
- Last years
   Gill — *Mayflower* p.86-93, 101, 118
- Life
   Marshall — *Mayflower* p.41-43, 45-47
- Medicine
   Marshall — *Mayflower* p.46
- Mutiny
   Willison — *Saints* p.138-142, 285
- Passengers
   See also **"Old comers"**
   Archer — *Mayflower* p.60-70
   Caffrey — *Mayflower* p.337-340

Gill — *Mayflower* p.191-193
Hills — *History (1)* p.20-22, 26-50
- Bachelors
   Hills — *History (1)* p.45-46
- Children
   Hills — *History (1)* p.51-53
- Crew
   Caffrey — *Mayflower* p.77-78
   Hills — *History (1)* p.23-25
   Willison — *Saints* p.135-136, 211
- Daughters
   Hills — *History (1)* p.47
- Heads of families
   Hills — *History (1)* p.44-45
- "Hired hands" and servants
   Leynse — *Preced.* p.270-271
   Willison — *Pilgrim* p.536-538
   Willison — *Saints* p.442-443
, Number of
   Dillon — *Pilgrims* p.121, 124-125
- Planters and families
   Hills — *History (1)* p.29, 36-41
- "Saints"
   Gill — *Mayflower* p.123
   Leynse — *Preced.* p.265-268
   Willison — *Pilgrim* p.531-534
   Willison — *Saints* p.437-440
- Sons
   Hills — *History (1)* p.46
- "Strangers"
   Leynse — *Preced.* p.268-271
   Willison — *Pilgrim* p.79-80, 90-91, 155, 295, 534-536
   Willison — *Saints* p.440-443; See also index p.510
- "Unattached persons"
   Hills — *History (1)* p.47-50
- Wives
   Hills — *History (1)* p.46-47
   Williams — *Demeter's* p.23-24
- Women
   Hills — *History (1)* p.55-61
   Williams — *Demeter's* p.21
- Young people
   Hills — *History (1)* p.53-54

MAYFLOWER (ship) (*continued*)

- *Preparations*
    See also **Mayflower** —Supplies
    taken
    Archer — *Mayflower* p.52-59
- *Return voyage*
    Caffrey — *Mayflower* p.145
    Dillon — *Pilgrims* p.159-160, 167
    Gill — *Mayflower* p.85-87
    Willison — *Pilgrim* p.137-139
    Willison — *Saints* p.180
    , *with "Speedwell"*
        Caffrey — *Mayflower* p.100-
        102
- *Route maps*
    Marshall — *Mayflower* p.31, 41
    , *Speculations on*
    Caffrey — *Mayflower* p.324-331
- *Supplies taken*
    Caffrey — *Mayflower* p.70-73
    Gill — *Mayflower* p.43-48, 57-58,
    129
- *Tonnage and displacement*
    Dillon — *Pilgrims* p.123
- *Voyage*
    Archer — *Mayflower* p.71-79
    Caffrey — *Mayflower* p.104-112
    Dillon — *Pilgrims* p.118-130
    Gill — *Mayflower* p.67-73
    Hills — *History (1)* p.62-65
    Marshall — *Mayflower* p.30-52
    Morris — *Ency.* p.31
    Starkey — *Land* p.46, 49-50
    Williams — *Demeter's* p.22
    Willison — *Pilgrim* p.89-102
    Willison — *Saints. See* index
    p.504

MAYFLOWER II (ship)
    Caffrey — *Mayflower* p.66-67, 88, 105
    Gill — *Mayflower* p.64-68
    Marshall — *Mayflower* p.32-38, 44
    Willison — *Saints* p.267-268, 270-
    271, 340, 470

- *Passengers (1629)*
    Hills — *History (1)* p.86-87
    - *"Saints"*
        Willison — *Pilgrim* p.545
        Willison — *Saints* p.450-451
    - *"Strangers"*
        Willison — *Pilgrim* p.313,
        316-317, 545-546
        Willison — *Saints* p.451

MAYFLOWER COMPACT (1620)
    Adams — *Album* p.42
    Amer. Her. — *Thirteen* p.90, 94
    Angle — *By* p.3-4
    Annals of America (1) p.64
    Bailey — *American (1)* p.26
    Caffrey — *Mayflower* p.114, 156, 332
    Carman — *History (1)* p.28
    Chitwood — *History (1)* p.98-100
    Collins — *Story* p.40
    Dillon — *Pilgrims* p.136-138, 223
    Hawke — *U.S.* p.88-89
    Hills — *History (1)* p.68-69
    Hope — *Nation* p.78
    Leynse — *Preced.* p.241, 250, 253-
    255, 273-274
    Marshall — *Mayflower* p.52, 160, 179-
    181
    Morison — *Story* p.44-45, 76, 87, 101,
    147-149
    Morris — *Ency.* p.31
    Pomfret — *Founding* p.121-123, 125-
    127
    Rozwenc — *Making (1)* p.28
    Willison — *Pilgrim* p.100-101
    Willison — *Saints* p.143-144, 286,
    366, 465
    , *as democracy*
        Nettels — *Roots* p.167-168
        Speare — *Life* p.39
    - *Signers*
        Hills — *History (1)* p.69
        Willison — *Pilgrim* p.554

MAYFLOWER COMPANY
    Willison — *Pilgrim* p.89-92

MAYHEW, THOMAS, JR.
    Vaughan — *New* p.243-244, 252, 258-
    259, 268, 273, 286-287, 295, 301
    Willison — *Saints* p.388, 410, 418

MAYHIEU, HESTER. *See* **COOKE, HES-**
TER MAYHIEU

MAYPOLES
    Dulles — *America* p.3
    Earle — *Customs* p.227-228
    - *Pilgrims*
        Willison — *Saints* p.47, 276-277,
        282-283, 462-463

MEAT
    - *Preservation*
        Gould — *Early* p.100
        Marshall — *Mayflower* p.89-91

- *Stripping and drying*
    Gould — *Early* p.103
- *Trade*
    Rutman — *Winthrop's* p.185,
    187-189

MEDICINE
See also **Indians — Medicine;**
Pilgrims — Medicine; Remedies;
related subjects
Adams — *Album* p.120
Bridenbaugh — *Cities* p.88-92
Chitwood — *History (1)* p.473
Earle — *Customs* p.340-352
Glubok — *Home* p.96-98
Hawke — *Colonial* p.300-301
Marshall — *Mayflower* p.119-132
Morison — *Intellect. See* index p.283
Wertenbaker — *First. See* index p.349
Williams — *Demeter's* p.116, 303
, *and astrology*
    Miller — *First* p.245
- *Boston, Mass.*
    Wertenbaker — *First* p.171
- *Connecticut*
    Wertenbaker — *First* p.171-172
- *Laws, early*
    Miller — *First* p.245-247
- *Massachusetts*
    Wertenbaker — *First* p.171-172
- *New Amsterdam*
    Bridenbaugh — *Cities* p.90-91
- *New England*
    Wertenbaker — *First* p.171-172
- *New Jersey*
    Wertenbaker — *First* p.172-173
- *Origin*
    Vaughan — *New* p.20-21
- *Philadelphia Pa.*
    Clark — *Old* p.75
- *Virginia*
    Wertenbaker — *First* p.172, 176-
    177
- *Women*
    Leonard — *Dear* p.210-211, 218-
    222, 471
    - *Virginia*
        Leonard — *Dear* p.480

MEETINGHOUSES
See also **Churches;** names of
meetinghouses
Adams — *Album* p.125
Earle — *Home* p.364-369
Hawke — *Colonial* p.152-153, 286
Rawson — *When* p.175-177, 204

Rutman — *Winthrop's. See* index
p.314
Scott — *Settlers* p.36
Wertenbaker — *Puritan* p.107-115
Willison — *Saints. See* index p.505
- *Connecticut*
    Johnston — *Conn.* p.48
- *New England*
    Morison — *Early* p.79-82

"MELTING POT"
See also **Nationalities**
Speare — Life p.67
- *New York and New Netherland*
    - *View from abroad*
        Axtell — *America* p.127-159

MEMBERTOU (Indian)
Snell — *Wild* p.72-73

MENIALS. *See* **Servants; Slaves and**
slavery

MENNONITES
Amer. Her. — *Thirteen* p.170-172
Calverton — *Awake.* p.186-187
Morris — *Ency.* p.549
Sweet — *Religion* p.213-214
Ver Steeg — *Formative* p.212
Willison — *Saints* p.32, 73, 79, 457
Wish — *Society (1)* p.94-95, 106
, *against slavery*
    Annals of America (1) p.274-275
- *Founding of Germantown*
    Leonard — *Dear* p.69
, *German*
    Sweet — *Religion* p.15

MERCANTILISM
Bailyn — *New England* p.113, 128,
130-131, 151, 182, 184
Chitwood — *History (1)* p.414-417
Hawke — *Colonial* p.66, 82, 174-177,
187, 203
Johnston — *Conn.* p.56-57
Morris — *Ency.* p.483
Rothbard — *Conceived (1)* p.260-262
Smith — *17th* p.100, 166-167, 171
Ver Steeg — *Formative* p.11-12, 31,
109-110
, *and empire*
    Goetzmann — *Colonial* p.120-
    121
, *British, and Virginia*
    Rothbard — *Conceived (1)* p.87-
    94

MERCHANTS
See also **Atherton Company; Fairs; Peddlers; Shops and shopkeepers**
Adams — *Provincial* p.43-47
Bridenbaugh — *Cities* p.38-41
Folsom — *Give* p.ix, 3, 24, 50, 53, 65-66, 68, 76, 86
Rothbard — *Conceived (1)* p.260-262
Rutman — *Winthrop's. See* index p.314
Ver Steeg — *Formative* p.63-65
Wertenbaker — *Puritan* p.195-200

- *Boston, Mass.*
    Rutman — *Winthrop's. See* index p.314
    Wertenbaker — *First* p.71-72
- *Bristol*
    Pomfret — *Founding* p.2-3, 13, 25, 132, 135-136, 140-142
, *Conflict with clergy*
    Wertenbaker — *First* p.111-113
- *Conflict with Puritan authorities*
    Bailyn — *New England* p.40-44, 105-111, 137-142
- *Connecticut*
    Bailyn — *New England* p.95-96
- *Correspondence*
    See also **Kinship**
    Bailyn — *New England* p.78-82, 87-91, 102, 142, 144, 147, 190
, *Differences among*
    Bailyn — *New England* p.15-16, 109-111, 134-135, 109-111, 122-125, 134-135, 190-191
- *Economic position*
    Nettels — *Roots* p.259, 261-264
- *"Gentleman" ideal*
    Bailyn — *New England* p.101-102, 194, 196
- *Influence*
    Bailyn — *New England* p.75, 98-99
- *Interests*
    Bridenbaugh — *New England* p.168, 170-190, 197
- *Ironworks*
    Bailyn — *New England* p.64, 67, 69-70
- *Maine*
    Bailyn — *New England* p.138
- *Massachusetts*
    Wertenbaker — *First* p.71-72

- *New England*
    Bailyn — *New England* p.33-34, 75, 92-93
    Wertenbaker — *First* p.53-55, 70-72
, *versus England*
    Nettels — *Roots* p.284-289
- *Northern towns*
    Nettels — *Roots* p.312
- *Political power*
    Bailyn — *New England* p.103-105, 142-143, 159-160, 169-170, 174-178, 180
- *Public offices*
    Bailyn — *New England* p.37-40
- *Recruitment*
    Bailyn — *New England* p.31, 35-37, 39, 82, 110-111, 125, 194-195
- *Rhode Island*
    Bailyn — *New England* p.95-96
- *Salem, Mass.*
    Gildrie — *Salem. See* index p.186
- *South*
    - *Education*
        Wertenbaker — *Old* p.23-24
- *Virginia*
    Goetzmann — *Colonial* p.127-128
- *Wealth and influence*
    Wertenbaker — *Puritan* p.203-206
    - *Names*
        Nettels — *Roots* p.310
- *West-country*
    Bailyn — *New England. See* index p.249
- *Women*
    Leonard — *Dear* p.439-440

MERCHANT'S HOPE (ship)
- *Passengers (1635)*
    Demos — *Remarkable* p.37-38

MERRIMAC(K) RIVER
Bailyn — *New England* p.26, 28, 51, 55-56, 173

MERIMAC(K) RIVER INDIANS
Beals — *John Eliot* p.133-134

MERRYMOUNT COLONY (Mt. Wollaston, Quincy, Mass.)
See also **Morton, Thomas**
Caffrey — *Mayflower* p.222-224, 226

Calverton — *Awake.* p.115-118
Dillon — *Pilgrims* p.201-203, 214
Gill — *Mayflower* p.122, 131, 134, 166, 180
Miller — *Colonial* p.108-112
Pomfret — *Founding* p.144-152
Sweet — *Religion* p.80-81
Vaughan — *New* p.89-90, 99
Willison — *Pilgrim* p.331-333
Willison — *Saints* p.273-274, 279-281
, *Confrontations at*
    Marshall — *Mayflower* p.184
- *Festivities*
    Dulles — *America* p.3-4

METACOM (BET). *See* **Philip, King (Indian)**

"METHEGLIN" (MATHOGLIN) (drink)
Earle — *Customs* p.169-171

MEY, CORNELIUS, CAPTAIN
Christensen — *Delaware* p.16

MIANTONOMO (H) (Indian)
Beals — *John Eliot* p.104-105, 156-157
Caffrey — *Mayflower* p.270-271
Vaughan — *New* p.55, 97, 127, 132, 143, 150-152, 155-157, 161-166, 258, 325, 340-341, 348
Willison — *Pilgrim* p.561-562

MICHAËLIUS, JONAS (JOHANNIS), DOMINE
Wright — *Cultural* p.85-86
- *"Attempts to Christianize the Indians" (1628)*
    Annals of America (1) p.92-94
- *"Letter from . . ." (1628)*
    Amer. Her. — *Thirteen* p.148-149
, *on Manhattan, N.Y.*
    Axtell — *America* p.69-72
, *on New Netherland*
    Axtell — *America* p.127-133

MICMAC INDIANS
Snell — *Wild* p.64-66, 72-73

MICUM McINTYRE GARRISON HOUSE (Scotland, Maine, 1640's)
Morrison — *Early* p.78-79

MIDDLE COLONIES
See also **New Netherland; New Jersey; Pennsylvania;** special subjects
- *Accomplishments & problems (1639)*
    Jernegan — *American* p.239-241
- *Class and status*
    Rozwenc — *Making (1)* p.49-51
- *Economic and social factors*
    Jernegan — *American* p.216
- *Industries and occupations*
    Jernegan — *American* p.222-224
- *Intellectual life*
    Jernegan — *American* p.234-238
- *People*
    Jernegan — *American* p.216-217
- *Settlements*
    Jernegan — *American* p.215-216
    Morris — *Ency.* p.41-49
- *Social conditions*
    Jernegan — *American* p.227-231
- *Trade and commerce*
    Jernegan — *American* p.225-227

MIDDELBURG, HOLLAND
Lynse — *Preced.* See index p.283

MIDDLEBORO, MASSACHUSETTS. *See* **Nemasket, Massachusetts**

MIDWIVES
Dexter — *Colonial* p.60-64
Leonard — *Dear* p.221-222, 473-475, 480
Rutman — *Winthrop's* p.136, 231
Wertenbaker — *First* p.177-178
Williams — *Demeter's* p.171
- *Boston, Mass.*
    Bridenbaugh — *Cities* p.90
, *Dutch*
    Leonard — *Dear* p.476-477
- *New Amsterdam*
    Bridenbaugh — *Cities* p.91
- *Plymouth*
    Demos — *Little* p.131, 150, 152

MIGRATION
See also **Indians — Migrations, Seasonal; Nationalities; Puritans — Migration**
Chitwood — *History (1)* p.104-109
Vaughan — *New* p.29-31, 55, 93, 116-117, 214, 335-337
Ver Steeg — *Formative* p.13, 35-38, 42-52, 65-67, 116, 120-121, 131, 158, 166-169

MIGRATION (*continued*)

, *English (1625–42)*
Rozwenc — *Making (1)* p.31-32
, *Non-English*
Ver Steeg — *Formative* p.164-
167
- *Reasons (1622)*
Demos — *Remarkable* p.25-31

MILBORNE, JACOB
Rothbard — *Conceived (1)* p.436,
441-442, 444, 446-447, 461, 466,
468

MILESTONES
Earle — *Home* p.335-336

MILITARY UNIFORMS
Speare — *Life* p.89

MILITIA
See also **Training Day**
Craven — *Colonies* p.30-31, 67, 123,
127, 155
Craven — *Southern. See* index p.444
Rutman — *Winthrop's. See* index
p.314
Vaughan — *New* p.95, 102-103, 138-
139, 153-154, 196-197, 289
- *Boston, Mass.*
Demos — *Remarkable* p.247-249
Rutman — *Winthrop's. See* index
p.314-315
- *Company, Oldest*
Adams — *Album* p.110
- *Exclusion of Jews, New Amsterdam*
Annals of America (1) p.221
- *Exemptions, law for*
Vaughan — *New* p.330
- *South*
Craven — *Southern* p.167, 170-
171, 276-277, 306-307, 364,
371n, 377
- *"Train bands"*
Adams — *Album* p.94-95
Speare — *Life* p.85-88

MILK ROOMS
Gould — *Early* p.37

MILKWEED
Earle — *Home* p.35, 211

MILLER, PERRY
Murdock — *Literature* p.35-36, 40, 91,
222

- *"Puritan state and Puritan society"*
Goetzmann — *Colonial* p.148-
159

MILLER, PETER
Calverton — *Awake.* p.203

MILLERS
Tunis — *Craftsmen* p.29-32

MILLINERS. *See* **Hats and hatters**

"MILLINERY WAR"
Willison — *Saints* p.66-68, 320, 457

MILLS AND MILLING
See also **Millers; Waterwheels;
Windmills**
Amer. Her. — *Treasury* p.152-155
Bridenbaugh — *Cities* p.36
Chitwood — *History (1)* p.380
Lawrence — *New* p.4-5
Leonard — *Dear* p.141-142
Morison — *Story* p.141, 167, 190n,
192, 224
, *Grist*
Earle — *Home* p.133
Wertenbaker — *First* p.79-80,
310
- *Boston*
Wertenbaker — *First* p.80
, *Hand*
Gould — *Early* p.107
- *New England*
See also **"Newport Tower"**
Morrison — *Early* p.92-95
- *New Netherland*
Tunis — *Colonial* p.72-73
- *Pennsylvania*
Adams — *Album* p.250
, *Tide*
Adams — *Album* p.119
- *Women*
Leonard — *Dear* p.464-465

MINES AND MINING
See also types of mines
Adams — *Provincial* p.40-41
Chitwood — *History (1)* p.378

MINISTERS. *See* **Clergymen**

"MINNEWIT." *See* **Minuit, Peter**

MINT
Bailyn — *New England* p.186-187
- *Massachusetts*
Langdon — *Everyday* p.195-196

MINTER, DESIRE
Hills — *History (1)* p.21, 29, 36, 38, 50-54, 60-61
Marble — *Women* p.24, 58-59, 86

MINUIT, PETER ("Minnewit")
Alderman — *Story* p.48, 103-104
Christensen — *Delaware* p.25-26, 28, 34-35
Hawke — *Colonial* p.217, 220, 227
Morris — *Ency.* p.41-42
Starkey — *Land* p.141, 144, 152-153, 157
- *Manhattan Purchase*
Leonard — *Dear* p.55

"MISLEN" (wheat and rye)
Hope — *Nation* p.85

MISSIONS AND MISSIONARIES
See also **Plymouth — Missionaries;**
names of missionaries
Vaughan — *New* p.185, 234-308, 333-334
- *Women*
Leonard — *Dear* p.352

MISSISSIPPI RIVER AND VALLEY
Amer. Her. — *Thirteen* p.19, 201
- *Bienville's army*
Collins — *Story* p.84
- *French expansion*
Morris — *Ency.* p.61
- *Joliet and Marquette*
Collins — *Story* p.80
- *La Salle*
See also **La Salle, René Robert, Cavelier, Sieur de**
Collins — *Story*

MITCHELL, EXPERIENCE
Willison — *Saints* p.446-447

MITCHELL, JANE COOKE
Willison — *Saints* p.505

MITTENS
Earle — *Home* p.262
Rawson — *When* p.120-121

MODESTY
- *Laws to enforce*
Wertenbaker — *Puritan* p.166-167

"MODESTY-PIECE"
Earle — *Home* p.270-271

MOHAWK INDIANS
Amer. Her. — *Thirteen* p.129, 132-133, 196
Caffrey — *Mayflower* p.263, 265, 272-273
Craven — *Colonies* p.122, 124-125
Morrison — *Story* p.165, 211, 237, 260-263, 269
Starkey — *Land* p.146-147, 207
Vaughan — *New* p.38, 58, 150, 291, 325
- *Albany, N.Y.*
Scott — *Settlers* p.12-13

MOHEGAN (MAHICAN) INDIANS
Alderman — *Story* p.71-72
Caffrey — *Mayflower* p.265, 270
Morison — *Story* p.209, 211-214, 264, 272
Vaughan — *New* p.55, 57, 182, 321;
See also index p.426

MOLINES. See Mullins

MONACAN INDIANS
Smith — *17th* p.43, 48-49, 55, 60n

MONEY
See also **Currency; Jamestown — Money; Wampum**
Carman — *History (1)* p.60, 81-83
Dow — *Every* p.166-171
- *Connecticut*
Johnston — *Conn.* p.55-57
- *Exchange, Bills of*
Bailyn — *New England* p.67, 80-81, 85, 91, 98, 104, 130, 182-183
, *in foreign trade*
Langdon — *Everyday* p.194-195
- *Paper*
Bailyn — *New England* p.188-189
Langdon — *Everyday* p.196-197
- *First*
Dow — *Every* p.172

MONEY (*continued*)
- *Scarcity*
    Hope — *Nation* p.87
- *Substitutes*
    Woodward — *Way* p.20-21

MONHEGAN ISLAND, MAINE
See also **Thanksgiving Day, First**
Adams — *Album* p.64
Gill — *Mayflower* p.82, 103, 114
Willison — *Pilgrim* p.291-292
Willison — *Saints* p.184, 260
- *Landings*
    Mitchell — *It's* p.62-65, 147, 148,
    184

MONMOUTH GRANT
Craven — *Colonies* p.82-83, 93-94

**MONOMOY (CHATHAM),
    MASSACHUSETTS**
Willison — *Saints* p.212–213

MONOPOLIES
See also **Council for New England**
Bailyn — *New England* p.34, 64, 133-
    134, 151
Rutman — *Winthrop's* p.131-132,
    181, 231-232, 249-251

MONOTO (Indian)
Caffrey — *Mayflower* p.389

MONTAUP. *See* **Mount Hope Neck,
    Rhode Island**

MONTFORT, ANN(E) (HANNAH). *See*
    Eliot, Ann(e) (Hannah) Montfort

MONTS, PIERRE DU GUA, SIEUR DE
Snell — *Wild* p.66-67, 72-73, 94

MOODEY, SAMUEL, REV.
Dow — *Every* p.103

MOODY, DEBORAH, LADY
Earle — *Colonial* p.51-52
Leonard — *Dear* p.56
Sweet — *Religion* p.131
Williams — *Demeter's* p.125-126, 188

MOORS (race)
, *in S.Delaware*
    Christensen — *Delaware* p.100-
    101

"MOOSE-COATS" (mooseskin coats)
Earle — *Two cent. (1)* p.178

MORALITY
See also **Punishment; Puritans —
    Morality; Religion; Sins and
    sinners;** names of clergymen; etc.
Nettels — *Roots* p.449-450, 452
Rutman — *Winthrop's. See* index
    p.315
Wertenbaker — *First. See* index
    p.349-350
Wertenbaker — *Puritan. See* index
    p.354
Wish — *Society (1)* p.44-45, 55, 61-
    62, 79-80
- *Connecticut*
    Lawrence *Not* p.20-30
- *Delinquency*
    Bridenbaugh — *Cities* p.71-72
- *Massachusetts Code*
    Wertenbaker — *First* p.189-192,
    194-200
- *New England*
    Wertenbaker — *First* p.109-110,
    192-195
    - *Regulation and control*
        Jernegan — *American*
        p.181, 184
    - *Views of John Winthrop*
        Jernegan — *American* p.181
    - *Views of William Bradford*
        Jernegan — *American* p.181
- *South*
    Wertenbaker — *First* p.203-207
    - *Courts*
        See also **County courts**
        Craven — *Southern* p.167-
        169
- *Standards*
    Jernegan — *American* p.102-103
- *Statute of 1647*
    Lawrence — *Not* p.28-29
- *Women, Books on*
    Spruill — *Women's* p.213-216

MORAVIANS
See also **Beissel, Johann Conrad**
Calverton — *Awake.* p.183-186

MORAY, ALEXANDER, REV.
Craven — *Southern* p.315-316

MORE, RICHARD
Hills — *History (1)* p.21, 29, 36, 39,
    49-50, 52, 54, 60, 89

Hills — *History (2)* p.188-189
Willison — *Saints* p.134-135, 443

MORE FAMILY
Hills — *History (1) See* index p.170

MORRELL, WILLIAM
Willison — *Saints* p.238-239

MORRIS, LEWIS
Alderman — *Story* p.55-56

MORRIS, MARY. *See* **Cushman, Mary Morris Allerton**

MORTALITY
See also **Death rate; Infant mortality**
, *from childbearing*
    Wertenbaker — *First* p.183-184
- *Hingham, Mass.*
    Wertenbaker — *First* p.181-182
, *Puritan view of*
    Morgan — *Puritan* p.15-16
- *Virginia*
    Wertenbaker — *First* p.179

MORTON, CHARLES
Morison — *Intellect.* p.236, 266-268

MORTON, EPHRAIM
Willison — *Saints* p.447, 460

MORTON, GEORGE
, *and family*
    Willison — *Pilgrim* p.103, 235
    Willison — *Saints. See* index p.505

MORTON, JOHN
Willison — *Saints* p.387, 447

MORTON, NATHANIEL
Dillon — *Pilgrims* p.105-107, 129
Morison — *Intellect.* p.12, 178-182, 257
Murdock — *Literature* p.92-94
Smith — *17th* p.210-211, 215, 218
Willison — *Pilgrim* p.96, 235-444n, 563-564
Willison — *Saints. See* index p.505

MORTON, PATIENCE. *See* **Faunce, Patience Morton**

MORTON, THOMAS
See also **Merrymount Colony**
Amer. Her. — *Thirteen* p.95-96

Caffrey — *Mayflower* p.117, 154, 198, 222-227, 231-232, 251
Collins — *Story* p.47
Dillon — *Pilgrims* p.166, 200-203, 205, 214, 221
Life — *New* p.78, 88
Marshall — *Mayflower* p.54, 81, 88-89, 184
Miller — *Colonial* p.103-107
Morison — *Story* p.106-110
Pomfret — *Founding* p.152, 165-166, 168-169
Vaughan — *New* p.31, 36-37, 43-46, 89-91, 98-99, 187, 220, 228
Wertenbaker — *First* p.17-18, 277-278
Willison — *Pilgrim* p.333-337; *See also* index p.578-579
Willison — *Saints. See* index p.505
- *"New England Canaan" (1637)*
    Amer. Her. — *Thirteen* p.145-146
    Miller — *Colonial* p.76
- *"On Puritan intolerance"*
    Annals of America (1) p.125-129
- *Views of William Bradford, et al*
    See also **Bradford, William — "Thomas Morton of Merrymount"**
    Vaughan — *Puritan* p.205-207

MORTON FAMILY
Caffrey — *Mayflower. See* index p.389

MORYSON, FRANCIS
Craven — *Southern* p.268-269n, 315n, 390, 403

MOSQUITOES
Scott — *Settlers* p.10-11

MOTHERS. *See* **Pilgrims — Mothers**

MOTTERSHED, T.
- *"Articles . . . against Charles Chauncey, 1630"*
    Demos — *Remarkable* p.32-36

MOUNT DESERT ISLAND, MAINE
Mitchell — *It's* p.58

MOUNT HOPE NECK, RHODE ISLAND
Willison — *Saints* p.394, 396, 398, 401-402

MOUNT WOLLASTON. *See* **Merrymount Colony**

MOUNTAINS
, and valleys — South
 Wertenbaker — Old p.8-9

MOUNTFORT, HANNAH. See Eliot,
 Ann(e) (Hannah) Montfort

MOURNING ATTIRE. See Funerals —
 Clothing and dress

MOURNING PIECES. See Funerals

MOURT, G. (pseud. of William Bradford
 and Edward Winslow)
 Dillion — Pilgrims p.139-141, 144,
 162, 164, 168
 - "Relation"
 Willison — Saints. See index
 p.505

MUDDY RIVER, MASSACHUSETTS
 Lawrence — New p.10-11
 Rutman — Winthrop's. See index
 p.315

MUGS AND JUGS. See Jugs

MULBERRY
 - Jamestown, Va.
 Adams — Album p.17

MULLINS, PRISCILLA. See Alden, Priscilla Mullins

MULLINS (MOLINES), WILLIAM
 Hills — History (1). See index p.171
 Hills — History (2) p.149, 156, 203,
 213-215, 217, 220, 224, 239
 Leynse — Preced. p.235, 253, 262,
 269
 Williams — Saints. See index p.505

MULLINS FAMILY
 Gill — Mayflower p.73, 81
 Hills — History (1). See index p.170-
 171
 Hills — History (2). See index p.267
 Leynse — Preced. See index p.269,
 283
 Marble — Women p.12, 72-74

MUNITIONS. See Guns

MURDER
 Vaughan — New p.14, 44, 87, 126-
 130, 132-134, 187, 192, 201-202,
 318

, First
 - Massachusetts
 Dow — Every p.202
 - Plymouth
 Willison — Saints p.285-286,
 297-299, 319, 443
 - Punishment for
 Wertenbaker — First p.214-216

MUSCOVY COMPANY
 Craven — Southern p.10, 15, 31, 37,
 38n, 43n, 65
 Rothbard — Conceived (1) p.35-40,
 43-45, 166

MUSIC
 See also Ballads; Hymns; Indians —
 Music; Plymouth — Music;
 Psalms and psalm singing; Puri-
 tans —Music; Singing; Songs; etc.
 Chitwood — History (1) p.476-477
 Goodrich — Colonial p.162-164
 Morris — Ency. p.614
 Wertenbaker — Puritan p.128-133
 Wish — Society (1) p.30, 47
 , Instrumental
 Howard — Our p.21-22
 , Secular — New England
 Howard — Our p.20-22
 - South
 Wertenbaker — First p.268-269

MUSICAL INSTRUMENTS
 Rawson — When p.98-99, 199

MUSKOGEANS (MUSKHOGEANS)
 (Indians)
 Hawke — Colonial p.80
 Nettels — Roots p.152

MUTILATION
 Jernegan — American p.182
 - Letters, wearing of — as punishment
 Miller — First p.255, 257
 - Massachusetts, law in
 Wertenbaker — Puritan p.213
 - New England
 Wertenbaker — First p.216-217
 - New Haven
 Wertenbaker — Puritan p.213-
 214
 - New Jersey
 Wertenbaker — First p.220

- *Quakers*
  Wertenbaker — *Puritan* p.234-237
- *South*
  Wertenbaker — *First* p.217-218

MYLES, JOHN
Sweet — *Religion* p.133-134

MYSTIC FORT
Vaughan — *New* p.122, 144-148, 310, 324-325

N

NAILS
Adams — *Album* p.77
Hope — *Nation* p.87
Johnston — *Conn.* p.48
Speare — *Life* p.123
Woodward — *Way* p.41
- *Scarcity*
  Earle — *Home* p.11

"NAKED SIGN" (Quaker rebellion)
Williams — *Demeter's* p.129

NAMES
Earle — *Colonial* p.277-278, 292-294
, *Anglicized (new flora and fauna)*
  Hawke — *Colonial* p.78
, *Children's*
  Earle — *Customs* p.24
, *Dutch, in New York*
  Hawke — *Colonial* p.221
, *Old and new*
  Hawke — *Colonial* p.305-306

NANSEMOND INDIANS
Smith — *17th* p.42, 55, 59

NANTASKET (HULL), MASSACHUSETTS
Willison — *Saints* p.249, 251-252, 346, 448-449, 458

NANTICOKE INDIANS
Smith — *17th* p.42, 59
- *Delaware, South*
  Christensen — *Delaware* p.100-101

NAPKINS
Earle — *Customs* p.133-134
Earle — *Home* p.77
Glubok — *Home* p.41-42

NARRAGANSETT BAY, RHODE ISLAND
See also **Fur trade**
Alderman — *Story* p.72, 94, 96-98, 101
Bailyn — *New England* p.14, 24, 26, 58-60, 139; *See also* index p.246
Rothbard — *Conceived (1)* p.373-374
Willison — *Saints* p.172, 287, 329, 351-352, 354, 382

NARRAGANSETT INDIANS
Alderman — *Story* p.29, 72, 93
Beals — *John Eliot* p.104-105, 147, 157
Beck — *Pilgrims* p.23, 37, 41, 45
Caffrey — *Mayflower* p.162-163, 261-263, 270, 272-274
Craven — *Colonies* p.119-121
Dillon — *Pilgrims* p.163, 168-170, 199, 212, 215
Folsom — *Give* p.16, 18, 36, 38-40
Johnston — *Conn.* p.24-26, 92
Marshall — *Mayflower* p.153
Morison — *Oxford* p.108
Morison — *Story* p.88, 132, 209-214, 237, 247, 263-269, 271
Snell — *Wild* p.126, 128, 135
Vaughan — *New. See* index p.426
Willison — *Pilgrim* p.172, 174-175, 304, 314, 477, 496n
Willison — *Saints. See* index p.505
Wish — *Society (1)* p.36-37, 39
, *and New England Confederation*
  Annals of America (1) p.85-86
- *Plymouth*
  Annals of America (1) p.70

NASHOBA (LITTLETON, MASS.) (praying town)
Vaughan — *New* p.291

NATICK, MASSACHUSETTS (praying town)
Beals — *John Eliot* p.138, 142-150, 152, 154, 157-159, 161, 170-171, 181-183
Vaughan — *New* p.263-270, 286, 289-290, 317, 321
, *Building of*
  Beals — *John Eliot* p.104-146
, *Destruction of*
  Beals — *John Eliot* p.170-172
- *Indian settlement*
  Amer. Her. — *Pioneer* p.60

148

NATICK INDIANS
- *Language, vocabulary*
  Demos — *Remarkable* p.255-276

NATIONALITIES
See also **Immigrants and immigration; "Melting pot"; Women — Nationalities; names of nationalities**
Bridenbaugh — *Cities* p.94-96
Carman — *History (1)* p.41-51
- *Distribution*
  Jernegan — *American* p.227
- *Race relations*
  Wish — *Society (1)* p.68-71, 76
- *Racial diversity*
  - *Middle Colonies*
    Jernegan — *American*
    p.227-230

NATIVE AMERICANS. *See* **Indians**

NATURAL HISTORY
Morris — *Ency.* p.528
- *Changing nature*
  - *Views of John Wise*
    Goetzmann — *Colonial*
    p.197-200
- *Flora and fauna*
  Hawke — *Colonial* p.78

NATURAL RESOURCES. *See* **New England — Natural resources; Plymouth — Natural resources**

NAUMKEAG, (SALEM) MASSACHUSETTS
Snell — *Wild* p.118, 124
Willison — *Saints* p.252-253, 267, 270, 272, 279, 283-286, 448, 458

NAUNTON, ROBERT, SIR
Willison — *Pilgrim* p.56-57
Willison — *Saints* p.100, 108

NAUSET (EASTHAM), MASSACHUSETTS
Willison — *Pilgrim* p.113, 482-483
Willison — *Saints* p.150-155, 169, 183-184, 217-219, 332

NAUSET INDIANS
Caffrey — *Mayflower* p.136
Dillon — *Pilgrims* p.144-145, 154, 164
Gill — *Mayflower* p.82, 141

Morison — *Story* p.50-52, 68, 78, 92-95, 115-116, 142, 145, 234, 242, 249
Vaughan — *New* p.57, 59-60, 65-67, 74-75, 85, 191, 301, 314-319
Willison — *Pilgrim* p.142-143, 200
Willison — *Saints* p.172, 183-184, 187, 213, 223, 229, 467

NAVIGATION
See also **Quadrant**
Caffrey — *Mayflower* p.92, 96-97
- *Astrolabe*
  Caffrey — *Mayflower* p.93
- *Charts and instruments*
  Caffrey — *Mayflower* p.93-94
  Marshall — *Mayflower* p.16, 38-40
- *Compass*
  Caffrey — *Mayflower* p.93
- *Lead and line*
  Caffrey — *Mayflower,* p.96-97
  - *"Shooting the sun"*
    Marshall — *Mayflower* p.38, 44
  - *Traverse board*
    Caffrey — *Mayflower* p.93

NAVIGATION ACTS
Abbot — *Colonial* p.54-55, 65, 70-71, 73, 75, 78
Adams — *Provincial* p.47
Alderman — *Story* p.15, 30
Amer. Her. — *Thirteen* p.136, 157-158, 177, 214-215, 217
Bailyn — *New England. See* index p.246
Carman — *History (1)* p.42, 77, 131-134
Chitwood — *History (1)* p.417-418
Goetzmann — *Colonial* p.120-125
Hawke — *Colonial. See* index p.746
Hawke — *U.S.* p.148-154
Hope — *Nation* p.122-123
Jernegan — *American* p.62-63, 260-261
Morris — *Ency.* p.484
Nettels — *Roots* p.280-285, 288, 372, 375, 550-551
Rothbard — *Conceived (1)* p.88-90, 268, 285, 287-289, 342-343, 355, 378, 413, 461-463, 469, 502-504
Rozwenc — *Making (1)* p.79-81, 116, 118, 127
Ver Steeg — *Formative* p.108-112

Wertenbaker — *First* p.11, 42-43, 81
Wertenbaker — *Puritan* p.199-200,
   307, 317-318, 321-323, 325-326
, *and royal charters*
   Craven — *Colonies* p.32-67
- *Maryland*
   Wertenbaker — *First* p.42-43

NAZIG, ENGLAND
Beals — *John Eliot* p.9-20, 26, 28, 31,
   43-46, 55, 62, 69, 77, 82, 138

NEALE, THOMAS
Langdon — *Everyday* p.262-263

NECKWEAR
See also **Cravats**
Earle — *Two cent. (1)* p.69-70, 197-
   213

NEEDLEPOINT
Rawson — *When* p.119

NEEDLEWORK
See also types of needlework
Glubok — *Home* p.221-227
Rawson — *When* p.111-138
Speare — *Life* p.81-82
- *Boston, Mass.*
   Clark — *Old* p.40-41
- *New York*
   Clark — *Old* p.63-64

NEFF, MARY
Williams — *Demeter's* p.163-165

NEGROES
See also **Music, Negro; Slaves and
   slavery**
Amer. Her. — *Thirteen* p.81-82, 140,
   155
Craven — *Colonies* p.20, 55, 102
Craven — *Southern. See* index p.445
Folsom — *Give* p.54, 65, 69, 88
Pomfret — *Founding* p.6, 40-41, 41n,
   86, 221, 270, 286, 321-322, 329-
   330
Wertenbaker — *First. See* index p.350
Willison — *Saints* p.370, 479-480
, *as commodities*
   Calverton — *Awake.* p.270-272
- *Carolinas*
   Craven — *Southern* p.327, 338n,
   341-342, 351, 358
   Starkey — *Land* p.229-231

- *Crime and criminals*
   Bridenbaugh — *Cities* p.68-69
- *First importation (1619, Va.)*
   Life — *New* p.98
- *Maryland*
   Rozwenc — *Making (1)* p.46-47
- *New Netherland*
   Starkey — *Land* p.165
- *Plymouth*
   Demos — *Little* p.110-111
- *Population*
   Calverton — *Awake.* p.273-274,
   278
- *Religion*
   Chitwood — *History (1)* p.452-
   453
   - *Views of Cotton Mather*
      Vaughan — *Puritan* p.267-
      271
- *South*
   Craven — *Southern* p.217-219,
   341-342, 402-403; *See also* in-
   dex p.445
- *Spanish origin of word*
   Williams — *Demeter's* p.66
- *Virginia*
   Craven — *Southern* p.128, 214,
   400-401, 404
   Pomfret — *Founding* p.40-41, 50
   Rozwenc — *Making (1)* p.45-47
   Starkey — *Land* p.69
- *Women*
   Spruill — *Women's* p.176-177

NEIGHBORS
See also **Hospitality**
Earle — *Home* p.388-420
Glubok — *Home* p.312-315
- *New England*
   Speare — *Life* p.24-51

**NEMASKET (MIDDLEBORO),
   MASSACHUSETTS**
Willison — *Saints* p.186-187, 201,
   213, 222, 224, 478

NEMASKET INDIANS
Willison — *Saints* p.186-187

NESUTAN, JOB (Indian)
Beals — *John Eliot* p.135-136, 150

NETHERLANDS. *See* **Holland**

NETTING
Glubok — *Home* p.226
Rawson — *When* p.127-128

NEW AMSTEL. *See* **New Castle, Delaware**

NEW AMSTERDAM
See also **New Netherland; Plymouth — New Amsterdam, trade**
Acheson — *America's* p.125-126, 128-129
Alderman — *Story* p.48-49, 51-53, 59-60, 76, 103, 108
Amer. Her. — *Pioneer* p.51, 68-69, 72-73
Amer. Her. — *Thirteen* p.125-126, 128, 130-131, 133-134, 136
Annals of America (1) p.234g
Collins — *Story* p.57-61
Folsom — *Give* p.22, 24-25, 53, 66
Hope — *Nation* p.100
Pomfret — *Founding* p.281-286, 289, 298, 301-302
Snell — *Wild* p.17, 101, 111-114, 138, 140-141
Speare — *Life* p.54-57
Starkey — *Land* p.149, 163-167, 172-174
Tunis — *Colonial* p.24, 73-74
Willison — *Saints* p.111, 264, 297, 311, 374, 383, 437, 451
, *Fall of*
Christensen — *Delaware* p.54
Collins — *Story* p.61
- *Regulations for colonists*
Annals of America (1) p.88
- *Trade*
Langdon — *Everyday* p.39-41
Wertenbaker — *First* p.53-54
- *Women*
Bridenbaugh — *Cities* p.73

NEW BEDFORD, MASSACHUSETTS.
See **Dartmouth, Massachusetts**

NEW CASTLE (NEW AMSTEL), DELAWARE
Alderman — *Story* p.106, 108-110
- *Public square*
Christensen — *Delaware* p.154

NEW ENGLAND
See also **Dominion of New England; New England Confederation;**
names of colonies & cities

Alderman — *Story* p.31, 41, 61, 63, 77-78, 84, 122-123
Amer. Her. — *Thirteen* p.59, 86, 95-98, 149-150, 157-158
Caffrey — *Mayflower. See* index p.389
Collins — *Story* p.40-56
Craven — *Colonies. See* index p.359
Earle — *Home. See* index p.462
Gill — *Mayflower. See* index p.204
Hawke — *Colonial* p.123-164; *See also* index p.747
National — *History.* p.62-91
Rutman — *Winthrop's* p.178, 182-183, 187-188, 272
Smith — *17th. See* index p.234
Tunis — *Colonial* p.29-64
Wertenbaker — *First. See* index p.350-351
Willison — *Saints. See* index p.505
- *Air*
Axtell — *America* p.18-22
, *and colonial wars*
Amer. Her. — *Thirteen* p.144, 163-164, 196-197
, *and "Glorious Revolution"*
Morris — *Ency.* p.39-40
- *Charter, loss of*
Jernegan — *American* p.158-160
- *Chronology*
, *before 1620*
Kraus — *U.S. (1)* p.46-47
- *1640*
Hawke — *U.S.* p.120-124
- *1640–1676*
Hawke — *Colonial* p.168-179
- *1643*
Jernegan — *American* p.142
- *Civil magistrates*
Hawke — *U.S.* p.133-134
- *Coasts*
Adams — *Album* p.72
- *Community blueprint*
Demos — *Remarkable* p.53-56
- *Consolidation plans*
Jernegan — *American* p.156-158
- *Counties, organization of*
Jernegan — *American* p.168-169
- *Drawbacks*
Axtell — *America* p.97-101
- *Early accounts*
See also **New England — Views of . . .**
Marshall — *Mayflower* p.53-54

- *Economy*
  Bailyn — *New England* p.1-13, 17, 46-48, 52, 61-65, 72-73, 75-76, 85-86
  Hawke — *Colonial* p.154-156
- *English relations*
  Jernegan — *American* p.152-153
  Rothbard — *Conceived (1)* p.355-360
- *Expansion*
  Kraus — *U.S. (1)* p.61-65
  Morris — *Ency.* p.34-37
  Ver Steeg — *Formative* p.43-46
- *Explorations*
  See also **New England — Settlements**
  Amer. Her. — *Thirteen* p.36, 58, 85, 87, 90, 94-95, 97-100, 151, 155
  Beck — *Pilgrims* p.17-23
  Marshall — *Mayflower* p.22-23
- *"First fruits" (1643)*
  Amer. Her. — *Thirteen* p.139-140
  Annals of America (1) p.175-179
- *Founding*
  Rothbard — *Conceived (1)* p.157-289
- *General court*
  Wertenbaker — *Puritan. See* index p.351
- *Government*
  Amer. Her. — *Thirteen* p.100-101, 158, 164, 166, 196
  Hawke — *Colonial* p.178
  Morris — *Ency.* p.41-42
  - *Representatives*
    Rozwenc — *Making (1)* p.61-62
- *Internal problems*
  Jernegan — *American* p.147-150
- *Investigation (1664–65)*
  Craven — *Colonies* p.66-67, 85-87, 168, 215
- *Life*
  See also **New England — Society**
  Dow — *Domestic* p.30
  Lawrence — *New* p.13-14
  Smith — *Colonial* p.3
- *Natural resources*
  Amer. Her. — *Thirteen* p.66, 87, 96, 106
  Caffrey — *Mayflower* p.19, 21-22, 116, 131-132
  Jernegan — *American* p.114
  Vaughan — *Puritan* p.65-72

, *Northern, Seizure of*
  Rothbard — *Conceived (1)* p.224-226
, *of Roger Williams*
  Wish — *Society (1)* p.24-62
- *People and institutions*
  Morison — *Oxford* p.69-74
- *Politics*
  Hawke — *Colonial* p.177-178
- *"The present state of New England, 1675"*
  Amer. Her. — *Thirteen* p.144
- *Purpose*
  Morison — *Intellect.* p.6-7
- *"Restoration" (1660–75)*
  Morris — *Ency.* p.37-38
  Rothbard — *Conceived (1)* p.277-289
- *Riches*
  See also **New England — Natural resources**
  - *Views of Francis Higginson*
    Annals of America (1) p.95-99
    Axtell — *America* p.13-21
- *Settlements*
  See also names of settlements
  Hope — *Nation* p.69-82
  Morris — *Ency.* p.30-40
- *Settlers, encouragement of*
  - *Views of John Smith*
    Annals of America (1) p.36-39
- *Social and economic development*
  Amer. Her. — *Thirteen* p.96, 101, 103, 106, 153, 165, 167
- *Society*
  Jernegan — *American* p.177-180
  - *Views of Judge Sewall*
    Holliday — *Woman's* p.190-192
- *Towns*
  Hawke — *Colonial* p.151-154
  Jernegan — *American* p.166-167
  Wertenbaker — *First* p.55-59
- *Trade. See* **Trade — New England**
, *Values of*
  Caffrey — *Mayflower* p.331-332
- *View from abroad*
  Axtell — *America* p.97-126
- *Views of John Brereton*
  Annals of America (1) p.11-14
- *Views of John Dunton*
  Axtell — *America* p.114-120

152

NEW ENGLAND (*continued*)
- *Views of John Smith (1600's)*
  Goetzmann — *Colonial* p.79-80
  Miller — *Colonial* p.66-75
  Scott — *Settlers* p.21
- *Views of Thomas Morton (1622)*
  Miller — *Colonial* p.76
- *Views of William Wood*
  Axtell — *American* p.22-23, 97-101
- *Waters*
  Axtell — *America* p.17-18, 23
- *Women*
  Wertenbaker — *First* p.84-85

NEW ENGLAND ALMANAC
  Woodward — *Way* p.33

NEW ENGLAND COMPANY
  See also **Massachusetts Bay Company**
  Bailyn — *New England* p.10, 17-19, 76, 119, 183
  Craven — *Colonies* p.117-118, 121, 123
  Gill — *Mayflower* p.127-128
  Morris — *Ency.* p.32
  Pomfret — *Founding* p.151-153, 164

NEW ENGLAND CONFEDERATION (1637–1684)
  See also **Narragansett Indians, and New England Confederation; Plymouth, and New England Confederation; United Colonies of New England**
  Annals of America (1) p.172-175
  Chitwood — *History (1)* p.138-140
  Craven — *Colonies* p.30, 47, 50, 121-123, 214
  Hawke — *Colonial* p.168-174, 179, 255, 262
  Jernegan — *American* p.145-147
  Morison — *Intellect.* p.38-39
  Morison — *Story* p.146, 157-158, 165, 213-215, 219, 263-264
  Morris — *Ency.* p.36
  Pomfret — *Founding* p.125, 218, 222-223, 226-227, 230, 238, 241-242, 253, 265, 268, 270, 299
  Rothbard — *Conceived (1)* p.230-236
  Rozwenc — *Making (1)* p.79
  Vaughan — *New. See* index p.422
  Williams — *Saints. See* index p.499

NEW ENGLAND COUNCIL. *See* **Council for New England**

NEW ENGLAND PRIMER
  Adams — *Album* p.122
  Annals of America (1) p.64
  Clark — *Old* p.43-44
  Drepperd — *Pioneer* p.117-118
  Hawke — *U.S.* p.231-233
  Langdon — *Everyday* p.318
  McClinton — *Antiques* p.79
  Miller — *First* p.226
  Morison — *Intellect.* p.79-82, 121, 126
  Rozwenc — *Making (1)* p.88-89
  Speare — *Life* p.106
  Vaughan — *Puritan* p.242-244

"NEW ENGLAND WAY" (Puritan churches of Massachusetts)
  Pomfret — *Founding* p.156-157, 161, 184-199, 237-238

NEW FRANCE
  See also **Canada and Canadians**
  Amer. Her. — *Pioneer* p.24-25
  Annals of America (1) p.232d; 300f-g
  Bailey — *American (1)* p.43-49
  Morison — *Oxford* p.57-58, 102-106
  Morris — *Ency.* p.60-62
  Snell — *Wild* p.36-40, 66-67, 70-73, 75, 94-95, 98

NEW HAMPSHIRE
  Acheson — *America's* p.112-113, 115
  Adams — *Album* p.67-75
  Alderman — *Story* p.39-42, 44, 46
  Amer. Her. — *Thirteen* p.106, 158, 160
  Bailyn — *New England. See* index p.246
  Chitwood — *History (1)* p.135-137
  Craven — *Colonies* p.18, 166-167, 169, 214-215, 234, 244
  Earle — *Home. See* index p.462
  Morris — *Ency.* p.32, 36
- *Founding*
  Fisher — *Men (1)* p.324-325
- *Royal government*
  Chitwood — *History (1)* p.137
  Morris — *Ency.* p.39
  Rothbard — *Conceived (1)* p.361-366
- *Settlements*
  Chitwood — *History (1)* p.135
  Jernegan — *American* p.137-138

NEW HAVEN, CONNECTICUT
Adams — *Album* p.105-106
Alderman — *Story* p.62, 73-76
Bailyn — *New England. See* index
p.246
Chitwood — *History (1)* p.127-128
Craven — *Colonies* p.4-7, 24-25, 28,
63, 87, 95
Fisher — *Men (1)* p.248-252
Gill — *Mayflower* p.135-136, 141-142,
145
Hawke — *Colonial* p.150-151; *See
also* index p.747
Jernegan — *American* p.138-142
Johnston — *Conn.* p.36-44
Miller — *First* p.64-67
Morison — *Intellect. See* index p.284
Nettels — *Roots* p.122, 131, 137, 142,
174-175, 201, 218, 266
Pomfret — *Founding* p.256-277; *See
also* index p.377-378
Sweet — *Religion* p.97-98
Wertenbaker — *First* p.55, 71, 102,
141
Willison — *Saints* p.311, 327-328,
331, 358, 384, 402, 437
- *Boundaries*
Pomfret — *Founding* p.266, 275-
278
- *Code of 1656*
Pomfret — *Founding* p.267, 272
- *Economy*
Pomfret — *Founding* p.270-272
- *Founding*
Morison — *Ency.* p.35
- *General Court*
, *on Quakers*
Vaughan — *Puritan* p.230-
234
- *Government*
Pomfret — *Founding* p.261-263,
270
- *Growth*
Pomfret — *Founding* p.263-266
- *Patent*
Pomfret — *Founding* p.260-261

NEW JERSEY
Alderman — *Story* p.59, 61-64, 67-68,
106, 108, 110
Calverton — *Awake.* p.375-389
Carman — *History (1)* p.30-31, 92
Chitwood — *History (1)* p.176-181
Craven — *Colonies. See* index p.359
Fisher — *Men (1)* p.377-388

Hawke — *Colonial* p.225-229; *See
also* index p.747-748
Hawke — *U.S.* p.174-179
Jernegan — *American* p.206-208
Kraus — *U.S. (1)* p.87
Morris — *Ency.* p.47-48
Nettels — *Roots* p.217-128
Starkey — *Land* p.179-180, 213
- *Carteret landing*
Collins — *Story* p.62
- *Criminal code*
Wertenbaker — *First* p.220-221
, *Division of*
See also **New Jersey — East
Jersey; New Jersey — West
Jersey**
Calverton — *Awake.* p.379
Chitwood — *History (1)* p.177-
179
Craven — *Colonies* p.167, 184,
188
Jernegan — *American* p.207-208
- *East Jersey*
Hawke — *Colonial* p.226-227
Hawke — *U.S.* p.174-177
- *Government (1674–88)*
Morris — *Ency.* p.47
, *Sale of*
Chitwood — *History (1)*
p.180-181
- *Turmoil (1678–86)*
Rothbard — *Conceived (1)*
p.390-396
- *First Assembly*
Jernegan — *American* p.207
- *Government controversy*
Chitwood — *History* p.179-180
- *Industry*
Jernegan — *American* p.224
- *Land, problem of*
Jernegan — *American* p.222
- *Nationalities*
Calverton — *Awake.* p.376
- *Proprietary grant and rights*
Chitwood — *History (1)* p.176-
177, 180
Craven — *Colonies* p.56, 82-85,
234, 243-244
Morris — *Ency.* p.47
- *Royal government*
Chitwood — *History (1)* p.181
- *Settlements*
Amer. Her. — *Thirteen* p.164-165
Chitwood — *History (1)* p.177
Jernegan — *American* p.206-207

NEW JERSEY (*continued*)
- *Social and economic institutions*
  Calverton — *Awake.* p.378
- *Trade*
  Jernegan — *American* p.227
- *Unification*
  Rothbard — *Conceived (1)* p.484-494
- *West Jersey*
  Alderman — *Story* p.59, 61, 63-64, 108
  Craven — *Colonies* p.107, 181-182, 184-189, 203-204
  Hawke — *Colonial* p.227-229
  Hawke — *U.S.* p.177-179
  - *Charter (1677)*
    Annals of America (1) p.262-264
  - *"Concessions and Agreements of West Jersey," by Wm. Penn (1676)*
    Craven — *Colonies* p.88-93, 186-188
    Morris — *Ency.* p.47-48
  - *Development*
    Rothbard — *Conceived (1)* p.397-401
  - *Government (1675)*
    Morris — *Ency.* p.47-48

NEW LONDON, CONNECTICUT
  Wertenbaker — *First* p.55, 190, 195

NEW NETHERLAND
  Alderman — *Story* p.47-49, 53, 60-61, 70-71, 103-104
  Chitwood — *History (1)* p.159-162
  Clark — *Old* p.52-53
  Craven — *Colonies* p.34, 47, 56-63, 65-66, 70-74, 200
  Folsom — *Give* p.24-25, 28, 88
  Hawke — *Colonial* p.169, 171-174, 199, 217-221, 239, 255
  Hawke — *U.S.* p.164-165
  Jernegan — *American* p.194-202
  Kraus — *U.S. (1)* p.65-69
  Life — *New* p.58, 83
  Monroe — *Founding (1)* p.69-73
  Morison — *Oxford* p.56-57, 75-77
  Morris — *Ency.* p.41-46
  Pomfret — *Founding* p.278-290; *See also* index p.378
  Snell — *Wild* p.105, 111-114
  Starkey — *Land* p.50, 138-140, 145, 167-168, 170-171, 176
  Tunis — *Colonial* p.64-76

  Wish — *Society (1)* p.92-102
- *Advice to planters (1650)*
  Demos — *Remarkable* p.44-52
- *Bush burnings. See* **Indians — Bush burnings (New Netherland)**
  "Charter of Freedoms and Exemptions"
    Hawke — *Colonial* p.217-218
    Morris — *Ency.* p.42
    Pomfret — *Founding* p.285, 298
- *Delaware lands*
  Snell — *Wild* p.113, 138-139, 141
- *Dutch occupation*
  Chitwood — *History (1)* p.160-161
- *English conquest*
  Chitwood — *History (1)* p.170-171
  Craven — *Colonies* p.59-60, 62-63, 65-66, 72-73
  Jernegan — *American* p.203-204
  Morris — *Ency.* p.44-45
- *Formation*
  Rothbard — *Conceived (1)* p.293-297
- *Freedoms and privileges*
  See also **New Netherland — "Charter of Freedoms and Exemptions"**
  Annals of America (1) p.88
- *Government and governors*
  Fisher — *Men (2)* p.25-27
  Jernegan — *American* p.200-201
  Pomfret — *Founding* p.287-289
  Rothbard — *Conceived (1)* p.298-310
- *Production*
  Axtell — *America* p.137-138
- *Religious meetings, restrictions on*
  Annals of America (1) p.90-91
- *Rise and fall*
  Rothbard — *Conceived (1)* p.293-328
- *Settlements*
  Christensen — *Delaware* p.14-15, 19
- *Society (social structure)*
  Pomfret — *Founding* p.286-287, 289
- *View from abroad*
  Axtell — *America* p.127-145
- *Views of Adriaen Van de Donck*
  Annals of America (1) p.204-209
  Axtell — *America* p.33-51

- *Views of David Pietersen de Vries*
  Axtell — *America* p.133-141
- *Views of Isaac Jogues*
  Axtell — *America* p.141-145
- *Views of Jonas Michaëlius*
  Axtell — *America* p.127-133

NEW NETHERLAND COMPANY
Willison — *Saints* p.111-112, 265

NEW PLYMOUTH COMPANY. *See*
"Undertakers"

NEW ROCHELLE, NEW YORK
Clark — *Old* p.83-93

NEW SWEDEN
Alderman — *Story* p.104-106
Amer. Her. — *Pioneer* p.70
Amer. Her. — *Thirteen* p.135-136,
146-147
Annals of America (1) p.300c
Chitwood — *History (1)* p.166-168
Jernegan — *American* p.201-202
Morris — *Ency.* p.42
Pomfret — *Founding* p.267-270, 290-
296
Rothbard — *Conceived (1)* p.311-317
Snell — *Wild* p.137-141
Starkey — *Land* p.153-156, 158-159,
161-162
Sweet — *Religion* p.203-205
Tunis — *Colonial* p.25-26
Wish — *Society (1)* p.101-102
- *Dutch conquest*
  Chitwood — *History (1)* p.167-
  168
- *Founding*
  Christensen — *Delaware* p.26-30
- *View from abroad*
  Axtell — *America* p.161-186
- *View of Israel Ackelius*
  Axtell — *America* p.173-177
- *View of Pehr Kalm*
  Axtell — *America* p.177-186

NEW SWEDEN COMPANY
Amer. Her. — *Thirteen* p.134-136
Christensen — *Delaware* p.25-26, 36
Pomfret — *Founding* p.291-293, 295-
296

NEW YEAR'S DAY
Earle — *Customs* p.228-229
- *Indians, Woodland*
  Northey — *American* p.89-90

- *Pilgrim legislation*
  Willison — *Saints* p.177, 241

NEW YORK
See also "Charter of Liberties";
Confederation of New York;
names of settlements and cities
Alderman — *Story* p.45, 57-58, 62-64,
67, 108, 118, 120
Bailyn — *New England. See* index
p.246
Calverton — *Awake. See* index p.468
Carman — *History (1)* p.32, 53, 63-64
Chitwood — *History (1)* p.479
Clark — *Old* p.52-71
Craven — *Colonies. See* index p.359-
360
Earle — *Home. See* index p.462
Folsom — *Give* p.26-27, 65-68, 88, 91
Gill — *Mayflower* p.118, 145, 147,
149, 154-155, 176, 178
Hawke — *Colonial* p.217-225; *See
also* index p.748
Hawke — *U.S.* p.164-173
Langdon — *Everyday* p.38-47
Wish — *Society (1)* p.92-100
, *and colonial wars*
Amer. Her. — *Thirteen* p.194-
197, 200-201
, *and Connecticut*
Craven — *Colonies* p.64, 71, 74-
75, 210-211, 216, 237
, *and "Glorious Revolution"*
Chitwood — *History (1)* p.225-
227
, *and New Jersey*
Craven — *Colonies* p.69, 84, 202-
205, 209-210, 216, 243
, *and the Delaware*
Craven — *Colonies* p.72-73, 78,
97, 200, 209
- *Assembly*
  Craven — *Colonies* p.65, 77, 208-
  209, 217
  Jernegan — *American* p.204-206
- *Chronology*
  - *1644–1691*
    Jernegan — *American*
    p.203-206
  - *1664–1675*
    Morison — *Oxford* p.77-79
  - *1676–1686*
    Rothbard — *Conceived (1)*
    p.380-389

NEW YORK (*continued*)
- *Dutch*
  - *Heritage*
    Hawke — *Colonial* p.221-222
  , *Reconquest by*
    Craven — *Colonies* p.78, 94, 104-105
- *Transition to English rule*
    Craven — *Colonies* p.70, 74-79
- *Economy*
    Calverton — *Awake.* p.327
    Wertenbaker — *First* p.306-307
- *English rule (1664–89)*
    Hawke — *Colonial* p.222-225
- *Estates*
    Nettels — *Roots* p.308-309
- *Feudalism*
    Wish — *Society (1)* p.92-100
- *Finance, problems of*
    Craven — *Colonies* p.201-202, 204-206
- *Garrison*
    Craven — *Colonies* p.73, 202, 204, 240
- *Government*
    Amer. Her. — *Thirteen* p.158, 164-167, 196
    Calverton — *Awake.* p.326-327, 336-337
  , *Proprietary*
    Craven — *Colonies* p.73, 76-78, 208
  , *in King William's War*
    Craven — *Colonies* p.237-240
- *Life*
    Amer. Her. — *Thirteen* p.165-167
  , *Reconstruction in (1690's)*
    Chitwood — *History (1)* p.243-245
- *View from abroad*
    Axtell — *America* p.145-159

NEWFOUNDLAND
    Bailyn — *New England* p.96, 129-131, 146, 192
    Pomfret — *Founding* p.2, 13, 15, 77, 101, 131-134, 147-148, 304-305

NEWGATE, JOHN
    Rutman — *Winthrop's* p.60, 73, 75, 82n, 193n, 215n

NEWPORT, CHRISTOPHER, CAPTAIN
    Craven — *Southern* p.65, 67-69, 80, 97, 100-101, 110
    Hawke — *Colonial* p.89, 91-92, 94-95, 103
  , *and Sir Thomas Dale*
    Phillips — *First* p.154

NEWPORT, RHODE ISLAND
    Alderman — *Story* p.97-100
    Amer. Her. — *Thirteen* p.106, 154-155
    Chitwood — *History (1)* p.131-132
    Folsom — *Give* p.26-28
    National — *History.* p.90-91
    Pomfret — *Founding* p.213-214, 216, 218-220, 222-223, 225

"NEWPORT TOWER" (mill)
    Morrison — *Early* p.94-95

NEWSPAPERS
  , *Lack of*
    Carman — *History (1)* p.107

NEWTOWN, MASSACHUSETTS
    Alderman — *Story* p.69-70

NIANTIC INDIANS
    Vaughan — *New* p.28, 55-58, 143, 147, 151, 169, 169n, 171-172, 174-176, 179, 188, 314

NICHOLSON, FRANCIS
    Amer. Her. — *Thirteen* p.166-167, 173, 179
    Craven — *Colonies* p.218, 225-227, 236, 243
    Hawke — *Colonial* p.262, 267-268, 270-271, 290, 332-333
    Rothbard — *Conceived (1)* p.148, 150-151, 420, 430-433, 435-437
    Smith — *17th* p.113, 126, 221, 223
    Wertenbaker — *First. See* index p.351

NICOLLS, RICHARD
    Chitwood — *History (1)* p.173-174
    Christensen — *Delaware* p.54-55
    Craven — *Colonies* p.62, 64-67, 71-83, 85-87, 92-94, 208-209
    Hawke — *Colonial* p.199, 220-221, 223, 228
    Hawke — *U.S.* p.165-168
    Nettels — *Roots* p.345
    Pomfret — *Founding* p.201-303

Rothbard — *Conceived (1)* p.282-285, 293, 323-328, 332-334, 338, 340, 353, 393-394, 490

"NINE, THE" (in New Netherland government)
Morris — *Ency.* p.43

NINIGRET (Indian)
Vaughan — *New* p.151, 169n, 171-172, 174-178, 188, 258, 324

NIPMUC(K) INDIANS
Beals — *John Eliot* p.155-157, 159, 167-168
Folsom — *Give* p.36, 38, 40
Morison — *Oxford* p.108
Morison — *Story* p.261-263, 269-271, 274
Starkey — *Land* p.207-208
Vaughan — *New* p.56, 179, 196, 258, 292-293, 313, 315, 320, 329

NOCAKE (food)
Earle — *Home* p.137-138
Glubok — *Home* p.75-76

NODDLES ISLAND
Rutman — *Winthrop's* p.70-71, 78, 78n, 90, 94, 238

NOGGINS (pitchers)
Gould — *Early* p.37

NOMENCLATURE. *See* **Names**

NONANTUM INDIANS
Beals — *John Eliot* p.110, 120-126, 128-129, 131, 133, 135, 137, 141, 143-144, 180

NON-CONFORMITY
Smith — *17th* p.87-88, 124, 163, 190

NOON-HOUSES
Earle — *Home* p.375-376

NORRIS, EDWARD
Gildrie — *Salem* p.72, 79-80, 82, 84-86, 88, 90, 123, 141-143, 150

NORTH
- *Colonies*
    Life — *New* p.75-85
    - *1660's–1690's*
        Rothbard — *Conceived (1)* p.331-506

NORTH AMERICA
- *European settlements, chronology of*
    Marshall — *Mayflower* p.22

NORTH CAROLINA
See also **Albemarle Sound Settlement, N.C.; Carolinas; etc.**
Alderman — *Story* p.124-128
Calverton — *Awake. See* index p.468
Craven — *Colonies* p.156-160, 232-233, 243
Craven — *Southern. See* index p.445
Folsom — *Give* p.75-77
Rothbard — *Conceived (1)* p.121-125, 127-130, 135, 138-140, 142-143
- *Contrast with South Carolina*
    Calverton — *Awake.* p.284
- *Contrast with Virginia*
    Calverton — *Awake.* p.286-287
- *Frontier*
    Calverton — *Awake.* p.284-285
- *Government*
    Calverton — *Awake.* p.290-291
- *Individualism of people*
    Calverton — *Awake.* p.287, 292, 303
- *Industry*
    Calverton — *Awake.* p.300-301
- *Insurrections*
    Chitwood — *History (1)* p.194-197
- *Proprietary conflicts*
    Nettels — *Roots* p.342
- *Regulators' revolt*
    Calverton — *Awake.* p.415-417
- *Settlements*
    Calverton — *Awake.* p.293
    Chitwood — *History (1)* p.183-186
- *Women, Industrious*
    Spruill — *Women's* p.82-83

NORTHERN NECK
Craven — *Southern* p.74, 246, 256, 271, 376, 398

NORTHWEST PASSAGE
, *English search for*
    Morris — *Ency.* p.23-24

NORTON, JOHN, REV.
Marshall — *Mayflower* p.183
Morison — *Intellect.* p.139, 152, 155n, 170

NORTON, JOHN, REV. (*continued*)
Sweet — *Religion* p.148-149
Tyler — *History* p.94, 188-189
Wertenbaker — *First* p.88, 91, 140, 238
Wertenbaker — *Puritan. See* index p.355
Willison — *Pilgrim* p.427-428, 497, 514, 562
Willison — *Saints* p.355-357, 364, 379, 459
- *Elegy on John Cotton*
  Vaughan — *Puritan* p.253-255

NORWOOD, RICHARD
Morison — *Intellect.* p.130, 139, 141

NOVA SCOTIA
Bailyn — *New England* p.60, 78, 101, 110, 115-116, 122, 128, 145-146, 157
- *French settlements*
  Snell — *Wild* p.66, 70-73, 75

NOVELS. *See* Fiction

NOWELL, ALEXANDER
Morison — *Intellect.* p.248, 252
Willison — *Saints* p.461-462

NOYES, NICHOLAS
Tyler — *History. See* index p.546
, *on periwigs*
  Demos — *Remarkable* p.212-220

NUICE, MRS.
, Williams — *Demeter's* p.154

NURSE, REBECCA
Williams — *Demeter's* p.140-141

NURSERY RHYMES
, *Dutch*
  Smith — *Colonial* p.120-121

NURSES AND NURSING
Leonard — *Dear* p.223, 382-483

NUTHEAD, DINAH
Dexter — *Colonial* p.166-167
Williams — *Demeter's* p.199-200, 203

O

OAKES, THOMAS, DR.
Dow — *Every* p.176
Wertenbaker — *First* p.171, 299-300, 317-318

OAKES, URIAN
Morison — *Intellect.* p.43, 156-158, 176, 195, 222-226, 243
Tyler — *History. See* index p.346
Wertenbaker — *Puritan. See* index p.355
- *Sermons*
  Tyler — *History* p.402-405

OATHS. *See* Profanity

OATHS OF ALLEGIANCE
- *Massachusetts*
  Fisher — *Men (1)* p.132-133

OCCAMEECHEE INDIANS
Craven — *Colonies* p.132, 136

OCCUPATIONS
See also "Calling"; Professions; Women — Occupations; names of occupations
Acheson — *America's* p.119
Hope — *Nation* p.87

OCTOBER
Gould — *Early* p.135

OGILBY, JOHN
Smith — *17th* p.215-216

OGLETHORPE, JAMES EDWARD
, *and Indians*
  Collins — *Story* p.70

OLD AGE. *See* Longevity

"OLD BRICK" CHURCH (meetinghouse)
Morrison — *Early* p.154-156
Wertenbaker — *Puritan* p.110-111

"OLD COLONIAL SYSTEM"
Chitwood — *History (1)* p.424-425

OLD COLONY CLUB
Willison — *Saints* p.409-415, 418, 420-421, 425

"OLD COMERS" (*Mayflower* **passengers, Plymouth)**
Morison — *Story* p.151, 154-155, 231-232
Willison — *Saints* p.237, 313-316

"OLD FIELD SCHOOLS" (Virginia)
Monroe — *Founding (1)* p.60-61

"OLD HUNDRED(TH)" (psalm)
Adams — *Album* p.60
Howard — *Our* p.6
Morison — *Oxford* p.74

"OLD SHIP" MEETINGHOUSE (Hingham, Mass.)
Morrison — *Early* p.80-81
Wertenbaker — *First* p.293, 318-319

"OLD SILVER NAILS." *See* Stuyvesant, Peter

"OLD STONE HOUSE AT GOWANUS" (Brooklyn, N.Y.)
Morrison — *Early* p.116

"OLD SWEDES" CHURCH
Christensen — *Delaware* p.93-95, 155

OLDHAM, JOHN ("Mad Jack")
Caffrey — *Mayflower* p.198-203, 206-207, 210, 261
Dillon — *Pilgrims* p.184-185, 190-193, 203, 214
Gill — *Mayflower* p.106-112, 129, 135
Johnston — *Conn.* p.14, 22-23
Marshall — *Mayflower* p.182-183
Morison — *Story* p.101-104, 111, 124-125, 150, 210
Willison — *Pilgrim. See* index p.579
Willison — *Saints. See* index p.506

OLDMIXON, JOHN
Smith — *17th* p.222-225

OLIVER, MARY
Dow — *Every* p.214-217

OLIVER, THOMAS
Rutman — *Winthrop's. See* index p.316

OLIVES AND OLIVE OIL
Craven — *Southern* p.19-20, 35, 44-46, 70, 141, 316-317, 336-337, 347

OMENS
- *Views of Mass. clergy*
Wertenbaker — *First* p.139-142

ONE HUNDRED ASSOCIATION (1628)
Amer. Her. — *Pioneer* p.24

ONEOTA (Oneida stone)
Northey — *America* p.102-103

OPECHANOUGH (Indian)
Chitwood — *History (1)* p.65-66
Craven — *Southern* p.143, 173, 232, 362
Hawke — *Colonial* p.104, 182-183
Pomfret — *Founding* p.42, 62-63
Snell — *Wild* p.82, 84-85
Willison — *Pilgrim* p.137n, 180n

"ORDEAL OF TOUCH" (guilt test)
Dow — *Every* p.202
Wertenbaker — *First* p.146

ORDINARIES. *See* Taverns

ORGANIZATIONS
See also names of organizations
Adams — *Provincial* p.22-23

ORGANS
Rawson — *When* p.199-200

ORPHANS
See also **County Courts; Plymouth — Orphans**
Craven — *Southern* p.272-273, 285, 304
, Apprenticeship of
Annals of America (1) p.59-61
- *Girls*
Glubok — *Home* p.113
- *Law*
Williams — *Demeter's* p.82
- *South*
Craven — *Southern* p.272-273, 285, 304

OUSAMEQUIN. *See* Massasoit (Indian)

OUTINA (Indian)
Folsom — *Give* p.4-5

OVENS
See also **Ash ovens; Bake ovens; Dutch ovens; Smoke ovens; "Tin kitchens"**
Dow — *Every* p.93

OVENS (*continued*)
    Earle — *Home* p.67
    Rawson — *When* p.12-13
    , *Brick*
        Dow — *Domestic* p.16-17
        Earle — *Colonial* p.287-288

OWEN, GRIFFITH, DR.
    Langdon — *Everyday* p.328

OXEN
    , *and oxcarts*
        Speare — *Life* p.139

OXENBRIDGE, MRS.
    , *on scholarship and influence*
        Williams — *Demeter's* p.122

OXENSTJERNA, AXEL
    Christensen — *Delaware* p.25

OXFORD UNIVERSITY
    Morison — *Intellect.* p.18, 38, 242-243, 245, 266

OYSTERS
    Glubok — *Home* p.66
    - *Brooklyn, N.Y.*
        Earle — *Home* p.118-119
    - *New Amsterdam*
        Smith — *Colonial* p.112-113

P

PABODIE, ELIZABETH ALDEN
    Marble — *Women* p.77-78

PABODIE, WILLIAM
    Marble — *Women* p.77-78

PABODIE FAMILY
    Hills — *History (1)* p.171
    Hills — *History (2)* p.204-205; *See also* index p.268

PADDY, ELIZABETH
    Earle — *Two cent. (1)* p.xv, 72

PADDY, WILLIAM
    Willison — *Saints* p.318, 336, 457, 460

PAINE, JOHN
    Bailyn — *New England* p.70-71

PAINE, WILLIAM
    Bailyn — *New England* p.53, 70-71

PAINTERS AND PAINTINGS
    See also **Limners; Portraits and portrait painting**
    Arts — *America* p.154-160
    Hawke — *Colonial* p.287-288, 309-310

PAINTS
    See also **Dyes**
    Gould — *Early* p.113

PALATINATES
    See also **Pennsylvania Dutch**
    Smith — *Colonial* p.5, 8
    Sweet — *Religion* p.24
    - *Jurisdiction*
        Craven — *Southern* p.186-187, 339-340

PALES. *See* **Fences**

PAMET INDIANS
    Caffrey — *Mayflower* p.173
    Dillon — *Pilgrims* p.141-142, 144
    Willison — *Pilgrim* p.140, 143

PAMPHLETS
    , *First — Boston (1690)*
        Carman — *History (1)* p.107
    , *Political*
        Morison — *Intellect.* p.197-200

PAMUNKEY INDIANS
    Craven — *Southern* p.380, 389, 392
    Smith — *17th* p.40, 46, 54-55, 57-58
    Snell — *Wild* p.79-82, 85
    Starkey — *Land* p.204-205

PANNAWAY, NEW HAMPSHIRE
    Alderman — *Story* p.38-39

PANTON, SALLY
    Williams — *Demeter's* p.178

PANTRIES. *See* **Closets**

PAPER CUTTING
    Rawson — *When* p.127

PAPER INDUSTRY
    Christensen — *Delaware* p.88-89
    - *Mill, First*
        Speare — *Life* p.126
        Tunis — *Craftsmen* p.132

PAPOUS COATS
Earle — *Two cent. (1)* p.178

"PAPYROTAMIA." *See* **Paper cutting**

PARAGON **(ship)**
Willison — *Pilgrim* p.229-230
Willison — *Saints* p.233

PARÉ, AMBROISE
- *Works*
Morison — *Intellect.* p.137-139

PARENTS
See also **Puritans — Parents**
, *Duty of*
Annals of America (1) p.170-171

PARISH SYSTEM
See also names of colonies
Chitwood — *History (1)* p.151-152
Wertenbaker — *First. See* index p.351

PARKER, THOMAS, REV.
Morison — *Intellect.* p.93, 97, 109n, 152

PARLIAMENTARY COMMISSION FOR PLANTATIONS
Morris — *Ency.* p.57

PARLORS
Dow — *Domestic* p.20-21
Dow — *Every* p.44-45
Morrison — *Every* p.47
- *South*
Goodwin — *Colonial* p.29

PARRISH, BETTY
Williams — *Demeter's* p.150

PARRISH, SAMUEL, REV.
Williams — *Demeter's* p.150

PARTRIDGE, GEORGE
Willison — *Saints* p.357-359, 363, 448

PARTRIDGE, RALPH
Willison — *Pilgrim* p.436-437, 461
Willison — *Saints* p.357-359, 363, 448

PASCATOWAY INDIANS
Starkey — *Land* p.112-113

PASKELL, THOMAS
- *"Letter from Philadelphia, Jan. 1683"*
Amer. Her. — *Thirteen* p.141-142

PASPAHEGH INDIANS
Starkey — *Land* p.17

PASSACONAWAY (Indian)
Beals — *John Eliot* p.133-134
Vaughan — *New* p.52, 159, 195, 252, 291

PASTORIUS, FRANCIS
Bridenbaugh — *Cities* p.131-132
Starkey — *Land* p.183-184, 186, 193-194

PASTORS. *See* **Clergymen**

PATCHWORK. *See* **Quilts and quilting bees**

PATENTS AND CHARTERS
See also names of colonies
Willison — *Pilgrim. See* index p.579
Willison — *Saints. See* index p.506

PATRIOTISM
, *and history*
Smith — *17th* p.197-198, 206

PATROONS AND PATROONSHIPS
Amer. Her. — *Treasury* p.180-181
Chitwood — *History (1)* p.163-164
Christensen — *Delaware* p.19-20, 25
Fisher — *Men (2)* p.20-22, 29
Hawke — *Colonial* p.217-219, 222
- *New Netherland*
Amer. Her. — *Thirteen* p.129
Amer. Her. — *Treasury* p.180-181
Jernegan — *American* p.197-198
Pomfret — *Founding* p.285-286
- *Rights and privileges (1629)*
Annals of America (1) p.104-106

PATTENS (shoes)
Earle — *Two cent. (1)* p.359-370

PATUXET INDIANS
Caffrey — *Mayflower* p.136, 183
Dillon — *Pilgrims* p.153-154, 156, 174
Morison — *Story* p.54-56, 70, 74, 238
Willison — *Pilgrim* p.131n-132
Willison — *Saints* p.172, 183, 202-203

PAUL REVERE HOUSE (Boston, 1676)
Morrison — *Early* p.59-62

PAUPER'S BADGES (poverty)
Earle — *Two cent. (1)* p.117-122

PAYNE FAMILY
- *History and genealogy*
Demos — *Remarkable* p.175-188

PEABODY. *See* **Pabodie**

PEACHES
Langdon — *Everyday* p.279-280

PEAGE. *See* **Wampum**

"PEARL PAINTING" (glass painting)
Rawson — *When* p.126

PECKSUOT (Indian)
Willison — *Pilgrim* p.220-221
Willison — *Saints* p.226-227

PEDDLERS
See also names of occupations, products
Adams — *Provincial* p.44-45
Gould — *Early* p.125-126
Speare — *Life* p.144-145

PEIRCE, JOHN
Caffrey — *Mayflower* p.49, 168, 183-184

PEIRCE, WILLIAM
Caffrey — *Mayflower* p.184, 199, 209, 231, 242, 245-246, 326
Willison — *Pilgrim* p.274n, 362, 378-379, 417
Willison — *Saints* p.242, 252, 256, 267, 450

PEMAQUID, MAINE
Adams — *Album* p.64
Snell — *Wild* p.117-118

PENDANTS (architecture)
Adams — *Album* p.99

PENHALLOW, SAMUEL
Tyler — *History* p.382-384

PENMANSHIP
Earle — *Customs* p.282-283

PENN, GULIELMA SPRINGETT
Earle — *Two cent. (1)* p.xix, 240
Earle — *Two cent. (2)* p.342-343, 602

PENN, HANNAH CALLOWHILL
Earle — *Two cent. (1)* p.xix, 242, 244
Earle — *Two cent. (2)* p.602

PENN, JAMES
Rutman — *Winthrop's* p.37, 48, 73, 81, 82n, 172-173, 174, 193n, 222, 247

PENN, WILLIAM
See also **Pennsylvania; Philadelphia; Quakers**
Acheson — *America's* p.141-145
Adams — *Album* p.228-230
Alderman — *Story* p.63, 108-110, 113-120
Amer. Her. — *Pioneer* p.51, 74-77
Calverton — *Awake.* p.179-180, 343-346
Chitwood — *History (1)* p.203
Christensen — *Delaware* p.60-61
Craven — *Colonies. See* index p.360
Fisher — *Men (1)* p.354-365
Folsom — *Give* p.49-54, 73, 91
Furnas — *Americans* p.39-40, 78-81, 83-84, 128, 130
Hawke — *Colonial* p.229-232; *See also* index p.752
Hope — *Nation* p.97-98
Jernegan — *American* p.208-209
Leonard — *Dear* p.66-69, 114, 180, 209, 272-273, 374, 394, 396-397
National — *History.* p.104-105, 110, 117
Nettels — *Roots* p.128-130; *See also* index p.740
Rothbard — *Conceived (1). See* index p.527
Rozwenc — *Making (1)* p.34, 49-50, 63, 74
Snell — *Wild* p.145-146, 148-149
Speare — *Life* p.64-65
Sweet — *Religion* p.158-162, 213, 330-331
Wish — *Society (1)* p.102-109
, *and Philadelphia*
Langdon — *Everyday* p.48-52
, *as founder of Pennsylvania*
Craven — *Colonies* p.191-199
- *Colonization*
Collins — *Story* p.64
Nettels — *Roots* p.160-161

- *"Concessions and agreements of West Jersey" (1676).* See **New Jersey — West Jersey**
- *Ethics of*
  Rozwenc — *Making (1)* p.37-38
- *"Frame of Government."* See **Pennsylvania — Government**
- *Houses*
  Langdon — *Everyday* p.53-57
  , *in England*
  Chitwood — *History (1)* p.211-212
- *Indian relations*
  Amer. Her. — *Thirteen* p.170
  Chitwood — *History (1)* p.207
  Starkey — *Land* p.184-186, 198
  - *"Great treaty"*
    Adams — *Album* p.230
    Collins — *Story* p.63
    Hope — *Nation* p.111
    Jernegan — *American* p.230
- *Land grants*
  Chitwood — *History (1)* p.204-205
  Jernegan — *American* p.221-222
  Morris — *Ency.* p.46
- *"The people called Quakers" (1696)*
  Annals of America (1) p. 299-30
- *Plan of union for colonies*
  Annals of America (1) p.308-309
- *Political philosophy*
  Bailey — *American (1)* p.40-41

PENNACOOK INDIANS
See also **Passaconaway (Indian)**
Vaughan — *New* p.52, 56, 159, 195, 216, 252, 291-292, 314

PENNSYLVANIA
See also **Penn, William; Philadelphia, Pennsylvania**
Acheson — *America's* p.143-145
Adams — *Album* p.228-231
Alderman — *Story. See* index p.185
Amer. Her. — *Pioneer* p.51, 75-77
Annals of America (1) p.300e
Calverton — *Awake.* p.341-356
Carman — *History (1)* p.58
Clark — *Old* p.72-82
Craven — *Colonies. See* index p.360
Earle — *Home. See* index p.463
Fisher — *Men (1)* p.340-349
Folsom — *Give* p.49-54, 73, 88, 90-91
Hawke — *Colonial* p.229-239; *See also* index p.753

Hawke — *U.S.* p.180-188
Morison — *Oxford* p.126-131
Morris — *Ency.* p.48-49
Nettels — *Roots* p.129-130; *See also* index p.740
Snell — *Wild* p.17, 24, 148-149
Starkey — *Land* p.181-182, 186-190, 195
, *and "Glorious Revolution"*
  Morris — *Ency.* p.49
, *and William Penn*
  Chitwood — *History (1)* p.204-205
  Jernegan — *American* p.209-210
  Scott — *Settlers* p.59-61, 64-65
, *as "Holy Experiment"*
  Kraus — *U.S. (1)* p.87-90
, *as royal province*
  Chitwood — *History (1)* p.212-213
- *Assembly*
  Craven — *Colonies* p.197-199
  Jernegan — *American* p.211
- *Boundary disputes*
  Chitwood — *History (1)* p.205
- *Charter*
  Craven — *Colonies* p.54, 164, 190-191, 198-199
  Hawke — *Colonial* p.232-233
  Jernegan — *American* p.210-211
  - *of liberties*
    Morris — *Ency.* p.49
- *Chronology*
  - *1681-1689*
    Jernegan — *America* p.208-212
  - *1685*
    Hawke — *U.S.* p.182-186
- *Founding*
  Rothbard — *Conceived (1)* p.402-411
- *Government*
  Morris — *Ency.* p.48-49
  , *First — Views of William Penn*
    Annals of America (1) p.265-271
  - *"Frames of government," by Penn*
    Annals of America (1) p.265-271
    Chitwood — *History (1)* p.208-209
    Hawke — *U.S.* p.180-182
    Leonard — *Dear* p.272

164

PENNSYLVANIA (continued)
- *Freeman's (1675)*
  Angle — *By* p.14-16
, *Return to*
  Rothbard — *Conceived (1)*
  p.495-506
- *Industry*
  Jernegan — *American* p.224
- *Life*
  Amer. Her. — *Thirteen* p.141-
  142, 150-151, 169-171
- *People, plain*
  National — *History.* p.108-111
- *Settlements*
  Amer. Her. — *Thirteen* p.169-172
  Chitwood — *History (1)* p.206
  Hawke — *Colonial* p.234-239
  Morris — *Ency.* p.49
- *Settlers*
  Bailey — *American (1)* p.41-42
, *Character of*
  Jernegan — *American*
  p.211-212
, *Non-English*
  Chitwood — *History (1)*
  p.209-211
- *Social ideals*
  Jernegan — *American* p.230
- *Trade, early*
  Jernegan — *American* p.227
- *"Twelve mile circle" (boundary)*
  Christensen — *Delaware* p.62-63
- *View from abroad*
  Axtell — *America* p.186-193
- *Views of Gabriel Thomas*
  Axtell — *America* p.186-193
- *Women*
  Starkey — *Land* p.189

PENNSYLVANIA DUTCH (Germans)
See also **Palatinates**
Acheson — *America's* p.144-145
Furnas — *Americans* p.83-90
Langdon — *Everyday* p.63-67

PENOBSCOT TRADING POST
Caffrey — *Mayflower* p.232-233, 242-
243, 253
Willison — *Pilgrim* p.359-360, 374-
375, 401-404
Willison — *Saints* p.288-289, 291,
293, 295, 299, 301, 305, 397, 451

PENOWAYANQUIS (Indian)
Morison — *Story* p.212, 241

PENROSE, BARTHOLOMEW
Langdon — *Everyday* p.229-233

PENTAGOET (CASTINE), MAINE
Willison — *Pilgrim* p.360n, 374-375,
401-404

"PEOPLE OF THE LONG HOUSE." *See*
**Iroquois Indians — "Long
House"**

PEPPERELL, WILLIAM
Wright — *Cultural* p.36

, *at Louisbourg*
  Collins — *Story* p.89

PEQUOT INDIANS
See also **Pequot War**
Acheson — *America's* p.173
Alderman — *Story* p.71-73
Beals — *John Eliot* p.92, 98, 103-105
Caffrey — *Mayflower* p.261-265, 267
Collins — *Story* p.44
Dillon — *Pilgrims* p.213, 215
Folsom — *Give* p.17-18, 34, 39
Johnston — *Conn.* p.3-4, 7, 9, 20-31
Morison — *Story* p.132, 209-211, 272
Snell — *Wild* p.135
Starkey — *Land* p.100, 131
Vaughan — *New* p.55-58, 98, 155-
156, 162-163, 170n, 172, 176-180,
188, 202, 207
Willison — *Pilgrim* p.304, 388, 413
Willison — *Saints* p.296, 304-306
Wright — *Everyday* p.219, 221

PEQUOT WAR
See also **Philip, King (Indian)**
Adams — *Album* p.104
Alderman — *Story* p.71-73
Amer. Her. — *Pilgrims* p.137
Amer. Her. — *Thirteen* p.163
Annals of America (1) p.82-84
Dillon — *Pilgrims* p.215
Hawke — *Colonial* p.149, 156-157,
163, 171, 252, 293
Jernegan — *American* p.140-141
Johnston — *Conn.* p.21-31
Morris — *Ency.* p.35-36
Pomfret — *Founding* p.184, 192, 218,
239-240, 256, 259
Rothbard — *Conceived (1)* p.227-229,
231, 257, 344
Scott — *Settlers* p.41-42

Vaughan — *New* p.115, 122-154, 188, 195-196, 201-203, 217, 246, 324-325, 329-330
Willison — *Pilgrim* p.273, 410-414
- *Connecticut*
    Chitwood — *History (1)* p.126-127
- *Views of Edward Johnson*
    Miller — *Colonial* p.244-247
- *Views of William Bradford*
    Miller — *Colonial* p.239-243

PERCY, GEORGE
Phillips — *First* p.63, 73
Starkey — *Land* p.12-14, 19, 22, 26
Tyler — *History* p.35-37
- *"Observations" (1607)*
    Amer. Her. — *Thirteen* p.59-60
- *Trials, in Virginia (1607)*
    Goetzmann — *Colonial* p.77-78

PERFECTION
- *Church (Dedham, Mass.)*
    Lockridge — *New* p.23-26
, *Policies of (Dedham, Mass.)*
    Lockridge — *New* p.3-26

PERFUME
Earle — *Customs* p.312-313
Earle — *Home* p.152, 424, 450
- *Revolt against, by Puritans*
    Earle — *Two cent. (1)* p.20

PERIODICALS. *See* **Magazines; Newspapers**

PERIWIGS. *See* **Wigs and wigmakers**

PERJURY
, *Punishments for*
    Wertenbaker — *First* p.217-218

PERKINS, WILLIAM
- *Doctrine of "Calling"*
    Vaughan — *Puritan* p.130-138

PERRY, MICHAEL
Morison — *Intellect.* p.105n, 106n, 129

PERSECUTION. *See* **Hutchinson, Anne Marbury; Intolerance; Quakers — Persecution; Religion — Sects — Persecution; Williams, Roger; Witchcraft**

PERSIMMONS
- *Jamestown, Va.*
    Adams — *Album* p.17

PERUKES (PERUKERS). *See* **Wigs and wigmakers**

PERUVIAN BARK. *See* **Cinchona bark**

PESSACUS (Indian)
Vaughan — *New* p.167-169, 188

PESTLES AND MORTARS
Gould — *Early* p.134

PETER, HUGH
Gildrie — *Salem* p.6, 38-40, 47-49, 51-54, 56, 64, 84, 86, 92
Morison — *Intellect.* p.66, 79, 115, 198
Pomfret — *Founding* p.151, 196, 258-259, 261
Rutman — *Winthrop's* p.14, 47, 51, 101, 103, 113, 124, 183

PETER TUFTS (CRADDOCK) HOUSE (Medford, Mass., 1675)
Morrison — *Early* p.72-75

PETER WYCKOFF HOUSE (Flatlands, Brooklyn, N.Y., 1639)
Morrison — *Early* p.121

"PETITION OF RIGHT" (of Sir Edward Coke)
Wish — *Society (1)* p.9-10

PETTICOATS
Earle — *Two cent. (1)* p.153-155
- *Plymouth*
    Demos — *Little* p.38, 55

PEWS. *See* **Churches — Pews**

PEWTER AND PEWTERERS
Dow — *Every* p.84-90
Drepperd — *Pioneer* p.179
Glubok — *Home* p.24, 45, 51
Gould — *Early* p.87
Langdon — *Everyday* p.169-174
Leonard — *Dear* p.153-154
Tunis — *Craftsmen* p.72-75
- *Lamps*
    Earle — *Home* p.44-45

PEWTER AND PEWTERERS (cont.)
- *Plates*
    Adams — *Album* p.89
- *Tableware*
    Earle — *Customs* p.139-142
- *Utensils*
    Earle — *Home* p.84-85

PHILADELPHIA, PENNSYLVANIA
See also under special subjects
Acheson — *America's* p.142-143
Alderman — *Story* p.63, 67, 109-110,
    114-115, 117-121
Chitwood — *History (1)* p.206-207,
    478-479
Christensen — *Delaware* p.68
Clark — *Old* p.72-73
Earle — *Home. See* index p.463-464
Folsom — *Give* p.49, 52-54
Langdon — *Everyday* p.48-52
Speare — *Life* p.65
Starkey — *Land* p.181-183, 187, 190-
    191

PHILIP, KING (METACOMBET) (Indian)
See also **King Philip's War**
Alderman — *Story* p.28-29, 99
Amer. Her. — *Pilgrims* p.136-141
Amer. Her. — *Treasury* p.41-55
Beals — *John Eliot* p.156-157, 159-
    160, 162-165, 168, 174, 180
Chitwood — *History (1)* p.140-142
Craven — *Colonies* p.118-120, 122
Folsom — *Give* p.35-41
Morison — *Story* p.232, 237-239, 243,
    246-280
Scott — *Settlers* p.42, 53, 58
Starkey — *Land* p.197, 206-209
Vaughan — *New* p.54, 113, 152, 185,
    210, 231, 310-312, 319, 325, 330
Willison — *Saints. See* index p.506
- *Death*
    Collins — *Story* p.87
    Hawke — *U.S.* p.195

PHILIPSE, FREDERICK
Craven — *Colonies* p.73, 227, 230,
    249

PHILIPSE, MARGARET RUDOLPHUS
Williams — *Demeter's* p.175-176

**"PHILIPSE MANOR HALL" (Yonkers,
N.Y., 1682)**
Morrison — *Early* p.116-117

PHILLIPS, GEORGE
Rutman — *Winthrop's* p.19, 27, 47-
    48, 48n, 52-53

"PHILOSOPHERS"
See also **Science and scientists**
Wright — *Cultural* p.223-224

PHILOSOPHICAL SOCIETY
Morison — *Intellect.* p.255, 271
Rozwenc — *Making (1)* p.93

PHIPS, MARY, LADY
Williams — *Demeter's* p.142-143

PHIPS, WILLIAM, SIR
Alderman — *Story* p.33-35
Craven — *Colonies* p.238-239, 245-
    246
Langdon — *Everyday* p.221
Morison — *Oxford* p.123-124
National — *History.* p.114
Rothbard — *Conceived (1)* p.371,
    426, 442-443, 449, 452-453, 455,
    457-461, 479
Rozwenc — *Making (1)* p.95-96, 108
Wertenbaker — *Puritan* p.271-272,
    278-282, 284-285
Wright — *Cultural* p.37-38, 44
Wright — *Everyday* p.119-120

, *and witchcraft*
    Morison — *Intellect.* p.260-263

PHOEBE LAMPS
Earle — *Home* p.44

PHOTOGRAPHERS
Gould — *Early* p.143

PHYSICIANS
Bridenbaugh — *Cities* p.192, 199,
    201, 330, 380, 409
Dow — *Every* p.174-177
Earle — *Customs* p.333-336
Hawke — *Colonial* p.292, 295, 300
Langdon — *Everyday* p.325-328
Leonard — *Dear* p.216-217
Morris — *Ency.* p.541
Wright — *Cultural* p.219-220

- *Boston*
    Bridenbaugh — *Cities* p.89-90
, *Ignorance of*
    Wertenbaker — *First* p.168-169

- *Instruments*
  Dow — *Every* p.179-181
- *New England*
  Wertenbaker — *First* p.171-172
- *New Jersey*
  Wertenbaker — *First* p.172-173
- *Qualifications*
  Dow — *Every* p.179
- *Salem*
  Dow — *Every* p.178-179
, *Training of*
  Marshall — *Mayflower* p.124
- *Virginia*
  Wertenbaker — *First* p.172, 176-177
- *Women*
  Leonard — *Dear* p.471-477, 479-480, 486

PHYSICS
  Morison — *Intellect.* p.243-244, 249-250, 267-268

PIAKO (Indian)
  Phillips — *First* p.111, 114-116

PICKERING, EDWARD
  Gill — *Mayflower* p.37-38

PIERCE, JOHN
  Willison — *Pilgrim* p.158n, 198, 229-331
  Willison — *Saints* p.233

PIERCE, WILLIAM, CAPTAIN
  Dillon — *Pilgrims* p.190, 192-193

PIERCE PATENT
, *and Pierce Associates*
  Pomfret — *Founding* p.107-109, 113, 117-118, 121

PIES
  Gould — *Early* p.94-95

PIETISM
  Nettels — *Roots* p.472

PIGEONS
  Earle — *Home* p.110
  Glubok — *Home* p.59-60

PILGRIM PRESS (Leyden). *See* Choir Alley Press

PILGRIMS
  See also **Mayflower;** **Plymouth; Pilgrim** subdivision under following subjects: **Boston, Massachusetts — Harbor; Christmas, First; Dolls; Fires and firefighting; Fishing and fishermen; Funerals; Furniture; Guns; Herbs; Lamps; Maypoles; New Year's Day; Provincetown Harbor; Ships and shipping**
  Alderman — *Story* p.21-23, 25, 96
  Amer. Her. — *Thirteen* p.61-62, 85-88, 90-91, 94-97, 99
  Caffrey — *Mayflower* p.372
  Carman — *History (1)* p.27-29, 38, 69
  Chitwood — *History (1)* p.90-101
  Demos — *Little* p.3-5
  Dillon — *Pilgrims. See* index p.248
  Folsom — *Give* p.8, 12, 15-16, 35
  Furnas — *Americans* p.26, 53-58, 64
  Gill — *Mayflower. See* index p.204
  Hawke — *Colonial* p.100, 102, 124-129, 133, 148-149, 253
  Hawke — *U.S.* p.87-165
  Leonard — *Dear* p.359-361
  Leynse — *Preced. See* index p.284
  Life — *New* p.76-77, 86-89
  National — *History.* p.62-69
  Nettels — *Roots* p.116-117
  Pomfret — *Founding* p.39, 103-114, 131, 144, 150, 156-157
  Rozwenc — *Making (1)* p.26-29
  Scott — *Settlers* p.26-27
  Snell — *Wild* p.99, 101-111
  Speare — *Life* p.24-30
  Willison — *Pilgrim. See* index p.580
  Willison — *Saints. See* index p.507
  Wish — *Society (1)* p.24-62
  Wright — *Everyday* p.163

- *Arrival. See* **Pilgrims — Landing**
- *Betrayal, imprisonment*
  Archer — *Mayflower* p.22-27
- *Beverages*
  Marshall — *Mayflower* p.94
  - *Beer*
    Marshall — *Mayflower* p.94-95
- *Books and reading*
  Wright — *Literary* p.27-29
- *Cape Cod adventures*
  Willison — *Pilgrim* p.142-143
  Willison — *Saints* p.211-212, 217, 220
, *Caution of*
  Willison — *Pilgrim* p.203-204

168

PILGRIMS (*continued*)
- *Charter*
  Caffrey — *Mayflower* p.55-56,
  130, 184
- *Children*
  Adams — *Album* p.61
  Hale — *Through* p.71-75
- *Churches*
  Adams — *Album* p.59-60
  Willison — *Saints* p.369-371
- *Clothing and dress*
  Caffrey — *Mayflower* p.72
  Earle — *Two cent. (1)* p.3-48
  Marshall — *Mayflower* p.107-118
  Willison — *Saints* p.7-8, 335, 480
- *Crops and grain*
  Marshall — *Mayflower* p.91, 94,
  171
- *Dancing*
  Willison — *Pilgrim* p.332-333
  Willison — *Saints* p.173, 277, 462
- *Declaration of Rights*
  Willison — *Saints* p.317-318
- *Difficulties. See* **Pilgrims —
  Hardships**
- *Emigration*
  Amer. Her. — *Pilgrims* p.74-90
  Caffrey — *Mayflower* p.45-46, 49,
  51-54
  Willison — *Pilgrim* p.24-26
  - *Decision and reasons*
    Archer — *Mayflower* p.46-51
    Hills — *History (1)* p.7-20
    Leynse — *Preced.* p.63-78
- *England*
  Willison — *Pilgrim* p.13-29, 80-82
  Willison — *Saints* p.123-124, 465,
  485
- *Exploration and discoveries*
  Archer — *Mayflower* p.89-99
  Calverton — *Awake.* p.99-102
  Marshall — *Mayflower* p.25-26
  Willison — *Pilgrim* p.104-115
- *Finance*
  Beck — *Pilgrims* p.9, 11-12, 44,
  51-53, 61
  Willison — *Saints. See* index
  p.500 (under Finances, Pilgrim)
- *Food*
  Caffrey — *Mayflower* p.146
  Leonard — *Dear* p.122-124, 128
  Willison — *Saints. See* index
  p.501
  - *Gardens*
    Marshall — *Mayflower* p.91

- *Preparation*
  Marshall — *Mayflower* p.88-
  118
- *Preservation*
  Marshall — *Mayflower* p.89-
  91
- *Hardships*
  Amer. Her. — *Pilgrims* p.90-103
  Chitwood — *History (1)* p.95-96
  Willison — *Pilgrim* p.116-127,
  225-232
- *Holidays*
  See also **"Forefather's Day"**;
  names of other holidays
  Caffrey — *Mayflower* p.282-283
- *Holland*
  See also names of Dutch cities
  , *Departure from*
    Bailey — *American (1)* p.24-
    25
    Beck — *Pilgrims* p.11-16
    Leynse — *Preced.* p.103,
    132, 179-189, 211-224
    Miller — *Colonial* p.46-53
  , *Flight to*
    Amer. Her. — *Pilgrims* p.38-
    51
    Archer — *Mayflower* p.16-
    21, 28-37
    Beck — *Pilgrims* p.3-9
    Leynse — *Preced.* p.79-101
    Marshall — *Mayflower* p.25
    Willison — *Pilgrim* p.26-29
  - *Life*
    Archer — *Mayflower* p.38-45
    Caffrey — *Mayflower* p.36-
    44
    Gill — *Mayflower* p.26-40
    Leynse — *Preced.* p.143-163
    Miller — *Colonial* p.43-46
    Morison — *Story* p.9-21
    Willison — *Pilgrim* p.30-48
- *Housekeeping*
  Marshall — *Mayflower* p.88-118
- *Houses*
  Marshall — *Mayflower* p.63-87
  Willison — *Saints* p.161, 165-166,
  265, 386, 483
- *Independence from Crown*
  Marshall — *Mayflower* p.182
- *Indian relations*
  See also **Indians — Trade;
  Pilgrims — Sabbath;** names of
  Indians

Caffrey — *Mayflower* p.14, 17-19,
22, 117-118, 124-126, 133-
134, 163-165, 244, 287-288
Hawke — *U.S.* p.53-59
Marshall — *Mayflower* p.134-136,
138-141, 151-153, 155, 159
Wish — *Society (1)* p.28, 39-41
- *Kitchen utensils*
Marshall — *Mayflower* p.96-97,
99
- *Landing*
Archer — *Mayflower* p.80-88,
112-118
Caffrey — *Mayflower* p.127-128
Collins — *Story* p.41
Dillon — *Pilgrims* p.148-149
Hale — *Through* p.63-64
Hawke — *U.S.* p.87-88
Leynse — *Preced.* p.254-263
Marshall — *Mayflower* p.49, 52-
54
- *Period following*
Dow — *Domestic* p.3
, *Last of the*
Willison — *Pilgrim* p.320-323
- *Laws*
Willison — *Saints* p.177, 285,
317-325, 359-366, 377, 392
- *Leadership*
See also names of leaders
Caffrey — *Mayflower* p.146-147
Marshall — *Mayflower* p.26-29
- *Letters to and from*
Caffrey — *Mayflower* p.342
- *Longevity*
Willison — *Pilgrims* p.469-471
- *Marriage*
Willison — *Pilgrim* p.149, 401,
420
Willison — *Saints* p.185, 300-301,
324, 380, 467, 473
- *Medicine*
Marshall — *Mayflower* p.119-132
- *Military orders*
Willison — *Pilgrim* p.118-130
- *Mothers*
Starkey — *Land* p.46-61
- *Music*
Howard — *Our* p.3-5
- *Negotiations for passage*
Leynse — *Preced.* p.225-241
- *Origin and faith*
Morison — *Story* p.6-7, 195-196
- *Patents*
Marshall — *Mayflower* p.178, 180

- *Plague*
Archer — *Mayflower* p.149-156
Demos — *Little* p.80-81, 109, 184
Morison — *Story* p.62-64, 76,
112, 215
Starkey — *Land* p.53-54
Wertenbaker — *First* p.166, 178-
179
Willison — *Pilgrim* p.124-126
Willison — *Saints* p.172, 202-203,
307, 315, 466
- *Prosperity*
Marshall — *Mayflower* p.163, 166
- *Puritans, Difference from*
See **Puritans, Difference from
Pilgrims**
- *Sabbath*
- *Lack of Indian trade*
Archer — *Mayflower* p.177-
185
- *Similarity to Boers*
Caffrey — *Mayflower* p.219
- *Sin*
Willison — *Pilgrim* p.455-466
Willison — *Saints. See* index
p.509
- *Society*
Willison — *Saints* p.421-426, 430,
434
- *Spiritual contribution*
Morison — *Story* p.292-293
- *Threats to rule*
Marshall — *Mayflower* p.182-183
- *Tools*
Wertenbaker — *First* p.58
- *Women*
See also **Pilgrims — Mothers**
Leonard — *Dear* p.47-52
- *Youth*
Caffrey — *Mayflower* p.280-281,
283-284

PILLORY. *See* **Stocks and pillory**

"PILLOW LACE"
Rawson — *When* p.137

PILOT TOWN, DELAWARE
- *Historic sites*
Christensen — *Delaware* p.155

"PINCHES" (pleating)
Earle — *Two cent. (1)* p.173-174

PINCUSHIONS
Glubok — *Home* p.99-100

"PINE BARRENS," NEW JERSEY
Snell — *Wild* p.148

PINE KNOTS. *See* Candlewood

PINE-TREE SHILLINGS
Dow — *Every* p.167-168
Speare — *Life* p.121
Woodward — *Way* p.21-22

"PINKSTER DAY"
Wish — *Society (1)* p.100
- *New York*
Wright — *Everyday* p.209, 211

PINNACES (sailing vessels)
Morison — *Story* p.123-124, 131, 136, 185, 201, 210

PIONEERS
See also **Colonies and colonists; Frontier; Women — Pioneers, in wilderness;** names of localities, etc.
Drepperd — *Pioneer* p.1-4
- *Life*
Lawrence — *New* p.1-18

PIPE-TONGS
Earle — *Home* p.68-69

PIPESTAVES
Bailyn — *New England* p.58, 83, 85-86, 100-101

PIRACY
See also **Bonnet, Stede; Kidd, William, Captain; Teach, Edward**
Collins — *Story* p.73
Dow — *Every* p.217-220
Fisher — *Men (2)* p.274-285
Goodwin — *Colonial* p.102-103
Life — *New* p.103
National — *History.* p.116-117
Nettels — *Roots* p.376-379
Willison — *Pilgrim* p.170-171, 183-184, 281, 484-486
Willison — *Saints* p.195, 256-257, 333
- *Plymouth*
Miller — *Colonial* p.101-102

PISCATAQUA RIVER (and settlement, Portsmouth, N.H.)
Alderman — *Story* p.38-39
Bailyn — *New England* p.14, 28, 50, 95, 121

Willison — *Pilgrim* p.243n, 291, 391n, 393n, 395
Willison — *Saints* p.249-250, 279, 297, 299-300, 438

PISCATAWAY INDIANS
Alderman — *Story* p.83-84

PITCH
Craven — *Southern* p.35, 48, 69, 140-141, 312, 313n
- *South*
Craven — *Southern* p.69, 140-141, 312-313

PLAGUE. *See* Pilgrims — Plague

PLANTATIONS AND PLANTERS
See also **Mansions — South**
Folsom — *Give* p.9-10, 44-45, 72, 75-76
Kraus — *U.S. (1)* p.72-74
Nettels — *Roots* p.306-308
Ver Steeg — *Formative* p.57
Wertenbaker — *First* p.352
- *Life*
Miller — *First* p.94-96
Speare — *Life* p.6-13
- *Maryland*
Wertenbaker — *First* p.44-47
, *"Particular"* — *Creation*
Pomfret — *Founding* p.36, 39, 106-107, 119, 145
- *People*
Tunis — *Colonial* p.91-93
- *South*
Jernegan — *American* p.88-91, 98-99
Tunis — *Colonial* p.80-81, 83-84
Wertenbaker — *First* p.26-31, 46-47
- *South Carolina*
Fisher — *Men* p.71
- *Virginia*
Life — *New* p.64
Rothbard — *Conceived (1)* p.67-69

PLANTING FESTIVALS. *See* Indians — Festivals

PLANTS
See also **Flowers; Herbs;** names of plants
, *Native and foreign*
Chitwood — *History (1)* p.360-363

PLAYING CARDS. *See* **Card playing**

PLEASURES. *See* **Amusements; Sports and games;** etc.

PLOCKHOY, CORNELIUS PIETER
Calverton — *Awake.* p.187-188

PLOWDEN, EDMUND, SIR
Pomfret — *Founding* p.294-295

PLOWS
Rutman — *Winthrop's* p.91, 177-178, 180
Wertenbaker — *First* p.38, 58
Woodward — *Way* p.50-51
"The Plough"
Calverton — *Awake.* p.191

PLYMOUTH
See also **Mayflower;** "Old Comers"; **Pilgrims; Plymouth Rock; Plymouth** subdivision under following subjects: **Cellars; Chairs; Chests; Childbearing; Children and childhood, Illegitimate; Christmas, First; Classes — Structure; Clergymen; Congregationalists — Origin; Corn; Dining tables; Dishes and utensils; Divorce; Fabrics; Fences; Fireplaces; Fires and firefighting; Fish and fishermen; Floors; Flowers; Forks; Furniture; Guns; Handkerchiefs; Hats and hatters; Indians, "Praying"; Iron industry; Kitchens; Knives; Liquor; Literacy; Livestock; Midwives; Murder; Negroes; Petticoats; Piracy; Population; Punishment; Rasieres, Isaac De; Sabbath; Servants; Shoes; Smallpox; Table cloths and linen; Thanksgiving Day; "Undertakers"; Warming pans; Whipping; Windows; Witchcraft; Woodenware**
Adams — *Album* p.43
Alderman — *Story* p.22-23, 25, 29, 33, 70, 93, 96
Amer. Her. — *Pilgrims* p.104-119
Amer. Her. — *Thirteen* p.90-97, 103
Annals of America (1) p.232e-232f
Bailey — *American (1)* p.24-31
Beals — *John Eliot* p.43, 81, 87, 90, 96, 103, 156-157, 159, 167, 179-180, 182
Beck — *Pilgrims* p.45-53
Caffrey — *Mayflower* p.127-129, 271-272, 294
Carman — *History (1)* p.27-29, 39
Craven — *Colonies* p.5-6, 24, 27-28, 50, 86, 118, 215, 234, 237, 244
Demos — *Little* p.10-11n, 80, 143-144, 173
Dillon — *Pilgrims* p.79, 148-175, 181-188, 205
Fisher — *Men (1)* p.119-124
Folsom — *Give* p.11-12, 14-18, 36-38, 41, 65, 157
Furnas — *American* p.54-58
Gill — *Mayflower* p.104-135; *See also* index p.104-135
Glubok — *Home* p.9-11, 94-95, 190, 284
Hawke — *U.S.* p.90-91
Hills — *History (1)* p.74-98
Kraus — *U.S. (1)* p.49-52
Leynse — *Prec.* p.12, 15, 29, 33, 46, 106, 149, 182, 238, 257
Miller — *Colonial* p.43-65
Miller — *First* p.30-38
Morison — *Oxford* p.54-56
Morison — *Story. See* index p.v
Morris — *Ency.* p.30-34
National — *History.* p.62-69
Pomfret — *Founding. See* index p.378
Rozwenc — *Making (1)* p.26-28
Rutman — *Winthrop's. See* index p.317
Snell — *Wild* p.17, 77, 99, 106-111
Tunis — *Colonial* p.22-24
Vaughan — *Puritan* p.41-53
Willison — *Pilgrim. See* index p.580
Willison — *Saints. See* index p.507
Wish — *Society (1)* p.25-33
- Adultery
Demos — *Little* p.96-98, 157
- Aggression
Demos — *Little* p.49, 135-138
- Agriculture
Demos — *Little* p.13-14
, and Mass. Bay Colony
Beck — *Pilgrims* p.81-83
Dillon — *Pilgrims* p.201-224
Starkey — *Land* p.128-130, 214
, and Dominion of New England
Craven — *Colonies* p.215, 234
, and New England Confederation
Life — *New* p.81
Vaughan — *New* p.160

172

PLYMOUTH (*continued*)

- *Apprenticeship*
  Demos — *Little* p.70-72, 105,
  120, 140-141, 146-147, 184
, *as a democracy*
  Nettels — *Roots* p.168
, *Assistants*
  Demos — *Little* p.7, 88, 173-174
- *Babies*
  Demos — *Little* p.131-134, 158-
  159
- *Bachelors*
  Demos — *Little* p.77-79
- *Beds and bedrooms*
  Demos — *Little* p.31, 38, 43-45,
  132
- *Boundaries*
  Marshall — *Mayflower* p.180
- *Buildings*
  See also **Plymouth — Houses**
  Caffrey — *Mayflower* p.130-131,
  137, 145, 162-163, 167
  Marshall — *Mayflower* p.54-55

  , *First (Storehouse, 1620)*
  , Morrison — *Early* p.89-90
- *Burial Hill*
  Gill — *Mayflower* p.79-81, 96, 147
  Willison — *Pilgrim* p.426-427, 448
- *Business*
  Beck — *Pilgrims* p.62-66
, *Centrifugal forces in*
  Marshall — *Mayflower* p.184-185
- *Children*
  Demos — *Little* p.25, 30, 32-33,
  57-58, 67-69, 74, 88-89, 100-
  106, 113-116, 120-122, 134,
  144, 182
  Morison — *Story* p.186-187, 190-
  192, 195-196
  - *Number per family*
  Demos — *Little* p.194
- *Chronology*
  - *1622*
  Willison — *Pilgrim* p.188-191
  - *1627 (Dutch view)*
  Willison — *Pilgrim* p.305-307
- *Church*
  Collins — *Story* p.43
  Marshall — *Mayflower* p.60
  Morison — *Story* p.117-120, 139-
  141, 145, 150-151, 217, 226
  Willison — *Pilgrim* p.415-438;
  See also index p.580
  Willison — *Saints. See* index
  p.506

- *Discipline*
  Demos — *Little* p.8-9, 13,
  158n
, *First*
  Hills — *History (1)* p.99-100
- *Clothing and dress*
  Beck — *Pilgrims* p.58, 71-74
  Demos — *Little* p.37-38, 52-58
  Morison — *Story* p.60-61, 126,
  178-181, 218
  , *Children's*
  Demos — *Little* p.57, 133,
  139-140
  - *Colors*
  Demos — *Little* p.53-54
  , *Women's*
  Adams — *Album* p.53
  Beck — *Pilgrims* p.73
  Demos — *Little* p.55-56
- *Cole's Hill*
  Willison — *Saints* p.162-163, 169,
  199, 321, 410, 412, 425, 431,
  433
- *Commerce and industry*
  Marshall — *Mayflower* p.160-177
- *"Common Course"*
  Caffrey — *Mayflower* p.181-182
  Morison — *Story* p.95-96, 128
  , *End of*
  Annals of America (1) p.72-
  73
  Bailey — *American (1)* p.26-
  27
- *Common house*
  Beck — *Pilgrims* p.31-32
  Willison — *Pilgrim* p.119-121
  Willison — *Saints* p.161-165,
  170-171, 190, 193, 200, 202
- *Corn Hill*
  Morison — *Story* p.47-49
  Willison — *Saints* p.151-153, 215
- *Corn trade*
  Caffrey — *Mayflower* p.170-172
- *Courtship*
  Demos — *Little* p.152, 156, 182
  Earle — *Customs* p.68-69
- *Crime and criminals*
  Lawrence — *Not* p.157-162
- *Crops and harvesting*
  Starkey — *Land* p.60-61, 83, 86,
  89
  Willison — *Pilgrim* p.151-152,
  182-183, 246
  Willison — *Saints* p.239-240

- *Festivals*
 See also **Thanksgiving Day**
 Dillon — *Pilgrim* p.158-175,
 186-187
- *Deaths*
 See also **Plymouth — Infant
 mortality**
 Caffrey — *Mayflower* p.132-133,
 140-141
 Demos — *Little* p.65-66, 131-132,
 193
 , *by age*
 Demos — *Little* p.193
 , *First*
 Archer — *Mayflower* p.117-
 118
 Willison — *Pilgrim* p.124-127
 , *Pattern of*
 Willison — *Pilgrim* p.126-127
- *Debts*
 Dillon — *Pilgrims* p.150-152, 196-
 197, 200
- *Decline and end of colony*
 Demos — *Little* p.17-18
 Dillon — *Little* p.216
 Rothbard — *Conceived (1)* p.273-
 276
- *Description*
 Marshall — *Mayflower* p.52-53,
 58
- *Drought*
 Willison — *Pilgrim* p.227-228,
 231-232
- *Dutch relations*
 Starkey — *Land* p.169
- *Economy*
 Demos — *Little* p.13-14
 Jernegan — *American* p.121-122
 Marshall — *Mayflower* p.170-171
 Willison — *Pilgrim. See* index
 p.574-575
 Willison — *Saints. See* index
 p.500
- *Education*
 See also **Plymouth — Schools**
 Demos — *Little* p.122, 142-144,
 183
 Monroe — *Founding (1)* p.124
- *English relations*
 Demos — *Little* p.16-18
- *Execution, first*
 Dillon — *Pilgrims* p.204
 Willison — *Pilgrim* p.355-356
- *Expansion. See* **Plymouth —
 Growth**

- *Exploration and discovery*
 See also **Pilgrims —
 Exploration and discovery**
 Morison — *Story* p.46-56
 Starkey — *Land* p.48, 51
 Willison — *Pilgrim* p.114-117
- *Families*
 Demos — *Little* p.179-190
 Marshall — *Mayflower* p.60-61
 Morison — *Story* p.182-187
 , *Size of*
 Demos — *Little* p.192, 194
- *Famine. See* **Plymouth —
 "Starving time", Plymouth —
 Winter, First**
- *Farm implements*
 Demos — *Little* p.45
- *Farmers and farming*
 Beck — *Pilgrims* p.39, 43, 58-62,
 77
 Wertenbaker — *Puritan* p.187-
 188
 Willison — *Pilgrim* p.146, 151-
 152, 182-183, 231-232, 246,
 296-297, 384-385
- *Finance*
 Willison — *Pilgrims. See* index
 p.575
- *Food*
 Dillon — *Pilgrims* p.160-161
 Morison — *Story* p.20, 62, 86-88,
 96-97, 114, 187-190
- *Fort Hill*
 Willison — *Saints* p.161-162,
 170-171, 190, 199, 201, 207,
 369, 401, 426
- *Forts and garrisons*
 Archer — *Mayflower* p.157-166
 Marshall — *Mayflower* p.55-57
 Miller — *Colonial* p.63-64
 Morison — *Story* p.245, 259-262,
 265, 271-273, 276
 Willison — *Pilgrim* p.198-199, 207
 Willison — *Saints* p.207, 225-226,
 228, 247, 251, 257
- *Founding*
 Chitwood — *History (1)* p.94-95
 Rothbard — *Conceived (1)* p.160-
 164
 Wertenbaker — *Puritan* p.28-29
- *Freemen*
 Hills — *History (1)* p.93-96
 Morison — *Story* p.101-103, 118,
 148-154, 159, 164-168, 171-
 173, 223

PLYMOUTH (*continued*)

Willison — *Pilgrim* p.378n, 420n,
558
- *French relations*
Morison — *Story* p.135-136, 237,
248, 288
- *Fruit*
Morison — *Story* p.62, 76, 114,
189, 200
- *Fur trade*
Bailyn — *New England* p.23-26,
28-29, 204 (n.34)
Caffrey — *Mayflower* p.152, 170,
181, 194-195, 209, 212-213,
218, 245, 258-259, 266
- *Gardens*
Morison — *Story* p.66, 95, 187,
228
- *General court*
Demos — *Little. See* index p.197
Morison — *Story. See* index p.iii
Willison — *Saints. See* index
p.501
- *Goats and sheep*
Morison — *Story* p.iii
- *Government*
Angle — *By* p.1-3
Beck — *Pilgrims* p.67-68, 70
Chitwood — *History (1)* p.96-98
Demos — *Little* p.6-8, 11n, 13
Dillon — *Pilgrims* p.218-219, 223-
224
Nettels — *Roots* p.167-168
Pomfret — *Founding* p.121-123,
125
Starkey — *Land* p.56
Willison — *Pilgrim. See* index
p.576
Willison — *Saints* p.319
- *Grandparents*
Demos — *Little* p.121-124
- *Growth*
Beck — *Pilgrims* p.62, 64
Caffrey — *Mayflower* p.283, 288,
304
Gill — *Mayflower* p.136-139
- *Guardians*
Demos — *Little* p.116, 121, 147
- *History*
Demos — *Little* p.1-18
- *Home furnishings*
Demos — *Little* p.36-51, 161
Morison — *Story* p.176-178, 230-
231

- *Horses*
Morison — *Story* p.112, 198, 202-
206, 228-232, 240
Willison — *Saints* p.314
- *Houses*
Adams — *Album* p.48-49
Beck — *Pilgrims* p.31, 39, 55-57
Demos — *Little* p.24-35
Dow — *Domestic* p.3
Dow — *Every* p.15
Furnas — *Americans* p.147-148
Marshall — *Mayflower* p.64-70
Morison — *Story* p.59-60, 174-
176, 230
Wertenbaker — *First* p.284-285
- *Maintenance*
Marshall — *Mayflower* p.107
- *Hunting and trapping*
Morison — *Story* p.63-66, 82, 87,
240
- *Hurricanes*
Willison — *Pilgrim* p.404-405
- *Husbands*
Demos — *Little* p.82-99
, *Indian name for*
Dillon — *Pilgrims* p.153
- *Indian Relations*
See also **Indians — Treaties,
Plymouth; Pequot War;**
names of tribes, individual
Indians
Annals of America (1) p.66-69
Archer — *Mayflower* p.101-111
Demos — *Little* p.5, 14-16, 110-
111
Life — *New* p.81
Marshall — *Mayflower* p.135-136,
140-141, 151, 161-163
Miller — *Colonial* p.61-62
Morison — *Story* p.46, 51-52,
104-108, 125-126, 181, 206,
209-214, 240-244
Vaughan — *New* p.57, 64-92,
187, 192-193, 199-201, 228,
310-313, 316, 327
Willison — *Pilgrim. See* index
p.577
Willison — *Saints. See* index
p.502-503
- *Indian Trade*
See also **Plymouth — Indian
relations**
Archer — *Mayflower* p.177-193
- *Infant mortality*
Willison — *Saints* p.385-386

- *Inheritance*
  Demos — *Little* p.85, 103, 117-120, 123-124, 149, 151, 160-161, 164-170, 189
- *"Inner room"*
  Demos — *Little* p.31-32, 34, 45, 131
- *"Inspectors of youth"*
  Willison — *Saints* p.371-372
- *Intolerance*
  Morison — *Story* p.163-166
- *Inventories*
  Demos — *Little* p.36, 52, 132
- *King Philip's war*
  Starkey — *Land* p.206-209
- *Kinship*
  Demos — *Little* p.118-125, 181
- *Kitchen utensils*
  Demos — *Little* p.40
- *Ladders*
  Demos — *Little* p.31
- *Land*
  Morison — *Story* p.236-239
  Willison — *Pilgrim* p.119-120, 158, 226-227, 239-240, 259-260, 294-297, 307
  - *Allotments*
    Demos — *Little* p.105-106, 109, 149, 160-161, 164, 166, 168-169
    Dillon — *Pilgrims* p.149-150, 181-182
    Hills — *History (1)* p.87-91
    Willison — *Pilgrim* p.194-196, 296-297
    Willison — *Saints* p.232
  - *Mortgage, and shareholder ownership*
    Dillon — *Pilgrim* p.196-197
  - *Laws*
    Beck — *Pilgrims* p.68
    Caffrey — *Mayflower* p.276-277
    Marshall — *Mayflower* p.60
    Morison — *Story* p.149, 152-153, 161-166, 170-171, 283
    Willison — *Saints* p.177, 285, 317-325, 359-366, 377, 392, 471-472
    - *Women's status*
      Williams — *Demeter's* p.82
  , *Laying out of*
    Willison — *Pilgrim* p.119-122
    Willison — *Saints* p.161-162
- *Leyden congregation*
  Caffrey — *Mayflower* p.230-231
- *Leyden street*
  Adams — *Album* p.62
  Willison — *Saints* p.161, 416, 425
- *Life*
  Beck — *Pilgrims* p.74-79
  Caffrey — *Mayflower* p.215
  Hills — *History (1)* p.104-107
  Marshall — *Mayflower* p.53-62
  Morison — *Story* p.182-183, 187-191
  , *Expectancy of*
    Demos — *Little* p.192
- *Longevity*
  Demos — *Little* p.75-77, 79, 171-178, 182, 184
- *Lydford-Oldham affair*
  Dillon — *Pilgrims* p.189-193
- *Main street*
  Willison — *Saints* p.162, 412-413
- *Marriage*
  Calverton — *Awake.* p.105-106
  Demos — *Little. See* index p.198-199
  Morison — *Story* p.162, 166, 183-186
  , *by age*
    Demos — *Little* p.193
  , *First*
    Annals of America (1) p.68
    Dillon — *Pilgrims* p.161
    Leonard — *Dear* p.75-76
    Miller — *Colonial* p.60
    Willison — *Pilgrim* p.149
    Willison — *Saints* p.185, 469
  - *Remarriage*
    Demos — *Little* p.67, 122, 194
- *Meat and dairy products*
  Marshall — *Mayflower* p.91
- *Medicine*
  Willison — *Saints* p.470-471
- *Missionaries*
  Vaughan — *New* p.295, 298-300
  , *Models of*
    Marshall — *Mayflower* p.56-59
- *Morality*
  Willison — *Pilgrim* p.455-476
- *Mosaic code*
  Willison — *Saints* p.317, 359-360
- *Mount Hope*
  Morison — *Story* p.233, 238-239, 247, 250-251, 276-277, 292
- *Music*
  Willison — *Saints* p.86, 463-464, 481, 483

PLYMOUTH (*continued*)

- *Natural resources*
  Caffrey — *Mayflower* p.131-132,
  285-286
- *Neighborhood tensions*
  Demos — *Little* p.49-51
- *New Amsterdam trade*
  Caffrey — *Mayflower* p.218-220
- *Newcomers*
  Dillon — *Pilgrims* p.168, 182-
  188
- *Officers*
  Caffrey — *Mayflower* p.359-363
  Willison — *Saints. See* index
  p.507
  , *Age of*
  Demos — *Little* p.172-174
- *Orphans*
  Demos — *Little* p.73, 115-116,
  120-122, 184
- *Parents*
  Demos — *Little* p.100-103, 134-
  136
- *Patent (old charter, 1630)*
  Beck — *Pilgrims* p.44
  Dillon — *Pilgrims* p.204
  Morison — *Story* p.16, 134, 141,
  151, 154-155
  Morris — *Ency.* p.32
  Willison — *Pilgrim* p.353-354,
  528-529
- *"Patriarchalism"*
  Demos — *Little* p.164, 169-170
- *Petition for rights*
  Wertenbaker — *Puritan* p.334-
  335
- *Pilgrim Hall*
  Willison — *Saints* p.424-425, 431,
  483, 485
- *Politics*
  Annals of America (1) p.75-76
  Marshall — *Mayflower* p.178-185
- *Profligates*
  Wertenbaker — *First* p.192-193
- *"Purchasers"*
  Willison — *Pilgrim* p.294-297,
  299, 308-309, 352
  Willison — *Saints* p.262-263, 317,
  437-449
- *Religion*
  See also **Plymouth — Church**
  Beck — *Pilgrims* p.46, 68, 70, 78
  Demos — *Little* p.12-13, 140,
  142n, 184

Caffrey — *Mayflower* p.40-41,
177, 186-187, 198, 219, 277-
282, 303
Calverton — *Awake.* p.104-105
Hall — *Religious* p.85-90, 95
Marshall — *Mayflower* p.60-61
Morison — *Story* p.163-166
Pomfret — *Founding* p.115-116,
119, 121, 129-130
- *Schools*
  Annals of America (1) p.243-244
  Demos — *Little* p.72, 143-144,
  182
  Caffrey — *Mayflower* p.290-291
  Hills — *History (1)* p.101-103
- *Seal*
  Morison — *Story* p.151-152
- *Settlements*
  Archer — *Mayflower* p.119-131
  Caffrey — *Mayflower* p.268
  Demos — *Little p.5*
  Gill — *Mayflower* p.78-82, 88-102
  Jernegan — *American* p.119-122
  Life — *New* p.49, 76-77, 86, 88,
  95
  Nettels — *Roots* p.157-158
  Starkey — *Land* p.53
- *"Seven Articles"*
  Caffrey — *Mayflower* p.46-47
- *"Seven-year plan"*
  Calverton — *Awake.* p.104-105
- *Sickness*
  See also **Pilgrims — Plague;**
  Smallpox — Plymouth
  Beck — *Pilgrims* p.26, 32-33
  Willison — *Pilgrim* p.124-127
  Willison — *Saints* p.166-168, 171,
  315, 467
- *Slavery*
  Morison — *Story* p.193, 241, 259,
  283-284
- *Spinsters*
  Demos — *Little* p.77-79
- *Spoons*
  Demos — *Little* p.42
- *Sports and games*
  Caffrey — *Mayflower* p.282-283
- *"Starving Time"*
  Annals of America (1) p.66, 74-
  75
  Archer — *Mayflower* p.298
  Gill — *Mayflower* p.88-102
  Hawke — *U.S.* p.89-90
  Miller — *Colonial* p.57-59, 64-65
  Miller — *First* p.32-34

Morison — *Story* p.86-88, 99
Willison — *Saints* p.198, 204,
206, 210-216, 231, 236-237
- *Stirring events*
Archer — *Mayflower* p.141-148
- *Strawberry Hill*
Willison — *Saints* p.170, 173-174,
177, 350
- *Sugar*
Adams — *Album* p.46
- *Summer, first*
Beck — *Pilgrims* p.39-42
- *Taxation*
Dillon — *Pilgrims* p.182, 196
Morison — *Story* p.160, 203, 286-
290
- *Town brook*
Willison — *Saints* p.161, 169,
174-176, 232, 262, 322, 411
- *Town square*
Willison — *Saints* p.369, 416,
421-422, 424
- *Trade*
See also **Plymouth — Corn
trade; — Fur trade; — Indian
trade; — New Amsterdam
trade**
Beck — *Pilgrims. See* index p.89
Caffrey — *Mayflower* p.212, 236-
242, 266, 268
Marshall — *Mayflower* p.169-170
Morison — *Story* p.92, 106, 126-
127, 136
Vaughan — *New* p.214-215, 228
Willison — *Pilgrim. See* index
p.583
- *Troop contributions*
Caffrey — *Mayflower* p.273
- *Views of Isaac De Rasieres*
Marshall — *Mayflower* p.55, 58
- *Views of William Bradford*
Annals of America (1) p.65-86
- *Wages*
Morison — *Story* p.168, 197-198
- *War*
Vaughan — *New* p.139-140, 169
- *Weather*
Demos — *Little* p.13, 46, 55
- *Wedding, first*
Caffrey — *Mayflower* p.147
- *Wickedness*
Annals of America (1) p.84-85
Caffrey — *Mayflower* p.268-269
- *Widows*
Demos — *Little* p.67, 73, 75-76,
85, 90, 177-178, 194

- *Winter, first*
See also **Plymouth — Sickness**
Adams — *Album* p.44-45
Beck — *Pilgrims* p.31-38
Caffrey — *Mayflower* p.130-141
Dillon — *Pilgrims* p.151
Leonard — *Dear* p.50-51
- *Wives*
Demos — *Little* p.82-99
- *Women*
Adams — *Album* p.53-55
Beck — *Pilgrims* p.23, 31, 50-51
Holliday — *Woman's* p.6-7
Willison — *Pilgrim* p.45
- *Duties*
Beck — *Pilgrims* p.58, 74, 77
- *Hardships*
Starkey — *Land* p.53
- *Legal status*
Demos — *Little* p.56, 82-91,
94-95, 181, 189
- *Woodcutting*
Morison — *Story* p.169-170, 187,
201
- *Youth*
Caffrey — *Mayflower* p.280-281,
283-284
- *Adolescence*
Demos — *Little* p.130, 145-
150

PLYMOUTH, ENGLAND
Gill — *Mayflower* p.48-59; *See also*
index p.204-205

PLYMOUTH COLONY COUNCIL
Willison — *Saints* p.3, 241-242, 245,
248-249, 254-255, 261

PLYMOUTH COMPANY
See also **"Adventurers"; Council for
New England; Virginia Company
of London**
Amer. Her. — *Thirteen* p.71, 85, 91,
94
Bailyn — *New England* p.2-5
Carman — *History (1)* p.27-28
Craven — *Southern* p.62, 83
Gill — *Mayflower* p.51, 57, 93, 103
Hawke — *Colonial* p.87-89, 108; *See
also* index p.754
Hills — *History (2)* p.219-244
Leynse — *Preced.* p.28-29, 33, 212
Marshall — *Mayflower* p.21, 23
Pomfret — *Founding* p.26, 109-110,
139-140

PLYMOUTH COMPANY (continued)
Rothbard — Conceived (1) p.42-44, 159
Rozwenc — Making (1) p.26-27, 31
- Early activities
Morris — Ency. p.30-31
- Reorganization
Hope — Nation p.61, 69, 76

PLYMOUTH COUNCIL (in England)
Alderman — Story p.38-40

PLYMOUTH ROCK
Gill — Mayflower p.187-189
Willison — Pilgrim. p.115n, 566
Willison — Saints. See index p.507

POCAHONTAS
See also **Rolfe, John; Smith, John, Captain**
Alderman — Story p.8-9, 11
Amer. Her. — Thirteen p.73-74, 81-82
Craven — Southern p.72, 108, 115-117, 132, 138
Earle — Two cent. (1) p.xvi, 68, 122, 201
Goodwin — Colonial p.46-47
Hawke — Colonial p.99, 103
Life — New p.54-55, 64-65
Marshall — Mayflower p.22
National — History. p.50, 53
Nettels — Roots p.156
Snell — Wild p.82-84, 94
Spruill's — Women's p.6-7
Starkey — Land p.20, 32-34, 38-44, 68
Williams — Demeter's p.10-11

, and Earl of Buckingham
Phillips — First p.193-194
, and James I
Phillips — First p.190-193
, and John Smith
Phillips — First p.57-58, 161, 178-181, 184
, and Queen Anne
Phillips — First p.167-171, 194
, as first Indian to cross Atlantic
Phillips — First p.154
- Bible, Knowledge of
Phillips — First p.191
- Books, Reading of
Phillips — First p.108

- Childhood and youth
Phillips — First p.17-21, 31-45, 49-56
- Clothing and dress
Earle — Two cent. (1) p.122, 125
Phillips — First p.126-127
- Conversion to Christianity
Phillips — First p.128-129
- Courtship by Samuel Dooling
Phillips — First p.135-136
- Death and funeral
Phillips — First p.199-200
- Disowned by Powhatan
Phillips — First p.120-121
- Education
Phillips — First p.130-131
- Food and drink (eating habits)
Phillips — First p.28-29, 125-126, 167
- Illness
Phillips — First p.195-199
, in Jamestown
Phillips — First p.97, 107-112, 114-154
, in London
Phillips — First p.115, 143-199
- Legends
Phillips — First p.35-36, 184-185
- Marriage. See **Pocahontas — Wedding (1614)**
- Party, in honor of
Phillips — First p.109-110
- Portraits and drawings
Phillips — First p.37-38
- Views of John Smith
Miller — Colonial p.231-238
- Wedding (1614)
Collins — Story p.36
Demos — Remarkable p.259-276
Phillips — First p.138-141

POCUMTUCK INDIANS
Vaughan — New p.56, 152, 179, 320, 329

POETS AND POETRY
See also **Funerals — Elegies;** names of poets
Earle — Customs p.265-266
Hawke — Colonial p.308
Morrison — Intellect. p.210-240
Morris — Ency. p.559
Ver Steeg — Formative p.97-98
Wertenbaker — First p.243-244
Wertenbaker — Puritan p.93-103

Wright — *Literary* p.84-90, 159-160, 162-164
- *Almanacs*
    Wright — *Literary* p.90
- *"Bermudas"*
    Annals of America (1) p.222
- *Best sellers, First*
    Wright — *Cultural* p.170-171
, *Controversial*
    Morison — *Intellect.* p.226-230
- *"If I were a Pilgrim child"*
    Hale — *Through* p.71-75
- *"The landing of the Pilgrims"*
    Hale — *Through* p.63-64
- *Massachusetts*
    Wertenbaker — *First* p.243-244
- *New England*
    Caffrey — *Mayflower* p.297-298
    Lawrence — *New* (Preface)
    Tyler — *History* p.227-253
    Wertenbaker — *Puritan* p.94-101
- *"New England ABC"*
    Annals of America (1) p.276
- *"New England's crisis"*
    Annals of America (1) p.245-246
- *"The Prologue"*
    Annals of America (1) p.197-198
- *Puritans*
    Morison — *Intellect.* p.23
    Tyler — *History* p.227-233
    Wertenbaker — *First* p.243-244
- *Women*
    Leonard — *Dear* p.491-495

POKANOKET INDIANS. *See*
Wampanoag Indians

POLITICS
    See also **Government;** names of localities, political parties
    Carman — *History (1)* p.125-130
, *Communal, Dedham, Mass.*
    Lockridge — *New* p.37-56
- *Culture*
    Rozwenc — *Making (1)* p.52-83

POLL TAX
    Craven — *Southern* p.165-166, 243-244, 283
- *South*
    Craven — *Southern* p.165-166
, *Alternatives to*
    Craven — *Southern* p.243-244, 283

POMEGRANATES
    Craven — *Southern* p.19, 119, 346

POMETACOM. **See Metacom(bet)**

POND, WILLIAM
    Miller — *First* p.44-46
- *Letter from Mass. (1630)*
    Demos — *Remarkable* p.73-75

PONKAPOAG, MASSACHUSETTS. *See*
Punkapog, Massachusetts

POOLE, ELIZABETH
    Williams — *Demeter's* p.30-31, 188

POPE'S DAY. *See* **Guy Fawke's Day**

POPHAM, GEORGE
    Hawke — *Colonial* p.88-89
    Vaughan — *New* p.11-14

POPLAR WOOD
    Earle — *Home* p.81-82

POPULATION
    See also **Birth rate**
    Amer. Her. — *Thirteen* p.107, 194
    Carman — *History (1)* p.41-42
    Craven — *Colonies* p.15-16, 60
    Hawke — *Colonial* p.167, 278
    Smith — *17th* p.5-6
    Vaughan — *New* p.93-94, 97, 153, 158, 185, 214, 312
- *Boston (1689)*
    Hawke — *Colonial* p.283
- *Chronology*
    - *1630–1690*
        Bridenbaugh — *Cities* p.6
    - *1680*
        Rothbard — *Conceived (1)* p.509
    - *1689*
        Jernegan — *American* p.300-301
    - *1690*
        Bridenbaugh — *Cities* p.143
        Nettels — *Roots* p.383
    - *1690's*
        Adams — *Provincial* p.2-3
- *Connecticut*
    Wertenbaker — *First* p.313
- *Dedham, Mass.*
    Lockridge — *New* p.4, 64n, 65-66, 66n, 68n

POPULATION (*continued*)
- *Economy*
    Pomfret — *Founding* p.114, 118-120, 123, 127
- *English*
    Carman — *History (1)* p.41
- *Growth*
    Wertenbaker — *First* p.8, 313-314
- *Male-female ratio*
    Williams — *Demeter's. See* index p.353
- *Maryland*
    Craven — *Colonies* p.15-16
- *Massachusetts*
    Pomfret — *Founding* p.201-202
- *New England*
    Craven — *Colonies* p.15-16, 109-110
    Hawke — *Colonial* p.251
    Jernegan — *American* p.165-169
    Morison — *Intellect.* p.17-18, 25-26
    - *Composition*
        Jernegan — *American* p.177-178
- *New Haven, Conn.*
    Pomfret — *Founding* p.270
- *New Netherland*
    Pomfret — *Founding* p.283, 297
- *New York*
    Hawke — *Colonial* p.225
- *Pennsylvania*
    Craven — *Colonies* p.192
    Hawke — *Colonial* p.236-237
- *Plymouth*
    Caffrey — *Mayflower* p.141, 228
    Dillon — *Pilgrims* p.184
    Hope — *Nation* p.79
    Pomfret — *Founding* p.114-115, 123
    Willison — *Pilgrim* p.234
    Willison — *Saints* p.261, 468-469, 318
- *Rhode Island*
    Craven — *Colonies* p.15
    Wertenbaker — *First* p.313
- *South*
    Jernegan — *American* p.82-83
- *Virginia*
    Craven — *Colonies* p.15-16
    Hawke — *Colonial* p.184
    Morison — *Intellect.* p.14, 25

    Pomfret — *Founding* p.33, 35, 38-40, 50, 55, 73
    Wertenbaker — *First* p.31

PORCHES
    Morrison — *Early* p.40-42
- *Virginia*
    Wertenbaker — *Old* p.76

PORRIDGE
    Gould — *Early* p.82, 93

PORRINGERS
    Earle — *Customs* p.140-141
    Earle — *Home* p.85-86
    Gould — *Early* p.86
    McClinton — *Antiques* p.32

PORT ROYAL, NOVA SCOTIA
    Morris — *Ency.* p.59, 62, 65
    Snell — *Wild* p.66, 72-73

PORT ROYAL ISLAND, SOUTH CAROLINA
    Alderman — *Story* p.136-138
    Craven — *Colonies* p.57, 89, 96, 135-136, 179
    Craven — *Southern. See* index p.446
    Morris — *Ency.* p.50, 53-54, 63, 101

PORTRAITS AND PORTRAIT PAINTING
    Wright — *Cultural* p.207-208
    Wright — *Literary* p.158
    , *as records*
        Glubok — *Home* p.281-283
    , *Children's*
        Glubok — *Home* p.281-283

PORTSMOUTH, NEW HAMPSHIRE
    See also **Piscataqua River; Strawberry Bank**
    Bailyn — *New England* p.50, 96, 124-125, 132

PORTSMOUTH, RHODE ISLAND
    Alderman — *Story* p.97-99
    Bailyn — *New England* p.40, 89, 179
    Chitwood — *History (1)* p.131-132
    Pomfret — *Founding* p.213-214, 216, 218-220, 223, 225
- *Deeds (1659)*
    Demos — *Remarkable* p.168
- *Indenture record (1663)*
    Demos — *Remarkable* p.128-129

PORTUGAL
Carman — *History (1)* p.13, 16
Pomfret — *Founding* p.1-2, 8, 11-12, 14

PORY, JOHN
Marshall — *Mayflower* p.88, 161
Tyler — *History* p.43-45; *See also* index p.547
Willison — *Pilgrim* p.185-193
- *The work of a colonial legislature"*
Annals of America (1) p.40-46

POSNETS (shallow porringers)
Earle — *Customs* p.141-142

POSTAL SERVICE
Bridenbaugh — *Cities* p.53
Earle — *Home* p.332-335
Langdon — *Everyday* p.255-263
Wright — *Cultural* p.240-241
, *First regular*
   Glubok — *Home* p.334-335
- *Intercolonial, first*
   Langdon — *Everyday* p.259
- *Massachusetts, first letter carrier*
   Langdon — *Everyday* p.261
- *New England*
   Tunis — *Colonial* p.61-63
- *New Netherland*
   Langdon — *Everyday* p.258
- *Post office*
   Chitwood — *History (1)* p.389-391
- *Post riders*
   Speare — *Life* p.144
- *Postmaster, first*
   Goodwin — *Colonial* p.115-116
- *South*
   Goodwin — *Colonial* p.114-116
- *Virginia, first letter delivered*
   Langdon — *Everyday* p.258

POTATOES
Craven — *Southern* p.21, 35, 107, 141, 346, 357
Earle — *Customs* p.153
Glubok — *Home* p.79-80
Gould — *Early* p.92-93
Hope — *Nation* p.86
Lawrence — *New* p.7-8
Woodward — *Way* p.52
, *Irish*

   - *Jamestown, Va.*
      Adams — *Album* p.16

, *Sweet (or Spanish)*
   - *Jamestown, Va.*
      Adams — *Album* p.16

POTOMAC RIVER
Alderman — *Story* p.11, 83-84
Amer. Her. — *Thirteen* p.74, 172, 177, 179
Craven — *Southern* p.73-74, 108, 190, 194-195, 363, 373

POTS AND PANS. *See* **Kitchen utensils**

POTT, ELIZABETH
Spruill — *Women's* p.233

POTT, JOHN
Wertenbaker — *First* p.172, 176, 179, 310

POTTERY AND POTTERS
Drepperd — *Pioneer* p.164, 174, 176
Tunis — *Craftsmen* p.119
- *Shops*
   Speare — *Life* p.47-48

POULTRY
See also names of types of poultry
Craven — *Southern* p.96, 99-100, 103, 212
- *New Amsterdam*
   Smith — *Colonial* p.112

POUNDERS (washing implement)
Gould — *Early* p.115

POVERTY
See also **Pauper's badges**
Bridenbaugh — *Cities* p.79-85
Dow — *Domestic* p.2
Morison — *Intellect.* p.25-26
Wertenbaker — *First* p.213-214
- *England*
   Wertenbaker — *First* p.211-212
- *Poor relief*
   Nettels — *Roots* p.461-463

POWDER AND POWDERING TUBS
Earle — *Colonial* p.292

POWHATAN (Indian)
Alderman — *Story* p.8-9
Craven — *Southern* p.79-81, 104, 108, 116
Goodwin — *Colonial* p.129
National — *History.* p.50, 55

POWHATAN (Indian) (*continued*)
Nettels — *Roots* p.155-156
Phillips — *First* p.1-5, 19, 44-45, 70-73, 88, 91, 96-97
Smith — *17th* p.22, 37, 41, 43-49
Starkey — *Land* p.33-37, 44, 62
Willison — *Pilgrim* p.137n
- *Ammunition demands*
    Phillips — *First* p.116-118
, *at Pocahontas' wedding*
    Phillips — *First* p.139
, *Coronation of*
    Hawke — *U.S.* p.66-68
- *First visit to Jamestown (1610)*
    Phillips — *first* p.107

POWHATAN CONFEDERATION
Smith — *17th* p.40-41, 46, 55, 59

POWWOWS. *See* **Indians — Powwows**

PRATT, MARY PRIEST
Willison — *Saints* p.446-447

PRATT, PHINEAS
Willison — *Pilgrim* p.218-219, 540
Willison — *Saints* p.225, 437, 446-447

"PRAYING INDIANS." *See* **Indians, "Praying"**

"PRAYING TOWNS"
See also **Nashoba; Natick; Punkapog; Wamesit**
Beals — *John Eliot* p.138, 144-146, 151, 156, 158, 182-183
Vaughan — *New* p.190-191, 289-290, 293-294, 296, 303, 314, 321, 325, 333

PRENCE, MARY COLLIER SOUTHWORTH
Willison — *Pilgrim* p.450n
Willison — *Saints* p.332, 445, 453

PRENCE, PATIENCE BREWSTER
Dillon — *Pilgrims* p.183
Gill — *Mayflower* p.104, 131
Marble — *Women* p.11, 37, 62
Morison — *Story* p.172
Willison — *Pilgrim* p.20, 79, 234, 299, 387n
Willison — *Saints* p.59-60, 122, 235, 314-315, 329, 445-446

PRENCE, THOMAS
Caffrey — *Mayflower. See* index p.390
Gill — *Mayflower* p.119, 130, 132, 135, 145
Hills — *History (1). See* index p.172
Hills — *History (2)* p.47-48; *See also* index p.172
Morison — *Story* p.76n, 86, 128, 130, 137-139, 145, 164, 171-172, 183, 219, 222-224, 248-249, 254
Willison — *Pilgrim. See* index p.581
Willison — *Saints. See* index p.507

PRENCE FAMILY
Hills — *History (1). See* index p.172
Hills — *History (2). See* index p.270

PRESBYTERIANS
Carman — *History (1)* p.35, 37, 39
Chitwood — *History (1)* p.433
Hall — *Religious* p.122-126, 141
Life — *New* p.76, 79
Nettels — *Roots* p.476
Pomfret — *Founding* p.102, 197-198, 309
Ver Steeg — *Formative* p.76
Willison — *Pilgrim* p.490, 499-500
Willison — *Saints* p.46, 61, 89, 97, 326, 334, 339

PRESERVING AND PICKLING
Earle — *Home* p.152
Glubok — *Home* p.84-85
Gould — *Early* p.138

PRESS. *See* **Newspapers**

PRESSES. *See* **Printers and printing; Publishers and publishing**

PRESTON, JOHN, REV.
Morison — *Intellect.* p.20-21, 140, 160

PRESTON, RICHARD
- *Petitions (servants)*
    Demos — *Remarkable* p.135-137

PRIBER, MR.
Calverton — *Awake.* p.303-307

PRICES
See also **Pilgrims — Prices;** individual products, and subjects
Bailyn — *New England. See* index p.247

Rutman — *Winthrop's. See* index
p.317
Tunis — *Craftsmen* p.17
- *Boston*
Woodward — *Way* p.22-23
- *Connecticut*
Annals of America (1) p.247-248
- *Controls*
Marshall — *Mayflower* p.171
, *Fair — Villages*
Bridenbaugh — *Cities* p.49-50

"PRICKING" (selectmen choice)
Dow — *Every* p.99-100

PRIEST, DEGORY
Caffrey — *Mayflower* p.41, 165, 185
Hills — *History (1)* p.22, 29, 38, 41,
46, 69, 74, 84
Hills — *History (2)* p.173
Leynse — *Preced.* p.206, 238, 267
Marshall — *Mayflower* p.28
Willison — *Pilgrim* p.36, 533
Willison — *Saints* p.91, 123, 439

**PRIEST, SARAH. See Coombs, Sarah
Priest**

PRIEST FAMILY
Caffrey — *Mayflower* p.390

PRIMARY SCHOOLS
Wertenbaker — *Puritan* p.146-147

PRIMERS
See also **New England Primer**
Morison — *Intellect.* p.79-82, 128

PRIMOGENITURE
Smith — *17th* p.108-109
Wish — *Society (1)* p.38, 44, 74

PRINCE, MARY
, *as Quaker martyr*
Williams — *Demeter's* p.124-125

PRINCE, THOMAS, REV.
Marshall — *Mayflower* p.160, 185
Willison — *Saints* p.4, 428-429

PRING, MARTIN
Amer. Her. — *Thirteen* p.66-67
- *"A voyage set out from the city of
Bristoll" (1603)*
Amer. Her. — *Thirteen* p.59

PRINTERS AND PRINTING
See also **Publishers and publishing**
Bridenbaugh — *Cities* p.130-131
Earle — *Customs* p.258-260
Folsom — *Give* p.x, 12, 19, 32, 44-
45, 49, 74, 86, 90-92
Hope — *Nation* p.115
Morison — *Intellect.* p.16, 113-127
Speare — *Life* p.126-127
Tunis — *Craftsmen* p.125-126
Ver Steeg — *Formative* p.96-97
Williams — *Demeter's* p.199
- *Boston (1690)*
Morison — *Intellect.* p.126-127
- *Massachusetts*
Wertenbaker — *First* p.239-240
, *First (1639)*
Carman — *History (1)* p.107
- *New England*
Wertenbaker — *First* p.242-244
- *Philadelphia*
Bridenbaugh — *Cities* p.132
- *Virginia*
Wertenbaker — *First* p.240, 255-
256
, *First*
Hawke — *Colonial* p.298
- *Women*
Leonard — *Dear* p.248, 458, 461

PRINTZ, JOHAN BJÖRNSON
Alderman — *Story* p.105-106
Amer. Her. — *Pioneer* p.70-71
Amer. Her. — *Thirteen* p.134-136,
146-147
Christensen — *Delaware* p.37-41
Morris — *Ency.* p.43-44
Snell — *Wild* p.137-141
Starkey — *Land* p.159-160
- *"Report of governor . . ." (1647)*
Amer. Her. — *Thirteen* p.147

PRISONS AND PRISONERS
See also **Punishment**
Bridenbaugh — *Cities* p.74-75
Rutman — *Winthrop's* p.167, 174-
176, 225, 242
Wertenbaker — *First* p.221-223
, *First*
Calverton — *Awake.* p.111-112

PRIVACY
Demos — *Little* p.31, 44, 46-47, 152
- *Unknown, in New England*
Miller — *First* p.58-59

PRIVATE ENTERPRISE
Furnas — *Americans* p.56

PRIVATE SCHOOLS
Morison — *Intellect.* p.71, 77-78
, *after Restoration (1660)*
Monroe — *Founding (1)* p.60

PRIVATEERS
See also **Piracy**
, *Dutch*
Amer. Her. — *Thirteen* p.125-
126, 177
, *English*
Amer. Her. — *Thirteen* p.41, 45-
46, 66, 121, 179-180

PROCTOR, ALICE
Williams — *Demeter's* p.154

PROCTOR, ELIZABETH
Williams — *Demeter's* p.140

PRODUCTION
, *Subsidized — Failure*
Rothbard — *Conceived (1)* p.263-
266

PROFANITY
See also **"Blue laws" (Conn.)**
Wertenbaker — *First* p.216-217
Wertenbaker — *Puritan* p.172-173,
179
- *Jamestown*
Wright — *Everyday* p.157
- *Virginia*
Morison — *Oxford* p.91

PROFESSIONS
See also **Women — Professions;**
names of professions
Chitwood — *History (1)* p.472-473

PROFITEERING
, *Women's*
Dexter — *Colonial* p.50

PROPHECY
Willison — *Pilgrim* p.45, 418-421
Willison — *Saints* p.87, 348

PROPRIETARY ASSOCIATES (1630)
Nettels — *Roots* p.138

PROPRIETARY COLONIES. *See*
Colonies and colonists, Proprie-
tary; names of colonies

PROTESTANT ASSOCIATION
Folsom — *Give* p.73-74

- *Maryland*
Craven — *Colonies* p.231

PROTESTANTS
See also names of denominations
Carman — *History (1)* p.13, 97
Chitwood — *History (1)* p.11, 89
Folsom — *Give* p.x, 3-5, 8, 19, 32,
64, 66-67, 72-74
Hall — *Religious* p.50, 107
Hawke — *Colonial* p.55-56; *See also*
index p.736
Leynse — *Preced.* p.118-119, 125-
126, 133, 145
Murdock — *Literature* p.8-10, 13-20,
23-24, 40-41
Willison — *Saints* p.19, 21-24, 481

, *Conventicle*
Hall — *Religious* p.87-94, 118-
120, 130-131
- *England*
Rozwenc — *Making (1)* p.20-22
- *Maryland*
Sweet — *Religion* p.176-181

, *Fears of*
Bailey — *American (1)* p.14
- *Sects*
Nettels — *Roots* p.470-479
- *Three groups of churches*
Nettels — *Roots* p.470

PROVIDENCE, RHODE ISLAND
Alderman — *Story* p.96, 98-99
Chitwood — *History (1)* p.130-131
Folsom — *Give* p.17-18, 22
Pomfret — *Founding* p.206, 211-212,
214, 219, 223-224
Snell — *Wild* p.126, 128-129, 134
Willison — *Pilgrim* p.425-426, 434,
479
Willison — *Saints* p.351-352, 459

- *Civil government, plan of*
Annals of America (1) p.160-162
- *Typical estate (1682)*
Demos — *Remarkable* p.122-124

PROVIDENCE COMPANY
Nettels — *Roots* p.121

"PROVIDENTIAL INTERPRETATION"
Smith — *17th* p.9-11, 196

PROVINCETOWN, MASSACHUSETTS
Beck — *Pilgrims* p.16, 23, 26
Gill — *Mayflower* p.67, 69, 75, 91, 139
- *Harbor, Pilgrims at*
  Willison — *Pilgrim* p.94, 99-115

PSALMS AND PSALM SINGING
See also **Bay Psalm Book;** Hymns
Adams — *Album* p.127
Rawson — *When* p.196-204
Wright — *Cultural* p.191-192
- *Books*
  - *"Sternhold and Hopkins"*
    Howard — *Our* p.5-7
- *New England*
  Howard — *Our* p.4-12
- *Versions*
  Willison — *Saints* p.86, 459, 464,
  474, 481, 483

PSYCHOLOGY
, *and history*
  Demos — *Little* p.128-130

"PUBLIC ESTATE," THE
- *South*
  Craven — *Southern* p.118, 120,
  128-129, 132, 140, 156, 159,
  337
- *Virginia*
  Craven — *Southern* p.128-129,
  132, 140, 156, 159

PUBLISHERS AND PUBLISHING
Carman — *History (1)* p.106-107
- *Censorship*
  Wertenbaker — *First* p.238-240
- *Massachusetts*
  Wertenbaker — *First* p.242-244
- *New England*
  Wertenbaker — *First* p.242-244
- *Religious books*
  Wertenbaker — *First* p.237-238
- *Virginians*
  Wertenbaker — *First* p.256

PUDDINGS
Earle — *Home* p.135

PUDEATOR, ANN
Williams — *Demeter's* p.152-153

PUMPKINS
Glubok — *Home* p.78-79
Gould — *Early* p.92

Morison — *Story* p.80, 114-115, 188-
189, 199
- *Cookery*
  Earle — *Customs* p.150-153
, *Drying of*
  Earle — *Home* p.143

PUNISHMENT
See also types of punishment and
  crimes
Adams — *Album* p.129
Chitwood — *History (1)* p.155-156
Clark — *Old* p.45-47
Furnas — *Americans* p.67-69
Nettels — *Roots* p.463
Wertenbaker — *First. See* index p.352
Woodward — *First. See* index p.352
Woodward — *Way* p.65
- *Boston*
  Clark — *Old* p.39
- *Children*
  Clark — *Old* p.81
  Glubok — *Home* p.130-137
- *Early forms*
  Miller — *First* p.255-259
- *Humiliation*
  Miller — *First* p.255-258
- *Maryland*
  Wertenbaker — *First* p.215, 217-
  220
- *Massachusetts*
  Fisher — *Men* p.178
  Wertenbaker — *First* p.215-218,
  222
- *New York*
  Jernegan — *American* p.182-183
- *Plymouth*
  Miller — *First* p.253-255
  Morison — *Story* p.161-163, 212
- *Servants*
  Glubok — *Home* p.137
- *Slaves and slavery*
  Nettels — *Roots* p.467-468
- *South*
  Goodwin — *Colonial* p.248-259
- *Virginia*
  Morison — *Oxford* p.90-91
- *Women*
  Earle — *Colonial* p.91-98
  Miller — *First* p.205
  Nettels — *Roots* p.463-464
  Spruill — *Women's* p.314-323

**PUNKAPOG, MASSACHUSETTS ("pray-
ing town")**
Vaughan — *New* p.270

PURCHAS, SAMUEL
Smith — *18th* p.206-208

PURITAN CHURCH (Dedham, Mass.)
Lockridge — *New* p.23-36

PURITAN PARTY (1635)
, *Women in*
Spruill — *Women's* p.236

PURITANS
See also Pilgrims; Separatists; Puritans subdivision under subjects; Carpenters; Chairs; Chests; Children and childhood — Discipline; Christmas; Clergymen; Congregationalists; Fashion; Law and lawyers; Miller, Perry; Mortality; Perfume; Poets and poetry; Pynchon, William; Sabbath; Science and scientists; Sermons; Servants; Superstitions; Teachers; Thanksgiving Day; Tribalism; Windows; Winthrop, John, on Puritans
Acheson — *America's* p.89-94
Adams — *Album* p.72-135
Alderman — *Story. See* index p.185-186
Amer. Her. — *Thirteen* p.99-101, 103-104, 139, 144, 151, 153-155, 157-158, 160, 162
Caffrey — *Mayflower. See* index p.390
Calverton — *Awake.* p.57-69
Carman — *History (1)* p.29, 35-41, 48, 86, 98-91, 93-95, 97, 102
Chitwood — *History (1)* p.88-101
Collins — *Story* p.46
Craven — *Southern* p.177-178
Demos — *Little* p.3, 12n, 135-139, 147, 162
Dillon — *Pilgrims. See* index p.249
Folsom — *Give* p.11-12, 14-19, 22, 28, 31, 33, 41, 44, 50, 70, 75, 78-79, 91
Gill — *Mayflower* p.20-21, 24-25, 31, 39, 48-49, 57, 64, 127
Greene — *Provincial* p.83-86, 88
Hall — *Religious* p.66-79, 99, 106, 118
Hawke — *Colonial* p.53-56, 167-204; *See also* index p.756
Jernegan — *American* p.180-181
Kraus — *U.S. (1)* p.47-49
Leynse — *Preced. See* index p.284
Life — *New* p.76-79, 82, 86-92

Marshall — *Mayflower* p.24-25
Miller — *First* p.50-61
Morison — *Oxford* p.61-64
Murdock — *Literature. See* index p.233
Pomfret — *Founding. See* index p.378
Rozwenc — *Making (1)* p.58-61; *See also* index p.650
Smith — *Colonial* p.6-7
Smith — *17th* p.5, 123, 165, 202
Snell — *Wild* p.117-119, 124, 126-129, 134-135, 144, 154
Vaughan — *New. See* index p.428
Ver Steeg — *Formative* p.37, 59-60, 75-80
Williams — *Demeter's. See* index p.355
Willison — *Pilgrim. See* index p.581
Willison — *Saints. See* index p.508
Wright — *Cultural. See* index p.287-288
Wright — *Everyday* p.28, 141, 152, 163-180, 200
- *Amusements*
Dulles — *America* p.8-12
Lawrence — *Not* p.177-178
Morison — *Intellect.* p.24-25
Smith — *17th* p.152
Wish — *Society (1)* p.45-47
, *and Cavaliers*
Amer. Her. — *Pilgrims* p.120-135
Hawke — *U.S.* p.120-154
, *and Quakers*
Wertenbaker — *First* p.101-105
- *Appearance*
See also Puritans — Clothing and dress
Glubok — *Home* p.266-267, 272-274
- *Art*
Morison — *Intellect.* p.12-14
Wright — *Cultual* p.207
, *as Anglicans*
Wertenbaker — *First* p.89-90
, *as "God's elect"*
Wertenbaker — *First* p.91-92
- *Asceticism*
Morgan — *Puritan* p.26-27
- *Babies*
- *Boston, Mass.*
Clark — *Old* p.27-28
.- *Bachelors*
, *Legislation against*
Morgan — *Puritan* p.85-86

- *Barbados*
  Starkey — *Land* p.218-219
- *Beliefs*
  Bailyn — *New England* p.39, 49
  Fisher — *Men (1)* p.124-186
  Life — *New* p.75-76, 86
  Morison — *Intellect.* p.8-9, 150-153
  Starkey — *Land* p.104
- *Censorship*
  Wertenbaker — *First* p.238-240
- *Character*
  Dow — *Domestic* p.22
  Starkey — *Land* p.80
- *Charity, ideals of Christian*
  Annals of America (1) p.109-114
- *Charter of 1629*
  Hawke — *Colonial* p.129-132
- *Children and childhood*
  Adams — *Album* p.121
  - *Boston, Mass.*
    Clark — *Old* p.28, 32-41
- *Churches*
  Adams — *Album* p.74
  National — *History.* p.77
  , *Discipline of*
    Smith — *17th* p.143-144
  - *Massachusetts. See* "**New England Way**"
  , *Membership in*
    Bailyn — *New England* p.30, 107-108, 115, 124, 137-139, 150-160
    Smith — *17th* p.144-145, 149
- *Clothing and dress*
  Earle — *Customs* p.315-318
  Earle — *Two cent. (1)* p.3-48, 179-180
  Wertenbaker — *First* p.279-281
  - *Colors*
    Earle — *Two cent. (1)* p.4-6, 27-28
  , *"Excessive," disapproved of*
    Willison — *Saints* p.8, 28-29, 66-68, 266, 320, 473
  , *Men's*
    Earle — *Two cent. (1)* p.4, 27
  , *Women's*
    Adams — *Album* p.123
    - *Grandmothers*
      Earle — *Two cent. (1)* p.137-159

- *Connecticut*
  National — *History.* p.86-87, 90
- *Courtship*
  Williams — *Demeter's* p.83
.- *Cultural superiority*
  Calverton — *Awake.* p.131-154
- *Dances and dancing*
  Dulles — *America* p.6, 8, 14, 19
- *Death penalty*
  Wertenbaker — *First* p.215-216
, *"Declension" of*
  Bailyn — *New England* p.109, 112, 139
- *Difference from Pilgrims*
  Sweet — *Religion* p.84
- *Drama*
  Morison — *Intellect.* p.12-13
  Wright — *Cultural* p.177-178
- *Economy*
  Morison — *Intellect.* p.9-10
- *Education*
  See also **Puritans — Schools**
  Life — *Nation* p.124-125
  Miller — *First* p.221-223
  Rozwenc — *Making (1)* p.88-90
  , *and humanism*
    Morison — *Intellect.* p.17-18
  , *Hostility to*
    Morison — *Intellect.* p,28-29
  , *Methods of*
    Morgan — *Puritan* p.54-57
  , *Purpose of*
    Morgan — *Puritan* p.45-48
- *England*
  Hall — *Religious* p.68-69, 71-72, 100, 105
  Starkey — *Land* p.81
  Sweet — *Religion* p. 18-22, 73-76
  - *Reasons for departure*
    - *Persecution*
      Demos — *Remarkable* p.32-36
      Life — *New* p.78, 86
  - *Views of John Winthrop*
    Vaughan — *Puritan* p.25-35
- *Establishment*
  Chitwood — *History (1)* p.102-121
- *Exclusion*
  - *Views of John Cotton v. Richard Saltonstall*
    Vaughan — *Puritan* p.199-205

PURITANS (continued)

- Expansion
  Chitwood — History (1) p.122-142
- Families
  , in social order
  Morgan — Puritan p.78-89
  , Well-ordered
  , Views of Benjamin Wadsworth
  Vaughan — Puritan p.184-192
- Fastings
  Earle — Customs p.221-222
- Fur trade
  Bailyn — New England p.26-30, 51-58
- Government, theories of
  Rozwenc — Making (1) p.64-66
- Hairdressing
  Miller — First p.56
- Heritage
  Hawke — Colonial p.157-160
  Life — New p.92
- History
  Smith — 17th p.202-206, 210-215, 217-219, 225
  , Conception of
  Smith — 17th p.11-12, 196
- Houses
  Adams — Album p.78-79
- Husbands, authoritative role
  Morgan — Puritan p.10-12
- Indian relations
  Nettels — Roots p.212, 218-219
  Vaughan — New p.4, 18-21, 23-65, 334
- Influence, repressive
  Dulles — America p.4-8, 12-13, 16, 18-21
- Intellectual life
  Wertenbaker — First p.237-238
  , Alternative to
  Morison — Intellect. p.14-17
- Intolerance
  See also **Morton, Thomas, "On Puritan intolerance"**
  Life — New p.78-79, 90, 92
  Wertenbaker — First p.89-92
- Law
  Wish — Society (1) p.42-45
- Libraries
  Wertenbaker — First p.240-241
  Wish — Society (1) p.33, 54, 60-61

- Life
  Glubok — Home p.298-300
  Morison — Intellect. p.8-12
  National — History. p.78-79
  - Views of John Winthrop
  Annals of America (1) p.132-138
- "Lighter side"
  Speare — Life p.34
- Literature
  Murdock — Literature p.204-205
  Rozwenc — Making (1) p.97-99
  Wright — Cultural p.127-145
- Love
  Morgan — Puritan p.9-27
- Marriage
  Earle — Customs p.79-81
  Morgan — Puritan p.9-27
  , and social rank
  Morgan — Puritan p.19-21
- Maryland
  Craven — Southern p.229, 234, 259-261, 296-297
  Pomfret — Founding p.89-90, 92-99
  Starkey — Land p.124
- Massachusetts
  Abbot — Colonial p.41-43, 68-70
  Bailyn — New England p.19-20, 39-40, 45, 47, 76, 91-92, 105-106, 159-160, 170
  Goetzmann — Colonial p.147-213
  National — History. p.70-85
  Pomfret — Founding p.184-199
  Wertenbaker — First p.87-90
- Migration
  Bailyn — New England p.14-18, 44-46, 61-62
  Morison — Story p.120, 138-140, 152
  Sweet — Religion p.81-89
  Vaughan — Puritan p.63-64
  , from Virginia to Maryland
  Chitwood — History (1) p.84
  , Motives of
  Wertenbaker — First p.49, 87-88
  , Misconceptions about
  Sweet — Religion p.116-117
- Model of state
  - Views of John Winthrop
  Goetzmann — Colonial p.169-179

- *Morality*
  Goetzmann — *Colonial* p.190
  Wertenbaker — *First* p.189-192,
  194-200
  Williams — *Demeter's* p.83
- *Music*
  Morison — *Intellect.* p.12-14
  Sweet — *Religion* p.116
  Wright — *Cultural* p.190-192
- *New England*
  Bailyn — *New England* p.92-93,
  131
  Rozwenc — *Making (1)* p.47-49
  , *on democracy*
  Wertenbaker — *First* p.93-98
  Wish — *Society (1)* p.34-35, 50
  , *on slavery*
  Wertenbaker — *First* p.231-233
- *Parents*
  Morgan — *Puritan* p.28-44
- *Philosophy. See* **Puritans — Beliefs**
- *Plymouth*
  Sweet — *Religion* p.76-81
- *Political control, challenge to*
  Vaughan — *Puritan* p.219-225
- *Preaching*
  See also **Hooker, Thomas, on**
  Puritan preaching
  Vaughan — *Puritan* p.82-92
- *Punishment of children*
  Morgan — *Puritan* p.38
- *Religion*
  See also **Congregationalists;**
  Puritans, as Anglicans;
  Puritans — Churches
  Holliday — *Woman's* p.10-28
  Life — *New* p.76
  Morgan — *Puritan* p.80
  Sweet — *Religion* p.98-192
  Vaughan — *New* p.18-22, 24,
  104, 138, 141
  Vaughan — *Puritan* p.82-92
  Wright — *Cultural* p.77-84
  Wright — *Everyday* p.180
- *Revolution*
  Rozwenc — *Making (1)* p.21-22,
  64
- *Rhode Island*
  National — *History.* p.86, 90-91
- *Salem, Mass.*
  Willison — *Pilgrim* p.315-319
- *Schisms*
  Wertenbaker — *First* p.98-101
- *Schools*
  Morison — *Intellect.* p.59-62
  Wertenbaker — *First* p.244-247

- *"Sin and sinners" (1670)*
  Morgan — *Puritan* p.93, 117
- *Society, restrictions on*
  Vaughan — *Puritan* p.179-184
- *South*
  Craven — *Southern* p.177-178
- *State and society*
  - *Views of Perry Miller*
  Goetzmann — *Colonial*
  p.148-159
- *Term*
  Amer. Her. — *Thirteen* p.87-88
- *Tobacco ban*
  Miller — *First* p.55-56
- *Trade*
  Bailyn — *New England* p.44, 75-
  76
- *Village (microcosm)*
  Vaughan — *Puritan p.192-198*
  Woodward — *Way* p.38-69
- *Virginia*
  Calverton — *Awake.* p.217-221
  Craven — *Southern* p.228-229
  Pomfret — *Founding* p.61-62, 65
  Starkey — *Land* p.121
  , *Factions in*
  Smith — *17th* p.124
- *Wives, submissive role of*
  Morgan — *Puritan* p.9-12
- *Women*
  Calverton — *Awake.* p.112-114
  Leonard — *Dear* p.249
  Morgan — *Puritan* p.9-12
  Williams — *Demeter's* p.25-31,
  38, 115-124, 187
- *Writers*
  Wertenbaker — *First* p.242-244

PUTNAM, ANN
Leonard — *Dear* p.389-390

"PUTTING OUT" (child apprenticeship)
Williams — *Demeter's* p.97

PYM, JOHN
Craven — *Southern* p.224-225, 249-
250

PYNCHON, JOHN
Bailyn — *New England* p.53-54, 95,
125
Beals — *John Eliot. See* index p. 191

PYNCHON , WILLIAM
Bailyn — *New England* p.19, 27, 29-
31, 53-55, 107-108

PYNCHON, WILLIAM (continued)
Earle — Two cent. (1) p.xviii, 200, 348
Morison — Intellect. p.169-170
, on the Puritan village
   Vaughan — Puritan p.192-198

Q

QUACKS
Drepperd — Pioneer p.226
Wertenbaker — First p.174-175

QUADEQUINA (WAMPANOAG) (Indian)
Beck — Pilgrims p.38
Marshall — Mayflower p.136
Morison — Story p.72-74
Willison — Pilgrim p.134-135, 137
Willison — Saints p.174-175, 177

QUADRANT
Caffrey — Mayflower p.93
Marshall — Mayflower p.38

QUAHOG SHELLS. See Wampum

"QUAKER HILL" (Wilmington, Delaware)
Christensen — Delaware p.89-90

QUAKERS
See also **Penn, William; Puritans, and Quakers;** special subjects, subdivision **Quakers**
Acheson — America's p.140-143
Adams — Album p.234-237
Alderman — Story p.33, 61, 63, 65, 88, 99, 108-109, 118-123
Amer. Her. — Pilgrims p.140, 143
Amer. Her. — Pioneer p.51, 63, 69, 75-77
Amer. Her. — Thirteen p.104, 107, 160, 165, 169-170, 173
Calverton — Awake. p.162-163
Carman — History (1) p.30, 45, 92
Chitwood — History (1) p.201-203, 435
Christensen — Delaware p.59-60
Craven — Colonies p.44, 95, 102, 175, 183-185, 193
Fisher — Men (1) p.158-162
Folsom — Give p.17, 23, 28, 31, 38, 49-54, 65, 76-77, 88, 91
Furnas — Americans p.78-82
Gill — Mayflower p.145-146
Hall — Religious p.101, 129-131, 138

Hawke — Colonial. See index p.756-757
Hope — Nation p.95-98
Langdon — Everyday p.57-62
Leonard — Dear p.66-67, 274-381, 392-395
Marshall — Mayflower p.178, 182
Miller — First p.73-83
Morison — Oxford p.128-131
Morison — Story p.8, 149, 163-165, 232-233, 251, 254, 259
Morris — Ency. p.549
Nettels — Roots p.473-474
Rozwenc — Making p.37-38, 49-50, 72-74, 87, 90
Smith — 17th p.87, 141, 150, 176, 214, 218
Snell — Wild p.137, 145, 148-149, 151, 154
Speare — Life p.63-65
Starkey — Land p.98, 177-179, 211-212, 214, 237, 241
Sweet — Religion p.22-23, 158-165; See also index p.365
Vaughan — Puritan p.230-234
Ver Steeg — Formative p.18, 91, 116-119, 213-214
Wertenbaker — Puritan. See index p.156
Williams — Demeter's. See index p.356
Willison — Pilgrim p.428, 503, 517-522
Willison — Saints. See index p.508
Wish — Society (1) p.44-45, 77, 91, 102-110
Wright — Everyday p.181-182
, and slave traffic
   Calverton — Awake. p.175-177
- Carolinas
   Craven — Southern p.342, 409
- Cooperative economics
   Calverton — Awake. p.174-175
- England
   Morison — Oxford p.126-127
- Founding
   Miller — First p.73-74
- Hangings
   Wertenbaker — First p.215-216
- Indian relations
   Calverton — Awake. p.177-180, 354-356
   Morison — Intellect. p.184-185
- Marriage
   Williams — Demeter's p.83-84

- *Martyrs*
  See also names of martyrs
  Sweet — *Religion* p.144-153
- *Maryland*
  Craven — *Southern* p.302
- *Meetinghouses*
  Adams — *Album* p.234-235
- *Missionaries, first*
  Sweet — *Religion* p.143-144
  - *Women*
    Snell — *Wild* p.145
- *New Jersey*
  Ver Steeg — *Formative* p.116-117
  , *West*
    Craven — *Colonies* p.184-189, 203
- *Organization*
  Sweet — *Religion* p.163-166
- *Pennsylvania*
  Chitwood — *History (1)* p.209-211
  - *Education*
    Wright — *Everyday* p.140-141
- *Persecution*
  See also **Quakers — Martyrs;** names of Quakers
  Bailey — *American (1)* p.30-31
  Calverton — *Awake.* p.171-173
  Chitwood — *History (1)* p.120-121
  Miller — *First* p.11, 75-79
  Wertenbaker — *First* p.351
  - *Massachusetts*
    Rothbard — *Conceived (1)* p.237-250
    Wertenbaker — *First* p.101-105
  - *New England*
    Jernegan — *American* p.184-185
    Wertenbaker — *First* p.101-105
  - *New Netherland*
    Rothbard — *Conceived (1)* p.318-320
- *Philadelphia, Pa.*
  Bridenbaugh — *Cities* p.103-104
- *Poetry*
  Morison — *Intellect.* p.226-228
- *Rhode Island*
  Miller — *First* p.73, 75-76
  , *Royal proclamation about*
  Spruill — *Women's* p.251-252
- *Salem, Mass.*
  Gildrie — *Salem* p.79-80, 117, 130-137, 140, 143, 145
  , *Tolerance of*
  Annals of America (1) p.223-224
- *Virginia*
  Craven — *Southern* p.229-230
- *Weddings. See* **Matthews, Margaret — Quaker wedding of; Quakers — Marriage**
  , *Welsh*
  Langdon — *Everyday* p.57-60
- *Women*
  See also **Quakers — Missionaries, First — Women**
  Adams — *Album* p.236
  Holliday — *Woman's* p.40-41
  Spruill — *Women's* p.249-251
  , *First*
  Dexter —·*Colonial* p.146-147

QUARLES, FRANCIS
  Morison — *Intellect.* p.23, 132, 228

"QUARNS" (hand-mills)
  Earle — *Colonial* p.293-294
  Lawrence — *New* p.4

"QUARTER COURT"
- *South*
  Craven — *Southern* p.133-135, 154, 270, 288, 397

QUARY, ROBERT
  Rothbard — *Conceived (1)* p.502-504

"QUASSIA CUPS" (wooden, medicinal)
  Drepperd — *Pioneer* p.226

QUEBEC, CANADA
  Morison — *Oxford* p.102-106
- *Attack (1690)*
  Collins — *Story* p.83
  Hawke — *U.S.* p.254-257
  Snell — *Wild* p.94-95, 98

"QUEEN OF APPOMATTOC" (Indian)
  Smith — *17th* p.56-57

"QUEEN OF PAMUNKEY" (Indian)
  Smith — *17th* p.56-57

"QUERNS" (CAIRNS). See "Quarns"

QUILTS AND QUILTING BEES
  Dow — *Every* p.52-59
  Glubok — *Home* p.292-293

QUILTS AND QUILTING BEES (*cont.*)
Gould — *Early* p.141
Rawson — *When* p.75-76, 129-130, 208-209
Speare — *Life* p.155-156

QUINCY, EDMUND
Rutman — *Winthrop's* p.73-74, 78-80

QUINCY, MASSACHUSETTS. *See* **Merrymount Colony**

QUINITIPARTITE DEED (1676), (East & West Jersey boundary)
Craven — *Colonies* p.188

QUINNETUKUT INDIANS
Snell — *Wild* p.135

QUINNIPIAC, CONNECTICUT
See also **New Haven, Connecticut**
Bailyn — *New England* p.29-30, 57-58
Johnston — *Conn.* p.38-44

QUITRENT SYSTEM
Adams — *Provincial* p.12
Alderman — *Story* p.125, 139
Carman — *History (1)* p.55
Craven — *Colonies* p.22-23, 81-83, 90-91, 93-94, 97-98, 152-153, 156, 194, 201, 221-222, 230, 246
Folsom — *Give* p.44, 50, 65
Morison — *Oxford* p.86
Pomfret — *Foundings* p.82-83, 117, 306
Starkey — *Land* p.182, 187-188, 235
- *Carolinas*
. Craven — *Southern* p.325, 327-328, 331, 338, 358
- *Maryland*
Craven — *Southern* p.192
- *"Red rose" token*
Adams — *Provincial* p.12
- *Virginia*
Craven — *Southern* p.127-128, 176, 255, 282, 397

QUONAHASSIT INDIANS
Beck — *Pilgrims* p.21

QUOTATIONS
- *Farms and farming*
Rawson — *When* p.60-62
- *New England writers*
Wright — *Literary* p.137-151

R

RACES. *See* **Nationalities**

RAG CARPETS
Rawson — *When* p.116

RAINMAKING
Willison — *Pilgrim* p.231-232

RAISING, HOUSE. *See* **House-raising**

RALEIGH, WALTER, SIR
See also **Roanoke Colony**
Amer. Her. — *Pioneer* p.49-50, 52-53
Amer. Her. — *Thirteen* p.31, 34-35, 37-42, 44, 46, 48, 66, 180
Amer. Her. — *Treasury* p.20-40
Craven — *Southern* p.23, 32n, 37n, 39-57
Earle — *Two cent. (1)* p.xiv, 20-21, 23-25, 455
Hawke — *Colonial* p.34-37; *See also* index p.757
Leynse — *Preced.* p.26-27, 211, 219
Marshall — *Mayflower* p.21
Morison — *Oxford* p.44-45
Phillips — *First* p.59-60
Smith — *17th* p.16-18, 24, 36-37, 39, 79

, *Visited by Pocahontas*
Phillips — *First* p.198-199
- *Works*
Morison — *Intellect.* p.134, 139, 144, 146

RAMUS, PETER
Morison — *Intellect.* p.43, 166, 243

RANDOLPH, EDMUND
Bailyn — *New England* p.143, 154-157, 160-166, 168-169, 174-182, 188, 225 (n.43)
Craven — *Colonies* p.147, 166-171, 215, 218, 224, 236
Hawke — *Colonial* p.256-260, 262, 266, 274
Morris — *Ency.* p.39
Nettels — *Roots* p.286-288
Rothbard — *Conceived (1). See* index p.528
Rozwenc — *Making (1)* p.81-83
Wertenbaker — *First* p.5, 7, 197
Wertenbaker — *Puritan. See* index p.356

- *Versus Massachusetts (1680–84)*
  Rothbard — *Conceived (1)* p.367-372

RAPAELJE, SARAH
, *on land grant petition*
  Williams — *Demeter's* p.51

RAPPAHANNOCK INDIANS
Smith — *17th* p.55, 59

RAPPAHANNOCK RIVER
Craven — *Southern* p.17, 73-74, 363-364, 374

RASIERES, ISAAC DE
Willison — *Pilgrim* p.300-301, 303, 305-307
Willison — *Saints* p.264-266, 383
- *"Letter of . . . to Samuel Blommaert"*
  Amer. Her. — *Thirteen* p.62-63
, *on Plymouth*
  Marshall — *Mayflower* p.55, 58, 170

RATCLIFFE, ROBERT
Sweet — *Religion* p.47, 47n

RATIONALISM
See also **"Age of Reason"**
Wertenbaker — *First* p.113, 162-163
Wertenbaker — *Puritan* p.252, 268-270, 289-290

RATTLESNAKE ROOT
Miller — *First* p.243-244

RAWSON, EDWARD
Vaughan — *New* p.271-272, 289, 306

RAWSON, REBECCA
Earle — *Two cent. (1)* p.xv, 66, 74-75
Earle — *Two cent. (2)* p.505

RECREATION. *See* **Amusements; Sports and games**

REDEMPTIONERS
Earle — *Colonial* p.10-11
Earle — *Two cent. (1)* p.110
- *Women*
  Leonard — *Dear* p.329-333

REED, JOHN, JR.
Adams — *Provincial* p.63-64

REFORMED DUTCH CHURCH (New York)
Bridenbaugh — *Cities* p.101

REGICIDES
Adams — *Album* p.130

REGULATORS
, *in Carolinas*
  Alderman — *Story* p.134-135

REHOBETH, MASSACHUSETTS
Morison — *Story* p.146, 155, 165, 224n, 226, 233, 240-241, 248, 252, 271

RELIGION
See also **Indians — Religion; Plymouth — Religion; Puritans — Religon;** names of religions and denominations
Calverton — *Awake.* p.165-168
Carman — *History (1)* p.85-97
Glubok — *Home* p.284-309
Hawke — *Colonial* p.301-395
Miller — *Colonial* p.115-117
Miller — *First* p.266-267
Morison — *Intellect.* p.20-23
Morris — *Ency.* p.546-549
Nettels — *Roots* p.453-454
Willison — *Pilgrim. See* index p.581
, *and morals*
  Jernegan — *American* p.231-234

- *New England*
  Jernegan — *American* p.180-185
- *South*
  Jernegan — *American* p.99-105
, *and poetry*
  Morison — *Intellect.* p.211-212, 216-220
, *as governing power*
  Rozwenc — *Making (1)* p.68-75
, *as intellectual interest*
  Morison — *Intellect.* p.3-4, 22-23, 150, 152-154
- *Books and reading*
  Morison — *Intellect.* p.11, 42, 48-49; *See also* index p.287 (under Theology)
  Murdock — *Literature* p.9-10
  Wertenbaker — *First* p.325-328
  Wertenbaker — *Puritan* p.78-79

RELIGION (*continued*)

    Wright — *Cultural* p.138-141, 174
    Wright — *Literary* p.83-85
- *Canada*
    Nettels — *Roots* p.206, 208-209
- *Carolinas*
    Jernegan — *American* p.105
- *Chesapeake colonies (1640–76)*
    Hawke — *Colonial* p.181-182
- *Conversion*
  - *Views of Thomas Shepard*
    Vaughan — *Puritan* p.92-97
- *Decay*
    Sweet — *Religion* p.108-109
- *Education*
    Morison — *Intellect.* p.79-80, 85-86, 90-91
    Wertenbaker — *Puritan* p.135-139
  - *Boston, Mass.*
    Clark — *Old* p.42
- *Factionalism, growth of*
  - *Views of John Woodridge, Jr.*
    Vaughan — *Puritan* p.299-305
- *Forms*
    Vaughan — *Puritan* p.78-81
- *Liberalism*
    Chitwood — *History (1)* p.445-446
- *Maryland*
    Amer. Her. — *Thirteen* p.173, 176, 217
    Jernegan — *American* p.163-164
    Sweet — *Religion* p.33-34
- *Massachusetts*
    Carman — *History (1)* p.86, 89-91, 93-97
    Hall — *Religious* p.96-109
- *Middle Colonies*
    Jernegan — *American* p.232-233
- *Motives in colonization*
    Rothbard — *Conceived (1)* p.157-159
    Sweet — *Religious* p.1-27
, *Natural*
    Morison — *Intellect.* p.269-270
- *New Amsterdam*
    Bridenbaugh — *Cities* p.101-102
- *New England*
    Amer. Her. — *Thirteen,* p.94, 103-104, 106, 155
    Hall — *Religious* p.83-95
    Hawke — *Colonial* p.178-179
    Jernegan — *American* p.180

    Morison — *Intellect.* p.159-161
    Vaughan — *Puritan* p.73-128
- *Pennsylvania*
    Wright — *Cultural* p.88-90
- *Salvation*
  - *Views of Cotton Mather*
    Vaughan — *Puritan* p.274-276
- *Sects*
  - *Persecution*
    Beals — *John Eliot. See* index p.192
    Chitwood — *History (1)* p.437-439
  - *Massachusetts*
    Amer. Her. — *Thirteen* p.101, 103-104, 106, 146, 154-157, 160
  - *New Netherland*
    Monroe — *Founding (1)* p.70-71
- *Racial groups*
    Jernegan — *American* p.302-303
- *South*
    Carman — *History (1)* p.97
- *Virginia*
    Hall — *Religious* p.110-126
    Holliday — *Woman's* p.64-65
    Jernegan — *American* p.99-101
    Rothbard — *Conceived (1)* p.78-80
- *Women*
    Holliday — *Woman's* p.10-28, 291-293
    Leonard — *Dear* p.349-390
, *Comfort in*
    Holliday — *Woman's* p.38-41

RELIGIOUS FREEDOM
  See also **Maryland Toleration Act (1649); Tolerance**
  Acheson — *America's* p.89-91
  Craven — *Colonies* p.9, 48, 52-53, 76-77, 92, 102, 179, 187, 195-196, 209, 220-221
  Folsom — *Give* p.12, 17-18, 22, 24-27, 49
  Hope — *Nation* p.93-98
  Snell — *Wild* p.101, 105, 124, 126-127, 137, 141, 144

, *and Roger Williams*
    Starkey — *Land* p.132
- *Carolinas*
    Starkey — *Land* p.221-222

- *Maryland*
  Pomfret — *Founding* p.82, 92-96
  Starkey — *Land* p.110, 124
- *New Amsterdam*
  Starkey — *Land* p.166
- *New England*
  Acheson — *America's* p.102
- *New Jersey*
  Jernegan — *American* p.233
- *Pennsylvania*
  Starkey — *Land* p.180
- *Rhode Island*
  Pomfret — *Founding* p.212, 227-228
, *Seeds of*
  Rozwenc — *Making (1)* p.73-75
- *Views of William Penn*
  Jernegan — *American* p.233-234
- *Virginia*
  Calverton — *Awake.* p.223-224

"RELIGIOUS SINK." *See* **Rhode Island**

RELIGIOUS WRITERS
Morris — *Ency.* p.559

REMEDIES
See also **Herbs; Medicine**
Beck — *Pilgrims* p.78
Earle — *Customs* p.336-348
Langdon — *Everyday* p.323-325
Lawrence — *New* p.2-4
Leonard — *Dear* p.214-215
Marshall — *Mayflower* p.124, 127
Rawson — *When* p.23-25
Speare — *Life* p.77-78
Wertenbaker — *First* p.167; *See also*
  index p.353
Woodward — *Way* p.56

, *Children's*
  Earle — *Customs* p.6-8
  Wertenbaker — *First* p.186-187
- *Herbs*
  Dow — *Every* p.190-198
- *Recipes*
  Dow — *Every* p.180-190
- *"Venice Treacle"*
  Woodward — *Way* p.46, 46n

RENTALS. *See* **Houses — Rentals**

REPRESENTATION
See also **Taxation**
Carman — *History (1)* p.128-129

"RESTORATION" (1660–1676)
See also under names of colonies
Hawke — *Colonial* p.192-202
- *England*
  Hawke — *Colonial* p.192-195
- *New England*
  Hawke — *Colonial* p.195-200

REYNER, JOHN
Willison — *Pilgrim* p.428-429, 461,
  480, 500-501
Willison — *Saints. See* index p.508

REYNOLDS, JOHN
Willison — *Saints* p.48, 94-95, 99

REYNOLDS, WILLIAM, CAPTAIN
Willison — *Pilgrim* p.74-84
Willison — *Saints* p.121, 126-128

RHETORIC
Morison — *Intellect.* p.106, 110-111,
  147

, *in schools*
  Morison — *Intellect.* p.42, 98,
  106, 163-166

RHODE ISLAND
Acheson — *America's* p.106-109
Adams — *Album* p.101-102
Alderman — *Story* p.33, 40, 61, 77,
  92, 99-102, 113, 121
Bailyn — *New England. See* index
  p.247
Calverton — *Awake.* p.146-148
Chitwood — *History (1)* p.130-134
Craven — *Colonies. See* index p.361
Folsom — *Give* p.14-17, 22-23, 28,
  31, 38, 52, 65
Jernegan — *American* p.134-137
Kraus — *U.S.(1)* p.61-64
Miller — *First* p.67-72
Morison — *Story. See* index p.vi
Nettels — *Roots* p.175-181
Pomfret — *Founding* p.210-231; *See*
  also index p.379
Starkey — *Land* p.90, 94-95, 103,
  131-134, 207, 214
Sweet — *Religion* p.122-127
Vaughan — *New. See* index p.428
Wertenbaker — *Puritan* p.218, 228-229
Willison — *Pilgrim* 430, 434, 458n,
  479, 491, 518

RHODE ISLAND (*continued*)

Willison — *Saints* p.328, 351-352, 376-379, 382, 401, 407

, *after "Glorious Revolution"*
  Rothbard — *Conceived (1)* p.478-481

, *and Dominion of New England*
  Craven — *Colonies* p.215-216

, *as "religious sink"*
  Fisher — *Men (1)* p.303

- *Boundaries*
  Pomfret — *Founding* p.226-229, 255

- *Charters*
  Chitwood — *History (1)* p.133-134
  Craven — *Colonies* p.51-54, 244
  Fisher — *Men (1)* p.311-313
  Jernegan — *American* p.150
  Morris — *Ency.* p.37
  Pomfret — *Founding* p.226-228
  Wertenbaker — *First* p.106-107

- *Chronology*

  - *1650's*
    Rothbard — *Conceived (1)* p.210-217

- *Commerce*
  Wertenbaker — *First* p.11, 52-55

- *Economy*
  Pomfret — *Founding* p.212, 228-230

- *Federation (4 colonies)*
  Chitwood — *History (1)* p.132-133

- *Founding*
  Morison — *Intellect.* p.7
  Pomfret — *Founding* p.211-216
  Rothbard — *Conceived (1)* p.185-209

- *"Fundamental Orders" (Acts and Orders of 1647)*
  Pomfret — *Founding* p.217, 220-222

- *Government*
  Jernegan — *American* p.148
  Pomfret — *Founding* p.220-223

- *Historic houses*
  Adams — *Album* p.102-103

, *in King Philip's War*
  Craven — *Colonies* p.119-121

- *Jews*
  Wertenbaker — *First* p.71

- *Patent of 1643*
  , Jernegan — *American* p.136-137

- *Settlements*
  Amer. Her. — *Thirteen* p.100, 103-104, 106
  Jernegan — *American* p.135-136
  Morris — *Ency.* p.35
  Snell — *Wild* p.117, 126, 128-129, 134-135

- *Towns*
  Pomfret — *Founding* p.216, 229-230

- *Unification*
  Pomfret — *Founding* p.224-228

RIBBONS
Earle — *Two cent. (1)* p.179-183

RICE
Craven — *Southern* p.19, 102, 140-141, 245, 315-316, 358
Woodward — *Way* p.52

- *North Carolina*
  Calverton — *Awake.* p.300-301

- *South*
  Craven — *Southern* p.19, 102, 140, 245, 315-316, 356

RICHES. See Wealth

RICHARDSON, ELIZABETH
Williams — *Demeter's* p.143

RIDDER, PETER HOLLENDER
Christensen — *Delaware* p.36-37

RIFLES. See Guns

RING FAMILY
Hills — *History (1)* p.143-149; *See also* index p.172
Hills — *History (2)*. *See* index p.271

RINGS
See also **Funerals — Rings and seals**

, *Thumb*
  Earle — *Two cent. (1)* p.57, 70

RISING, JOHAN CLASSEN
Christensen — *Delaware* p.42-43, 47
Morris — *Ency.* p.44

RIVER INDIANS
Johnston — *Conn.* p.3, 6-9, 21

RIVERS
See also names of rivers, settlements
Wertenbaker — First p.6-8, 12, 117
- South
  - Transportation
    Wertenbaker — Old p.7-8
- Trade
  Speare — Life p.120-121

ROADS
See also **Highways; Indian trails**
Glubok — Home p.322-323
Langdon — Everyday p.242-246
- Bay Path
  Earle — Customs p.199-200
, "Breaking of" bees
  Rawson — When p.66-67
- Connecticut
  Earle — Customs p.199
- Old Plymouth or Coast
  Earle — Customs p.199
- South
  Goodwin — Colonial p.105-106

ROANOKE COLONY
See also **Raleigh, Walter, Sir**
Amer. Her. — Pioneer p.50, 52-53
Annals of America (1) p.58
Craven — Southern p.27-59, 69n, 75
Furnas — Americans p.24-25, 27-28, 50
Marshall — Mayflower p.21
Morison — Oxford p.45
Morris — Ency. p.25-26
Smith — 17th p.36-37, 39, 42, 198
Snell — Wild p.17, 53-58, 86
Tunis — Colonial p.20-21

"ROASTING KITCHENS." See **Dutch ovens**

ROBBINS, CHANDLER
Willison — Saints p.419, 421, 426, 483-484

ROBINSON, BRIDGET WHITE
Leynse — Preced. p.106-107, 149, 174-175, 204
Willison — Pilgrim p.322-323
Willison — Saints. See index p.508

ROBINSON, ISAAC
Willison — Saints. See index p.508

ROBINSON, JOHN
Beck — Pilgrims p.5-7

Caffrey — Mayflower. See index p.390
Demos — Little p.x, 83-84, 91, 95-96, 99, 134-137
Dillon — Pilgrim p.75, 77, 82, 91, 93, 98-100, 113, 115, 119, 125-183, 195, 203, 223
Hills — History (1) p.9-10, 12, 19, 32, 43
Hills — History (2) p.123-127; See also index p.271
Leynse — Preced. See index p.285
Marble — Women p.10, 14, 57, 100
Marshall — Mayflower p.25-26, 183
Morison — Story p.8-12, 16-18, 102, 117-119, 217, 233, 242
Willison — Pilgrim. See index p.581
Willison — Saints. See index p.508
- Death
  Gill — Mayflower. p.113-115; See also index p.205
  Willison — Pilgrim p.286-289
  Willison — Saints p.258-259, 340, 345, 442, 458
- "Spiritual advice to Pilgrim planters" (1620)
  Annals of America (1) p.61-63

ROBINSON, WILLIAM
Wertenbaker — Puritan p.234-236

ROBINSON FAMILY
Caffrey — Mayflower. See index p.390
Hills — History (1). See index p.173
Hills — History (2) p.122-127; See also index p.271
Leynse — Preced. See index p.285

"THE ROCKS" (near Wilmington, Del.)
Christensen — Delaware p.27-29, 155

ROGERS, JOSEPH
Willison — Saints p.380, 439

ROGERS, THOMAS
Caffrey — Mayflower p.41, 140, 306
Hills — History (1) p.131-133; See also index p.173
Hills — History (2) p.40, 56, 58, 149, 156, 217, 239
Leynse — Preced. p.206, 238, 267
Willison — Saints p.91, 122-123, 439

ROGERS FAMILY
Hills — History (1) p.130-136; See also index p.173
Hills — History (2). See index p.271

ROLFE, JOHN
Alderman — *Story* p.11-12
Amer. Her. — *Thirteen* p.79-82, 140
Marshall — *Mayflower* p.22
Phillips — *First* p.136-139, 146-147
Starkey — *Land. See* index p.273
- *Marriage to Pocahontas*
Phillips — *First* p.138-141
Starkey — *Land* p.41-42
, *Letter on*
Demos — *Remarkable*
p.258-262
- *Retirement and death*
Phillips — *First* p.201-202
- *Tobacco interests*
Phillips — *First* p.149, 153, 159,
200-201, 203
Starkey — *Land* p.41, 76-77

ROOFS
Glubok — *Home* p.11
Gould — *Early* p.20, 38-40
Morrison — *Early* p.35-39
- *Framing*
Morrison — *Early* p.36
, *Shingle*
Dow — *Every* p.20-21
, *Thatched*
Dow — *Every* p.19
Marshall — *Mayflower* p.81, 83,
87
Wertenbaker — *First* p.285-286
- *Types*
Morrison — *Early* p.36-39

ROOMING HOUSES
Bridenbaugh — *Cities* p.111

ROOMS
Dow — *Domestic* p.14-15, 21-22
Morrison — *Early* p.48
"Common"
Langdon — *Everyday* p.25-26

ROTTERDAM, HOLLAND
Leynse — Preced. p.36, 49, 116, 128,
130, 133, 135, 137-139, 145, 192,
239

"ROUNDHEAD" (haircut)
Earle — *Two cent. (1)* p.34, 39-40,
42

ROUS, JOHN
Wertenbaker — *Puritan* p.232-234

ROWLANDSON, MARY WHITE
Leonard — *Dear* p.110, 518-520
Morison — *Intellect.* p.123, 128, 154,
188-191, 194
Tyler — *History* p.379-380
Williams — *Demeter's* p.154-159
Wish — *Society (1)* p.40-41
- *Captivity and restoration*
Demos — *Remarkable* p.286-310
Dexter — *Colonial* p.131-133
Scott — *Settlers* p.44-58
- *"Captured by Indians"*
Miller — *Colonial* p.257-289

ROXBURY, MASSACHUSETTS
Beals — *John Eliot. See* index p.192
Rutman — *Winthrop's. See* index
p.318
Willison — *Saints* p.312, 388, 417
- *Birth, first*
Beals — *John Eliot* p.69, 74, 76-
77, 80, 82-84
- *Wedding, first*
Beals — *John Eliot* p.84

ROYAL AFRICA COMPANY
Scott — *Settlers* p.104, 106, 111, 113-
114

ROYAL SOCIETY OF LONDON
Morison — *Intellect. See* index p.286
Rozwenc — *Making (1)* p.93, 96
- *American fellows*
Wright — *Cultural* p.221-223
, *and John Winthrop, Jr.*
Hawke — *U.S.* p.238-247

RUDOLPHUS, MARGARET. See
Philipse, Margaret Rudolphus

RUFFS AND BANDS
Earle — *Two cent, (1)* p.195-213
- *Starch*
Earle — *Two cent. (1)* p.198-199

RUGS
, *as bed furnishings*
Dow — *Domestic* p.20-21

RULE, MARGARET
Wertenbaker — *Puritan* p.283-289

RUM
See also **Flip**
Carman — *History (1)* p.79

Earle — *Customs* p.174-175
Earle — *Home* p.163-164, 410
Gould — *Early* p.107
- *New England*
　　Miller — *First* p.171-172

RURAL LIFE. *See* Country life; Farmers
　　and farming

RUSHLIGHTS
Drepperd — *Pioneer* p.199
Gould — *Early* p.124
Marshall — *Mayflower* p.107

RUSSELL, DANIEL
Morison — *Intellect.* p.138, 232-235

S

SABBATARIANISM
Dow — *Domestic* p.27
Glubok — *Home* p.292-294, 302
Miller — *First* p.86-92
Wertenbaker — *First* p.190-191, 262
Willison — *Saints* p.47, 103, 243, 368,
　　462, 477
- *South*
　　Craven — *Southern* p.107, 178,
　　216n

SABBATH
Beck — *Pilgrims* p.70
Bridenbaugh — *Cities* p.76-77
Dulles — *America* p.5, 7-8, 10-12, 19
Glubok — *Home* p.302
Lawrence — *New* p.242-248
Leonard — *Dear* p.355, 365
Rawson — *When* p.175-206
Wertenbaker — *Puritan* p.160-162,
　　171-172, 179
Wish — *Society (1)* p.7-8, 14, 78
- *Boston, Mass.*
　　Clark — *Old* p.29
- *Breaking*
　　Dow — *Every* p.207
　　Rutman — *Winthrop's* p.52, 225,
　　233, 239
- *New England*
　　Earle — *Home* p.378-384
- *New York*
　　Clark — *Old* p.64-65
- *Plymouth*
　　Morison — *Story* p.161, 169, 190,
　　241

- *Puritans*
　　Speare — *Life* p.30-33
　　Wright — *Everyday* p.170-171
, *Sleeping on*
　　Rawson — *When* p.223-225
- *Virginia*
　　Clark — *Old* p.10-11
- *Women*
　　Holliday — *Woman's* p.31-33

SACK (drink)
Earle — *Customs* p.168

SACJES (church bells)
Earle — *Home* p.386-387

SAFFIN, JOHN
Morison — *Intellect.* p.222-224
Morison — *Story* p.184-185, 208

SAGADAHOC, MAINE
See also Fort St. George
Adams — *Album* p.36
Hawke — *Colonial* p.88-89, 91, 93,
　　108, 119
Marshall — *Mayflower* p.23
Rozwenc — *Making (1)* p.26-27
Vaughan — *New* p.12-15, 211

SAGAMORE, JOHN
Vaughan — *New* p.96, 98-101, 103,
　　242

"SAGAMORE TOM" (Indian)
Beals — *John Eliot* p.177-178

SAILING VESSELS. *See* Ships and
　　shipping

SAILMAKERS
Marshall — *Mayflower* p.40, 42

SAILORS
Wertenbaker — *Puritan. See* index
　　p.356
- *Behavior and superstitions*
　　Caffrey — *Mayflower* p.74-76
- *Clothing and dress*
　　Caffrey — *Mayflower* p.72, 74
- *Duties*
　　Caffrey — *Mayflower* p.94-95
- *Wages*
　　Caffrey — *Mayflower* p.76

ST. AUGUSTINE, FLORIDA
Collins — *Story* p.72
Starkey — *Land. See* index p.273

200

ST. JOHN'S, NEWFOUNDLAND
Snell — *Wild* p.61-63, 66

ST. LAWRENCE RIVER AND VALLEY
Morris — *Enc.* p.59
Snell — *Wild* p.67, 94-95, 114-115

ST. LUKE'S CHURCH (Smithfield, Va.)
Wertenbaker — *First* p.293-294, 319

ST. MARY'S, MARYLAND
Alderman — *Story* p.83, 86, 89
Chitwood — *History (1)* p.80-81
Leonard — *Dear* p.65-66
Morrison — *Early* p.157
Nettels — *Roots* p.158-159
- *Founding*
  Starkey — *Land* p.113-114
- *Old State House (1676)*
  Morrison — *Early* p.159-160
- *Settlements*
  Spruill — *Women's* p.10-11
  , *First Catholic (1634)*
    Acheson — *America's*
    p.136-137
- *Women*
  - *Land settlement*
    Leonard — *Dear* p.65-66

"SAINTS" (passengers)
See also names of ships
Carman — *History (1)* p.87-89, 94-95
Willison — *Pilgrim* p.546-547
Willison — *Saints. See* index p.508

SALEM (NAUMKEAG),
MASSACHUSETTS
Amer. Her. — *Thirteen* p.97-99, 103
Bailyn — *New England. See* index
p.247
Earle — *Home. See* index p.465
Folsom — *Give* p.14-16, 76, 78-87
Gill — *Mayflower* p.123, 127-129, 136
Glubok — *Home. See* index p.355
National — *History.* p.72-75
Pomfret — *Founding* p.150, 156-157,
161, 173,190-191, 207, 211
Rutman — *Winthrop's. See* index
p.318
Snell — *Wild* p.118, 125
Wertenbaker — *First* p.51-52, 55-56,
98-99, 157-162, 317, 319
Wertenbaker — *Puritan. See* index
p.356
Williams — *Demeter's* p.145

Willison — *Pilgrim* p.267n, 271, 275,
324, 430
Willison — *Saints.* See index p.508
Wish — *Society (1)* p.24, 32-33, 36,
42, 52
- *Churches*
  Gildrie — *Salem. See* index p.186
  Willison — *Pilgrim* p.315-319,
  416, 422-425
- *Commerce*
  Gildrie — *Salem* p.105-109, 155,
  167-169
- *Court of Assistants*
  Gildrie — *Salem* p.37-38, 47, 88-
  92, 94-98
- *Deputies*
  Gildrie — *Salem* p.90-92, 95-97,
  99-100, 151
- *General court*
  Gildrie — *Salem. See* index p.186
- *Quarterly court*
  Gildrie — *Salem* p.41, 46-47, 78,
  97, 129-131, 134-135, 140
- *Views of Francis Higginson*
  Dow — *Domestic* p.5-8
- *Witchcraft*
  Miller — *Colonial* p.179-192
  Morison — *Intellect.* p.256, 259-
  265
  Wertenbaker — *Puritan* p.270-
  283

SALOONS. *See* **Taverns**

SALT
Bailyn — *New England* p.67, 74, 127,
149, 152, 164, 174
Gould — *Early* p.86
Willison — *Pilgrim* p.358-359
Wilison — *Saints* p.242, 252
- *New England*
  Wertenbaker — *First* p.81-82

SALTONSTALL, RICHARD
Earle — *Two cent. (1)* p.xiii, xxi, 18,
164, 324
Earle — *Two cent. (2)* p.690
Pomfret — *Founding* p.151, 154, 160,
164, 176, 198, 203, 233-234
, *on Puritan theory of exclusion*
Vaughan — *Puritan* p.200-201

"SALTS" (silver)
Earle — *Customs* p.135
Earle — *Home* p.78-79

Glubok — *Home* p.42-43
Gould — *Early* p.86

"SAMARES" (jackets, waists)
Earle — *Two cent. (1)* p.103

SAMOSET (Indian)
Archer — *Mayflower* p.167-176, 180-185
Marble — *Women* p.21-22, 24, 59
Marshall — *Mayflower* p.135, 138, 155
Miller — *First* p.35
Morison — *Story* p.69-70, 74
Snell — *Wild* p.108
Willison — *Pilgrim* p.130-134, 137, 139n
Willison — *Saints* p.171-174, 176-178, 183-184, 484-485

"SAMP" (corn-food)
Earle — *Home* p.131-132, 134

"SAMP CLOTHS." See Samplers

SAMPLERS
Glubok — *Home* p.221-224
Gould — *Early* p.141
McClinton — *Antiques* p.186-189
Rawson — *When* p.117-119
Speare — *Life* p.102

SAMPSON (SAMSON), HENRY
Hills — *History (1)* p.21, 29, 37, 40, 46, 54, 89, 96
Willison — *Saints* p.122, 439, 442

SAMPSON (SAMSON) FAMILY
Caffrey — *Mayflower* p.390
Hills — *History (2)* p.97, 144, 170-171, 211

SANDERS, JOHN
Willison — *Pilgrim* p.201-203, 205, 219
Willison — *Saints* p.215-217, 219

SANDWICH, MASSACHUSETTS
Morison — *Story* p.142-143, 153, 164, 226, 231, 242
Willison — *Pilgrim* p.142, 205-207, 452n, 522, 558
Willison — *Saints. See* index p.509

SANDYS, EDWIN, SIR
Abbot — *Colonial* p.20-31
Bailyn — *New England* p.7-8

Chitwood — *History (1)* p.56-68
Craven — *Southern. See* index p.448
Folsom — *Give* p.8-10, 12-13
Hawke — *Colonial* p.101-105, 115, 125, 181
Hills — *History (2). See* index p.272
Morison — *Oxford* p.53-54
Pomfret — *Founding* p.31, 37-39, 43, 45, 47, 106-107, 307-308
Sweet — *Religion* p.30n
Willison — *Pilgrim* p.51-52, 56-58, 63, 181n, 187
Willison — *Saints. See* index p.509
- *"Letter to . . . , 1620"*
   Amer. Her. — *Thirteen* p.140
- *Revolt*
   Calverton — *Awake.* p.222-226

SANITATION
Bridenbaugh — *Cities* p.85-86
Langdon — *Everyday* p.322-323
- *Pilgrims*
   Marshall — *Mayflower* p.104
, *Shipboard*
   Marshall — *Maynard* p.44

SARAH CONSTANT (ship)
Leynse — *Preced.* p.211-212

SASSACUS (Indian)
Caffrey — *Mayflower* p.390
Morison — *Story* p.209-211
Vaughan — *New* p.115, 126, 143-144, 147-150, 166, 203, 325, 330

SASSAFRAS
Caffrey — *Mayflower* p.20-21
Craven — *Southern* p.17, 48, 56, 108
- *Jamestown*
   Adams — *Album* p.16

SASSAMON, JOHN (Indian)
Craven — *Colonies* p.118-119
Morison — *Oxford* p.108
Morison — *Story* p.249-250

SATURIOVA (Indian)
Folsom — *Give* p.3-5

SAUGUS, MASSACHUETTS
- *Ironworks*
   National — *History.* p.82-85

SAUNAS
, *Early, in Delaware*
   Christensen — *Delaware* p.33-34

SAUSAGE AND SAUSAGE MAKERS
Earle — *Home* p.154-155
Gould — *Early* p.78

SAVAGE, THOMAS
Bailyn — *New England* p.35, 39-40,
88, 156
Morison — *Story* p.257-260

"SAVING FAITH" ("Saving Grace")
Pomfret — *Founding* p.185-188, 199

SAWMILLS
Lawrence — *New* p.27
Nettels — *Roots* p.245
Tunis — *Colonial* p.89-91
- *New England*
Wertenbaker — *First* p.80-81
, *First — Berwick, Me. (1631)*
Mitchell — *It's* p.3

SAWS
Marshall — *Mayflower* p.71-78, 80-81,
84

SAWYERS
Tunis — *Craftsmen* p.26

SAY AND SELE, WILLIAM, LORD
Johnston — *Conn.* p.15-17, 81
Willison — *Saints* p.298-299, 375

SAYBROOK, CONNECTICUT
Adams — *Album* p.101
Chitwood — *History (1)* p.125
Johnston — *Conn.* p.17, 36, 59-64
Nettels — *Roots* p.121-122
Vaughan — *New* p.117, 128, 130, 133,
141-143, 147, 218

SAYINGS. *See* **Quotations**

SCALIGER, J. J.
Morison — *Intellect.* p.20, 135, 244

SCALPING
Axtell — *America* p.177

SCANDINAVIANS
See also names of special
nationalities
Wish — *Society (1)* p.101-102

"SCARLET LETTER"
Adams — *Album* p.120

SCHOLARS AND SCHOLARSHIP
Wertenbaker — *First. See* index p.354
, *Reverence for*
Miller — *First* p.223

SCHOOL BOOKS. *See* **Textbooks**

"SCHOOL DAMES." *See* **Teachers —
"School dames"**

SCHOOL LAW OF 1647
- *New England*
Hawke — *U.S.* p.230-231

SCHOOLHOUSES
Earle — *Customs* p.32-33
Glubok — *Home* p.120
Rawson — *When* p.139-141, 145-151
- *Boston, Mass.*
Clark — *Old* p.45
- *Virginia*
Clark — *Old* p.18

SCHOOLMASTERS. *See* **Teachers**

SCHOOLS
See also **Dame Schools; Plym-
outh — Schools; Puritans —
Schools; Town schools;** types of
schools
Acheson — *America's* p.92-93, 118-
119
Langdon — *Everyday* p.317-318
Leonard — *Dear* p.286
Morison — *Intellect.* p.57-58
Rawson — *When* p.139-173
Ver Steeg — *Formative* p.100
Wertenbaker — *Puritan. See* index
p.356-357
- *Architecture, four-square*
Morison — *Early* p.82
- *Boston, Mass.*
Clark — *Old* p.39-46
Rutman — *Winthrop's* p.72-73,
75, 200, 200n-221, 221n-222,
247
- *Cambridge, Mass.*
Morison — *Intellect.* p.65, 72, 90,
99, 101-102
- *Church-state, Middle Colonies*
Monroe — *Founding (1)* p.69-104
- *"Collapse"*
Morison — *Intellect.* p.96-97
- *Connecticut*
Johnston — *Conn.* p.51-53
Morison — *Intellect.* p.72-73

- *Dedham, Mass.*
  Morison — *Intellect.* p.65, 76n, 93
- *Discipline*
  Wright — *Everyday* p.138-139
- *Dorchester, Mass.*
  Morison — *Intellect.* p.64-65, 89, 100-101
  Vaughan — *Puritan* p.238-241
, *Dutch, under English rule*
  Monroe — *Founding* p.80
- *Duxbury, Mass.*
  Morison — *Intellect.* p.98
, *Elementary*
  Morison — *Intellect.* p.57-85
, *Endowed*
  Monroe — *Founding(1)* p.65, 67
- *Franciscans*
  Leonard — *Dear* p.296-297
, *Girls' — First, in Dorchester (1639)*
  Monroe — *Founding (1)* p.130-131
, *Grammar*
  Morison — *Intellect.* p.86-112
  Speare — *Life* p.105, 107
  Wertenbaker — *Puritan* p.143-146

  - *Distribution and duration*
    Morison — *Intellect.* p.97-102
  - *New England*
    Hawke — *Colonial* p.295-296
    Wright — *Literary* p.23
- *Hingham, Mass.*
  Morison — *Intellect.* p.97, 107n
, *in wilderness*
  Vaughan — *Puritan* p.235-244
- *Ipswich, Mass.*
  Morison — *Intellect.* p.65, 72, 100-101
- *Laws*
  Morison — *Intellect.* p.73-76
  , *Execution of*
    Morison — *Intellect.* p.69-75
  - *Massachusetts*
    Annals of America (1) p.184, 203
    Monroe — *Founding (1)* p.124, 126
- *Massachusetts*
  Vaughan — *Puritan* p.235-238
  Wertenbaker — *First* p.244-247
  Wright — *Everyday* p.136-138

- *New Amsterdam*
  Monroe — *Founding (1)* p.73, 75-77, 78-80
- *New England*
  Hawke — *Colonial* p.296
  Morison — *Intellect.* p.62-65
  Wertenbaker — *First* p.244-247
  - *Systems (Act of 1647)*
    Jernegan — *American* p.190-191
- *New Jersey*
  Monroe — *Founding (1)* p.89-91
- *Newbury, Mass.*
  Morison — *Intellect.* p.72, 92, 97, 109n
- *Northampton, Mass.*
  Morison — *Intellect.* p.73, 97, 107
- *Pennsylvania*
  - *Church control*
    Monroe — *Founding (1)* p.93, 95
  , *First (1683)*
    Holliday — *Woman's* p.78-79
- *Punishment*
  Rawson — *When* p.169-171
- *Religious purpose*
  Morison — *Intellect.* p.58-59, 76
- *Salem, Mass.*
  Glubok — *Home* p.117-118
  Morison — *Intellect.* p.72, 100, 107n
- *Seats and arrangement*
  Rawson — *When* p.146-148
- *South*
  Wertenbaker — *First* p.250-254
- *Taunton, Mass.*
  Morison — *Intellect.* p.92
- *Terms and vacations*
  Rawson — *When* p.166
- *Tuition*
  Morison — *Intellect.* p.76, 107
, *Undemocratic*
  Morison — *Intellect.* p.76-77
- *Virginia*
  Adams — *Provincial* p.136-137
  Glubok — *Home* p.115-116
  , *First (1635)*
    Wright — *Everyday* p.135-136
- *Watertown, Mass.*
  Morison — *Intellect.* p.96, 100
- *Woburn, Mass.*
  Morison — *Intellect.* p.93-95

SCHOONERS. *See* **Ships and shipping — Schooners**

SCHUYLER, PETER
Fisher — *Men* p.94-95

SCIENCE AND SCIENTISTS
See also **Books and reading — Science; Inventions and inventors;** special subjects
Hawke — *Colonial* p.298-301
Hawke — *U.S.* p.238-241
Morison — *Intellect. See* index p.286
Rozwenc — *Making (1)* p.91-96
Wertenbaker — *First* p.237-238, 258-261
Wertenbaker — *Puritan. See* index p.356

, *and witchcraft*
Rozwenc — *Making (1)* p.93-96
- *Lack of specialization*
Wright — *Cultural* p.218-219
- *Puritans*
Morison — *Intellect.* p.141-142
Rozwenc — *Making (1)* p.91-93
Wright — *Cultural* p.223-224, 226
- *Revolution*
Rozwenc — *Making (1)* p.91

SCIENTIFIC WRITERS
Tyler — *History* p.532-533

SCITUATE, MASSACHUSETTS
Morison — *Story* p.118, 140-142, 152-153, 156, 176, 190, 203, 224, 227, 231, 271, 274, 291
Willison — *Pilgrim* p.377n, 436-438, 521, 562
Willison — *Saint. See* index p.509

SCOTCH-BOARDMAN HOUSE (Saugus, Mass.)
Morrison — *Early* p.54-56

SCOTCH-IRISH
See also special subjects
Alderman — *Story* p.119, 129
Carman — *History (1)* p.57
Furnas — *Americans* p.91-97
Hall — *Religious* p.122-126, 142-146
Nettels — *Roots* p.386-387
Sweet — *Religion* p.254-255

- *Migration*
Ver Steeg — *Formative* p.168
- *Pennsylvania*
Chitwood — *History (1)* p.210

SCOTS
See also **Scotch-Irish**
Bailyn — *New England* p.23, 45, 127, 148-149, 154, 178
Craven — *Colonies* p.179-180, 190
- *Carolinas*
Craven — *Southern* p.408
- *South*
Craven — *Southern* p.315-316, 408
- *Virginia*
Craven — *Southern* p.315-316

"SCOT'S CHARITABLE SOCIETY"
Bridenbaugh — *Cities* p.81-82

SCOTT, CATHERINE
Rothbard — *Conceived (1)* p.196-197, 216-217, 241-242

SCOTT, JOHN
Bailyn — *New England* p.117-118

SCOTTISH CHURCH (Leyden)
Willison — *Saints* p.89-90, 94, 340-341, 374

SCOTTOW, JOSHUA
Tyler — *History* p.341-342

"SCRIBBLING." *See* Books and reading — "Scribbling"

SCROOBY, ENGLAND
Adams — *Album* p.38
Gill — *Mayflower* p.21-26; *See also* index p.205
Leynse — *Preced.* p.35-62; *See also* index p.285
Willison — *Saints. See* index p.509

- *Church*
Beck — *Pilgrims* p.3-9
- *Congregation*
Willison — *Pilgrim* p.17-18, 22-27, 30, 90, 235
Willison — *Saints. See* index p.509

SCRUBBING AND SCOURING
Speare — *Life* p.76-77

"SCRUTOIRES" (cabinets)
Earle — *Customs* p.17-118

SCULPTURE
Arts — *America* p.175-180
Morris — *Ency.* p.597

SCURVY
Dow — *Domestic* p.7-8

SEA CAPTAINS
- *Virginia*
Clark — *Old* p.16-17

SEABORNE, WINIFRED
Williams — *Demeter's* p.32

SEARLE, DANIEL
Pomfret — *Founding* p.316-317

SEDAN CHAIRS
Chitwood — *History (1)* p.387
Earle — *Customs* p.193
Glubok — *Home* p.344

SEDGWICK, ROBERT
Bailyn — *New England* p.37, 51, 79-80, 82, 94, 106
Wright — *Cultural* p.35-36

SEINING (net fishing)
Wright — *Everyday* p.198-199

SEISMOLOGY
Morris — *Ency.* p.528

SELDEN, JOHN
Morison — *Intellect.* p.44, 144-145, 148

SELECTMEN
- *Dedham, Mass.*
Lockridge — *New* p.38-46, 80
- *Duties*
Wertenbaker — *Puritan* p.69-70

"SENATE HOUSE" (Kingston-on-Hudson, N.Y. 1676–1695)
Morrison — *Early* p.114-114

SENECA INDIANS
- *Dinner*
Northey — *American* p.63-64
, *in Bacon's Rebellion*
Smith — *17th* p.53-54

SENNERT, DAVID
- *Works*
Morison — *Intellect.* p.136-137

SEPARATISTS
See also **Barrowism; Brownisms; Franciscans; Pilgrims; Puritans; "Saints"**
Acheson — *America's* p.84-85
Alderman — *Story* p.20-21, 25-26, 96
Amer. Her. — *Pilgrims. See* index p.153
Amer. Her. — *Thirteen* p.88, 101, 103
Beck — *Pilgrims* p.4-12, 16, 32
Caffrey — *Mayflower* p.23-24, 26, 28, 299-300, 304
Dillon — *Pilgrims* p.49, 60, 64, 67-69, 103, 111, 119, 126, 192-193, 209
Folsom — *Give* p.12-13, 15, 17
Furnas — *Americans* p.57
Hawke — *Colonial* p.54, 124-129, 142
Marshall — *Mayflower* p.25-26
Morison — *Story* p.5, 8-9, 15, 119
Pomfret — *Founding* p.23, 29, 101-108, 111-130, 154, 156-158, 185-189
Rutman — *Winthrop's* p.16-17, 52, 56, 99, 101, 103, 112, 126, 285
Scott — *Settlers* p.19-20, 23, 25, 93
Snell — *Wild* p.118, 125

- *Doctrines*
Willison — *Pilgrim* p.420-421
Willison — *Saints* p.9-10; *See also* index p.509
- *Emigration to Holland*
Caffrey — *Mayflower* p.30-35
- *England*
Hall — *Religious* p.68, 71-72
- *Holland*
Beck — *Pilgrims* p.5-12
- *Religious practices*
Annals of America (1) p.125-128
- *Salem, Mass.*
Gildrie — *Salem* p.21-22, 24, 31-39, 48-49, 52-53, 142, 146
- *Scrooby, England*
Amer. Her. — *Pilgrims* p.24-37
- *Terminology*
Willison — *Pilgrim* p.418-419

SEQUIN (Indian)
Vaughan — *New* p.57, 203-205

SERMONS
See also **Books and reading — Sermons; Funerals — Sermons; "Jeremiads"; names of clergymen**
Hawke — *Colonial* p.45-46, 289, 306-307

206

SERMONS (*continued*)
Morison — *Intellect.* p.42, 59, 158-
159, 166, 168, 173-175
Wertenbaker — *Puritan* p.79-87

- *"Election and artillery"*
Morison — *Intellect.* p.174-176
- *Expression and influence*
Morison — *Intellect.* p.166-172
- *Puritans*
Miller — *First* p.92-93

SERVANTS
See also **Slaves and slavery**
Bailyn — *New England* p.13, 16, 33,
72, 127, 144
Craven — *Southern. See* index p.448
Earle — *Customs* p.82-84
Morison — *Story* p.149, 162-173, 170-
171, 183, 186-187, 193-195, 232
Rutman — *Winthrop's* p.318-319
Speare — *Life* p.8-12
Williams — *Demeter's. See* index
p.356

, *Advice to*
Hawke — *U.S.* p.227-228
, *Indentured*
See also **"Redemptioners"**
Adams — *Album* p.113
Amer. Her. — *Thirteen* p.82, 107,
149, 169-170, 173, 175, 178,
180
Carman — *History (1)* p.46-48
Dillon — *Pilgrims* p.26, 126-127,
136
Earle — *Customs* p.97-102
Folsom — *Give* p.9, 13, 44-45,
75, 82, 86, 88
Furnas — *Americans* p.97-110
Goodwin — *Colonial* p.169-174
Hawke — *Colonial* p.289-290
Jernegan — *American* p.86-87
Nettels — *Roots* p.140-145, 231-
232, 319-322; *See also* index
p.733 (under Indentured. . .)
Pomfret — *Founding* p.35, 39-41,
81, 86, 110-111, 117, 202, 270,
272, 310
Rozwenc — *Making (1)* p.44-45
Smith — *17th* p.69-80
Ver Steeg — *Formative* p.61
Wertenbaker — *First. See* index
p.346 (under Indentured. . .)
Willison — *Pilgrim* p.90, 296,
332n

Willison — *Saints. See* index
p.502
Wish — *Society (1)* p.67-68
- *Children, Abducted*
Monroe — *Founding (1)* p.38
- *Criminals*
Monroe — *Founding (1)*
p.37-38
- *"Freedom dues"*
Smith — *17th* p.69
- *Maryland*
Wertenbaker — *First* p.24-26
- *Nationalities, origins*
Monroe — *Founding (1)*
p.35-36
- *North Carolina*
Calverton — *Awake.* p.294
- *Political prisoners*
Monroe — *Founding (1)* p.37
- *Portsmouth, R.I.*
Demos — *Remarkable*
p.128-129
- *South*
Tunis — *Colonial* p.79-80
- *South Carolina*
Calverton — *Awake.* p.294
- *Women*
Smith — *17th* p.70-71
- *Liberties*
Annals of America (1) p.166
- *Maryland*
Morison — *Oxford* p.82-83
- *Petitions, Calvert Co., Md. (1663)*
Demos — *Remarkable* p.135-137
- *Plymouth*
Demos — *Little* p.69-75, 105,
107-117, 120-122, 181, 185,
194
- *Puritans*
Morgan — *Puritan* p.62-77
- *Boldness*
Morgan — *Puritan* p.73-75
- *Compensation*
Morgan — *Puritan* p.70-71
, *Indentured*
Morgan — *Puritan* p.71-73
- *Life*
Morgan — *Puritan* p.65
, *Types of*
Morgan — *Puritan* p.62-63
- *South*
Craven — *Southern. See* index
p.448
- *Treatment*
Calverton — p.128-130

- *Virginia*
  Clark — *Old* p.12-13
, *White*
  Chitwood — *History (1)* p.340-344
- *Women, and children*
  See also **Servants, Indentured**
  Earle — *Colonial* p.12-13
  Leonard — *Dear* p.329-333, 337-348
  Rutman — *Winthrop's* p.91, 141, 196, 243
  - *Rewards of Labor*
    Leonard — *Dear* p.346-348

SESSIONS, COURT OF
Craven — *Colonies* p.76-78

SETTLERS. *See* **Colonies and colonists; Immigrants and immigration;** names of nationalities and colonies

"SETTLES" (boxed seats)
Gould — *Early* p.25

"SEVEN ARTICLES" (confession of faith)
Leynse — *Preced.* p.225-228
Willison — *Pilgrim* p.53-57

SEVEN YEAR'S WAR. *See* **French and Indian War**

SEVENTEENTH CENTURY
- *Bibliographical essay*
  Rothbard — *Conceived (1)* p.512-518
- *Significance*
  Smith — *17th* p.3-12

SEVENTH DAY BAPTISTS
Bridenbaugh — *Cities* p.104

SEWALL, BETTY
Williams — *Demeter's* p.78-79

SEWALL, SAMUEL
Adams — *Album* p.111
Bailyn — *New England* p.134-135, 183, 190, 192-193, 195
Dulles — *America* p.13-15
Morison — *Intellect. See* index p.286
Morris — *Ency.* p.560-561
Murdock — *Literature* p.106-109, 194-195, 209-210
Tyler — *History* p.345-348

Wertenbaker — *First* p.80, 161, 185, 231, 277-278
Willison — *Saints. See* index p.509
- *Apology for witchcraft*
  Goetzmann — *Colonial* p.204-213
- *Diary*
  Dexter — *Colonial* p.84-86
  Earle — *Two cent. (1)* p.249-250, 331-333
, *on drama*
  Wright — *Cultural* p.178-179
- *Wedding with Betsy Hull*
  Dow — *Every* p.170-171
- *"Witchcraft in Salem"*
  Miller — *Colonial* p.190-192

SEWING
Gould — *Early* p.141

SEWING BEES
Gould — *Early* p.142

"SHADOW WORK" (needlework)
Rawson — *When* p.136

SHAFTSBURY, ANTHONY ASHLEY COOPER, EARL OF
Craven — *Colonies* p.56, 97-100, 159, 178
Craven — *Southern. See* index p.438-439
Hawke — *Colonial* p.209-215, 251, 335

SHALLOPS
See also **Sparrow** (ship)
Marshall — *Mayflower* p.48-49
Morison — *Story* p.45, 50-54, 62, 78, 89-90, 108, 111, 115-116, 127, 131, 139, 202
Speare — *Life* p.114-115
Willison — *Pilgrim* p.177-180, 540

SHAWMUT. *See* **Boston, Massachusetts**

SHEEP
See also **Wool**
Earle — *Home* p.188-189, 401
Gould — *Early* p.127
Leonard — *Dear* p.176
- *Massachusetts*
  Glubok — *Home* p.241
  Gould — *Early* p.127
- *Shearing festivals*
  Earle — *Customs* p.232-233

SHELDON, GILBERT, ARCHBISHOP
Smith — *17th* p.168, 171-172, 181

SHEPARD, THOMAS
Morison — *Intellect.* p.5, 120, 140, 152, 155n, 158-159, 161, 167, 169
Rutman — *Winthrop's* p.103, 114-115, 117, 119, 124, 151, 259, 263
Vaughan — *Puritan* p.35-39
Wertenbaker — *Puritan* p.32, 34, 209, 214, 243
- *"Letter . . . to his son" (1672)*
    Demos — *Remarkable* p.130-138
, *on conversion experience*
    Vaughan — *Puritan* p.92-97

SHEPARD, THOMAS, JR.
Morison — *Intellect.* p.75, 81, 225-226

SHEPARD, MRS. THOMAS
Williams — *Demeter's* p.30

SHERIFFS. *See* Constables and sheriffs

SHERLEY, JAMES
Caffrey — *Mayflower* p.48, 208, 220-221, 232, 235-236, 238-241, 243, 258-260, 325-326
Morison — *Story* p.126, 129-130, 156, 194, 198
Willison — *Pilgrim* p.448-453; *See also* index p.582
Willison — *Saints. See* index p.509

SHINGLES
Earle — *Home* p.316-318

SHIPBUILDING
Adams — *Provincial* p.41-42
Amer. Her. — *Thirteen* p.67, 106, 154-155, 165, 188
Carman — *History (1)* p.76-77, 80
Chitwood — *History (1)* p.377-378
Langdon — *Everyday* p.212-215
Nettels — *Roots* p.245-247
Wright — *Everyday* p.82, 91-95, 112-113
- *Boston, Mass.*
    Wertenbaker — *First* p.51
- *Connecticut*
    Wertenbaker — *First* p.51-52
- *Marblehead, Mass.*
    Wertenbaker — *First* p.51, 81, 191
- *Massachusetts*
    Jernegan — *American* p.173
    Wertenbaker — *First* p.51-52

- *New England*
    Wertenbaker — *First* p.11-12, 51-52
- *Philadelphia, Pa.*
    Langdon — *Everyday* p.229-233

SHIPS AND SHIPPING
See also **Pinnaces; Shallops;** names of ships
Adams — *Album* p.111
Caffrey — *Mayflower* p.86-87
Craven — *Colonies* p.35, 37-38, 40
Dow — *Every* p.143, 154-155
Gill — *Mayflower. See* index p.205
Goodwin — *Colonial* p.100-101
Marshall — *Mayflower* p.17-18, 32, 167
Nettels — *Roots* p.263-264
Rutman — *Winthrop's* p.319
Wish — *Society (1)* p.52, 113-116

- *Armament*
    Marshall — *Mayflower* p.48
- *Designs*
    Caffrey — *Mayflower* p.67-69, 74, 94-96
- *Development*
    Caffrey — *Mayflower* p.62-63
, *Emigrant*
    Dow — *Every* p.3-12
    Nettels — *Roots* p.145-146
, *Ghost (Maine)*
    - *Superstitions*
        Mitchell — *It's* p.88
, *Medicine on*
    Marshall — *Mayflower* p.46
- *New England*
    Langdon — *Everyday* p.211-223
- *Officers*
    See also **Sea captains**
    Caffrey — *Mayflower* p.76-78
    , *Duties of*
        Marshall — *Mayflower* p.39-40
- *Passage cost*
    Dow — *Every* p.6
- *Passengers*
    See also **Mayflower — Passengers;** names of other ships
    Demos — *Remarkable* p.37-43
    Willison — *Plymouth* p.549

    - *Accomodations*
        Dow — *Every* p.7, 158-165

, *Pilgrim*
  See also **Mayflower;** names of
    other ships
  Archer — *Mayflower* p.298-305
  Willison — *Pilgrim* p.74, 79, 88,
    154-155, 177-178, 234, 313,
    321-322
- *Sanitary and cooking facilities*
  Marshall — *Mayflower* p.44
- *Schooners*
  Speare — *Life* p.114-116
- *Shipboard clothing*
  Marshall — *Mayflower* p.44, 46
- *Shipboard provisions*
  Dow — *Every* p.6, 9-10

    - *New England*
      Wertenbaker — *First* p.17,
        20-21
, *Small*
  Marshall — *Mayflower* p.49,167

SHIPWRIGHTS
  Tunis — *Craftsmen* p.111

SHOEMAKERS
  See also **Cordwainers**
  Chitwood — *History (1)* p.374
  Rutman — *Winthrop's* p.92, 188, 194,
    232, 247, 249-251
  Speare — *Life* p.46-47
  Tunis — *Craftsmen* p.105-108

SHOES
  See also **Batts and broags; Clogs;**
    Galoshes; Pattens
  Earle — *Two cent. (1)* p.371-388

, *Children's*

    - *Buckles*
      McClinton — *Antiques* p.62-
        63
- *Pegs*
  Earle — *Home* p.315-316
- *Plymouth*
  Demos — *Little* p.55, 57

SHOPS AND SHOPKEEPERS
  See also **Artisans; Merchants;** etc.
  Bridenbaugh — *Cities* p.41-42
  Leonard — *Dear* p.443-444
  Speare — *Life* p.45-49

- *Boston, Mass.*

    - *Inventory (1660)*
      Dow — *Every* p.244-245

- *Roxbury, Mass.*
  - *Inventory (1646–47)*
    Dow — *Every* p.242-243
- *Salem, Mass.*
  Dow — *Every* p.262, 270
- *Towns*
  Tunis — *Craftsmen* p.39-56

SHORT, MERCY
  Williams — *Demeter's* p.150-151, 160

SHORTHAND
  Wertenbaker — *First* p.237-238

SHOVELS
  Gould — *Early* p.75

SHRIMPTON FAMILY
  Bailyn — *New England. See* index
    p.248

"SHROVE TUESDAY"
  Earle — *Customs* p.228
  Wright — *Everyday* p.228

SICKNESS
  See also **Diseases; Epidemics;**
    Smallpox; Pilgrims — Plague;
    names of other diseases; related
    subjects
- *Care*
  Rutman — *Winthrop's* p.175,
    217-220, 242, 242n, 258
- *South*
  Goodwin — *Colonial* p.273-282

SILK
  Craven — *Southern. See* index p.448
  Leonard — *Dear* p.165-166

- *South*
  Craven — *Southern. See* index
    p.448

SILKWORMS
  Glubok — *Home* p.207-208

SILVER
  See also **Currency; Silverware;** etc.
  Glubok — *Home* p.48-49
  Leonard — *Dear* p.154

- *New York*
  Arts — *America* p.322-326
  Clark — *Old* p.56-57

SILVERSMITHS
- *Boston, Mass.*
  Langdon — *Everyday* p.179
- *New England*
  Arts — *America* p.319
- *New York*
  Langdon — *Everyday* p.181-182

SILVERWARE
Drepperd — *Pioneer* p.179-180
, *from coins*
  Langdon — *Everyday* p.176-177

SILVESTER, DINAH
Williams — *Demeter's* p.137

SIMMES, SARAH
Williams — *Demeter's* p.75

SIMMONS (SYMONSON), MOSES
Willison — *Pilgrim* p.155, 539
Willison — *Saints* p.90, 191, 314, 444

"SIMPLES." *See* **Remedies**

SIN AND SINNERS
See also **Morality; Puritans;** etc.
Furnas — *Americans* p.66-69
Woodward — *Way* p.60-61
- *Massachusetts*
  Calverton — *Awake.* p.123-127
- *Repentance*
  Smith — *17th* p.144-146

SINGING
See also **Psalms; Songs**
Rawson — *When* p.99-100

SINGLETON, MARY CLARKE. *See*
Cushman, Mary Clarke Singleton

1600's. *See* **Seventeenth Century**

SKATES AND SKATING
Glubok — *Home* p.195-196
Rawson — *When* p.84-85

"SKEELS" (milk and cream tubs)
Earle — *Colonial* p.293

SKELTON, SAMUEL
Willison — *Pilgrim* p.318, 346, 423
Willison — *Saints* p.271, 346, 350, 470
- *"Accompte" (1629–30)*
  Dow — *Every* p.239-241

SKILLETS
Gould — *Early* p.76

"SKIPPETS" (dippers)
Earle — *Colonial* p.293

SLANDER (gossip)
- *Punishment, of women*
  Earle — *Colonial* p.89-91
  Goodwin — *Colonial* p.258

SLAVES AND SLAVERY
See also **Plymouth — Slavery; Puritans, on slavery; Royal Africa Company**
Amer. Her. — *Thirteen* p.81-82, 128, 140, 155, 175, 180, 182
Calverton — *Awake.* p.268-274
Carman — *History (1)* p.48-51, 129
Chitwood — *History (1)* p.344-355
Dillon — *Pilgrims* p.40-43, 122, 135, 142, 156-157, 193-194
Folsom — *Give* p.6-7, 10, 26-27, 32, 41, 44-45, 47, 54, 69, 75, 80-81, 88-89, 92
Furnas — *Americans* p.42-43, 81-82, 115-117
Hawke — *Colonial* p.289-290; *See also* index p.762
Hope — *Nation* p.112-113
Jernegan — *American* p.87-88
Life — *New* p.98-99
Morris — *Ency.* p.512
Scott — *Settlers* p.106, 115
Smith — *17th* p.108-111, 128, 131
Ver Steeg — *Formative* p.190-194
Wertenbaker — *First. See* index p.354
Williams — *Demeter's. See* index p.356-357
Willison — *Saints. See* index p.509
- *Advantages and disadvantages*
  Chitwood — *History (1)* p.353-355
- *Carolinas*
  Starkey — *Land* p.229-231
- *Connecticut*
  Johnston — *Conn.* p.55
- *Crime and punishment*
  Miller — *First* p.155
- *Delaware*
  Christensen — *Delaware* p.9
, *English*
  Scott — *Settlers* p.104-106
, *French and Dutch*
  Scott — *Settlers* p.106

- *Maryland*
Calverton — *Awake.* p.249-252
Wertenbaker — *First* p.23, 233-235
- *Massachusetts*
Wertenbaker — *First* p.231-233
- *New England*
Hawke — *U.S.* p.229
Langdon — *Everyday* p.216
- *New Jersey*
Calverton — *Awake.* p.380-381
- *North Carolina*
Calverton — *Awake.* p.294
, *Opposition to*
Chitwood — *History (1)* p.352-353
- *Prices*
Calverton — *Awake.* p.270-272
- *South*
Goodwin — *Colonial* p.168-169, 174-184
- *South Carolina*
Calverton — *Awake.* p.302
Chitwood — *History (1)* p.189
, *Spanish*
Scott — *Settlers* p.104
, *Traffic of (1688)*
Annals of America (1) p.274-275
- *Treatment*
Chitwood — *History (1)* p.348
- *Virginia*
Clark — *Old* p.12-13
Fisher — *Men (1)* p.36-37
Hawke — *U.S.* p.229
Morison — *Oxford* p.90
- *Laws (1660–69)*
Annals of America (1) p.225-226
, *White*
Calverton — *Awake.* p.257-268
- *Women*
Leonard — *Dear* p.339-340

SLEDS
Glubok — *Home* p.188-189
Rawson — *When* p.85-86

"SLEEPY HOLLOW CHURCH" (Tarrytown, N.Y., 1699)

Morrison — *Early* p.117-119

SLEEVES
Earle — *Two cent. (1)* p.81-86, 171, 186

SLEIGHS AND SLEIGHING
Chitwood — *History (1)* p.387
Earle — *Customs* p.209-210

SLOUGHTER, HENRY
Hawke — *Colonial* p.269, 326
Rothbard — *Conceived (1)* p.437, 444-447, 461

SLUYTER, PETER
- *Visits to Maryland, Virginia*
Axtell — *America* p.214-216
- *Visits to New England*
Axtell — *America* p.88-95, 107-113, 145-159

SMALLPOX
See also **Innoculation**
Wertenbaker — *First* p.167, 180-181
- *Boston, Mass.*
Bridenbaugh — *Cities* p.86-87
Wertenbaker — *First* p.180-181
- *Plymouth*
Caffrey — *Mayflower* p.248
Willison — *Pilgrim* p.386-387

SMEDES, JOHANNES
Hale — *Through* p.85

SMITH, HENRY
Smith — *Colonial* p.35-47

SMITH, JOHN, CAPTAIN
Acheson — *America's* p.68-70
Adams — *Album* p.14-15
Alderman — *Story* p.5-6, 8-10
Amer. Her. — *Pioneer* p.50, 54-57
Amer. Her. — *Thirteen* p.60-61, 65, 71, 73-75, 78-79, 86-87, 98-99, 106, 117
Caffrey — *Mayflower. See* index p.391
Chitwood — *History (1)* p.55-57
Christensen — *Delaware* p.12
Craven — *Southern* p.68-69, 72-73, 79-80, 98, 100, 114
Earle — *Home* p.115-116, 127, 381-382
Fisher — *Men (1)* p.19-28
Furnas — *Americans* p.25-26, 48-49, 52, 54, 58, 107
Gill — *Mayflower* p.45, 52, 55, 57-59, 64-65, 73, 124
Glubok — *Home* p.64, 69-70, 293
Hawke — *Colonial. See* index p.762

SMITH, JOHN, CAPTAIN (cont.)

Hawke — *U.S.* p.65-70
Hills — *History (1)* p.6, 26-27, 30, 43, 108
Hills — *History (2)* p.53, 56, 59-60, 157, 161, 230-232, 238-240
Langdon — *Everyday* p.5-7, 9
Leynse — *Preced.* p.12, 29-34, 212, 214, 220-221, 223, 257
Life — *New* p.50, 54-55, 64-65
Marshall — *Mayflower* p.22-23, 27, 52-54, 133, 171, 177
Morison — *Story* p.15, 22, 50, 63, 81, 218
National — *History.* p.49-53, 55, 65
Phillips — *First* p.63-67, 72-100, 178-185
Pomfret — *Founding* p.27-30, 32-34, 43-44, 109
Smith — *17th* p.1, 20, 42, 45, 47, 199-202, 220
Snell — *Wild.* See index p.203
Starkey — *Land.* See index p.273
Tyler — *History* p.15-34; *See also* index p.548
Vaughan — *New* p.5, 16-18, 26, 59, 235
Willison — *Pilgrim* p.37n, 65, 98, 136n, 143, 145
Willison — *Saints* p.129, 145, 153, 183, 261, 468
Wish — *Society (1)* p.22-23, 76, 84-85
Wright — *Everyday* p.27-28, 32, 38, 81-82, 157

, *and Barbara Courtenay*
    Phillips — *First* p.183-184
, *and Indians*
    Nettels — *Roots* p.155-156
, *and Pocahontas*
    Collins — *Story* p.35
    Miller — *Colonial* p.231-238
    Phillips — *First* p.57-58, 161, 178-181, 184
- *Biography*
    Morris — *Ency.* p.715
- *Books*
    Phillips — *First* p.84, 86, 98-100, 178-183
- *Character and weakness*
    Phillips — *First* p.64-65, 98-99, 181
- *"A description of New England"*
    Miller — *Colonial* p.66-75
    Phillips — *First* p.100
- *"Encouragement of settlers in New England" (1616)*
    Annals of America (1) p.36-39
- *"General Historie"* . . .
    Phillips — *First* p.181-182
- *"The Indians in Virginia"*
    Miller — *Colonial* p.221-230
- *"A map of Virginia" (1612)*
    Amer. Her. — *Thirteen* p.60-61
    Phillips — *First* p.86, 99
, *on American abundance: Virginia*
    Goetzmann — *Colonial* p.75
, *on New England (1614)*
    Goetzmann — *Colonial* p.79-80
, *on New World vistas*
    Phillips — *First* p.72
, *on Virginia hardships (1608)*
    Bailey — *American (1)* p.7-9
, *on Virginia Indians*
    Axtell — *American* p.53-69
- *"Starving time in Virginia" (1607–14)*
    Annals of America (1) p.21-31
- *"True relation"*
    Phillips — *First* p.84, 98, 179-180, 183
- *Visits to England*
    Phillips — *First* p.98-100

SMITH (SMYTH), JOHN, REV.
Gill — *Mayflower* p.22, 25-26, 29-30
Leynse — *Preced.* p.67, 146, 149, 155-157, 163, 204, 208-209
Willison — *Pilgrim* p.17, 25n, 32, 45, 422n
Willison — *Saints.* See index p.509

SMITH, MARY GOODALL MASTERSON
Willison — *Saints* p.268, 354, 451, 458

SMITH, RALPH
Morison — *Story* p.117-118, 163
Willison — *Saints* p.299, 346-348, 353-355, 451, 458

SMITH, SAMUEL
Smith — *Colonial* p.48-57

SMITH, THOMAS, SIR
Chitwood — *History (1)* p.66-67
Craven — *Southern* p.60, 82, 86n, 90, 102, 111, 117, 125-126
Pomfret — *Founding* p.5, 11-12, 17, 19, 25, 31, 34, 37, 45, 107, 305-307
Rothbard — *Conceived (1)* p.40-41, 43-44, 57, 65
Willison — *Pilgrim* p.57-58

SMITH, WILLIAM
Rothbard — *Conceived (1)* p.445,
465, 468, 473, 475-476

SMITH FAMILY
Hills — *History (1)*. See index p.174
Hills — *History (2)*. See index p.273

SMOKE OVENS
Gould — *Early* p.55-56, 58

"SMOOTHING." See Ironing

SMUGGLING
See also **Navigation Acts**
Bailyn — *New England* p.122, 127,
130, 153, 157, 164

SMYTH (SMYTHE). See Smith

SNAKES
Scott — *Settlers* p.10

**SNOW, CONTANCE (CONSTANCIA)
HOPKINS**
Caffrey — *Mayflower* p.111, 306
Marble — *Women* p.9, 16, 23, 30-31,
68, 71, 88-89
Willison — *Saints* p.133, 332, 441, 450

SNOW, NICHOLAS
Hills — *History (1)* p.126-129; *See
also* index p.174
Hills — *History (2)* p.24, 52, 54
Willison — *Saints* p.332, 450

SNOW FAMILY
Hills — *History (1)* p.126-129; *See
also* index p.174
Hills — *History (2)* p.24; *See also*
index p.273-274

SNOW (winter)
Adams — *Album* p.91

SOAP AND SOAP MAKING
Dow — *Every* p.97
Earle — *Colonial* p.301-303
Earle — *Customs* p.311-312
Glubok — *Home* p.200-201
Gould — *Early* p.113-114
Leonard — *Dear* p.101
Marshall — *Mayflower* p.101-103
Nettels — *Roots* p.241
Williams — *Demeter's* p.47-48

- *Ashes*
Craven — *Southern* p.69, 108,
141
, *Dutch*
Smith — *Colonial* p.115-116

SOCIAL CLASSES. See Classes

SOCIETY
See also **Aristocracy; Classes**
Hawke — *Colonial* p.288-291
Holliday — *Woman's* p.174-175
Miller — *First* p.108-111
Smith — *17th* p.61-115
Vaughan — *Puritan* p.129-198

, *Chesapeake*
Hawke — *Colonial* p.114-119
, *Communal*
See also names of communities
- *Pattern (Dedham, Mass.)*
Lockridge — *New* p.37-78
- *Contracts*
Demos — *Remarkable* p.191-193
, *English*
Rozwenc — *Making (1)* p.42-43
- *Instability*
Smith — *17th* p.4, 6, 8-9, 12, 90-
91
- *Massachusetts*
Dow — *Every* p.107-108
- *New England*
Hawke — *Colonial* p.151-160
Jernegan — *American* p.178-179
- *Salem, Mass.*
Gildrie — *Salem* p.56-74, 155-
169
- *South*
See also **Plantations and
planters**
Arts — *America* p.5-11, 15-16
Jernegan — *American* p.95-99
Wertenbaker — *Old* p.10-11
- *Structure*
Adams — *Provincial* p.1-24
Pomfret — *Founding* p.40-41, 52-
53, 56-60, 68
- *Villages*
Bridenbaugh — *Cities* p.94-139

**SOCIETY FOR PROMOTING CHRISTIAN
KNOWLEDGE (Propagation of
the Gospel in New England)**
Beals — *John Eliot* p.136-137
Wright — *Cultural* p.146

**"SOCIETY OF PARTICULAR ADVEN-
TURERS FOR TRAFFIQUE WITH
VIRGINIA"**
Hawke — *Colonial* p.99

SOIL
- *Exhaustion*
Craven — *Southern* p.22, 363-
364

**"SOJOURNERS" (newcomers,
strangers)**
See also **"Strangers"**
Rutman — *Winthrop's. See* index
p.319

SOMERS, GEORGE, SIR
Craven — *Southern* p.85, 92-93, 96-
97, 100-101, 110

SONGS
See also **Ballads; Hymns; Psalms;
Singing**
Annals of America (1) p.116-117
- *"Lileburlero"*
Morison — *Oxford* p.125
- *"Tate and Brady song book"*
Sweet — *Religion* p.117
- *"Vexilla regis"*
Morison — *Oxford* p.106
- *"Vive Henri Quatre"*
Morison — *Oxford* p.46
- *We gather together"*
Annals of America (1) p.117

SOTHEL, SETH
Rothbard — *Conceived (1)* p.129-130,
135-137

SOULE, GEORGE
Hills — *History (1)* p.21, 37, 39, 50,
69, 90, 94
Hills — *History (2)* p.162
Willison — *Saints* p.134, 314, 443, 448

SOULE, MARY BECKET
Willison — *Saints* p.443, 448

SOULE (SOWLE) FAMILY
Hills — *History (1). See* index p.174

SOUTH
See also names of southern colonies;
special subjects
Rothbard — *Conceived (1)* p.53-153
Tunis — *Colonial* p.76-96

- *Economy*
Wertenbaker — *First* p.22-48,
304-306
- *First colonies*
Collins — *Story* p.32, 67-72
- *Local government*
Jernegan — *American* p.76-78
- *Martial law*
Craven — *Southern* p.105-106,
133-134, 200
- *Nationalities*
Wertenbaker — *Old* p.348
- *Plantations and planters. See*
Plantations and planters — South
- *Puritans. See* **Puritans — South**
- *View from abroad*
Axtell — *America* p.195-232
- *Views of John Hammond*
Axtell — *America* p.195-211
- *Women*
Goodwin — *Colonial* p.43-56

- *Home occupations*
Spruill — *Women's* p.44-45
- *Plantation domestic life*
Goodwin — *Colonial* p.33
- *Status*
Spruill — *Women's* p.44

SOUTH CAROLINA
Acheson — *America's* p.151-154
Alderman — *Story* p.126, 128, 133,
136-138
Amer. Her. — *Thirteen* p.19, 26-27,
55, 154, 180, 182
Axtell — *America* p.216-232
Calverton — *Awake. See* index p.472
Craven — *Colonies. See* index p.362
Craven — *Southern. See* index p.448
Rothbard — *Conceived (1)* p.121-125,
135-138, 140-142
Wish — *Society (1)* p.91-92

, *Barbadian influence in*
Craven — *Colonies* p.102-103
- *Contrast with North Carolina*
Calverton — *Awake.* p.284-285
- *Government*
Calverton p.290-291
- *History*
Chitwood — *History (1)* p.186-
191
- *Individualism*
Calverton — *Awake.* p.303
- *Nationalities*
Calverton — *Awake.* p.288

- *Plantations and planters. See*
  Plantations and planters—South Carolina
- *Proprietary conflicts*
  Nettels — *Roots* p.339-342
- *Settlements*
  Calverton — *Awake.* p.293
  Craven — *Colonies* p.97-99
- *Spanish conflict, in Florida*
  Chitwood — *History (1)* p.190-191

SOUTHWORTH, ALICE. *See* **Bradford, Alice Carpenter Southworth**

SOUTHWORTH, CONSTANT
  Willison — *Pilgrim* p.235, 451n, 510
  Willison — *Saints. See* index p.509

SOUTHWORTH, EDWARD
  Hills — *History (1)* p.64, 116
  Hills — *History (2)* p.40-41, 98-100, 105, 156, 167, 205, 212
  Willison — *Pilgrim* p.84, 514
  Willison — *Saints* p.88, 127, 464

SOUTHWORTH, ELIZABETH COLLIER
  Willison — *Pilgrim* p.450n-451n
  Willison — *Saints* p.452-453

SOUTHWORTH, MARY COLLIER. *See* **Prence, Mary Collier Southworth**

SOUTHWORTH, THOMAS (the younger)
  Willison — *Pilgrim* p.235, 510, 514
  Willison — *Saints. See* index p.509-510

SOUTHWORTH FAMILY
  Caffrey — *Mayflower* p.61, 185-186, 281, 306
  Hills — *History (1)* p.64, 83, 85-86, 116
  Hills — *History (2). See* index p.274

SOWAMS (SOWAMET), RHODE ISLAND (Barrington, R.I.)
  Beck — *Pilgrims* p.39-40
  Dillon — *Pilgrims* p.212-213
  Vaughan — *New* p.73-74, 80, 118, 214
  Willison — *Pilgrim* p.134, 139-141, 209-214
  Willison — *Saints. See* index p.510

SPAIN AND SPANIARDS
  Amer. Her. — *Thirteen. See* index p. 383

Craven — *Southern. See* index p.448
Hawke — *Colonial* p.21-31; *See also* index p.763
Pomfret — *Founding* p.1-2, 5-8, 10, 14, 17-18, 311-312, 318-322
Starkey — *Land. See* index p.273-274

- *Women*
  Williams — *Demeter's* p.17-18

SPARROW (ship)
  Archer — *Mayflower* p.296-297
  Caffrey — *Mayflower* p.165-166
  Willison — *Pilgrim* p.178-179
  Willison — *Saints* p.204-205, 208, 446, 454

SPARROWHAWK (ship)
  Caffrey — *Mayflower* p.216-217
  Gill — *Mayflower* p.114-115
  Marshall — *Mayflower* p.163, 166
  Morison — *Story* p.115-117

SPEEDWELL (ship)
  Beck — *Pilgrims* p.11-13
  Caffrey — *Mayflower* p. 63-65, 80, 86-88, 98-99, 101-104
  Dillon — *Pilgrims* p.117-121
  Gill — *Mayflower* p.39-41, 43-48, 57-58, 123
  Leynse — *Preced.* p.11, 15, 17, 28, 233, 236-241, 244-245
  Marshall — *Mayflower* p.31-32, 49
  Morison — *Story* p.20, 23-24, 86
  Willison — *Pilgrim* p.74-88
  Willison — *Saints. See* index p.510

- *Passengers*
  Caffrey — *Mayflower* p.353-355

SPICES
  Adams — *Album* p.119

SPINNING
  Adams — *Album* p.114-115
  Drepperd — *Pioneer* p.87
  Earle — *Colonial* p.310
  Glubok — *Home* p.233-236, 238, 246-250
  Gould — *Early* p.128
  Hope — *Nation* p.90
  Speare — *Life* p.78-79

- *Connecticut*
  Fisher — *Men (1)* p.273-274
- *New England*
  Tunis — *Colonial* p.46-50

SPINSTERS
See also **Plymouth — Spinsters**
Earle — *Customs* p.38-39
Holliday — *Woman's* p. 262-263
Spruill — *Women's* p.138-139
Williams — *Demeter's* p.188

SPITS (for roasting)
Dow — *Domestic* p.18
Gould — *Early* p.70-72

SPOONS
See also **Indians — Spoons; Plymouth — Spoons**
Earle — *Customs* p.135-136
Earle — *Home* p.87-90
Gould — *Early* p.87-88

SPORTS AND GAMES
See also **Amusements; Indians — Sports and games; Plymouth — Sports and games; Women — Sports and games;** names of sports and games; special subjects
Clark — *Old* p.36-37
Dow — *Every* p.110-112
Drepperd — *Pioneer* p. 97-98
Earle — *Customs* p.234-241
Miller — *First* p.84-93
Speare — *Life* p.156
Wertenbaker — *First* p.191, 197, 269-270, 273, 275
Wish — *Society (1)* p.46, 80-81, 100
Wright — *Everyday* p.186-191
- *Boston, Mass.*
  Clark — *Old* p.35-37
- *Boys*
  Rawson — *When* p.79-109
, *Children's*
  Beck — *Pilgrims* p.74
  Glubok — *Home* p.171-191
  Speare — *Life* p.103-104
- *Connecticut*
  Fisher — *Men (1)* p.271
, *Dutch*
  Glubok — *Home* p.188-189
- *"I catch you without green"*
  Glubok — *Home* p.184-185
- *South*
  Wertenbaker — *First* p.262-267
- *Virginia*
  Calverton — *Awake.* p.212-213
  Clark — *Old* p.13-15, 20-24

SPRAGUE, FRANCIS
Willison — *Saints* p.235, 321-322, 450, 457

SPRAGUE, JOHN
Willison — *Saints* p.231-322, 450

SPRING
Gould — *Early* p.108-128

SPRINGFIELD, MASSACHUSETTS
Bailyn — *New England* p.29-30, 53-55, 60
Pomfret — *Founding* p.210, 240-242
- *Articles of Agreement (1636)*
  Demos — *Remarkable* p.53-56

SPRY, MRS.
Williams — *Demeter's* p.174

SQUANTO (Indian)
Alderman — *Story* p.23, 25
Amer. Her. — *Thirteen* p.87, 90
Archer — *Mayflower* p.190-197, 203
Beck — *Pilgrims* p.22-23, 34, 38-39, 41-42, 45, 48, 61, 77
Caffrey — *Mayflower. See* index p.391
Dillon — *Pilgrim* p.154-157, 159-160, 163, 168-171, 174-175
Earle — *Home* p.117, 130
Marshall — *Mayflower* p.134-136, 138, 140-141, 148-149, 153, 155
Morison — *Story* p.70-74, 77-81, 88-89, 92, 125, 181, 238
Phillips — *First* p.99-100
Rozwenc — *Making (1)* p.26, 29
Snell — *Wild* p.99, 106, 108, 110
Starkey — *Land* p.59-61
Vaughan — *New* p.22-23, 44, 54, 60, 68, 70-71, 73-74, 76-83, 241, 325
Willison — *Pilgrim* p.134, 137-139, 141, 144-145, 174-177
- *Death*
  Archer — *Mayflower* p.309-311
, *Loss of*
  Willison — *Pilgrim* p.199-201
- *Power*
  Archer — *Mayflower* p.272-281
- *Rescue, by Standish*
  Archer — *Mayflower* p.238-244
- *Treachery*
  Archer — *Mayflower* p.282-289, 290—296

SQUASHES
- *Names*
  Earle — *Home* p.144

"SQUAW SACHEM" (of Mass.)
Williams — *Demeter's* p.12, 14

STAGECOACHES AND STAGE LINES
Lawrence — *New* p.77-80

STAMFORD, CONNECTICUT (Toquams)
Pomfret — *Founding* p.264-266, 270, 273

"STANDING SALT" (salt bowl)
- *Below the salt*
  Woodward — *Way* p.28

STANDISH, ALEXANDER
Willison — *Pilgrim* p.507-508
Willison — *Saints* p.336

STANDISH, BARBARA
Marble — *Women* p.37, 98-100
Willison — *Pilgrim* p.236, 507
Willison — *Saints* p.235, 314, 335-336, 442, 448

STANDISH, MILES, CAPTAIN
Alderman — *Story* p.22-23
Amer. Her. — *Pioneer* p.59
Amer. Her. — *Thirteen* p.90-91, 93, 95, 97, 145-146
Beck — *Pilgrims* p.12, 25, 32-34, 41, 48-52
Caffrey — *Mayflower. See* index p.391
Dillon — *Pilgrims. See* index p.249-250
Hills — *History (1). See* index p.175
Hills — *History (2)* p.66, 99, 102, 132, 141, 145
Leynse — *Preced.* p.215-216, 246, 253, 256-257, 261-263
Marble — *Women* p.12, 28-29, 37, 45-46, 48, 55, 98-100
Marshall — *Mayflower* p.23, 27, 31, 107, 114, 120, 135, 153, 155, 167-168, 181, 184
Morison — *Story. See* index p.vi
Rozwenc — *Making (1)* p.28
Snell — *Wild* p.101, 106, 108, 110-111
Starkey — *Land* p.60-61, 92
Vaughan — *New* p.68, 71, 76, 80, 85-87, 89, 139, 169, 239
Willison — *Pilgrim. See* index p.583
Willison — *Saints. See* index p.510
, *as soldier*
  Archer — *Mayflower* p.86-87
- *Death (1656)*
  Willison — *Pilgrim* p.506-508
  Willison — *Saints* p.335

- *Indian relations*
  Archer — *Mayflower* p.316-324, 331-341
- *Inventory*
  Marshall — *Mayflower* p.114-117

STANDISH, ROSE
Willison — *Pilgrim* p.91, 125, 536
Willison — *Saints* p.132, 166, 235, 442, 448

STANDISH FAMILY
Hills — *History (1). See* index p.175
Hills — *History (2). See* index p.274
Marble — *Women* p.8, 12, 44, 54, 98-100

STAPLE ACT OF 1663
Rozwenc — *Making (1)* p.80-81

STARBUCK, MARY COFFIN
Williams — *Demeter's* p.129-130

STARCH
Gould — *Early* p.92-93

STARESMORE, SABIN
Willison — *Pilgrim* p.55-56
Willison — *Saints* p.108, 110

STATE HOUSE (later Independence Hall)
Collins — *Story* p.66

STEINWYCK, CORNELIUS
Earle — *Two cent. (1)* p.xix, 232, 234

STEVENSON, MARMADUKE
Wertenbaker — *Puritan* p.234-236

STEWART'S TOWN, SOUTH CAROLINA
Chitwood — *History (1)* p.188-189

STOCK MARKET
- *Collapse (1641)*
  Willison — *Pilgrim* p.448-450

STOCKS AND PILLORY
Lawrence — *Not* p.135-136
Wertenbaker — *First* p.220, 225

STODDARD, MRS. SIMEON
Earle — *Two cent. (1)* p.xv, 75-76

STODDARD, SOLOMON
Tyler — *History* p.407-408

STONE, JOHN
Vaughan — *New* p.123-126, 128-129

STONE, VERLINDA BURDETTE BREWSTER
Earle — *Colonial* p.49

STONE, WILLIAM
Craven — *Southern* p.234, 257-261, 297
Pomfret — *Founding* p.94, 96-99

STONE
See also **Houses, Stone**
, *as building materials*
Langdon — *Everyday* p.15

STOUGHTON, ISRAEL
, *on evolution of government*
Vaughan — *Puritan* p.151-156

STOUGHTON, WILLIAM, LIEUT. GENERAL
Morison — *Intellect.* p.76n, 200, 260, 264-265
Rothbard — *Conceived (1)* p.461-463; *See also* index p.529
Tyler — *History* p.400-402
Wertenbaker — *Puritan* p.272, 282-283, 320-321, 325

STOVES
See also **Footstoves**
Furnas — *Americans* p.162-163

STRACHEY, WILLIAM
Tyler — *History* p.37-40

"STRANGERS" (passengers on ships)
Alderman — *Story* p.20-21
Willison — *Saints. See* index p.510

STRANGERS (wayfarers)
- *Prohibitions against "(Warning out")*
Bridenbaugh — *Cities* p.46, 79-80
Earle — *Home* p.392-394
Glubok — *Home* p.314-315
Wertenbaker — *First* p.112

STRAW
, *Manufacture of*
Earle — *Home* p.259-260
Earle — *Two cent. (2)* p.569-470

STRAWBERRY BANK (PORTSMOUTH), NEW HAMPSHIRE
Alderman — *Story* p.39-42, 44-45

STREETS
Bridenbaugh — *Cities* p.17-19
Earle — *Home* p.362-363
- *Charlestown*
Bridenbaugh — *Cities* p.12-13
- *Philadelphia, Pa.*
Bridenbaugh — *Cities* p.13

STUBBS, PHILIP
, *on clothing and dress*
Earle — *Two cent. (1)* p.13-19

STUDLEY, DANIEL
Willison — *Pilgrim* p.33-35
Willison — *Saints. See* index p.510

STUYVESANT, PETER
Alderman — *Story* p.49, 51-54, 60-61, 103, 106
Amer. Her. — *Pioneer* p.68-70, 72
Amer. Her. — *Thirteen* p.131, 133-136
Bailey — *American (1)* p.38-40
Christensen — *Delaware* p.40-48
Collins — *Story* p.60-61
Craven — *Colonies* p.31, 60-62, 66, 70-71, 73
Fisher — *Men (2)* p.50-51, 60-61, 65-67, 70, 75, 108-109, 117
Folsom — *Give* p.24-26,53
Hawke — *Colonial* p.190, 219-221, 228, 240
Jernegan — *American* p.199
Johnston — *Conn.* p.69-72, 85
Morris — *Ency.* p.43
National — *History.* p.96-97, 99
Pomfret — *Founding* p.295-299
Rothbard — *Conceived (1)* p.235, 297, 308-310, 312-315, 317-320, 322-324, 332
Snell — *Wild* p.140-141
Starkey — *Land. See* index p.274
Wish — *Society (1)* p.93-94, 102
- *Administration*
Chitwood — *History (1)* p.168-170
, *and religion*
Wright — *Cultural* p.86-87
- *Views of Henry Hudson*
Bailey — *American (1)* p.38-39

SUDBURY, MASSACHUSETTS
Woodward — *Way* p.38-69

SUFFRAGE
See also **Women — Suffrage**
Bailyn — *New England* p.107, 115-
116, 124-125, 139, 159
Carman — *History (1)* p.128-130
Chitwood — *History (1)* p. 156-158
Craven — *Colonies* p.28, 48, 52-53,
76-77, 92, 102. 179, 187, 195-196,
209, 220-221
Pomfret — *Founding. See* index p.380
Wertenbaker — *Puritan. See* index
p.350
- *Ballots, corn and beans*
Earle — *Home* p.141
- *Dedham, Mass.*
Lockridge — *New* p.47-49
- *Laws*
Adams — *Provincial* p.19-21

SUGAR
See also **Maple sugar; Plymouth —
Sugar**
Amer. Her. — *Thirteen* p.27, 44, 154,
179
Bailyn — *New England* p.83, 85, 101,
129-130, 149-150, 152, 182, 187
Craven — *Colonies* p.35-37, 55, 98
Craven — *Southern. See* index p.449
Gould — *Early* p.86
Morison — *Story* p.114, 131-132, 189,
229
- *Cutting of sugar loaf*
Earle — *Home* p.155-156
- *South*
Craven — *South. See* index p.449

SUGAR BOWLS
Gould — *Early* p.86-87

SUMMER
Gould — *Early* p.128-133

**SUMPTUARY LAWS (fancy-clothing
restrictions)**
Bridenbaugh — *Cities* p.97
Earle — *Customs* p.316
- *Massachusetts*
Earle — *Home* p.281-284
- *New England*
Annals of America (1) p.210-211
Jernegan — *American* p.179-180
- *Northampton, Mass.*
Earle — *Home* p.283-284

SUNDAY. *See* **Sabbath**

SUNDIALS
Earle — *Home* p.442-443

SUPERNATURAL
See also **Witchcraft**
Demos — *Remarkable* p.349-380
Wertenbaker — *First. See* index p.355
Wertenbaker — *Puritan. See* index
p.357

SUPERSTITIONS
Glubok — *Home* p.300-301
- *Pennsylvania*
Clark — *Old* p.74-75
- *Puritans*
Fisher — *Men (1)* p.165

SUPPERS. *See* **Dinners**

SURGERY
- *Instruments*
Marshall — *Mayflower* p.132

SURNAMES. *See* **Names**

"SURPRISE PARTIES"
Rawson — *When* p.92-93

SURVEYORS
Craven — *Southern* p.278-279, 293,
326, 349
- *South*
Craven — *Southern* p.278-279,
295, 326, 349

SUSAN CONSTANT (ship)
Hawke — *Colonial* p.89
Phillips — *First* p.82-83, 87, 89, 154-
155

SUSQUEHANNA INDIANS
Craven — *Colonies* p.107, 114, 124-
128, 131, 134
Craven — *Southern* p.232, 373-374,
380-381, 392
Folsom — *Give* p.46-47
Goodwin — *Colonial* p.127-128
Smith — *17th* p.42, 53-55
Starkey — *Land* p.133, 123, 201
- *South*
Craven — *Southern* p.232, 373-
374, 380-381, 392

"SWAN"
Dillon — *Pilgrims* p.172, 174-175, 179-
180

"SWAN" (*continued*)
Gill — *Mayflower* p.96, 98, 100
Morison — *Story* p.90
Willison — *Pilgrim* p.241n
Willison — *Saints* p.207, 210-214, 219, 226, 228, 239, 446

SWANSEA, MASSACHUSETTS
Willison — *Saints* p.357-358, 390, 396, 439, 443, 451-452

SWEARING. *See* Profanity

SWEDISH
See also **New Sweden; Women, Swedish and Finnish**
Acheson — *America's* p.127-129
Alderman — *Story* p.61, 65, 103-104, 111, 113
Amer. Her. — *Thirteen* p.116, 128, 134-136, 172
Calverton — *Awake.* p.358-359
Carman — *History (1)* p.16, 45
Nettels — *Roots* p.198-200
Pomfret — *Founding* p.292-296
Wish — *Society (1)* p.101-102
Wright — *Cultural* p.50-51
- *Delaware*
Bailyn — *New England* p.51-52, 57
Calverton — *Awake.* p.364-369
National — *History.* p.102
- *New York*
Fisher — *Men (2)* p.35-36

SWEDISH SOUTH COMPANY
Chesterton — *Delaware* p.18

SWEEP AND MORTAR MILLS
Glubok — *Home* p.73-74

SWEETS
See also **Maple sugar; Sugar**
Earle — *Custom* p.25
Glubok — *Home* p.86-88

SWISS
Alderman — *Story* p.119, 127

"SWITCHELL" (mild drink)
Earle — *Customs* p.173

SYMMS (SYMES) SCHOOL
Monroe — *Founding (1)* p.65
Wertenbaker — *Old* p.25

SYMONDS, REBEKAH
Earle — *Two cent. (1)* p.140-159

SYMONDS, SAMUEL
Marshall — *Mayflower* p.68

SYMONDS, WILLIAM
"Britain's claim. . . . justified" (1609)
Annals of America (1) p.32-35

SYMONSON, MOSES. *See* **Simmons, Moses**

SYNODS
Rutman — *Winthrop's. See* index p.320
Sweet — *Religion* p.108-109
Vaughan — *Puritan* p.305-313
Wertenbaker — *Puritan. See* index p.357

T

TABLECLOTHS AND LINEN
See also **"Board-Cloths"**
Earle — *Customs* p.132-142
- *Plymouth*
Demos — *Little* p.37-38, 42

TABLES
Gould — *Early* p.83-85
Langdon — *Everyday* p.26-27
, *Hutch*
Gould — *Early* p.84

TABLEWARE
See also **Pewter and pewterers; Silverware: Tinware and tinsmiths; names of tableware**
Clark — *Old* p.7-8
Glubok — *Home* p.42, 47
Marshall — *Mayflower* p.99-100
Spruill — *Women's* p.25
Woodward — *Way* p.55
- *Jamestown*
Adams — *Album* p.29

TAHATAWAN (Indian)
Beals — *John Eliot* p.133

TAILORS AND TAILORING
Tunis — *Craftsmen* p.37
- *Ipswich, Mass.*
Demos — *Remarkable* p.79-88

- *Work and prices*
  Earle — *Two cent. (1)* p.91-92,
     95-96

TALBOT (ship)
  Willison — *Pilgrim* p.313, 316-317,
     546
  Willison — *Saints* p.267-270,346, 454,
     458, 461
- *Food supplies*
  Dow — *Every* p.5, 11-12

TALON, JEAN
  Chitwood — *History (1)* p.300-301

TAMBOUR WORK (embroidery)
  Rawson — *When* p.135-136

TANKARDS
  Earle — *Home* p.83-84, 99

TANNERS AND TANNING
  See also **Leather**
  Christensen — *Delaware* p.86-88
  Rutman — *Withrop's* p.188, 197-200,
     207, 247
  Tunis — *Craftsmen* p.32-34

TAR
  Craven — *Southern* p.35, 48, 69, 140-
     141, 313n
  Earle — *Home* p.33
  Glubok — *Home* p.16-17
  Marshall — *Mayflower* p.171

TARENTINE (TARRANTINE) INDIANS.
  See **Abnaki Indians**

TARTS
  Gould — *Early* p.94

"TASTERS" (small cups)
  Earle — *Customs* p.137
  Earle — *Home* p.86-87

TAUNTON, MASSACHUSETTS
  Morison — *Story* p.153, 162, 180, 207-
     208, 226-227, 239, 248-249, 257,
     286-287, 291

TAVERNS
  See also **Inns and innkeepers;**
     Jamestown — Taverns; Plym-
     outh — Taverns
  Adams — *Album* p.109
  Bridenbaugh — *Cities* p.107-115

Chitwood — *History (1)* p.388-389
Earle — *Customs* p.193-196
Earle — *Home* p.356-357, 360-361
Glubok — *Home* p.346-347
Miller — *First* p.127-130
Morrison — *Early* p.91-92
Speare — *Life* p.48-49, 149-153
Wertenbaker — *First* p.196, 201-203,
     299-301
Woodward — *Way* p.13-14, 66
- *Boston, Mass.*
  Wertenbaker — *First* p.299-300
- *Hostesses*
  Dexter — *Colonial* p.1-6
- *Keepers, Typical*
  Wertenbaker — *First* p.299-300
- *New England*
  Wertenbaker — *First* p.299-300
- *South*
  Wertenbaker — *First* p.300-301
- *Women*
  Dexter — *Colonial* p.1-6
  Leonard — *Dear* p.426-428, 435-
     436
  Spruill — *Women's* p.295

TAXATION
  See also **Plymouth — Taxation**
  Carman — *History (1)* p.53, 126-127
  Craven — *Colonies* p.29, 130, 138,
     154, 201, 219-220
  Craven — *Southern. See* index p.449
  Folsom — *Give* p.44-45, 76
  Pomfret — *Founding* p.46, 61, 174-
     175, 205, 271, 289, 315
  Rutman — *Winthrop's. See* index
     p.320
  Willison — *Pilgrim* p.382
- *Boston*
  Rutman — *Winthrop's. See* index
     p.320
- *Collectors*
  Folsom — *Give* p.66, 71, 73-77
- *Dedham, Mass.*
  Lockridge — *New* p.16, 65, 73,
     81, 86
- *Midwout, N.Y.*
  - *Rate list (1683)*
    Demos — *Remarkable*
       p.201-202
, *Poll*
  Nettels — *Roots* p.333
- *South*
  Craven — *Southern. See* index
     p.449

TAXATION (*continued*)
- *Virginia*
  Calverton — *Awake.* p.228-229
- *Watertown, Mass.*
  , *Resistance to*
  Wertenbaker — *First* p.95-96

TAYLOR, EDWARD
Miller — *Colonial* p.367-369
Morison — *Intellect,* p.15, 235-240
Murdock — *Literature* p.19, 150, 152-171; *See also* index p.234

TEA
Earle — *Home* p.164-165
Glubok — *Home* p.92-93
Miller — *First* p.188

TEACH, EDWARD ("Blackbeard")
National — *History.* p.116-117

TEACHERS
See also **Tutors**
Dexter — *Colonial* p.78-80
Monroe — *Founding* p.131-132, 134
Rawson — *When* p.162-163, 168
Speare — *Life* p.108
Wright — *Everyday* p.139
- *Braintree, Mass.*
  Morison — *Intellect.* p.96-97
, *Dutch*
  Glubok — *Home* p.119-120
- *Flatbush, L. I.*
  Glubok — *Home* p.119-120
- *New York*
  Clark — *Old* p.60-61
- *Puritans*
  Earle — *Customs* p.33-34
- *Salaries*
  Morison — *Intellect.* p.93-95, 104
- *"School dames"*
  Monroe — *Founding (1)* p.132
, *Scottish*
  Glubok — *Home* p.119
- *Selection*
  Wertenbaker — *Puritan* p.143-144
- *Women. See* **Teachers — "School dames"**

TEETH
See also **Dentistry**
- *Women*
  Miller — *First* p.247

TEMPERANCE
- *Maryland*
  Wertenbaker — *First* p.201
- *Virginia*
  Wertenbaker — *First* p.200-201

"TEST ACT" (religion, N.Y., 1691)
Craven — *Colonies* p.106, 163, 223
Sweet — *Religion* p.36

TEXTBOOKS
Chitwood — *History (1)* p.457-458
Glubok — *Home* p.138-140
Vaughan — *Puritan* p.242-244
- *Elementary schools*
  Morgan — *Puritan* p.56
- *Grammar schools*
  Morison — *Intellect.* p.79, 109-112

TEXTILES. *See* **Fabrics**

THAMAYEISON (Indian)
Northey — *American* p.8-9

THANKSGIVING DAY
Beck — *Pilgrims* p.43-44
Chitwood — *History (1)* p.489-490
Dillon — *Pilgrims* p.165-166, 168, 186-187
Earle — *Colonial* p.287-288
Gill — *Mayflower* p.92, 94
Marshall — *Mayflower* p.143
Miller — *First* p.85-86
Morison — *Story* p.82-84, 97
Rawson — *When* p.229-230
Snell — *Wild* p.108
Speare — *Life* p.159
Sweet — *Religion* p.115
Vaughan — *New* p.78
Wertenbaker — *First* p.273-274
Wish — *Society (1)* p.31-32
Wright — *Cultural* p.188
Wright — *Everyday* p.205-206
, *First*
  - *Monhegan Island, Me.*
    Earle — *Customs* p.216
    Mitchell — *It's* p.64
  - *Plymouth*
    Alderman — *Story* p.25
    Annals of America (1) p.69
    Archer — *Mayflower* p.254-257
    Caffrey — *Mayflower* p.152-153

Earle — *Customs* p.216-218
Hale — *Through* p.65-70
Hope — *Nation* p.78-79
Miller — *Colonial* p.63
Willison — *Pilgrim* p.152-153
Willison — *Saints* p.188-190
- *Public, Boston, Mass. (1630)*
Earle — *Customs* p.219-220
Wertenbaker — *First* p.273-274
, *Regular (Proclamation 1677, Mass.)*
Earle — *Customs* p.223
- *Indians*
Dillon — *Pilgrims* p.165-166
Gould — *Early* p.98
- *Green corn ceremony*
Northey — *American* p.57
- *Maple ceremony*
Northey — *America* p.73-74
- *Massachusetts*
Wertenbaker — *First* p.273-274
- *New England*
Holliday — *Woman's* p.203
- *Puritans*
Earle — *Customs* p.222-223
- *Stories of early celebrations*
- Earle — *Customs* p.222-223

THATCHING
See also **Tools, Thatching**
Marshall — *Mayflower* p.63, 81, 83, 87
Wertenbaker — *First* p.285-286

THEATER
Morris — *Ency.* p.589

THEOCRACY
Wertenbaker — *First. See* index p.355

- *Dissolution*
Rothbard — *Conceived (1)* p.251-253, 263-266
- *Massachusetts*
Rothbard — *Conceived (1)* p.174-181, 341-343

THEOLOGY. *See* **Religion; Religious writers**

THIEVES AND THIEVERY
Bridenbaugh — *Cities* p.69-70
Vaughan — *New. See* index p.429

THOMAS, GABRIEL
Tyler — *History* p.458-461

- *"An historical and geographical account of . . . New Jersey" (1698)*
Amer. Her. — *Thirteen* p.150-151
, *on Pennsylvania*
Axtell — *America* p.186-193

THOMAS, WILLIAM
Willison — *Saints* p.315, 409, 420, 453, 456

THOMPSON (TOMSON), BENJAMIN
Morison — *Intellect.* p.228-230
Tyler — *History* p.272-276
- *"New England's crisis" (1675)*
Annals of America (1) p.245-247

THOMPSON, DAVID
Alderman — *Story* p.37-38
Gill — *Mayflower* p.103, 106, 114, 119
Willison — *Saints* p.249-250, 279, 297

THORPE, GEORGE
Starkey — *Land* p.62-64, 198

"THREE RIVER TOWNS"
See also **Hartford, Wethersfield, Windsor, Conn.**
Johnston — *Conn.* p.20, 32-36

"THREE SISTERS" (Indian corn, squash and beans)
Northey — *American* p.57

THRESHING
Earle — *Home* p.313-314
Gould — *Early* p.133

THRIFT
Earle — *Home* p.321-324

TICKENS, JANE WHITE
Willison — *Saints* p.86, 106

TICKENS, RALPH
Willison — *Saints* p.88, 106, 341

TILLAM, THOMAS
Vaughan — *Puritan* p.63-64

TILLEY, BRIDGET VAN DER VELDE
Willison — *Saints* p.90, 122, 410, 439, 486

TILLEY, EDWARD
Hills — *History (1)* p.21, 34, 37, 40,
43-44, 53, 59-60, 67, 69-71, 119
Hills — *History (2)* p.162, 220
Leynse — *Preced.* p.256-257, 267
Willison — *Pilgrim* p.105, 110, 533
Willison — *Saints* p.122, 148, 153,
439, 441

TILLEY, ELIZABETH. *See* Howland,
Elizabeth Tilley

TILLEY, JOHN
Caffrey — *Mayflower* p.41, 54, 117,
124, 140, 312
Hills — *History (1)* p.21, 34, 37-38, 40,
43-44, 59-60, 69, 71, 119
Leynse — *Preced.* p.257, 267
Willison — *Pilgrim* p.110, 533
Willison — *Saints* p.90, 122, 153, 439,
441

TILLEY FAMILY
Caffrey — *Mayflower* p.391
Hills — *History (1).* *See* index p.175
Hills — *History (2)* p.162, 220
Marble — *Women* p.12, 59

TILLY, ALICE
Williams — *Demeter's* p.171

TIMBER *See* Forest; Lumbering; Wood

TIMUCUA INDIANS
Folsom — *Give* p.3-5

"TIN KITCHENS" (ovens)
Earle — *Colonial* p.286-287

TINDERBOXES
Dow — *Domestic* p.18
Earle — *Home* p.48-50
Glubok — *Home* p.25
Gould — *Early* p.66

TINKERS
Tunis — *Craftsmen* p.38

TINWARE AND TINSMITHS
Drepperd — *Pioneer* p.178-179
Earle — *Customs* p.142

TIPSTAVES
Glubok — *Home* p.346-347

TISQUANTUM. *See* Squanto

TITHABLES
Craven — *Southern* p.165, 219, 302n

TITHING-MEN (Sunday policemen)
Earle — *Home* p.372-373
Lawrence — *Not* p.128-132
Morgan — *Puritan* p.87-88

TITUBA (Barbadian slave)
Folsom — *Give* p.81-83, 87
Williams — *Demeter's* p.150

TOASTERS
Gould — *Early* p.79

TOBACCO
See also **Puritans — Tobacco ban**
Alderman — *Story* p.11-24
Bailyn — *New England* p.85-86, 101,
127, 130, 144-145, 147-151, 164,
182
Caffrey — *Mayflower* p.21, 258
Carman — *History (1)* p.65-67
Craven — *Colonies* p.19, 35, 37-40,
55, 129, 155, 230
Craven — *Southern. See* index p.449
Folsom — *Give* p.9-10, 44-45, 47, 75-
77
Furnas — *Americans* p.25, 35-36, 41,
43
Langdon — *Everyday* p.313
Leonard — *Dear* p.158-159
Miller — *First* p.242-243
Morris — *Ency.* p.25-30, 477, 517
Nettels — *Roots* p.231
Pomfret — *Founding* p.34-35, 43-45,
47, 50, 53, 57-58, 61, 85, 87, 208,
230, 272, 300, 308, 310, 314, 317
Scott — *Settlers* p.92-96
Smith — *17th* p.49, 83n, 97, 121, 128,
132, 222
Snell — *Wild* p.92, 94, 127, 131
Starkey — *Land* p.13, 41, 76-77, 119
Wertenbaker — *First. See* index p.355
, and James I
Phillips — *First* p.193
- English import
Goetzman — *Colonial* p.126-127
- Festivals. See **Indians — Festivals**
- Jamestown
Adams — *Album* p.19-20
- Maryland
Starkey — *Land* p.119
Wertenbaker — *First* p.6, 12-13
- North Carolina
Calverton — *Awake.* p.301

- *South*
  Craven — *Southern. See* index
  p.449
  Jernegan — *American* p.89-90,
  95
  Tunis — *Colonial* p.76-79
  Wertenbaker — *Old* p.10
- *Trade*
  Hawke — *U.S.* p.84-85
  Nettels — *Roots* p.252-258
- *Virginia*
  Calverton — *Awake.* p.232-237
  Fisher — *Men (1)* p.32-33, 45-46,
  110-111
  Morison — *Oxford* p.52
  Pomfret — *Founding* p.34-35, 43-
  44, 57-58, 70
  Starkey — *Land* p.76-77
- *"Plant-cutters' rebellion"*
  Calverton — *Awake.* p.235-
  237
  Chitwood — *History (1)* p.79

TOKAMAHAMON (Indian)
  Marshall — *Mayflower* p.141
  Vaughan — *New* p.75-76

TOLERANCE
  See also **Toleration Act of 1649;**
  Women — Tolerance
  Abbot — *Colonial* p.94-96
  Annals of America (1) p.87-91
  Bailyn — *New England* p.106-108
  Carman — *History (1)* p.92
  Chitwood — *History (1)* p.435-436
  Hall — *Religious* p.127-146
  Hope — *Nation* p.114
  Smith — *17th* p.167-168, 174, 215
  Wertenbaker — *First* p.89-90, 92, 98,
  238-239
  Wertenbaker — *Puritan* p.32-33, 75,
  208-215
  Willison — *Pilgrim. See* index p.583
  Willison — *Saints. See* index p.511

  , *Doctrine of*
  Wish — *Society (1)* p.36-38, 77-
  78, 88, 91
- *Holland*
  Sweet — *Religion* p.185-189
- *Maryland*
  Hall — *Religious* p.134-135
  Hope — *Nation* p.94
- *Massachusetts*
  , *Opposition*
  Wertenbaker — *First* p.89-92

- *New Jersey*
  Calverton — *Awake.* p.376-378
- *North Carolina*
  Calverton — *Awake.* p.285-288
- *Views of Roger Williams*
  Miller — *Colonial* p.169-174

TOMBSTONES
  Earle — *Customs* p.381-384
- *Inscriptions*
  See also **Epitaphs**
  Goodwin — *Colonial* p.297-299

TOMOCHICHI (Indian)
  Starkey — *Land* p.245, 252

TOMPSON. *See* **Thompson**

TOOLS
  See also **Farm implements**
  Adams — *Album* p.118
  , *Boring*
  Marshall — *Mayflower* p.73
  , *Carpenter's*
  Marshall — *Mayflower* p.73
  , *Garden*
  Marshall — *Mayflower* p.144-145
  , *Harvesting*
  Marshall — *Mayflower* p.92
  , *Household*
  See also **Kitchen utensils**
  Marshall — *Mayflower* p.93
  , *Sharpening*
  Marshall — *Mayflower* p.81, 85
- *Storage*
  Marshall — *Mayflower* p.105
  , *Thatching*
  Marshall — *Mayflower* p.87
- *Woodworking*
  Marshall — *Mayflower* p.70-71,
  77

TOQUAMS, CONNECTICUT. *See*
  Stamford, Connecticut

TORREY, SAMUEL
  Wertenbaker — *Puritan* p.71, 148-
  149, 170-171, 203, 215, 223, 280,
  314-315

TOWN BROOK (in Plymouth)
  Morison — *Story* p.54, 57-58, 62, 72-
  74, 112, 190n

TOWN CRIERS
- *Boston, Mass.*
  Lawrence — *New* p.212-213

TOWN MEETINGS
Craven — *Colonies* p.17-20, 24-25, 77, 95, 220
Rutman — *Winthrop's* p.61-61n, 64, 66, 81, 160, 162, 197, 232
- *Dedham, Mass. (1636–86)*
Lockridge — *New* p.37-56
- *Democracy*
Speare — *Life* p.39-40
- *New England*
Abbot — *Colonial* p.48-49
Jernegan — *American* p.168
Speare — *Life* p.39-40
- *Origin*
Willison — *Pilgrim* p.101
- *Salem, Mass.*
Gildrie — *Salem* p.42-44, 46, 148-149, 153-154

TOWN SCHOOLS
- *Compulsory system*
- *Massachusetts (1647)*
Monroe — *Founding (1)* p.109-110
- *New England*
Monroe — *Founding (1)* p.105-118, 130-135
- *Control*
Monroe — *Founding (1)* p.114-116
- *Free school development*
Monroe — *Founding (1)* p.110-114
- *Taxation*
Monroe — *Founding (1)* p.112-114

"TOWN WATCHES"
- *Boston, Mass.*
Lawrence — *New* p.138-141

TOWNS
See also **Town meetings**
Chitwood — *History (1)* p.152-153
Morrison — *Early* p.50-51
Rutman — *Winthrop's. See* index p.321
Wertenbaker — *Puritan. See* index p.358

, *as settlement pattern*
Crane — *Southern* p.55, 88n, 95, 122, 129-132, 312-313, 342, 347-349, 352-353
- *Character and relation to trade*
Bailyn — *New England* p.96-98

- *Development*
Carman — *History (1)* p.108-110
- *General courts*
Hawke — *Colonial* p.152-153
- *Government*
Demos — *Remarkable* p.194-199
Rutman — *Winthrop's. See* index p.321
- *Life*
Chitwood — *History (1)* p.478-480
Hawke — *Colonial* p.151-154, 281-285
- *New England*
Tunis — *Colonial* p.55-56
Ver Steeg — *Formative* p.58
- *Massachusetts*
Jernegan — *American* p.167-168

TOYS
See also **Dolls**
Drepperd — *Pioneer* p.116
Williams — *Demeter's* p.93

TRADE AND TRADERS
See also **Commerce; Indians — Trade; Industry; Plymouth — Trade; Puritans — Trade; Triangular Trade;** types of trade
Bailyn — *New England* p.32-33, 46, 59, 75, 89-91
Hope — *Nation* p.113
Rutman — *Winthrop's. See* Index p.321
Ver Steeg — *Formative* p. 63-65; *See also* index p.341

, *Aristocracy of*
Wright — *Cultural* p.30-38
, *Balance of*
Bailyn — *New England* p.13, 62, 66, 77, 100, 143, 182-183
- *Boston, Mass.*
Rutman — *Winthrop's* p.182-183, 187-188, 191, 194, 199-201, 248-249, 253-254
- *Chesapeake colonies*
Hawke — *Colonial* p.180-181
- *Conditions after 1660*
Bailyn — *New England* p.114-115
- *Extension in 1670's*
Bailyn — *New England* p.144-145
- *Influence on society*
Bailyn — *New England* p.75-76, 94-98, 134-135, 159

- *London complaints*
    Bailyn — *New England* p.152-153
- *Middle Colonies*
    Jernegan — *American* p.226-227
- *New England*
    Amer. Her. — *Thirteen* p.154-155
    Jernegan — *American* p.174-177
    Nettels — *Roots* p.258-260
    , *with Southern colonies*
        Craven — *Southern* p.184,
            240-241, 358, 401, 409
- *Orbits*
    Bailyn — *New England* p.58, 89,
        95, 98
- *Overseas*
    Morris — *Ency.* p.486
    , *Regulation of*
        Bailyn — *New England* p.126-
            127, 149
- *South*
    Jernegan — *American* p.93-95
- *Specialization*
    Bailyn — *New England* p.99-101
- *Trading posts*
    See also names of localities
    Willison — *Pilgrim. See* index
        p.583
    Willison — *Saints* p.295-297,
        299-304, 471

TRADES
See also **Crafts and craftsmen; Oc-
cupations;** names of trades
Dow — *Every* p.120-121
- *New England*
    Tunis — *Colonial* p.57-61

TRADITION
Rozwenc — *Making (1)* p.72-73

TRAFFIC
- *Boston, Mass.*
    Lawrence — *New* p.127-128

TRAILS
See also **Indian trails**
- *Footpaths*
    Glubok — *Home* p.332-333
    Speare — *Life* p.135-136

TRAIN BANDS. *See* Militia

"TRAINING DAY"
Beals — *John Eliot* p.105
Earle — *Customs* p.223-225

- *Boston, Mass.*
    Clark — *Old* p.38-39
    Wertenbaker — *First* p.275
- *Massachusetts*
    Wertenbaker — *First* p.274-275
- *New England*
    Wertenbaker — *First* p.274-275

TRAMMELS (fish-cooking holders)
Glubok — *Home* p.28-29, 31
Gould — *Early* p.79

TRAMPS
Speare — *Life* p.145

TRANSPORTATION
See also **Horses; Rivers; Travel and
travelers;** types of transportation
Wertenbaker — *First. See* index p.356

TRANTON, MARY
Williams — *Demeter's* p.32

TRAPPING. *See* Hunting and trapping

TRAVEL AND TRAVELERS
See also **Books and reading —
Travel;** names of travelers, types
of traveling and transportation
Earle — *Customs* p.184-186, 199-200
Wertenbaker — *First. See* index p.356
- *Massachusetts*
    Wertenbaker — *First* p.297-298
- *New England*
    Tunis — *Colonial* p.61-63
    , *Primitive*
        Lawrence — *New* p.61-68
- *Restrictions, legal*
    Vaughan — *New* p.95, 189, 197,
        330
    , *Sea*
        Speare — *Life* p.134
- *South*
    Goodwin — *Colonial* p.106-109
    , *Water, early means*
        Spruill — *Women's* p.88

TREATIES. *See* Indians — Treaties;
names of treaties

TREATY OF HARTFORD
Pomfret — *Founding* p.299-300
Vaughan — *New* p.150-151, 153, 170-
    170n, 178, 340

TREATY OF WESTMINSTER
Nettels — *Roots* p.345

TREES
See also **Wood;** types of trees
Adams — *Provincial* p.32-33
Rawson — *When* p.43-44
- *Blazing*
  Earle — *Home* p. 330
- *Debarking, by Indians*
  Marshall — *Mayflower* p.158
, *Early*
  Adams — *Album* p.28
- *Felling*
  Marshall — *Mayflower p.71, 77*
  , *by Indians*
    Marshall — *Mayflower* p.142
- *New England*
  Axtell — *America* p.23-26
- *New Netherland*
  Axtell — *America* p.33-37

TRENCHERS (wooden plates)
Earle — *Customs* p.138
Glubok — *Home* p.43-45

TRIALS
See also **Witchcraft — Trials**
Folsom — *Give* p.8, 16, 18, 21-22, 26, 28-29, 34, 49-50, 65, 69, 72, 77-78, 81, 83-92
Holliday — *Women's* p. 197-200

TRIANGULAR TRADE
- *Northern colonies*
  Morris — *Ency.* p.486
- *West Indies*
  Wish — *Society (1)* p.52

TRIBALISM
, *Puritans*
  Morgan — *Puritan* p.90-104

TRICO, CATALINA
Williams — *Demeter's* p.51-52

TRIVETS
Glubok — *Home* p.30-31

TRUNK-PEDDLERS. See **Chapmen**

TRYON, WILLIAM
Alderman — *Story* p.134-135

TUNXIS INDIANS
Hope — *Nation* p.83

TURKEYS
Earle — *Customs* p.154
Earle — *Home* p.109-110
Glubok — *Home* p.58-59
Gould — *Early* p.139
- *"Shoots"*
  Rawson — *When* p.90-92

TURNER, JOHN
Caffrey — *Mayflower* p.41, 54, 59, 140
Willison — *Saints* p.91, 123, 439

TURNER, NATHANIEL, CAPTAIN
Pomfret — *Founding* p.260, 264, 267-268, 293

"THE TURNER HOUSE." See **House of Seven Gables**

TUSCARORA INDIANS
Alderman — *Story* p.127-128
Phillips — *First* p.2-3, 44-45

TUTORS
Monroe — *Founding (1)* p.61
- *Fees*
  Morison — *Intellect.* p.76
- *Virginia*
  Jernegan — *American* p.107

TYNG(E), MERCY
Bailyn — *New England* p.137-138

TYNG(E), WILLIAM
Bailyn — *New England* p.36, 51, 61, 108, 110, 135
Rutman — *Winthrop's. See* index p.321
- *Largest estate (1653)*
  Wright — *Literary* p.37-38

TYNG(E) FAMILY
Bailyn — *New England* p.36-37, 135, 137-138

U

UNCAS (Indian)
Beals — *John Eliot* p.158
Caffrey — *Mayflower* p.265, 270-274
Johnston — *Conn.* p.21-26, 29, 31
Morison — *Story* p.213-214

Vaughan — *New* p.56, 141, 150, 155-
156, 159, 162-170, 172, 174, 177,
179, 181, 210, 258, 292-293, 301,
305, 314, 325
Willison — *Pilgrim* p.561-562

UNDERHILL, JOHN, CAPTAIN
Rutman — *Winthrop's* p.48n, 63, 74,
80, 123, 137, 174, 216-217, 225n
Vaughan — *New* p.102, 129, 139,
141-142, 145, 148

**"UNDERTAKERS" (Massachusetts Bay
Company)**
Bailyn — *New England* p.19, 26-27,
32, 76, 204 (n10), 206 (n39), 207
(n64)
Beck — *Pilgrims* p.52
Caffrey — *Mayflower* p.220-221
Morison — *Story* p.128-130, 134-137,
171, 218
- *Plymouth*
    Bailyn — *New England* p.10, 12-
    13, 23-26
    Willison — *Pilgrim* p.297-299,
    304, 307-308, 313n, 352, 379n,
    388n, 399n, 452-454

UNITED COLONIES OF NEW ENGLAND
See also **New England
Confederation**
Chitwood — *History (1)* p.139-140
Starkey — *Land* p.127-128, 170
Willison — *Pilgrim* p.477-480, 517-
522, 524-526, 559-562

UNITY (ship)
Willison — *Saints* p.273-274

UPPER CLASSES. *See* **Aristocracy**

URBAN PROBLEMS. *See* **Cities**

USHER, HEZEKIAH
Morison — *Intellect.* p.128, 130-131

USHER, JOHN
Bailyn — *New England* p.135, 137-
138, 175, 177, 190
Morison — *Intellect.* p.128, 130-131
Rothbard — *Conceived (1)* p.376-377,
415-416, 424, 428-429, 460, 464,
466-467, 472-474
Wertenbaker — *First* p.241, 247
- *Books imported (1679–85)*
    Wright — *Literary* p.120-123

USHER FAMILY
Bailyn — *New England* p.128, 135,
137

USSELINX, WILLIAM
Christensen — *Delaware* p.24
Jernegan — *American* p.201-202

USURY
Bailyn — *New England* p.21-22
- *Keayne's trial*
    Bailyn — *New England* p.41-44

UTTAMATOMAKKIN (Indian)
Starkey — *Land* p.43-44

V

**"VALLEY OF SWANS" (Zwaanendael,
Delaware)**
Christensen — *Delaware* p.18-20

VAN CORTLAND, STEPHANUS
Rothbard — *Conceived (1)* p.434-437,
445, 465, 468, 473

VAN CURLER, JACOB
Johnston — *Conn.* p.6-8

VAN DE DONCK, ADRIAEN
- *"Criticism of New Netherland"
(1650)*
    Annals of America (1) p.204-212
, *on New Netherland*
    Axtel — *America* p.33-51

VAN RENSSELAER, KILIAEN
Amer. Her. — *Pioneer* p.69
Fisher — *Men (2)* p.21-25, 50, 64, 93-
94, 99, 114

VAN TIENHOVEN, CORNELIUS
Jernegan — *American* p.199
- *"Information . . . . taking up land"*
    Demos — *Remarkable* p.44-52
- *"Report on agriculture in New Neth-
erland" (1650)*
    Amer. Her. — *Thirteen* p.141

VAN TWILLER, WOUTER
Fisher — *Men (2)* p.25-34
Hawke — *Colonial* p.218-219
Morris — *Ency.* p.42

VANDERDONCK, MARY
Williams — *Demeter's* p.174

VANE, HENRY (HARRY), SIR
Pomfret — *Founding* p.193-194, 210, 223, 259-261
Rothbard — *Conceived (1)* p.190-191, 203, 210-214, 228, 277
Starkey — *Land* p.94-95, 97, 99-100, 120, 134, 175
Wertenbaker — *First* p.100-101

VANITY
, *of clothing and dress — punishment*
Wertenbaker — *Puritan* p.166-168

VARKENS KILL (Salem, N.J.)
Pomfret — *Founding* p.267-268, 293-294

VASSALL, WILLIAM
Willison — *Pilgrim* p.492-498
Willison — *Saints* p.361, 475

VAUGHAN, WILLIAM
Bailyn — *New England* p.133, 138, 161, 190

VAUGHAN FAMILY
Bailyn — *New England* p.137

VEGETABLES
Adams — *Album* p.93
Furnas — *Americans* p.173-174
Gould — *Early* p.92
Leonard — *Dear* p.132-133
- *Cooking methods*
Glubok — *Home* p.29-30
- *Gardens*
Dow — *Domestic* p.7
Langdon — *Everyday* p.277-279

VEHICLES
See also **Transportation;** types of vehicles
Wertenbaker — *First* p.298-299

VEILS
Earle — *Two cent. (1)* p.67-68
, *Black*
Earle — *Two cent. (2)* p.658-659

VERMONT
- *New Hampshire graves*
Alderman — *Story* p.45-46

VERRAZANO, GIOVANNI DA
Christensen — *Delaware* p.10-11
Collins — *Story* p.74

VESTRIES
Smith — *17th* p.133, 136, 138, 183
Wertenbaker — *First* p.126-127, 129-131, 135-136
- *Virginia*
See also **Virginia — Parishes**
Sweet — *Religion* p.31-32

VICE-ADMIRALTY COURTS
Morris — *Ency.* p.58

VILLAGES
See also **Towns**
Wertenbaker — *Puritan. See* index p.358
- *Commercial expansion*
Bridenbaugh — *Cities* p.52-53
- *Economy*
Bridenbaugh — *Cities* p.26-54
Demos — *Remarkable* p.200-202
- *Engineering problems*
Bridenbaugh — *Cities* p.19-20
- *Physiognomy*
Bridenbaugh — *Cities* p.3-25
, *Planting of*
Bridenbaugh — *Cities* p.135-139

VILLIERS, GEORGE. *See* **Buckingham, Earl of**

VIRGINIA
See also **Jamestown, Virginia; Roanoke Island;** special subjects
Acheson — *America's* p.161-164
Alderman — *Story. See* index p.187
Amer. Her. — *Thirteen. See* index p.384
Caffrey — *Mayflower* p.14-15, 166, 304-305
Clark — *Old* p.3-24
Craven — *Colonies. See* index p. 362
Craven — *Southern* p.138-182; *See also* index p.450
Dillon — *Pilgrims. See* index p.250
Earle — *Home. See* index p.468
Folsom — *Give* p.8, 32, 44, 70, 72, 75, 77
Gill — *Mayflower. See* index p.206
Hall — *Religious. See* index p.347

Hawke — *Colonial* p.94-107; *See also* index p.768-769
Hawke — *U.S.* p.50-81
Leynse — *Preced.* p.20, 27, 31, 35, 208, 211, 220-221, 228-229, 232-233, 248, 251
Miller — *First* p.15-29
Morison — *Story. See* index p.vii
Pomfret — *Founding. See* index p.380
Smith — *17th. See* index p.238
Wertenbaker — *First. See* index p.356
Willison — *Pilgrim. See* index p.583
Willison — *Saints. See* index p.511

- *Advantages, natural*
  Goetzmann — *Colonial* p.139-141
- *Assembly*
  Goetzmann — *Colonial* p.107
  Hawke — *U.S.* p.73-76
  Jernegan — *American* p.58-59
  Pomfret — *Founding* p.37-38, 49-50, 65, 68, 70-72
  Rozwenc — *Making (1)* p.56-57, 78, 87
  Sweet — *Religion* p.30-32
  Willison — *Pilgrim* p.186-187
- *Charters*
  Annals of America (1) p.15-17
  Craven — *Southern* p.61-63, 75, 82, 84, 88, 90, 111-112, 190n; *See also* index p.450
  Goetzmann — *Colonial* p.97-100
  Hawke — *Colonial* p.86-88
  Jernegan — *American* p.55-56
  Nettels — *Roots* p.164
  Pomfret — *Founding* p.26-27, 31-32
  Rozwenc — *Making (1)* p.55-56
- *Chronology*

  - *1604–1625*
    Morison — *Oxford* p.49-54
  - *1607–1676*
    Fisher — *Men (1)* p.34
  - *1609–1624*
    Jernegan — *American* p.55-59
  - *1610–1619*
    Jernegan — *American* p.56-58
  - *1649*
    Jernegan — *American* p.90-91
  - *1652–1660*
    Jernegan — *American* p.61-62

  - *1660–1676*
    Jernegan — *American* p.62
- *Contrast with Massachusetts*
  Calverton — *Awake.* p.215-221
- *Contrast with North Carolina*
  Calverton — *Awake.* p.286-287
- *Council*
  Amer. Her. — *Thirteen* p.70-71, 74-75
  Craven — *Southern. See* index p.441 (under Governor's Council)
  Rozwenc — *Making (1)* p.23, 56
- *Death rate. See* **Death rate — Virginia**
- *Economy*
  Abbot — *Colonial* p.78-79
- *Famous Families*
  See also **Aristocracy — Virginia**
  Calverton — *Awake.* p.211-213
  Starkey — *Land* p.27-45
- *Feudalism*
  Wish — *Society (1)* p.63-86
- *Founding*
  Morison — *Intellect.* p.14
  Nettels — *Roots* p.110-113
  Pomfret — *Founding* p.25-48
  Wertenbaker — *First* p.16
- *Frontier*
  Wish — *Society (1)* p.63-86
- *"General Muster"*
  Clark — *Old* p.11-12
- *Government*
  See also **Virginia — Assembly; — Chronology; — House of Burgesses; — Laws; etc.**
  Abbot — *Colonial* p.79-82
  Morison — *Oxford* p.85-93
  Nettels — *Roots* p.164-165
  Pomfret — *Founding* p.27, 31, 35, 49-74
  Rothbard — *Conceived (1)* p.81-86
  Ver Steeg — *Formative* p.70-72
- *Governors*
  See also names of governors
  Hawke — *Colonial* p.106-107
- *Growth*
  See also **Virginia — Chronology**
  Bailey — *American (1)* p.15-19
  Goetzman — *Colonial* p.83-144
  Pomfret — *Founding* p.54-56, 63-64, 69

VIRGINIA (continued)

- *Hardships*
  Chitwood — *History (1)* p.74-75
  Fisher — *Men (1)* p.30-31
  Goetzmann — *Colonial* p.77-79,
  101-104, 133-138
  Hawke — *U.S.* p.63-70
- *House of Burgesses*
  Craven — *Colonies* p.27, 138,
  145, 151-152, 154, 234
  Miller — *First* p.28-29, 88-89
  Starkey — *Land. See* index p.274
- *Indian relations*
  See also **Indians — Virginia;
  Virginia — Massacre of 1622**
  Goetzmann — *Colonial* p.109-
  113
  Rothbard — *Conceived (1)* p.95-
  102
- *Institutions*
  Kraus — *U.S. (1)* p.74-76
  - *Views of Herbert S. Klein*
    Goetzmann — *Colonial* p.85-
    96
- *Landmarks*
  National — *History.* p.60-61
- *Laws*
  See also **Virginia — Statutes**
  Hawke — *U.S.* p.70-76
  Wertenbaker — *First* p.174, 227-
  228
  - *"Lawes divine, morall and mar-
    tiall, etc., 1612"*
    Amer. Her. — *Thirteen* p.138
- *Letters (1623)*
  Demos — *Remarkable* p.68-73
- *Massacre of 1622*
  Goetzmann — *Colonial* p.109
  Miller — *First* p.16, 29
- *New England trade*
  Wertenbaker — *First* p.53-54
  , *of William Fitzhugh*
  Wish — *Society (1)* p.63-86
- *Ordinance of 1621*
  Goetzmann — *Colonial* p.107-
  109
- *Parishes*
  Smith — *17th* p.122, 126-130,
  136-137, 139, 142
  Wertenbaker — *First* p.117-119
  Wish — *Society (1)* p.71-72
- *People*
  Goetzmann — *Colonial* p.141-
  144
  Morison — *Oxford* p.89-90

- *Plantations and planters. See*
  **Plantations and Planters —
  Virginia**
- *Politics*
  See also **Virginia —
  Government**
  Craven — *Colonies* p.149-156
  Jernegan — *American* p.60-65
  Smith — *17th* p.90-115
- *Private property*
  Morison — *Oxford* p.52
- *Prosperity*
  Wertenbaker — *First* p.41-42
- *Revolution of 1639*
  Morris — *Ency.* p.28
- *Servants and slaves*
  Rothbard — *Conceived (1)* p.70-
  88
- *Settlements*
  Jernegan — *American* p.52-55
  Snell — *Wild* p.79-94, 128, 151,
  154
  , *Reasons for*
  Calverton — *Awake.* p.209-
  210
  Chitwood — *History (1)* p.48-
  50
- *Society*
  Goetzmann — *Colonial* p.139-
  144
  Rothbard — *Conceived (1)* p.67-
  77
  Rozwenc — *Making (1)* p.43-47
- *Stafford Co. (1686)*
  Demos — *Remarkable* p.124-126
- *Statehouses*
  Wertenbaker — *First* p.292
- *Statutes*
  Amer. Her. — *Thirteen* p.143
  Hawke — *U.S.* p.137-143
- *Success, Factors of*
  Morison — *Oxford* p.52-53
- *Tidewater region*
  Alderman — *Story* p.11-12
- *Towns, incentives for building (1661)*
  Annals of America (1) p.227-231
- *"True Declaration of Virginia"*
  Goetzmann — *Colonial* p.101-
  104
- *Views of Berkeley (1671)*
  Bailey — *American (1)* p.15-16
- *Views of John Smith*
  Goetzmann — *Colonial* p.75
  Scott — *Settlers* p.82

- *Women*
  Fisher — *Men (1)* p.79
  Goodwin — *Colonial* p.50-51
  Starkey — *Land* p.69-72
- *Yeomanry*
  Wertenbaker — *First* p.34-44

"VIRGINIA ACT FOR TRAINING OF POOR CHILDREN"
Annals of America (1) p.171

VIRGINIA COLLEGE OF LANDS
Starkey — *Land* p.62-63

VIRGINIA COMPANY OF LONDON (Merchant Adventurers)
See also **Plymouth Company of Virginia**
Abbot — *Colonial* p.14, 16, 18, 20, 31
Acheson — *America's* p.63, 66-68, 72, 74-77
Amer. Her. — *Pilgrims* p.66-73
Amer. Her. — *Thirteen* p.70-71, 74-75, 78-82, 85-86, 94
Bailyn — *New England* p.2-4, 7
Caffrey — *Mayflower* p.47-48, 51, 54, 101; *See also* index p.389, under Merchant Adventurers
Carman — *History (1)* p.26-28, 54
Craven — *Southern* p.93-137; *See also* index p.450
Folsom — *Give* p.8-10, 12-13
Gill — *Mayflower* p.24, 38, 51, 58
Hawke — *Colonial. See* index p.739
Hawke — *U.S.* p.60-62
Hills — *History (2)* p.11-23
Hope — *Nation* p.61, 63
Leynse — *Preced.* p.28-30, 33, 211-213, 225, 228, 230-233, 235, 240, 243, 251
Marshall — *Mayflower* p.21-22, 26, 30, 63, 160, 167, 169, 182
Miller — *First* p.15-16, 18, 23-24, 26-30
Morison — *Oxford* p.50-54
Morison — *Story* p.17-19, 27, 45, 87, 90, 95, 99, 105, 124-130, 134-135, 141, 150-151
Nettels — *Roots* p.111-113, 134-135, 156, 164-165, 167, 222-223, 231, 278, 290-291
Pomfret — *Founding* p.26-27, 31, 35, 39-40, 43-48, 106-110, 132-133, 139-141, 304, 306

Rothbard — *Conceived (1)* p.44-45, 53-66, 83, 96, 160, 166, 171
Rozwenc — *Making (1)* p.22, 25-27, 32, 55-57, 62, 78
Scott — *Settlers* p.83, 86, 89, 91-92
Starkey — *Land* p.14-16, 22-23, 70, 74-76
Sweet — *Religion* p.30-31
Wertenbaker — *First* p.1, 16-17, 179
Willison — *Pilgrim. See* index p.547-548
Willison — *Saints. See also* index p.505 (Adventurers; Merchant Adventurers)
- *Charter (1612)*
  Abbot — *Colonial* p.25-26
  Beck — *Pilgrim* p.8, 16, 44
- *Dissolution, annulment*
  Abbot — *Colonial* p.31
  Chitwood — *History (1)* p.66-68
  Hope — *Nation* p.64
  Jernegan — *American* p.59
  Morris — *Ency.* p.32
- *Fund raising (1611)*
  Abbot — *Colonial* p.24-25
- *Land policy*
  Goetzmann — *Colonial* p.104-106
- *Patent of 1606*
  Jernegan — *American* p.51
- *Reforms of 1618–19*
  Abbot — *Colonial* p.28-31
- *Reorganization (1609)*
  Abbot — *Colonial* p.20-24
- *Trade aspect*
  Jernegan — *American* p.52

VIRGINIA COMPANY OF PLYMOUTH.
See **Plymouth Company**

VOTING. *See* **Suffrage**

W

WABAN, THOMAS
Beals — *John Eliot. See* index p.192

WABENAKI INDIANS. *See* **Abnaki Indians**

WADSWORTH, BENJAMIN
- *"The well-ordered family"*
  Vaughan — *Puritan* p.184-192

WAFER IRONS (waffle irons)
Gould — *Early* p.79-80

WAFERS (waffles)
Gould — *Early* p.97

WAGES
See also **Plymouth — Wages;
Prices; Women — Wages**
Bailyn — *New England* p.32-33, 66,
207-208, 208(n70)
Morris — *Ency.* p.517
Rothbard — *Conceived (1)* p.254-259
Rutman — *Winthrop's* p.44, 52, 63,
75, 159, 211-212, 215, 222-223,
239, 248
Wertenbaker — *First* p.69, 120-124
- *Connecticut, regulation (1676)*
Annals of America (1) p.247-248
- *Massachusetts, laws (1670)*
Demos — *Remarkable* p.251-254
- *Pennsylvania*
Axtell — *America* p.188-190

WAGINCUT (Indian)
Johnston — *Conn.* p.1-6, 19

WALDRON, RICHARD
Bailyn — *New England* p.114, 137-
138, 161-162
Rothbard — *Conceived (1)* p.353,
361-364, 428-429

WALDRON FAMILY
Bailyn — *New England* p.124, 137,
175

WALKER, "WIDOW"
Dexter — *Colonial* p.79-80, 85

"WALKING PURCHASE"
Acheson — *America's* p.143
Adams — *Album* p.231
Alderman — *Story* p.122
Folsom — *Give* p.54

WALLING, WAITSTILL
- *Life in Sudbury (1680)*
Woodward — *Way* p.38-69

WALLOONS
Alderman — *Story* p.48
Amer. Her. — *Thirteen* p.126-128
Fisher — *Men (2)* p.19
Pomfret — *Founding* p.280-281
Snell — *Wild* p.111, 113-114
Willison — *Puritan* p.235

WALLS
Rawson — *When* p.51-56
- *Clapboard siding*
Morrison — *Early* p.30-31
- *Construction*
Morrison — *Early* p.30-35
- *Sheathing*
Morrison — *Early* p.31-32
- *Shingles*
Morrison — *Early* p.32-33
, *Stone*
Gould — *Early* p.112

WALTER, NEHEMIAH
Beals — *John Eliot* p.184-185

**WAMESIT, MASSACHUSETTS (praying
town)**
Vaughan — *New* p.291-292

WAMPANOAG INDIANS
See also **Massasoit (Indian); Quade-
quina (Indian); Sowams, Rhode
Island**
Alderman — *Story* p.25, 94
Amer. Her. — *Pilgrims* p.138
Beck — *Pilgrims* p.21, 23, 34, 37, 39,
73
Demos — *Little* p.14-16
Dillon — *Pilgrim* p.15, 181, 199
Folsom — *Give* p.35-38, 40-41
Morison — *Oxford* p.108
Morison — *Story* p.69-74, 82-84, 246-
251, 254-255, 261-263, 271, 276,
279-280
Vaughan — *New. See* index p.430
Willison — *Pilgrim* p.132-137, 139-
142, 523-526
Willison — *Saints. See* index p.511

WAMPUM
Adams — *Album* p.19, 46
Bridenbaugh — *Cities* p.52
Caffrey — *Mayflower* p.221-222
Johnston — *Conn.* p.56
Langdon — *Everyday* p.194
Lawrence — *New* p.42
Marshall — *Mayflower* p.170
Morison — *Story* p.78, 132-134, 146,
158, 211-214, 230, 239
Northey — *American* p.79-82
Speare — *Life* p.121
Vaughan — *New* p.34, 125, 132, 213,
220-224, 233
Willison — *Pilgrim* p.291-307
Willison — *Saints* p.266, 304

WAMSUTTA (ALEXANDER) (Indian)
Willison — *Pilgrim* p.523
Willison — *Saints* p.390

WAR
See also names of wars
Abbot — *Colonial* p.116

WARD, EDWARD
Wertenbaker — *First* p.197-198
, *on New England*
Axtell — *America* p.120-126

WARD (JOHN) HOUSE
Dow — *Domestic* p.12, 15-16, 24, 28

WARD, NATHANIEL
Gildrie — *Salem* p.90, 92, 94-96, 98
Lawrence — *Not* p.24-26
Morison — *Intellect.* p.152-153, 155n, 198
Tyler — *History* p.196-198; *See also* index p.550
- *"In defense of intolerance"*
  Miller — *Colonial* p.175-178
- *"The simple cobbler of Aggawam" (1647)*
  Annals of America (1) p.185-189

WARDEL, LYDIA
Williams — *Demeter's* p.129

WAREHOUSES
- *Inventory (1660)*
  Dow — *Every* p.258

WARHAM, JOHN, REV.
Rutman — *Winthrop's* p.19, 47-48, 51, 53, 91-93

WARMING PANS
Earle — *Colonial* p.290
- *Plymouth*
  Demos — *Little* p.39

WARNER, THOMAS, SIR
Pomfret — *Founding* p.14, 311-312, 318

WARREN, ELIZABETH MARCH
Marble — *Women* p.16, 37, 93-94
Willison — *Saints* p.235, 399, 450, 486

WARREN, JAMES
Willison — *Saints* p.410, 414-418

WARREN, RICHARD
Caffrey — *Mayflower* p.117, 124, 312
Hills — *History (1)* p.18, 21, 28-29, 34, 37, 40, 43-44, 67, 69, 71, 81, 83, 90-91, 119
Hills — *History (2)* p.47, 150-154
Marble — *Women* p.16, 36, 93
Willison — *Pilgrim* p.110, 236, 248n, 536
Willison — *Saints* p.133, 143, 153, 235, 241, 399, 442, 450, 456, 486

WARREN FAMILY
Hills — *History (1). See* index p.176
Hills — *History (2). See* index p. 278-279

WARWICK, ROBERT RICH (2nd Earl of)
Craven — *Southern* p.19, 119, 125, 148, 234, 239, 249
Pomfret — *Founding* p.45, 77, 122, 151, 153, 164, 167, 233-235, 261, 306-307, 309-311

WARWICK, RHODE ISLAND
Chitwood — *History (1)* p.132
Pomfret — *Founding* p.215-216, 219, 222-224, 226
- *Patent*
  Pomfret — *Founding* p.23, 234, 251-252, 254-255, 258-259, 261, 264

"WASHBALLS" (soap substitute)
See also **Soap and soap making**
Earle — *Customs* p.310

WASHBOARDS
Gould — *Early* p.115-116

WASHHOUSES
Gould — *Early* p.60

WASHING. *See* **Laundry**

"WASSAIL BOWLS"
Gould — *Early* p.106

WATCHES (defense watchmen)
Glubok — *Home* p.346-347
- *Citizens*
  Bridenbaugh — *Cities* p.65-66
, *Military*
  Bridenbaugh — *Cities* p.64-65
- *"Rattle"*
  Bridenbaugh — *Cities* p.65, 67

WATER AND WATER SUPPLY
Bridenbaugh — *Cities* p.61-63
Furnas — *Americans* p.142
Gould — *Early* p.82-83, 105
Rawson — *When* p.35-39
- *Connecticut*
Johnston — *Conn.* p.51
- *New England*
Miller — *First* p.183-184
- *Power*
Furnas — *Americans* p.145
- *Springs*
Bridenbaugh — *Cities* p.61-62
, *Well*
Bridenbaugh — *Cities* p.62-63

WATER TRANSPORTATION
See also **Rivers; etc.**
Bridenbaugh — *Cities* p.53-54
Chitwood — *History (1)* p.386
Furnas — *Americans* p.144-147

WATERTOWN, MASSACHUSETTS
Rutman — *Winthrop's* p.27, 29-30, 43,
48n, 51, 73, 99-100, 100n, 102,
181n, 191, 216, 281
Wertenbaker — *First* p.79, 95-96, 317

WATERWHEELS
See also **Mills and milling**
- *Saugus, Mass.*
National — *History.* p.82-83

WATSON, JOHN
Willison — *Saints* p.409, 420-421

WATSON, PHEBE HICKS
Willison — *Saints* p.449

WAYSIDE INN
Earle — *Home* p.357-358

WEALTH
Carman — *History (1)* p.58
Rutman — *Winthrop's* p.5, 7-8, 72, 74-
75, 199-200, 244-248
Wertenbaker — *First* p.70-72
Wright — *Literary* p.157-158
, *and division of land*
Nettels — *Roots* p.163
, *and power*
Nettels — *Roots* p.163
- *Pioneers*
Wright — *Literary* p.77-79

WEAPONS. *See* **Guns**

WEATHER
See also **Plymouth — Weather**
Furnas — *Americans* p.22
Lawrence — *New* p.49-50
, *and soil*
Ver Steeg — *Formative* p.32-33
- *New Sweden*
Axtell — *America* p.183-184

WEAVERS AND WEAVING
Adams — *Album* p.114-115
Dow — *Every* p.94-95
Earle — *Home.* *See* index p.469
Gould — *Early* p.140-141
Leonard — *Dear* p.166-167
Speare — *Life* p.80-81
Tunis — *Craftsmen* p.37, 101-103
Wright — *Everyday* p.128
- *Beaming*
Earle — *House* p.218
- *Bier*
Earle — *Home* p.220
- *Bouts*
Earle — *Home* p.218
- *Chain*
Earle — *Home* p.250
- *Dents, of sley*
Earle — *Home* p.219-220
- *Design and patterns*
Earle — *Home* p. 243-244, 250-
251
Glubok — *Home* p.264
, *Hand*
Glubok — *Home* p.254-264
- *Indians*
Marshall — *Mayflower* p.155
- *Looms*
Earle — *Home* p.213-214
- *New England*
Tunis — *Colonial* p.50-52
- *Warping*
Earle — *Home* p.217-219

WEBSTER, MARY REEVE
Williams — *Demeter's* p.138

WEDDINGS
See also **Marriage; Plymouth —
Wedding First**
Chitwood — *History (1)* p.497
Earle — *Customs* p.72-76
- *Banns and ceremony*
Holliday — *Woman's* p.258-259

237

- *Boston, typical*
    Woodward — *Way* p.32-36
, *First English (1608)*
    Goodwin — *Colonial* p.47-48
- *Hospitality*
    Wertenbaker — *First* p.270-271
- *"Sewall-Hull"*
    - *Views of Hawthorne*
        Dow — *Every* p.169-171
- *South*
    Wertenbaker — *First* p.270-271
- *Virginia*
    Miller — *First* p.102
    Spruill — *Women's* p.87

WEIGHTS AND MEASURES
    Adams — *Provincial* p.45
    Bridenbaugh — *Cities* p.50-51

WELDE, THOMAS
    Vaughan — *New* p.252-253, 273-274
, *on defection in the Laity*
    Vaughan — *Puritan* p.212-218

WELLS
    Bridenbaugh — *Cities* p.62-63
    Rawson — *When* p.36-40
- *New England*
    Tunis — *Colonial* p.33-34

WELSH
    Alderman — *Story* p.119, 129
    Carman — *History (1)* p.45
    Starkey — *Land* p.182, 190
    Wish — *Society (1)* p.105
- *Pennsylvania*
    Chitwood — *History (1)* p.211
- *Quakers*
    Adams — *Provincial* p.6

WENTWORTH, BENNING
    Alderman — *Story* p.44-45

WENTWORTH FAMILY
    Bailyn — *New England* p.176, 181,
    196-197

WEQUAPAUGE (Indian town)
    Vaughan — *New* p.177

WESSAGUSSET, MASSACHUSETTS
    See also **Weymouth,
    Massachusetts**
    Dillon — *Pilgrims* p.173-181, 187-188

Morison — *Story* p.92-95, 104-105,
    242
Snell — *Wild* p.110-111, 117, 125
Vaughan — *New* p.82-87, 96, 136
Willison — *Pilgrims. See* index p.584
Willison — *Saints. See* index p.511
- *Massacre*
    Willison — *Pilgrim* p.205-223

**WESSAGUSSET (WEYMOUTH)
INDIANS**
    Caffrey — *Mayflower. See* index p.391

WEST, JOHN
    Rothbard — *Conceived (1)* p.412-413,
    415, 418, 424

WEST, JOSEPH
    Craven — *Colonies* p.98-99, 103, 176,
    180-181
    Craven — *Southern* p.336-338, 343,
    346-347, 356

WEST, WILLIAM
    Langdon — *Everyday* p.229

WEST INDIA COMPANY
    Acheson — *America's* p.125-126
    Alderman — *Story* p.47-49, 60
    Amer. Her. — *Thirteen* p.121, 125-
    134, 136, 148
    Craven — *Colonies* p.31, 34, 61-62,
    228
    Fisher — *Men (2)* p.17-21
    Leonard — *Dear* p.28
    Nettels — *Roots* p.196, 198, 201, 203-
    205, 227-228
    Pomfret — *Founding* p.280-282, 284,
    292, 296, 300-302
    Snell — *Wild* p.111-113
, *and Delaware*
    Christensen — *Delaware* p.19,
    24-25
, *and New Netherland*
    Demos — *Remarkable* p.51-52
    Jernegan — *American* p.196
- *Charter of Privileges*
    Jernegan — *American* p.197-198
- *Founding*
    Morris — *Ency.* p.41

WEST INDIES
    See also **Fisheries**
    Alderman — *Story* p.7, 12, 28, 41, 51,
    57, 67, 80, 101, 131, 137

WEST INDIES (continued)
Bailyn — New England p.16, 54, 84-86, 88-91, 98, 128-129, 146-147, 157
Morison — Oxford p.59-60
, Non-Spanish
Morison — Oxford p.98-102
- Trade
Carman — History (1) p.77-79
Chitwood — History (1) p.397-400
Jernegan — American p.176-177
Morison — Story p.201-203, 228, 291
Wertenbaker — Puritan p.197-198, 200, 206

WEST JERSEY. See New Jersey — West Jersey

WESTCHESTER COUNTY, NEW YORK
Wertenbaker — First p.59, 150, 234

WESTO INDIANS
Craven — Southern p.272, 344, 406

WESTON, ANDREW
Caffrey — Mayflower p.108-109, 167
Willison — Pilgrim p.196, 221-222
Willison — Saints p.208

WESTON, THOMAS
Beck — Pilgrims p.8-9, 11-12, 44, 51
Caffrey — Mayflower. See index p.392
Dillon — Pilgrims p.113-114, 119, 127, 166-167, 171-175, 177, 179-182, 187-188
Gill — Mayflower p.37-39, 43, 61, 86, 93, 95-96, 98, 100-101, 106
Marshall — Mayflower p.30, 153, 161, 183
Morison — Story p.17-22, 87-90, 104-105, 126
Willison — Pilgrim. See index p.584
Willison — Saints. See index p.511

WESTON'S COMPANY
- Articles of Agreement
Willison — Pilgrim p.64-71, 80-82, 97-99, 157-158

WETHERSFIELD, CONNECTICUT
Pomfret — Founding p.233, 236, 239, 264, 266

Vaughan — New p.117, 133, 139, 174, 203-205, 218
- Life
Smith — Colonial p.34-57

WEYMOUTH, GEORGE
, on Kennebec
Collins — Story p.56

WEYMOUTH, MASSACHUSETTS
See also **Wessagusset, Massachusetts**
Beck — Pilgrims p.48-50
- Disbandment
Archer — Mayflower p.342-346
- Immigrants (1635)
Demos — Remarkable p.39-41

WEYMOUTH INDIANS. See Wessagusset Indians

WHALING
Adams — Album p.112
Carman — History (1) p.75
Morison — Story p.49-50, 224-226, 286
Speare — Life p.117-118
Wright — Everyday p.86-90

WHALLEY, EDWARD
Alderman — Story p.75-76
Johnston — Conn. p.75-77

"WHANG" (women's cooperative housecleaning)
Leonard — Dear p.100, 102-103

WHARTON, RICHARD
Bailyn — New England. See index p.249
Rothbard — Conceived (1) p.270, 289, 372-374, 376-379, 413-415, 417

WHARVES AND DOCKS
Bridenbaugh — Cities p.22-24

WHEAT
Craven — Southern p.19, 211, 253, 316, 346
Earle — Customs p.150
Langdon — Everyday p.277
Morris — Ency. p.477
Nettels — Roots p.233-236

Rutman — *Winthrop's* p.88, 93, 177, 180, 184-185, 188-189, 191, 199, 207, 227

WHEELER, THOMAS, CAPTAIN
Morison — *Intellect.* p.191-194

WHEELOCK'S INDIAN CHARITY SCHOOL
Hope — *Nation* p.84

WHEELWRIGHT, JOHN, REV.
Acheson — *America's* p.111-112
Morris — *Ency.* p.34
Pomfret — *Founding* p.193-195, 210
Rothbard — *Conceived (1)* p.190-191, 198, 225-226, 247
Starkey — *Land* p.96, 98-99, 126-127
Wertenbaker — *First* p.65, 100-101
Wertenbaker — *Puritan* p.220-221

WHEELWRIGHTS
Glubok — *Home* p.235-236
Gould — *Early* p.142

WHIPPING
Lawrence — *Not* p.136-138
Miller — *First* p.256-257, 259
Wertenbaker — *First* p.219-220, 227-230, 268
- *Plymouth*
Willison — *Saints* p.322-323

WHIPPLE HOUSE (Ipswich, Mass., 1639)
Morrison — *Early* p.54-55

WHISKEY
Earle — *Customs* p.175

"WHISKS" (straight lace collars)
Earle — *Two cent. (1)* p.76-77

"WHISTLE-BELLY VENEGEANCE" (strong drink)
Earle — *Customs* p.179

WHITAKER, ALEXANDER
Tyler — *History* p.41-43

WHITE, ANDREW, FATHER
Tyler — *History* p.53

WHITE, CATHERINE. *See* Carver, Catherine White

WHITE, ELEANOR. *See* Dare, Eleanor White

WHITE, JOHN
Amer. Her. — *Thirteen* p.41-46, 48, 57, 96-97
Craven — *Southern* p.49, 51-52, 54-56, 58, 79, 99
Morris — *Ency.* p.32
Pomfret — *Founding* p.149-151, 154, 158-160, 174
Snell — *Wild* p.42, 54-55, 58, 86-90
Williams — *Demeter's* p.18-19

WHITE, PEREGRINE
Caffrey — *Mayflower* p.119, 306, 308
Dillon — *Pilgrims* p.141, 216
Hills — *History (1)* p.22, 37, 40, 46, 53, 57, 81, 88
Marble — *Women* p.7, 24, 62
Willison — *Pilgrim* p.110, 386n, 534
Willison — *Saints* p.324, 440, 475

WHITE, RESOLVED
Caffrey — *Mayflower* p.41, 54, 306, 308
Hills — *History (1)* p.22, 37, 40, 46, 52-53, 88
Willison — *Pilgrim* p.78, 492, 534
Willison — *Saints* p.122, 440, 475

WHITE, ROGER
Willison — *Pilgrim* p.287-288

WHITE, SUSANNA FULLER. (See Winslow, Susanna Fuller

WHITE, WILLIAM
Hills — *History (1)* p.22, 29, 37, 39, 45, 50, 69, 76
Hills — *History (2)* p.128
Willison — *Pilgrim* p.78, 125, 534
Willison — *Saints* p.122, 134, 143, 166, 439-440, 443

WHITE FAMILY
Hills — *History (1). See* index p.176
Hills — *History (2). See* index p.278
Marble — *Women* p.9, 24, 29, 64
Morison — *Story* p.36, 140, 183, 217, 220

***WHITE ANGEL* (ship)**
Morison — *Story* p.123-125
Willison — *Pilgrim* p.362-376, 379, 399, 401, 452-453
Willison — *Saints* p.290-294, 301, 306, 310, 345

"WHITE APRONS" (Bacon's defenders)
Goodwin — *Colonial* p.53
Spruill — *Women's* p.235

WHITESMITHS (tinsmiths)
Tunis — *Craftsmen* p.65-67

WHITING, SAMUEL
, *on John Cotton*
Hawke — *U.S.* p.99-102

WHITMAN, WILLIAM
- *House and furnishings*
Smith — *Colonial* p.10-11

WHITMAN HOUSE (Farmington, Conn.)
Morrison — *Early* p.56-57

WHITTLING. *See* **Wood carving**

WIAT, "OLD WIDOW"
Williams — *Demeter's* p.172

WICKHAM, GOODWIFE
Wright — *Cultural* p.104

WIDOWERS
Spruill — *Women's* p.156-158

WIDOWS
See also **Courtship — Widows;
Plymouth — Widows**
Earle — *Colonial* p.30-33, 39-40
Earle — *Customs* p.44-54
Rutman — *Winthrop's* p.217-218, 258
- *Land grants, Mass.*
Leonard — *Dear* p.53
- *Rights*
Leonard — *Dear* p.316-318
Spruill — *Women's* p.359-361

"WIDOW'S PEAK" (hood and hair)
Earle — *Two cent. (1)* p.243

WIGGLESWORTH, MICHAEL
Glubok — *Home* p.305-306
Miller — *Colonial* p.357-366
Morison — *Intellect. See* index p.287
Murdock — *Literature* p.31, 104-106,
145-146, 176, 193
Tyler — *History* p.276-288
Wright — *Cultural* p.170-171
Wright — *Everyday* p.176-177
- *"Diary"*
Goetzmann — *Colonial* p.190-
197

- *Letter (1691)*
Demos — *Remarkable* p.142-145

WIGS AND WIGMAKERS
Earle — *Customs* p.300
Earle — *Home* p.296-297
Earle — *Two cent. (1)* p.327-333
Glubok — *Home* p.127-128, 272-274
Lawrence — *Not* p.12-13, 18-19
Miller — *First* p.115-117
Tunis — *Craftsmen* p.41-42
Wertenbaker — *Puritan* p.174-176

, *Men's*
Dow — *Domestic* p.24
- *Names*
Earle — *Two cent. (1)* p.338-339
- *Periwigs*
Earle — *Two cent. (1)* p.321-348
- *Perukes*
Earle — *Two cent. (1)* p.335
- *Views of Nicholas Noyes*
Demos — *Remarkable* p.213-220
, *Women's*
Earle — *Two cent. (2)* p.509-510

WIGWAMS
Dow — *Domestic* p.4-5
Dow — *Every* p.18
Gould — *Early* p.15-16
Marshall — *Mayflower* p.141-142
Morrison — *Early* p.9

, *English*
Langdon — *Everyday* p.5
Snell — *Wild* p.118, 124
- *Indians*
Northey — *American* p.45-47
- *Salem, Mass.*
Dow — *Every* p.16-17

WILBERFORCE, SAMUEL
Willison — *Pilgrim* p.564-565

WILD, SARAH
Williams — *Demeter's* p.140

WILD STRAWBERRY FESTIVALS. *See*
Indians — Festivals

WILDERNESS
See also **Frontier**
Wright — *Everyday* p.33-55

WILLARD, JOHN
Williams — *Demeter's* p.140

WILLARD, SAMUEL
  Morison — *Intellect.* p.36, 161-164, 169, 173-175, 255
  Tyler — *History* p.405
  Wertenbaker — *Puritan* p.154, 156, 278, 312-313
  - *Account of . . . Elizabeth Knapp of Groton (1672)*
    Demos — *Remarkable* p.358-371

WILLARD, SIMON
  Bailyn — *New England* p.28, 30, 55-57
  Vaughan — *New* p.175-176, 215, 251-252, 317

WILLET, MARY BROWNE
  Willison — *Saints* p.451-452

WILLET, THOMAS
  Willison — *Pilgrim* p.360n-361n, 374, 402
  Willison — *Saints* p.268, 289, 291, 295, 301, 374, 383, 451-452, 456

WILLIAM III (king of England)
  Abbot — *Colonial* p.58-59, 61, 74, 107, 115
  Amer. Her. — *Thirteen* p.157-158, 162, 166-167, 173, 193-194

WILLIAM AND MARY COLLEGE
  Chitwood — *History (1)* p.466-467
  Folsom — *Give* p.54, 66-67, 73-74
  Hawke — *U.S.* p.236-237
  Jernegan — *American* p.107-108
  Monroe — *Founding (1)* p.167
  Morison — *Intellect.* p.28
  National — *History.* p.118-119
  Rozwenc — *Making (1)* p.86, 90
  Wertenbaker — *Old* p.26-27
  Wish — *Society (1)* p.83-84
  Wright — *Cultural* p.118-119
  Wright — *Everyday* p.147-148
  - *Founding (1693)*
    Adams — *Album* p.30
    Wertenbaker — *First* p.136-137, 255

"WILLIAM DAMME" GARRISON HOUSE (Dover, N.H., ca.1675)
  Morrison — *Early* p.77

WILLIAMS, ABIGAIL
  Williams — *Demeter's* p.141

WILLIAMS, JOHN
  Tyler — *History* p.379-381

WILLIAMS, ROGER
  Abbot — *Colonial* p.47, 51
  Acheson — *America's* p.105-107
  Alderman — *Story* p.33, 93-94, 96-100
  Amer. Her. — *Pioneer* p.51, 62-63
  Amer. Her. — *Thirteen* p.103-104, 146
  Annals of America (1) p.81-82
  Bailyn — *New England* p.58-59, 118
  Beals — *John Eliot. See* index p.192
  Caffrey — *Mayflower* p.247, 257, 267, 271-272, 301
  Calverton — *Awake. See* index p.474
  Carman — *History (1)* p.29, 90-92
  Craven — *Colonies* p.21, 52-53, 116, 120
  Dillon — *Pilgrims* p.210-211
  Fisher — *Men (1)* p.140-150, 303-311
  Folsom — *Give* p.14-18, 22, 36
  Gildrie — *Salem* p.6, 15, 24-25, 30-38, 89
  Hawke — *Colonial* p.143-145; *See also* index p.772
  Hawke — *U.S.* p.105-112
  Hope — *Nation* p.81-82
  Jernegan — *American* p.131-132, 135-137
  Life — *New* p.78-79
  Morison — *Intellect.* p.5, 23, 125, 142, 152-153, 155n, 197
  Morison — *Story* p.119, 163, 212-214, 247, 271, 284
  Nettels — *Roots* p.175-178
  Pomfret — *Founding. See* index p.380
  Rothbard — *Conceived (1). See* index p.531
  Rozwenc — *Making (1)* p.38, 69-71
  Rutman — *Winthrop's* p.88, 99, 103, 113-114, 127, 144
  Smith — *17th* p.25, 156, 203, 215, 218
  Snell — *Wild* p.1, 4, 126, 128-129, 134-135
  Starkey — *Land. See* index p.275
  Sweet — *Religion* p.13, 76, 81, 85, 90-92, 122-127, 154-156
  Tyler — *History. See* index p.550
  Vaughan — *New. See* index p.430
  Ver Steeg — *Formative* p.47-49
  Wertenbaker — *First* p.98-99, 103, 231
  Wertenbaker — *Puritan* p.215-218, 228-229
  Willison — *Pilgrim. See* index p.584

WILLIAMS, ROGER (continued)
  Willison — Saints. See index p.512
  Wright — Cultural p.81-82, 84-85
  - Answer to John Cotton (1644)
      Hawke — U.S. p.107-111
  - Arrival in Rhode Island
      Collins — Story p.48
  - Banishment
      Chitwood — History (1) p.115-117
      Hawke — U.S. p.106-107
      Morris — Ency. p.33
  - Biography
      Morris — Ency. p.731-732
  , Flight of
      Rothbard — Conceived (1) p.182-189
  - "The hireling ministry — none of Christ's" (1652)
      Annals of America (1) p.213-216
  , in England
      Wish — Society (1) p.1-23
  , in New England
      Wish — Society (1) p.24-62
  - Indian relations
      Nettels — Roots p.176-177
  - Letter to townsmen of Providence (1655)
      Angle — By p.12-13
      Hawke — U.S. p.111-112
  - "Liberty is not license" (1655)
      Angle — By 10-12
  , on liberty
      Bailey — American (1) p.35-37
      Rothbard — Conceived (1) p.210-217
      Wright — Cultural p.85
  , on religious freedom and tolerance
      Chitwood — History (1) p.134
      Miller — Colonial p.169-174
  - Views of William Bradford
      Hawke — U.S. p.106

WILLS
  Spruill — Women's p.352-355
  - Isle of Wight Co., Va., 1655
      Demos — Remarkable p.171-173
  - Virginia (1684)
      Demos — Remarkable p.153-155
  - Watertown, Mass. (1668)
      Demos — Remarkable p.169-170

WILMINGTON, DELAWARE
  Christensen — Delaware p.89-90
  - Historic sites
      Christensen — Delaware p.155

WILSON, DEBORAH
  Williams — Demeter's p.129

WILSON, EDWARD
  Caffrey — Mayflower. See index p.392

WILSON, JOHN, REV.
  Morison — Intellect. p.125, 145, 152, 155n, 169, 212n
  Rutman — Winthrop's. See index p.322
  Tyler — History p.162-163, 233
  Vaughan — New p.242, 245, 253-254, 257, 264
  Wertenbaker — Puritan p.34, 63, 203, 220-221, 230-231, 235-236
  Willison — Pilgrim p.326-327n, 395n, 416-417, 428, 519

WILSON, MRS. JOHN (wife of Rev. Wilson)
  Williams — Demeter's p.28

"WIMPLES"
  Earle — Two cent. (1) p.207-208

WINCOB PATENT
  Willison — Pilgrim p.62-63

WINDMILLS
  Adams — Album p.119
  Earle — Home p.130, 133
  Morrison — Early p.92-94
  , First — Virginia (1621)
      Gould — Early p.134
  - New York
      Clark — Old p.55

WINDOWS
  Beck — Pilgrims p.55-56
  Dow — Every p.20
  Earle — Home p.23
  Glubok — Home p.11-12
  Miller — First p.174
  Morrison — Early p.34-35
  Wertenbaker — First p.286, 289-290
  - Casement
      - Jamestown
          Adams — Album p.26
  , Dormer
      Morrison — Early p.38-39
  - Oiled paper
      Glubok — Home p.11-12, 286
  - Plymouth
      Demos — Little p.25, 28-29

- *Puritans*
  Adams — *Album* p.82
- *Virginia*
  Wertenbaker — *Old* p.79

WINDSOR, CONNECTICUT
Pomfret — *Founding* p.233-234, 239

WINE
Bailyn — *New England* p.81, 83, 85, 101, 107, 127, 149, 152-153, 155
Earle — *Customs* p.168-169
Miller — *First* p.187-188
Rutman — *Winthrop's* p.32, 89, 171, 187-188, 209n, 221, 223, 231-232, 249
- *South*
  Craven — *Southern. See* index p.451

"WINE ISLANDS"
Bailyn — *New England* p.78, 80-81, 85-86, 98, 127, 129

WINGFIELD, EDWARD MARIA
Goodwin — *Colonial* p.192-194
Phillips — *First* p.62, 74, 78, 81
- *Discourse of Virginia (1608)*
  Demos — *Remarkable* p.57-67

WINNISIMMET, MASSACHUSETTS
Rutman — *Winthrop's* p.24, 39, 48n, 70, 94, 200, 208

WINSLOW, EDWARD
Beck — *Pilgrims* p.9, 34, 39, 48, 51-52, 67
Dillon — *Pilgrims. See* index p.250
Earle — *Two cent. (1)* p.xiii, 7
Gill — *Mayflower. See* index p.206
Hills — *History (1). See* index p.177
Hills — *History (2). See* index p.279
Johnston — *Conn.* p.2, 6-9
Leynse — *Preced.* p.152, 206, 213, 216-217, 232, 241, 246-247, 253, 257, 261-262, 268
Marble — *Women* p.11-12, 14, 24, 29, 43, 45-47, 53, 55, 63-67
Marshall — *Mayflower* p.135-137, 140, 149, 161, 163, 167
Morison — *Intellect.* p.179, 198
Morison — *Story. See* index p.vii
Pomfret — *Founding* p.115, 119, 166, 181, 198-199, 211, 232-233, 261
Snell — *Wild* p.101, 106, 108, 110-111, 128, 135

Starkey — *Land* p.54, 56-57, 95
Vaughan — *New. See* index p.430
Willison — *Pilgrim. See* index p.584
Willison — *Saints* p.512
- *Death (1655)*
  Willison — *Pilgrim* p.504-506
  Willison — *Saints* p.504-506
- *"Letter to a friend in England" (1623)*
  Amer. Her. — *Thirteen* p.141
, *on survival and success*
  Vaughan — *Puritan* p.50-53

WINSLOW, ELIZABETH BARKER
Marble — *Women* p.12, 29, 55
Willison — *Pilgrim* p.125, 534
Willison — *Saints* p.102, 122, 134, 166, 440

WINSLOW, ELLEN NEWTON ADAMS
Willison — *Saints* p.445, 449, 451

WINSLOW, JOHN
Marble — *Women* p.16, 34-35, 82-85
Willison — *Pilgrim* p.445n, 540
Willison — *Saints. See* index p.512

WINSLOW, JOSIAH
Gill — *Mayflower* p.145-146
Willison — *Pilgrim* p.514, 518, 524, 527
Willison — *Saints. See* index p.512

WINSLOW, KENELM
Willison — *Saints* p.386, 449, 451, 480

WINSLOW, MARY CHILTON
Hills — *History (1)* p.21, 29, 37, 40, 47, 52-54, 57-61, 80, 82
Hills — *History (2)* p.101
Marble — *Women* p.82-85
Williams — *Demeter's* p.23
Willison — *Pilgrim* p.445n, 525
Willison — *Saints* p.133, 191, 336, 405, 411, 441, 446

WINSLOW, PELHAM
Willison — *Saints* p.409-410, 414-415, 420

WINSLOW, PENELOPE
Earle — *Two cent. (1)* p.xvi, 146
Earle — *Two cent. (2)* p.505
Willison — *Saints* p.394, 420, 455

WINSLOW, SUSANNA FULLER WHITE
Caffrey — *Mayflower* p.41, 54, 119, 147, 279, 306

244

WINSLOW, SUSANNA FULLER WHITE
(*continued*)

Dillon — *Pilgrims* p.141, 161
Gill — *Mayflower* p.75, 88, 91
Hills — *History (1)* p.22, 37, 39, 47,
    56-57, 61, 78
Leynse — *Preced.* p.267
Marble — *Women* p.44, 62-67
Starkey — *Land* p.47, 55-57
Willison — *Pilgrim* p.78, 110n, 149
Willison — *Saints* p.122, 134, 185,
    440, 480

WINSLOW FAMILY

Caffrey — *Mayflower* p.392
Hills — *History (1). See* index p.177
Hills — *History (2). See* index p.279

WINTER

Gould — *Early* p.140-144

WINTER SPORTS

See also **Sports and games;** names
    of sports
Rawson — *When* p.84-86
Speare — *Life* p.158

WINTHROP, FITZ-JOHN

Craven — *Colonies* p.1, 218, 238, 240
Earle — *Two cent. (2)* p.691
Rothbard — *Conceived (1)* p.336,
    374, 376-377, 379, 418-419, 429,
    443, 466, 481-482

WINTHROP, JOHN

Abbot — *Colonial* p.39, 43, 46-47, 49-
    52, 61, 64
Amer. Her. — *Pilgrims* p.122-124
Amer. Her. — *Thirteen* p.98-104, 138-
    139, 144-145
Bailyn — *New England* p.18-22, 24,
    26, 35, 39, 49, 64, 78, 85, 93, 106,
    109, 134, 160
Beals — *John Eliot. See* index p.192
Bridenbaugh — *Cities* p.128-129
Caffrey — *Mayflower. See* index p.392
Chitwood — *History (1)* p.105-107
Dillon — *Pilgrims* p.204, 207-210, 212-
    215
Dow — *Every* p.9, 16, 18, 34, 106
Earle — *Two cent. (1)* p.xiii, 9-11, 14,
    49, 170, 177-179, 198, 300
Earle — *Two cent. (2)* p.354, 461, 618
Gildrie — *Salem* p.17, 22, 34, 38-41,
    63, 79, 81, 88, 90-93, 95-99

Glubok — *Home* p.18, 30, 42, 75, 164,
    344
Hawke — *Colonial. See* index p.773
Hawke — *U.S.* p.92-99
Johnston — *Conn.* p.2, 7, 12, 14-15,
    22, 73
Life — *New* p.75-78, 96
Morison — *Intellect.* p.30, 155n, 165,
    177, 181
Morison — *Story* p.120, 140, 147, 161,
    201, 207, 210, 218-219
Morris — *Ency.* p.33
Nettels — *Roots* p.74, 119-120, 136-
    137, 158, 168-170, 174, 178, 217,
    246, 455-456
Pomfret — *Founding* p.62, 82, 158-
    162, 166-168, 170, 172-174, 184,
    187, 203-204, 210-211, 259, 268,
    310
Rothbard — *Conceived (1). See* index
    p.531
Rozwenc — *Making (1)* p.48, 58-60,
    65-66, 69-70
Rutman — *Winthrop's. See* index
    p.322-323
Smith — *17th* p.84, 91, 199, 202-204
Snell — *Wild* p.119, 124-125, 127-
    128, 135, 140
Starkey — *Land. See* index p.275
Vaughan — *New. See* index p.430
Ver Steeg — *Formative* p.37
Wertenbaker — *First. See* index p.357
Wertenbaker — *Puritan. See* index
    p.359
Williams — *Demeter's* p.25-26, 28;
    See also index p.358
Willison — *Pilgrim. See* index p.584-
    585
Willison — *Saints. See* index p.512
Wish — *Society (1)* p.34-36, 41, 47,
    49, 59-60
- *Biography*
    Morris — *Ency.* p.733
- *"Edifying incidents"*
    Miller — *Colonial* p.113
- *"The exclusion of heretics" (1637)*
    Annals of America (1) p.154-156
- *Expedition*
    Jernegan — *American* p.127-128
- *Ideal society*
    Rutman — *Winthrop's. See* index
    p.323
- *"Journal" (1630-49)*
    Amer. Her. — *Thirteen* p.138-
    139, 144-145
    Rozwenc — *Making (1)* p.97-98

- *"Letters" (1600's)*
  Miller — *Colonial* p.77-82
- *Liberty concepts (1645)*
  Bailey — *American (1)* p.28-29
- *"Little speech on liberty"*
  Hawke — *U.S.* p.97-99
- *Love and marriage*
  Morgan — *Puritan* p.16-17
- *"A model of Christian charity" (1630)*
  Annals of America (1) p.109-115
  Hawke — *U.S.* p.96-97
  Vaughan — *Puritan* p.138-146
- *"A negative view of democracy"*
  Annals of America (1) p.168-169
- *Objections to laws*
  Hawke — *U.S.* p.124
, *on Anne Hutchinson*
  Williams — *Demeter's* p.29, 115, 117-118
, *on defection in the clergy*
  Vaughan — *Puritan* p.207-211
, *on economic ethics*
  Vaughan — *Puritan* p.172-176
, *on Margaret Jones*
  Williams — *Demeter's* p.135-136
, *on Mary Dyer's child*
  Williams — *Demeter's* p.147-148
, *on migration*
  Williams — *Demeter's* p.28
, *on Puritans*
  Vaughn — *Puritan* p.25-35
- *Selections*
  Goetzmann — *Colonial* p.169-179
- *Trial of Anne Hutchinson*
  Goetzmann — *Colonial* p.181-184

WINTHROP, JOHN, JR.
  Bailyn — *New England* p.27, 30, 62-67, 74, 84, 100, 106-107, 109, 118, 135, 139
  Craven — *Colonies* p.7, 12-13, 20, 26, 62, 64, 74, 218
  Johnston — *Conn.* p.15-17, 59, 78-82, 88, 95
  Morison — *Intellect.* p.101n, 134-136, 155n, 201, 242, 247, 249-251
  Morison — *Story* p.198-199, 249, 263
  Morris — *Ency.* p.34, 37
  Pomfret — *Founding* p.205, 224, 226-227, 234-235, 237, 239, 251-256, 258, 275, 286, 302
  Rothbard — *Conceived (1)* p.218-219, 233, 264-266, 278-280, 284, 336, 338, 374

Wertenbaker — *First* p.81-82, 167-169, 241-242
Wertenbaker — *Puritan* p.261-262
Wright — *Cultural* p.221-223
, *and Royal Society*
  Hawke — *U.S.* p.238-241
- *Letter (1658)*
  Demos — *Remarkable* p.139-142
- *Library, scientific*
  Wright — *Cultural* p.135-136, 138
- *Mission to England*
  Craven — *Colonies* p.6-9, 32, 44-47, 49-51

WINTHROP, MARGARET
  Beals — *John Eliot* p.64-65, 68, 72, 80-81, 83, 127
  Earle — *Colonial* p.110-111
  Starkey — *Land* p.4-5, 85-86
  Williams — *Demeter's* p.26, 39
- *"Letters" (1600's)*
  Miller — *Colonial* p.77-82
, *on Anne Hutchinson*
  Williams — *Demeter's* p.116

WINTHROP, MARTHA COYTMORE
  Williams — *Demeter's* p.89-90

WINTHROP, MARY. *See* **Dudley, Mary Winthrop**

WINTHROP, WAIT
  Rothbard — *Conceived (1)* p.376-377, 379, 424-425, 449, 463, 466-467, 471-472

WINTHROP FAMILY
  Bailyn — *New England. See* index p.249

WINTHROP FLEET
  Rutman — *Winthrop's. See* index p.323

WISE, JOHN
  Morris — *Ency.* p.40
  Tyler — *History* p.349-360
, *on natural law*
  Goetzmann — *Colonial* p.197-200

WISWALL, ICHABOD
  Willison — *Pilgrim* p.527-529
  Willison — *Saints* p.373, 403, 405-406, 481

246

WITAWAWMUT (Indian)
Morison — *Story* p.94-95

WITCHCRAFT
See also **Science and scientists, and Witchcraft**
Adams — *Album* p.128-129
Amer. Her. — *Pilgrims* p.133-135
Calverton — *Awake.* p.142-145
Chitwood — *History (1)* p.235-238
Dow — *Every* p.210-213
Earle — *Colonial* p.103-105
Fisher — *Men (1)* p.166-173
Folsom — *Give* p.52, 78-87
Furnas — *Americans* p.69, 72, 78
Glubok — *Home* p.300-301
Hawke — *Colonial* p.73, 300, 303-305
Hope — *Nation* p.106
Johnston — *Conn.* p.100-101
Morison — *Intellect.* p.249, 255-265
Rozwenc — *Making (1)* p.93-95
Speare — *Life* p.33-34
Wertenbaker — *First. See* index p.357-358
Wertenbaker — *Puritan. See* index p.359
Williams — *Demeter's. See* index p.359
Wish — *Society (1)* p.18-19, 31, 41-43, 80

- *Boston, Mass.* — *Executions*
  Dow — *Every* p.211
- *Connecticut*
  Wertenbaker — *First* p.151-155
- *Hartford, Conn.*
  Wertenbaker — *First* p.152-153
- *Maryland*
  Wertenbaker — *First* p.148-149
- *Massachusetts*
  Hawke — *U.S.* p.243-249
  Ver Steeg — *Formative* p.145-146
  Wertenbaker — *First* p.151-160
- *Mass. General Court Resolution (1957)*
  Williams — *Demeter's* p.152
- *New England*
  Jernegan — *American* p.185-187
  Morison — *Oxford* p.124-125
  Wertenbaker — *First* p.150-162
- *New York (1665)*
  Hawke — *U.S.* p.242-243
- *on Delaware River*
  Starkey — *Land* p.103-104

- *Origin*
  Wertenbaker — *First* p.142-143
- *Plymouth*
  Demos — *Little* p.21-22, 83
- *Salem, Mass.*
  See also **Sewall, Samuel — Witchcraft in Salem; Witchcraft — Trials**
  Amer. Her. — *Thirteen* p.160, 162
  Bailey — *American (1)* p.34-36
  Jernegan — *American* p.186-187
  National — *History.* p.72-85
  Rothbard — *Conceived (1)* p.452-463
  Starkey — *Land* p.214-215, 217
  Wertenbaker — *First* p.157-162
- *Trials*
  See also **Witchcraft — Views of Thomas Brattle**
  Hawke — *U.S.* p.245-249
  Smith — *17th* p.146, 154-155
  Vaughan — *Puritan* p.277-282
  Willison — *Pilgrim* p.428, 430-431
  Willison — *Saints* p.319-320, 356, 472
- *Views of Cotton Mather*
  Goetzmann — *Colonial* p.204-213
  Miller — *Colonial* p.185-189
- *Views of Increase Mather*
  Annals of America (1) p.293-296
  Miller — *Colonial* p.179-185
- *Views of Samuel Sewall*
  Miller — *Colonial* p.190-192
- *Views of Thomas Brattle*
  Annals of America (1) p.285-292
- *Virginia*
  Wertenbaker — *First* p.145-148
- *Women*
  See also names of accused witches
  Holiday — *Woman's* p.47-63
  Leonard — *Dear* p.350-351, 355-358, 367-368, 381-390

WITHER, GEORGE
, *and Pocahontas*
  Phillips — *First* p.161

WITUWAMAT (Indian)
Vaughan — *New* p.86-87, 202
Willison — *Pilgrim* p.206-207, 220-221, 223
Willison — *Saints. See* index p.512

WIVES
See also **Mayflower — Wives;**
Plymouth — Wives; Puritans —
Wives, Submissive role of
Hawke — U.S. p.226-227
, Beating of
Miller — First p.203
- Duties
Spruill — Women's p.163-175
- Imported to Virginia
Earle — Colonial p.2-6
Goodwin — Colonial p.48
Leonard — Dear p.300-301
- Land. See **Land, Virginia — Wives**
- Marital rights
Spruill — Women's p.359-360
- New England
Earle — Colonial p.16-17
Hawke — U.S. p.226-227

"WOEFUL DECADE." See **Witchcraft —**
New England

WOLCOTT, ROGER
Tyler — History p.297-299

WOLLASTON, CAPTAIN
Dillon — Pilgrims p.201
Willison — Pilgrim p.331-332
Willison — Saints p.273-275

WOLLASTON, MASSACHUSETTS. See
Merrymount Colony

WOLSTENHOLME, JOHN, SIR
Willison — Pilgrim p.54-56
Willison — Saints p.107-108

WOLVES
Glubok — Home p.60-61
Lawrence — New p.56-59
- Hunts (drives or routs)
Earle — Customs p.236-237
Speare — Life p.83-84
- New Netherland
Axtell — America p.40

"WOMAN IN THE WILDERNESS" (cooperative colony)
Calverton — Awake. p.199

WOMEN
See also **Appendix — Women of the**
17th Century; Casket girls; Child-
bearing; Cosmetics; "Femme co-
vert"; Housekeepers; Midwives;

Widows; Wives; Women, etc.,
subdivision under following subjects: **Authors — New England**
women; Bacon's Rebellion,
Women in; Books and reading;
Business; Carolinas; Churches;
Clothing and dress; Convicts;
Crime and criminals; Divorce —
Women's rights; Dutch; Educa-
tion; **England and English; Eti-**
quette; Food; French; Germans;
Hair dressing; Huguenots; Inven-
tions and inventors, First; Jamestown; Labadists; Land; Law and
lawyers; Libraries; Louisiana;
Marriage; Massachusetts;
Mather, Cotton, on female educa-
tion; **Mayflower — Passengers;**
Medicine; Merchants; Mills and
milling; Missions and missionar-
ies; Morality; Negroes; New Am-
sterdam; New England; North
Carolina; Pennsylvania; Physicians;
Pilgrims: Plymouth; Poets; Print-
ers and printing; Profiteering;
Punishment; Puritan Party; Puri-
tans; Quakers; "Redemptioners";
Religion; Sabbath; St. Mary's
Schools, Girls'; Servants —
Indentured; Slander; South;
Spain and Spaniards; Taverns;
Teeth; Virginia; Witchcraft
Hawke — Colonial p.289, 310
Leonard — Dear. See index p.641-658
Miller — First p.58-59
Willison — Saints p.157, 240, 368-
369, 376, 385-387, 418
- Advantages
Leonard — Dear p.31-36
, and Roger Williams
Hawke — U.S. p.107
- Books praising
Spruill — Women's p.227-228
- Churches
Holliday — Woman's p.68-69
Rutman — Winthrop's p.57, 65,
131, 133
Spruill — Women's p.246-247
- Classes
Nettels — Roots p.446-447
- Colonies and colonists
Smith — 17th p.73
Wertenbaker — First p.303

WOMEN (*continued*)
- *Courage*
  See also **Women — Indian relations**
  Earle — *Colonial* p.20-22
  Leonard — *Dear* p.93-94, 538-539
- *Duties*
  Miller — *First* p.201-202
  Spruill — *Women's* p.214-215
  - *Views of John Hammond*
    Hawke — *U.S.* p.228
- *Foibles and religion*
  Holliday — *Woman's* p.33-38
- *Health (survival)*
  Leonard — *Dear* p.208-214
- *Hingham, Mass., Vital statistics in*
  Wertenbaker — *First* p.181-182
- *Historians*
  Leonard — *Dear* p.519-520
- *Homes*
  Leonard — *Dear* p.73-77
- *Husbands*
  , *Business partnership with*
    Leonard — *Dear* p.233-234
  , *Control by*
    Spruill — *Women's* p.342
  , *in courts*
    Spruill — *Women's* p.347
  , *in defense of*
    Spruill — *Women's* p.233-236
  , *in "Body of Liberties"*
    Hawke — *U.S.* p.127
- *Indian relations*
  See also **Indians, Captives of — Women; Indians — Cookery; Indians — Women**
  Leonard — *Dear* p.109-112, 540-541
  , *Intellectual — Masculine opinion*
    Woodward — *Way* p.48
- *Labor, division between husbands and wives*
  Williams — *Demeter's* p.36-54
- *Legal status*
  See also **Brent, Margaret, and women's rights**
  Folsom — *Give* p.9, 20, 44, 78
  Leonard — *Dear* p.298-322
  Miller — *First* p.201-205
  Nettels — *Roots* p.446
  - *Maryland*
    Goodwin — *Colonial* p.49-50
    Leonard — *Dear* p.299-300

, *Liberties of*
  See also **Women, in "Body of Liberties"**
  Fisher — *Men (1)* p.283
- *Life*
  Rawson — *When* p.112-113
  - *Isolation*
    Leonard — *Dear* p.234-235
- *Literacy*
  Morison — *Intellect.* p.82-84
- *Markets*
  Leonard — *Dear* p.442-443
- *Nationalities*
  Leonard — *Dear* p.24-36
- *Nervousness*
  Holliday — *Woman's* p.28-31
- *Occupations*
  See also **Crafts and craftsmanship; Women — Professions**
  names of occupations and crafts
  Leonard — *Dear* p.439-440
  - *Cooperative endeavors*
    Leonard — *Dear* p.235
  - *Spinning and weaving*
    Leonard — *Dear* p.156-184
  , *Status of*
    Smith — *17th* p.73
  , *Titles of*
    Glubok — *Home* p.240
- *Petitions*
  Rutman — *Winthrop's* p.231
- *Pioneers, in wilderness*
  Leonard — *Dear* p.37-69
- *"Place in home"*
  Holliday — *Woman's* p.142-143
- *Politics*
  Leonard — *Dear* p.542-546
- *Professions*
  Spruill — *Women's* p.255
- *Property, personal*
  Leonard — *Dear* p.315-316
- *Public affairs*
  Rutman — *Winthrop's* p.65, 136
- *Rebellion*
  Holliday — *Woman's* p.41-47
- *Social welfare*
  Rutman — *Winthrop's* p.217-218, 258
- *Sports and games*
  Spruill — *Women's* p.108-109
- *Suffrage*
  Williams — *Demeter's. See* index p.357 (under Voting)
  - *Limited, in Virginia (1699)*
    Leonard — *Dear* p.322

- *Survival*
      Leonard — *Dear* p.237-249
, *Swedish and Finnish*
      Leonard — *Dear* p.57, 131-132
, *Synod of 1637, on*
      Hawke — *U.S.* p.114
- *Titles, old-time*
      Earle — *Home* p.187
- *Tolerance*
      Leonard — *Dear* p.391-397
- *Views of John Cotton*
      Hawkes — *U.S.* p.105
- *Violence*
      Holliday — *Woman's* p.287-290
- *Virtues*
      Spruill — *Women's* p.214
- *Wages*
      Smith — *17th* p.74

WOOD. *See also* **Atwood; Attwood**

WOOD, ABRAHAM
      Craven — *Southern* p.362, 370-372,
      379, 392

WOOD, WILLIAM
      Morison — *Intellect.* p.153, 155n, 178,
      212n
, *on New England*
      Axtell — *American* p.22-33, 97-
      101

WOOD
      See also names of woods
      Earle — *Home. See* index p.469
      Rutman — *Winthrop's* p.6, 35, 67, 88,
      92, 178, 180
- *Boards*
      - *Sawing, clapboards*
            Marshall — *Mayflower* p.79-
            80
- *Firewood*
      Bridenbaugh — *Cities* p.11-12
, *Horn leather*
      Rawson — *When* p.9
- *Pegs*
      Woodward — *Way* p.41
- *Products*
      Furnas — *Americans* p.28-29
      Rutman — *Winthrop's* p.39, 185,
      187, 193, 207, 227
- *Turning*
      Earle — *Colonial* p.295-296
- *Uses*
      Glubok — *Home* p.195, 212-217

WOOD CARVING
      See also **Tools, Woodworking**
      Glubok — *Home* p.212-216
- *Whittling*
      Earle — *Colonial* p.296-297

WOODBERRY, MARY DODGE
      Williams — *Demeter's* p.122

WOODBRIDGE, JOHN, JR.
, *on growth of nationalism*
      Vaughan — *Puritan* p.299-305

WOODENWARE
      See also **Dishes and utensils;**
      Trenchers
      Adams — *Album* p.89
      Drepperd — *Pioneer* p.269, 272, 278
      Earle — *Colonial* p.295-297
      Gould — *Early* p.37, 85
      Langdon — *Everyday* p.169-170
      Wertenbaker — *First* p.83-85
- *Plymouth*
      Adams — *Album* p.56

WOODLAND INDIANS. *See* **Indians —**
      Festivals

WOODS HOLS (HOLE),
      MASSACHUSETTS
      Morison — *Story* p.233

WOODWARD, HENRY
      Alderman — *Story* p.138
      Craven — *Colonies* p.135-136
      Snell — *Wild* p.155-156

WOOL
      See also **Sheep; Spinning; Weavers**
      and weaving
      Earle — *Home. See* index p.469
      Gould — *Early* p.127-128
      Leonard — *Dear* p.164-165
      Nettels — *Roots* p.379-380
- *Culture*
      Glubok — *Home* p.241-242
- *Exports, prohibited*
      Glubok — *Home* p.244-245
- *New England*
      Tunis — *Colonial* p.46

WOOLEN ACT OF 1699
      Morris — *Ency.* p.484
      Nettels — *Roots* p.380
      Sweet — *Religion* p.16

WORDS
See also **Names**
, *New*
Hawke — *Colonial* p.306

WORK. *See* **Labor**

"WORKHOUSE SCHOOLS"
Monroe — *Founding (1)* p.56-57

WORMELEY, RALPH
Wertenbaker — *First* p.45, 47, 258, 287

WRIGHT, PRISCILLA CARPENTER
Marble — *Women* p.35, 101
Willison — *Saints* p.444-445

WRIGHT, SUSANNA
Williams — *Demeter's* p.211-212

WRIGHT, WILLIAM
Hills — *History (1)* p.80, 83, 88, 93
Hills — *History (2)* p.122
Marble — *Women* p.35, 95, 101
Morison — *Story* p.6-7, 79, 185, 197
Willison — *Saints* p.444-446

WRIGHT FAMILY
Hills — *History (1)* p.80, 83, 88, 93, 153-154, 158
Hills — *History (2)* p.122, 134, 169

WRITERS AND WRITING
See also **Authors; Puritans — Writers;** names of writers; names of special types of writers, and subjects
Glubok — *Home* p.156
Williams — *Demeter's. See* index p.359
- *Chronology (1676–)*
Tyler — *History* p.256-257
- *New England*
Miller — *First* p.224
- *Virginia*
Tyler — *History* p.15-80

WRITING SCHOOLS
, *Children's*
McClinton — *Antiques* p.84

WYATT, FRANCIS, SIR
Morris — *Ency. p.27*
Smith — *17th* p.92-93, 97, 120

WYCLIF, JOHN
Hall — *Religious. See* index p.348

WYNCOP, JOHN
, *and Wyncop patent*
Pomfret — *Founding* p.107-108, 112

X

Y

YALE, ELIHU
Earle — *Two cent. (1)* p.xix, 228

YALE COLLEGE
- *Books and reading*
Morison — *Intellect.* p.39, 146-148, 150, 267

YAMACRAW INDIANS
Starkey — *Land* p.243

"YARBS." *See* **Herbs**

YARMOUTH, MASSACHUSETTS
Morison — *Story* p.92, 143-144, 153, 226-227, 238, 242
Willison — *Saints. See* index p.513

YARN
Earle — *Home* p.197-199, 202

YEAMANS (YEOMANS), JOHN, SIR
Craven — *Colonies* p.89, 96, 99, 103, 176
Craven — *Southern* p.330-332, 336, 342-343, 351

"YEAR OF DISCOVERY" (1699)
Hawke — *Colonial* p.339

YEARDLEY (YARDLEY), GEORGE, SIR
Acheson — *America's* p.75
Craven — *Southern* p.64, 121, 127, 131n, 138, 146, 154, 160
Goetzmann — *Colonial* p.114-116
Starkey — *Land* p.68, 73, 75-76

YELLOW FEVER
Wertenbaker — *First* p.141, 166, 178-179

251

- *Charleston, N.C.*
    Starkey — *Land* p.232-233
- *Philadelphia, Pa.*
    Starkey — *Land* p.195

YEOMANRY
Wertenbaker — *First. See* index p.358
- *Maryland*
    Wertenbaker — *First* p.34-44

YONG, THOMAS, CAPTAIN
- *Trip on Delaware River (1634)*
    Axtell — *America* p.161-172

YORK, JAMES, DUKE OF
Christensen — *Delaware* p.53-55
Craven — *Colonies* p.34, 56, 59-60, 62-63, 84-85, 94, 163, 175, 189
, *as proprietor of N.Y.*
    Craven — *Colonies* p.65, 199-200, 202, 204-205, 207-209
- *Charter of 1664*
    Craven — *Colonies* p.54, 63-65, 72, 80-83, 106, 210, 216

- *Territory, granted by*
    Chitwood — *History (1)* p.171-173

YOUTH
See also **Pilgrims — Youth; Plymouth — "Inspectors of youth"; Plymouth — Youth**
Bridenbaugh — *Cities* p.117
Demos — *Remarkable* p.127-137
Lawrence — *Not* p.96-105

Z

ZENGER, JOHN PETER
Alderman — *Story* p.55-56

ZWAANENDAEL (colony)
- *Massacre*
    Christensen — *Delaware* p.20-23

"ZWAANENDAEL HOUSE" (Lewes, Delaware)
Christensen — *Delaware* p.153

Appendix

Noted Women
of
The 17th Century
A Selection

(exclusive of some accused witches, midwives, etc., also found in this book)

A
Alcock, Sarah
Alden, Priscilla Mullins
Allerton, Fear Brewster
Armine, Mary, Lady
Attwood, Anne
Austin, Ann(e)
Avery, Mary Tappan

B
Bacon, Elizabeth Duke
Bangs, Lydia Hicks
Bartlett, Mary Warren
Bellingham, Mrs. Richard
Berkeley, Frances, Dame
Blossom, Anne
Bradford, Alice Carpenter Southworth
Bradford, Dorothy May
Bradstreet, Anne Dudley
Brent, Margaret
Brent, Mary
Brewster, Love
Brewster, Mary
Brown, Lydia Howland
Browne, Martha Ford
Burras, Anne

C
Carver, Catherine White
Chandler, Isabella Chilton
Chiesman, Lydia
Clark(e), Katherine
Conant, Elizabeth Weston
Cooke, Damaris Hopkins
Cooke, Elizabeth
Cooke, Hester Mayhieu
Cooke, Sarah Warren
Coombs, Sarah Priest
Cooper, Humility

Cotton, Anne
Crespin, Jean
Cushman, Mary Clarke Singleton
Cushman, Mary Morris Allerton
Cuthbertson, Sarah Allerton Vincent

D
Dale, Arabella, Lady
Dandy, Ann
Dare, Eleanor White
Dare, Virginia
Davenport, Elizabeth Wooley
De La Warr, Lady
DeVries, Mrs. Rudolphus
Dennison, Margaret
Digges, Elizabeth
Dillingham, Sarah
Dotey, Faith
Drummond, Sarah
Dudley, Dorothy
Dudley, Mary Winthrop
Dustin, Hannah
Dyer, Mary

E
Eaton, Martha Billington
Eaton, Sarah
Eliot, Ann(e) Montfort (Hannah Mountfort)
Eliot, Sarah Curtis

F
Farmer, Mary
Faunce, Patience Morton
Fisher, Mary
Flowerdieu, Temperance
Flynt, Margery Hoar
Forrest, Anne
Fuller, Bridget Lee